THE CLIMATE IS CHANGING, CAN HUMANS?

Center for Corporate Rehabilitation

DAVID L. HAWK

ISBN 978-1-967361-34-2 (Paperback)
ISBN 978-1-967361-47-2 (Hardback)
ISBN 978-1-967361-35-9 (Ebook)

Inquiries and Book Orders should be addressed to:

Leavitt Peak Press
17901 Pioneer Blvd Ste L #298, Artesia, California 90701
Phone #: 2092191548

Contents

12. Understanding Dimensional Platforms

Appendix: Into Life's Continuance

Biography

Introduction to the Ominous

The content found herein is to help humans understand how, and perhaps why, they knowingly created conditions that threaten their lives. These climate change conditions came from CO2 increases in the atmosphere from industrial processes built to meet human bio-physical needs and psycho-wants. From this the question becomes why do humans expands life-threatening process even after knowing they threaten planetary life?

Industrial development was based on machines, many of which were massive. Most appear to exhibit values of the masculine that exaggerate the value of size. This may be a clue to the basis of our planetary tragedy.

Eunice Newton Foote illustrated the scope of a climate change tragedy in her research as presented to the 1856[1] American Association for Advancement of Science annual meeting. Most attending were men. A man sitting next to her was asked to read her paper. Humans disregarded her warnings, except for a few men that plagiarized her awesome research. They addressed her concern but didn't mention Foote in their references. She was a woman. Most humans became very busy building their industrial dream. Believing it would make them rich and famous they proceeded to realize the disaster Foote warned of. Men somehow preferred creating heavy versions of machinery. It would intimidate nature and other men being conquered. Nature needed to become subservient, as did other

---

[1] The Irony in my research on climate change was that Exxon's Chief Scientist and CEO of the time were the ones to teach me most about the danger awaiting humans from climate change, as they had learned it in their reading of Foot's 1856 work.

men. The Donald Trump ideology was integral to human behavior a long time ago.

My work since 1975 has been on the above, with emphasis coming to focus on how the masculine has focused on creating the above problem while the feminine is coming to be seen as key to rediscovery of the role of nurture in nature. This is not about women versus men although women do tend to embrace the feminine easily, but both can emphasize nurture while making fun of ideas about destruction of that which doesn't obey.[2] The theory herein is metaphorical but seems to capture the essence of human behavior during centuries of troubled lives in making sense of life's mission, and their role in it. Expanded knowledge about the Foote warning of a disaster on the horizon did little to reduce human actions. Much in science actually increased the pending danger via that false optimism about the importance of the masculine in the universe.

In a prior book I tried to explain the above via European metaphors. Titled "Short-Term Gain, Long-Term Pain,"[3] it outlined the legacy of humans going for short-term personal gain while ignoring community wellbeing. The long-term price, climate change, was building and great but insufficient to call for a changed direction.

That look was written for students. They seemed to fear a future where debts would come due. They felt the elders had made serious errors in over-valuing the short-term. Students used the term "Faustian Bargain" to denote negotiations by elders with the devil. Via their bargaining humans had proposed a means to override the universal law of entropy via the devil's assistance. Coming to be known as "negative entropy" this idea would invite faith in immorality, reversing the irreversible and allowing men to override the law of entropy. Adults simply ignored the lawful role of the university and turned to their design of legal systems, that proved to be trivial and hasten entropy. A pre-mature death was arriving for life on

---

[2] I learned of the human ability to destroy nature and others during my 16 months in a Vietnam war.

[3] David L Hawk, "Short-term Gain, Long-term Pain: Climate Change as a Faustian Tragedy," Eliva Press, 2022.

the planet. What adults received for their bargain in the short-term proved to be trivial and would shorten planetary life.

Somehow, the Elders, having endorsed that masculine model for human development, created conditions of climate change. By then much planetary nature has deteriorated and is about to cross irreversible tipping points. Youth were questioning if there would even be a future. It's interesting that most Americans didn't know of the Faustian Bargain then Tragedy. In addition their concerns for an ominous end via climate change is small. Few Americans know of the Faustian dilemma where a man ignores his soul, and thus the soul of natural existence, then moves on to the pleasures of short-term treasures in the artificial. If there were to be long-term costs, then "new technologies" would be invented to "fix them." In American terms the situation focused on there being fortune and fame out there waiting to be had. If gaining access could be helped via a devil, then so be it. "Life is short, actions are cheap. Wants are many, thus let's go for it." If it helps to sell off the soul, then so be it. Had anyone actually seen a soul? What's wrong with selling what doesn't exist to gain access to knowledge, beautiful girls, and success in the eyes of parents and society? Why not?

The original story of Faust focused on the aspirations of wanting to climb that proverbial ladder quickly, to be nearer those attractive stars. This was an ancient storyline about Faust as written in 1550. Faust was subsequently recast in European literature in 1808 by a truly great writer, Goethe. Faust spread throughout art and music. The theme became key to many movies and books attempted to explain humans on earth, in search of meaning in life.

German youth seem to have been early in applying that classic story for the present. This is where human development came to be defined via industrial accomplishments in meeting bio-needs and psycho-wants. These were seen to bring great success to human life, but at a cost. By the turn of the 21st Century the costs were much greater than the products of the industrial. Life on the planet was threatened.

Seeking short-term gains seems to threaten valuation of the human soul, as created and nurtured by nature. This was especially apparent during growth of the industrial model of man. Industrializing gain also brought deterioration expense to the process. Clearly seen in the line between the industrial and the natural, this is where life's soul negotiates. At that line we see warnings about life's continuance but ignore them. Much depends on the continued health of nature. With reflection we see that a relation between life and the planet is not guaranteed. If we look, we see how our 20th Century short-term gains were very expensive to a larger sense of life on the planet, almost like our soul had gone for our temporary psycho-needs.

The prior book arose from conversations with students who saw their future questionable. They felt a loss of their hope, their inner self as hollow, and no secure feelings about life having a purpose. Their sadness came via discussions of 19th Century humans setting out on an optimistic journey in adoption of the significant potential in technological development. That dream had expanded into extensive industrialization of human beings attempting to be human. By the early 21st Century the optimism for and success from the industrial was questionable. It was becoming apparent that very serious consequences were approaching for life on planet earth. Discussion began on a 6th extinction of life on the planet. The 1850 model was seen as seriously wrong. Humans needed to rethink their bio-needs and psycho-wants.

Inherent in the 1850 model was almost purposeful ignorance of knowledge that the industrial will include much of an irreversibility process, and thus have consequences. Early science on the subject suggested fatal damage awaited life if continued. Much later, in 2010, it was obvious that life was supported by the natural environment, and that human actions were endangering it. Humans have greatly expanded their activities in search of expanding their short-term gains. The longer-term costs were hinted at, and seemed grim, but mostly ignored. The entire process was reminiscent of that 1550 story of Faust and the tragedy he negotiated with his devil. Perhaps the devil was upset with humans and the natural processes on which their lives depended.

Somehow the devil had attracted humans to a model of development where emphasis was on the 1st Law of Thermodynamic and its idea of changelessness. There was little mention of the 2nd Law[4] and its fundamental importance to all activities in the universe. By going with the devil the humans came to emphasize changelessness and its stability. By 1990 humans were beginning to see that the short-term personal gains were had at long-term costs. A grim future was approaching. Resources for continuance of life would then be less available and of lower quality per the 2nd Law. At the same time the atmosphere around the planet would fill with CO^2 that threatened life as it warmed up the surface of the planet. Sadly, a young woman warned of this process in 1856 via her research into such. In a paper prepared for the 1856 annual meeting of the American Association for the Advancement of Science she outlined such. Enice Newton Foote was a female, and not seen as a manly scientist, thus a man sitting near her in the audience was asked to read her paper to the audience. Her research suggestion that the industrial model beginning to be used, as designed by the masculine, would come to warm the earth. No one seemed to care.

Via their agreement with the devil humans could forget the aesthetic nature of the non-rational environment. Its well-being was not important. Work was instead invested in ways to become more productive in the meeting of "today's needs." Emphasis was directed to rational development of technology to improve productivity. A furnace for melting iron ore was seen as tangibly attractive, therefore important. Foote's vague notions of CO^2 entering and being trapped in the atmosphere thus heating the planet were set aside. The rational basis of the science of nature was seen as too logical to worry about.

Ideas about life-ending, mortal, events for entities were coupled to life-renewal processes, immortal, at the species level. The nature of this and the role of nature in it were mysterious. Thus, humans moved on to something they felt they would have more control over.

---

[4]   The 1st t Law of Thermodynamics - Energy cannot be created or destroyed. 2nd Law of Thermodynamics - For a spontaneous process, the entropy of the universe increases

They worked to develop technological replacements that could be better managed. Peculiarities of nature, such as birth leading to death, were seen as unfortunate and in need of change. Negative entropy became the doorway into the land of the immortal. Yes, nature was clearly the key to life on the planet, and metaphorically it's soul but humans came to invest much in development of religious hierarchies to contain the human soul. Via these humans came to believe in an afterlife after a small death period. Technology then became important via dreams of its aid to immortality of the individual not just the specific entity.

In this way, the soul, as a dynamic metaphor of the non-rational, was filed away awaiting a technological fix. So too was the concern for how life leads to death via the cosmic role of the 2nd Law of Thermodynamics. The First Law was more consistent with humans dreaming of infinite processes that worked to meet needs despite nature's Second Law, that of Entropy. The technology to be developed would seem to have been to ultimately give human control over all things, including those non-rational peculiarities like death. Via the emphasis on life being cheap it was easy to work out a Faustian deal with that phenomenon called nature. Via such everything could be bought or sold, and its context could serve as a stage set for human plays that followed.

We can learn much from looking to the European students that had begun to fear climate change conditions, then consequences. In classes they had mentioned this via that metaphoric payback via the devil (the bad). In essence their elders had forsaken the longer-term hope for life. Humans had come to give emphasis to the cheap from the short-term. Soul-selling had been formalized prior to the 1850s articulation of those thermodynamic laws of the cosmos but after that is expanded. Prior to knowing of the 2nd Law humans could believe they had access to infinite free-will, materials, time, and energy. Now humans just pretend they don't know of the 2nd Law as its deterioration activities continue.

1

The Economic & Technological Versus Life

Major Problems From Human Worship of Negative-Entropy

If humans continue to use natural resources to enhance their lives, should they show more concern for the deterioration accompanying the process? Can concern direct change? Of course it's pleasant to assume there to be gain and no pain, but can such ever be true in a universe governed by *entropy*? Readers of the *Economist* like to presume that productivity enhancements overshadow signs of mounting deterioration that necessarily accompanies production and consumption. Where problems emerge from raw material scarcity many have come to believe they can just turn to recycling, reusing, and alternative inputs consistent with dreams of *negative entropy*. It is dreamed that intelligence, via natural and artificial methods, will provide ever better ways to avoid the dictates of the 2nd Law of Thermodynamics. A few have argued with such presumptions and thus become economic outcasts to those who rejoice in their thinking of continuing human progress. Examples are Socrates and more recent philosophers such as Nicholas Georgescu-Roegen.[5] To the dreams of the emotional he added the nightmares of the physical. He argued against Adam Smith' belief in creating national wealth. From this the contextual disruption issues, such as environmental deterioration, from product

---

[5] Nicholas Georgescu-Roegen, *The Entropy Law and the Economic Process*, Harvard University Press, 1971.

making then use, could, via Smith, become effectively managed with more innovative societal regulations. Thus, humans using business as usual can find happiness assured.

Even the 1971 formalization of why this couldn't continue to govern economic models, by Nicholas Georgescu-Roegen, didn't bring much concern to there being a flaw in the logic of the human mission. After his book was published by Harvard Press, "The Entropy Law and The Economic Process," Roegen came to be harshly abused via comments of American economists. In other parts of the world, such as Europe and Asia, he gained respect.

As long as energy and materials were available in nature humans felt they could prosper indefinitely. They argued that science would come to solve all human problems associated with limitations. Nobel prizes were annually awarded for signs of this. Humans were discovering ways to forgo concern over limits on energy and material inputs to the industrial system. They were also thinking there were ways to avoid the obvious signs of deterioration from their relations to the natural environment. Humans came to believe in the central thesis of the book on "Wealth of Nations[6]" that provided an infinite development model. Smith even talked of recycling in his formalized dream of economic development in 1776.

Smith's economic model appeared during the same year as the human fantasy that humans could create a meaningful democratic nation. Called the United States, the 1776 attempt was to provide a social context where occupants would be free to seek the ever-cheaper life. This would make use of the nature as stolen from peoples who had long cared for nature and the land.[7] The gains would then be spread to major parts of the world, including Europe.

Meanwhile, elders feeling secure about the industrial process they had created and expanded, were telling youth to forget about their concern. "Forget that damned climate change crap, it's a hoax." Youth should simply "Keep on keeping on and follow their education."

---

[6] Adam Smith, "An Inquiry into the Nature and Causes of the Wealth of Nations," two volumes, W. Strahan and T. Cadell Publishers, London, 9 March, 1776.

[7] David Hawk, "Human Nature and the Potential in Nurture," Writer's Banding, 2022.

Education had prepared them for success in a "business as usual" context. Sadly, the situation of climate change's consequences has since become more serious yet diffuse. Except for some misinformed, or ignorant, leaders most humans now sense an approaching tragedy for life via the climate changing they initiate.

A new context was emerging, one that threatened the process of life on earth. Its conditions required "business as unusual" ventures for continuance. To worsen the situation adults were advising youth to simply ignore ideas of context mattering. Youth were taking note that context not only mattered but was becoming everything. Key scientists on the subject were saying "The stage set was becoming more important to the play on climate change then the actors." Youth noticed how when context is included answers are different, as well as the questions that define the play. Without context included there seemed to be no meaning.

Emery and Trist: Environmental Turbulence — Humans

A 1965 Emery and Trist science article illustrated how ignoring context increases the chances for failure. Many management theorists of the time were upset with that thesis, which they thought complicated things. Emery and Trist then went on to argue how ignoring context created conditions leading into a turbulent environment. By 2000 the revolutionary Emery and Trist idea had become common sense, then classical wisdom. Both were my advisors during the 1975-77 Swedish based climate change project central to this book.

Climate change consequences are now creating conditions of turbulence. On the horizon there is a strong suggestion of chaos. Climate change science is now attracting similar criticism to that leveled against Emery and Trist in 1965. Such critics now comment: "The weather is always changing, so why worry about climate change?"

Youth are thus perplexed. Scientists say there will be radical environmental changes, that threaten life on the planet, but parents and neighbors tell them to forget about it. Elders become more upset when science illustrates how it was the past and present activities of elders that brought about the dangers. Business as usual may be helpful to humans meeting their present bio-needs and psycho-wants, but the manner in which they have been doing it is not complementary to life. Just now the system relies on egocentric mannerisms as described and marketed in Adam Smith's "Wealth of Nations." Perhaps he did not realize that such will require that a future price be paid, perhaps one that is unaffordable.

Environmental disaster reports attract more of the attention of youth with time. Increasingly numerous and expanding droughts, fires, floods and storms are the most powerful in history. The religiously initiated, culturally driven arguments of elders against climate change become more humorous with time. Optimistic platitudes such as "Don't worry. When the going gets tough the tough get going." Once a cute phrase, it depicts a future for humans dying via droughts and hurricanes.

The emphasis on management in modern society is with the masculine, and its capabilities for coming to the rescue during trouble. The feminine, on the other hand, is mostly a dutiful follower from the Garden of Eden. She follows along to work at cleaning-up messes. Just now society is beginning to see the feminine spirit as key to avoidance of wrong and maintenance to repair that which was not avoided. Such was becoming more crucial to life's survival than just doing things. Early indications were that leadership must contain feminine values, and perhaps be defined by such values. Masculinity had become an unsupportable expense.

We should keep in mind that adult intentions are steeped in a long history of guiding youth to do better than the adults did, or at least better than the adult neighbors. Competition was assumed to house a crucial motivator for continuous improvement in a social group. Such processes depend on definitions of "doing well" although under conditions of climate change there will be a radical redefinition, including of doing, of well, and of extinction. Even the definition of attempting to define will change.

Somehow humans mostly presume the future is a continuation of their past. Change occurs but its manageable; especially so with new technologies. Limitations in education illustrate the problem clearly. Change is allowed but not encouraged. The answers being taught can by modified but not the questions. Climate change is now beginning to change the definition of change not just climate.

The education system was set up to give emphasis to memorization of fixed answers to historic questions. Sadly, via change both were irrelevant and possibly dangerous in a dynamic world. Adults, including teachers, argued for stability in answers as well as the questions needing to be answered. Students preferred the more dynamic and responsive alternative. In the many courses I taught in many subjects I found students to consistently enjoy improving questions more than memorizing former answers from the past. We called this learning as distinct from education, this encouraged working to redefine the future while defining ways to manage it. With climate change conditions coming to affect life such attempts seemed appropriate. The fragmented educational process was simply a fragment of a larger process. Analytic divisions between subject areas, that were not recombined, were an additional problem.

Sitting in classrooms watching streams of disconnected parts go by as they defined the future was not very meaningful to learning of "systems of life." Parts called words, math, sciences, history, and ethics were abstracted from context, thus less than meaningful. As students advanced in school, they watched parts be continually subdivided into additional parts. This resulted in abstract disintegrations of meanings hidden behind the concept of analysis. Learning is different. It attempts integration of knowledge in a search for meaning.

Education, not learning, depends on parts and their hierarchies. Hierarchy is introduced on the first day of a term. A manifestation of many rows of seats and/or desks facing a central and higher position reserved for a teacher that is expected to be in charge is central to education. Such hierarchies are unnatural but posed as essential to an efficient education, even if the subjects were nonessential or wrong. Being natural, when brought up in student questions, is seen as an obstacle to efficient education defined as memorization of accepted axions and postulates. Student questions are mostly dealt with via a gaze that says "shut-up and listen." Students are thus introduced to acceptance of the artificial. Here I present a different model, one that avoids the limitations in reliance on hierarchies of knowledge absent in nature.

Sexuality is apparent in the ordering then management of education. Masculinity assumes an important role in the idea of hierarchy and then does battle with ideas of the natural that mostly ignore hierarchy. The basis for the continuance and nurturing of the natural, i.e., the feminine, is mostly ignored or used for humor. Definitions of success and reoccurring value are built from emphasis on the masculine. Order is thus defined by management via the masculine. Masculine defines the ordering system with authority placed in the first three letters of management. From this humans move to create machines in support of the masculine. Thus, we see piles of machinery call industrial. Thus, we see the beginnings of what is now called climate change and seen to have severe consequences for life.

As such the ideas of industrial processes were defined to be "manageable." Implicit to measures of success in such comes to include size representations where it's always better to be faster and larger. Thus, humans felt they could declare war on the natural, then move on to war with each other.

From this the human came to develop and believe in the existence of competitive advantages, especially over other forms of life, and others. Such were to be praised. In this way humans would board the train of industrialization that would head towards a drop-off cliff, off into a climate change ending. This was soon seen as a problem as the process grew, but then humans proposed repairs. One followed by many was to make the train more sustainable, as it approached the drop-off. Youth, thought to be inexperienced and uneducated, failed to see the science of sustainability, and felt there needed to be another way, one without the train and its certain end state regardless of sustainability of the process.

Measures of Success as Entrees to Failure

Career status and measures of success linked to a bank account were somehow linked to ownership of ever larger quantities of material objects and the energy required in their use. Key to this was the industrial production of the stage set of human life. Expanding industrial production was an unquestioned necessity. It was seen as very manly and thus under manly management. This all began about 1850 and grew exponentially. Youth in general and some adults in particular came to notice that the accepted model of the industrial had unacceptable environmental costs associated with it. An industrial ideology, even a religion, was emerging. By the advent of the 21st Century most youth began to notice there were problems awaiting in their futures from what was being called climate change.

Critics of the industrial model of human progress were/are rare. Where they did emerge, they tended to arise from feminine values. A 19th Century version of the epic Joan of Arc seemed in order. One arose in 1856, Eunice Newton Foote, via a critic of the industrial process in her work on the science of climate change emerging from CO2. She warned of the future costs of expanding use of coal and other energy sources. Her research illustrated how CO2 from fossil fuel burning would warm the planet. When she was to present her findings at an 1856 AAAS Annual Meeting a man sitting near to her was asked to read the presentation. Her "womanly" work was not discussed until a man plagiarized it three years later then another man plagiarized both thirty years later. The "work" of both men was reviewed but no change in the industrial model emerged at the time. Only in the 1960s did we begin to see serious criticism of the accepted model of the industrial in human affairs, as it hinted at a future defined by environmental deterioration. Later, that industrial phenomenon became synonymous with climate change.

Youth were seeing that the contemporary manner of development brought problematic consequences with it. Climate change conditions, as noted in 1856 research was emerging 125 years later. It then became obvious that its consequences were serious and brought devastating events. Our species thus seems at war with systems of living order. We are part of that natural context and thus depend on its healthfulness, yet how is it that we show pride in its destruction? To what end is such being sought?

Since the "Short-Term Gain" book was written the situation has changed. It's much worse. This book is edited and modified to account for six of ten major tipping points of life's collapse having already been crossed. Several species crucial to human life have already died off. Humans are clearly responsible for an against-life trend on the planet. Much of this is collected under the title of climate change. Humans can change the climate of the planet but seem incapable of changing themselves to support life.

Youthful concern seems especially apparent in Europe and has expanded since the publication of the "Short-Term Gain" book. Climate change consequences have arrived sooner than expected and with greater intensity. The future of civilization has become questionable. Adam Smith's articulation of human happiness via expanding personal wealth now seems more questionable than 100 years ago. We begin to question Smith's idea of economics as: *"...our individual need to fulfill self-interest results in societal benefit."*

In much of youth this Smith idea is questionable if not dead. They see climate change's consequences from individualized behaviors. Smith's dream of short-term gains having priority while longer-term costs could be dealt with when they arise is now under serious review where believed. Belief centers are becoming rarer. He went easy in his writing on the longer costs although he noted that continuation of industrial expansion would require "reuse" of material and energy recourses as depended upon. He somehow trusted that via increasing knowledge and expanding technology there could be an infinite expansion of the "wealth of nations. The timeline and morality of Smith's idea of economic development have proved to be problematic. A good friend, Nicholas Georgescu-Roegen, stook up against the Adam Smith intellect and thus became quite unpopular. His 1971 book, "The Entropy Law and The Economic Process," may become the last economics book of relevance by 2050. The situation of 2025 is proving to be far worse than his warnings of 1971. The cost of ignoring such becomes greater each day.

2

Descriptors of the Ominous

Business as Usual Will Insure a Future of No Business

Threats to life from business-as-usual activities, that generate climate change issues, were key to the original book. Students were interested in business as unusual in their lives, and what such could do to alleviate climate change. Change of humans to meet change of environment was key. Seeing their future defined by an unfortunate version of industrial development needed changing. A clue to how bad students felt about their prospects in life is hinted at via Amy Macdonald in her song "Where are you going to sleep tonight," as recorded on *This is the Life*. Where could they find or create business as unusual?

Central to business as usual are ideas connected to being more strategically successful in doing the usual. Humans have been taught during the past two centuries to think strategically. Doing so was key to success. Today this continues in an exaggerated format, where almost all pronouncements, commercials and interviews involve questions about the quality of the strategy each participant holds. While early ideas of strategic thinking were seen as key to expanding the valuation of the individual they were constrained by social interaction with others and nature. The situation has changed. Via the wholesale adoption of the philosophies of Adam Smith, Frederic Taylor, and Thomas Hobbes via his thesis on centralized authority being essential. He believed humans were selfish and brutish,

9

thus without powerful central authorities' anarchy would emerge. Consistent with this was the thinking of John Locke's Second Treatise of "Political power is "a right of making laws with penalties of death and consequently all less Penalties." Strategic thinking was key to the thinking of all our men.

The strategic approach to enhancement of individuality is now seen to act against life and its continuance. The concern about this was mentioned by James Madison in 1788 in his Federalist paper, then placed in the context of 1968 with a paper by Garrett Hardin titled "The Tragedy of the Commons." Those early warnings of consequences of strategic thinking were mostly ignored until climate change results materialized. As founder of contemporary strategic thinking, Carl von Clausewitz argued for the key role of strategic thinking in warfare. He argued that warfare was part of a long-term political process of physical and mental fights between humans. Via the industrial revolution unfolding this fight was expanded to include nature. His book on conduct of warfare, On War of 1832, elaborated on how to win in the violent context of conflict. He argued that deceit with others was key to achieving a strategic intent. Deceit expanded to strategic defeat of nature was used in the sense depicted in the Garden of Eden's image and story.

Regardless of its breath the depth of strategic thinking in human affairs offered humans a framework for many actions, including those we call business. Herein business references many activities of the human, not just the production and selling of goods and services as taught in business school curriculum. The results of all these activities are now seen as consequences unacceptable to life's continuance. It's seen in most curricula but especially in that of BS, MBA, and EMBA training. Therein the strategic is widely accepted, even revered, as central to success in the missions of **business-as-usual**.

Climate Change Arrives, with Consequences

Climate change concerns are growing from reflection on consequences awaiting in their present. Global temperatures at the surface are rising. Droughts, floods and storms are becoming more frequent and harmful. Concern is growing, especially in the youth. They wonder if there will be a future. Ideas for significant changes seem essential for access to a future. Herein such is called **business-as-unusual**. It is urgently called for, even as ill defined.

Natural Strength Illustrating Human Weakness

"Change ideas," for finding business as unusual, remain at the edge, the front not the back edge. When suggested they appear hard to implement. More innovation of a special type is essential. Following is an image of the significance of the early stages of climate change resulting from strategic human behavior. The future of business-as-unusual will include knowledge of the 2nd Law of Thermodynamics and its unhappy centerpiece, entropy. Much of emergent concern and marketing to ignore it centers on the strategy of being sustainable. As greenwashing is wrong and counterproductive to continuing life it is contradictory to universal entropy. Even relying on science for wisdom is problematic. Its estimates for climate change timing and damage are consistently slow and less serious than what arrives. One consistent truth is that continuation of business, even as sustainable, will end in no business, metaphorically speaking.[8]

The human war against nature, as stimulated from 1850s mechanization would have unforeseen costs. We now see these human activities as unthoughtful, and from a weakness implicit in humans. The machines invented to improve provision for human needs, especially biological, could also be used to seek fulfillment of psycho-wants. This second category is the essence of the human problem whose solution led to what we now call climate change. This was mentioned in the early book but herein we go much deeper into the change required of humans to survive the change in environment thus created by our weaknesses.

Changelessness: Dreaming of Negative Entropy Discoveries

Climate change consequences can now be seen to arise from *business as usual.* Much of this book presents how this happens in contemporary society, as well as how it was known to be in the human future since 1856 via an emerging interest in and emphasis for a particular industrial paradigm. The contents of this book focus on how long-term costs were known yet were ignored. Instead, via a desire to avoid changing contexts, humans ignored the 1856 warning from an early climate change scientist. Assuming she was wrong, men concentrated on their work in short-term gains while avoiding evidence of long-term expenses for such. Ideas of death-defining "sustainability" emerged to do battle with natural laws that insured the continuation of entropy. On the following page is a 21st Century image of a "sustainability" fix to infrastructure.

---

[8] Please listen to Dana Winner sing "Let the Children Have a World"

Sustainability arguing with Entropy

Later sections of the book provide hints of what *business as unusual* might look like to be effective, as well as the prospects for humans going there even if it's too late to reverse the damages of the time. These areas of hope arose from 1979 conclusions presented in a book resulting from a study of the science of climate change. This was back when climate change was mostly announced as a hoax. At that time it was said that continuation of the current model of business as usual would create conditions of *no business* This came in the results of a 1975 to 1977 research project. Therein results of efforts to control environmental deterioration were studied via extraordinary assistance of 20 international companies and 6 governments attempting to regulate them.

Conclusions from the seventies research project, as presented in a 1979 book, were seen as too early by some, and simply a hoax by others. Those results were republished in 2019 and came to be seen as "too late." The consequences were becoming too harsh to manage via 1977 ideas. In 2019 few still saw climate change to be a hoax, except perhaps for a US president of 2020 and his believers.

DAVID L. HAWK

This book differs from the 1979 European text. It was seen as unsuitable for American business students. Americans were less concerned about environmental deterioration then their European and Asian contemporaries. US students were taught to amass sufficient wealth by any means possible to then afford a private climate change resistive bunker in Hawaii. This was in the style of the richest US CEOs. Americans were not taught about the message in the book's subtitle: "Climate Change as a Faustian Tragedy?" Upon seeing that book's cover they would ask, "What is this Faust stuff?" The answer was Faust was central to a European metaphor articulated in a book of 1550 where the devil negotiated with a man wanting to be rich and famous at any cost thus was willing to sell his end-of-life soul for short-term gains of intelligence, a beautiful woman (like the one in Garden of Eden), and great wealth. After this was presented to a class, some American students asked: "What the hell is this soul thing all about? Does it have anything to do with business success?"

The content of this book is a bit different. It's for a more international and less European audience. Some years have passed since 1979. The ominous nature of consequences of human's war with nature now has more evidence. Climate change consequences are now "tangible." The emphasis herein is no longer on long-term loss of a soul to capture short-term gains. It is on the long-term cost of short-term thinking via business-as-usual. It is urgent to notice the immediate costs arising each day and night in weather pattern changes brought on by flawed values and the thinking they encouraged. The passion for watching stock futures needs replacement with business as unusual negotiations around human ideas on their needs and wants.

Change becomes the qualifier of the most important kind in responding to our long-term initiation of climate change problems. Business as unusual becomes key to improvement of what is, business as usual. This includes philosophy, science, learning, family, and regulation of self. Students will need to learn about the conditions that define our universe and the systemic, not analytic, processes that manage it. This includes knowing more of the fundamental process of entropy and its role in the pessimism coming from our past behaviors. Such sets the conditions for life and its continuance. Change is a context in which life is limited yet allows aspirations for continuation. Humans can thus act out via ideas of great potential while wearing the dog tags of approaching death. It reminds one of their beginnings in life while avoiding the shadows of certain death.

As humans we engage the initial enthusiasm as well as the end of state sorrow. We think about the unlimited potential against a context of guaranteed limitations. Change is natures force that motivates our avoidance of death. How then do we manage change? If we can't manage it where then can we seek knowing how it comes to limit our operations?

We avoid change's end state via the non-rational dreams found in culture, family, children and soft sciences that suggest "Go ahead, it will be alright." We visit places where optimism is apparent such as places of worship, bedrooms, soft-science laboratories, and coffee shops. The hard sciences show we can't avoid evidence of threats coming from humanly caused change. Therein we see change as a process that limits life. Key to the nightmares found therein is a fundamental process that came to be called entropy in 1850. Entropy signifies the universal process of order being dissipated in time. Entropy defines time, although many humans hope it is time that defines entropy. Time has some traits that are negotiable. Entropy does not. Entropy stands at the conceptual core of the 2nd Law of Thermodynamics.

Entropy limits life, movement, change, and evolution in the cosmic process. Beginning with the "big bang" dissipation of order moves forward. As such, entropy denotes a serious limit on human aspirations. It defines a constant dissipation of order over time on everything, including human work and the aspirations driving it. Entropy cannot be overturned or disrupted. It simply is.

Via some level of arrogance humans generally ignore the idea of entropy governing their context and their operations in that context. Some humans go further backward to defeat entropy via dreams of "negative entropy." the more fuel they add to the entropy process. Removing coal, oil and gas reserves locked in the ground to do battle with processes that naturally increase disorder only serves to amplify the extent of that disorder. As many renown scientists have argued

15

during the last 150 years, since humans began to develop and expand on industrialization and the energy input it requires:

> "The law that entropy always increases holds, I think, the supreme position among the laws of Nature. If someone points out to you that your pet theory of the universe disagrees with Maxwell's equations - then so much the worse for Maxwell's equations. If it is found to be contradicted by observation - well, these experimentalists do bungle things sometimes. But if your theory is found to be against the Second Law of Thermodynamics, I can give you no hope; there is nothing for it but to collapse in deepest humiliation."[9]
>
> – Sir Arthur Eddington Lectures –
> When Masculine Management Can't

Feminine values tap into processes that nurture life. This supports life's continuance. Masculine values differ. They tend to deny some aspects of life while being selective about its continuance. What the masculine comes to oppose they do battle with or attempt blockage of. Attempts to nurture as a natural process should have no opposition. To act out via the masculine encourages an opposition mentality, even in support of warfare.

The masculine is drawn to doing battle with the idea of entropy. Such is drawn to fighting against what appears to limit the quantity of their life. As such they initiate and expand ideas that we might best call negative entropy. One is to do war with nature who is seen to be the manager of entropy. Others relate to denial of entropy just as many past scientists have done. Many in the systems science community have done this by arguing that life is negative entropy and thus an effective opposition to death. While attending funerals of

---

[9] Sir Author Eddington, *New Pathways in Science*, Cambridge University Press, 1934.

friends and family such people argue how such in not the end, as the individuals have children that carry on? The dilemma from this attitude is that in not understanding entropy they ignored its role and therefore operate to expand the entropic process. Thus, humans become an even larger threat to life by not internalizing its process. Negative entropy beliefs thus become ideals. Thus what humans do via ignorance only serves to enhance the entropic processes. This can now be seen as the rationale behind the major contributors to an ominous process that threatens life on our planet – climate change. This comes from 1970s research that was not well received by the human need for optimism as seemingly offered by marketing of negative entropy.

The subject herein, humanly created and driven climate change consequences, expands noticeably via secured ignorance in changelessness. It takes pride in ignoring the entropy law in humans carrying out their motivations for technological and economic innovation. None-the-less, many humans hold strong faith in the positivism allowed in concepts of "changelessness" and defiance of entropy in encourages. From this, they soon believe in the dreams of "negative entropy" and disregard the warnings from scientists such as Sir Eddington. Virtually all occupants of marketing and political endeavors place much faith in the rewards of negative entropy.

Why do such humans feel they can halt or even reverse change? Why must they hold such faith in changelessness? Acting to instill and install anti-change in their context thus comes to counter conditions of life and movement of nature. Virtually all marketing and most politicians strongly guarantee negative entropy if only you are willing to "buy it." If this is so, why do these semi-independent forms parading around as humans feel they can halt or even reverse change? a need to exhibit changelessness in their passion for being? Acting to instill and install anti-change soon becomes counter to conditions of life. Many argue that they need stability in life thus a break from change is essential for mental health. As you may have heard, "It may be bad but with change it will be worse." If you watch them, you will see how they are rather passionate about moving backwards and un-doing some changes yet not too far back. It somehow represents something that bothers them in a socio-political sense. Anti-action is not the intent. In fact they work very hard to undo changes that challenge prior models of change they favored. They even favor leadership that will ruthlessly oppose the unfolding change.

For example they rise to oppose those who question the merit of a model of economic exchange as connected to a model of industrial production for that economic system. These individuals somehow had come to appreciate the industrial economic system that was at war with nature even though it had come to endanger the natural, a phenomenon on which they were part of and on which their life depended. They supported its continuance, not its change. Their sense of masculinity stood on continuance of that war with nature. They could not come to understand the idea that without context there is no meaning. This masculinity then relies on a manly model of ego-centric economics where: "I have what I have. You are not welcome to it. It is mine. Leave it and me alone."

Selfish ideals have expanded from individuals into a social phenomenon. This is seen in many countries. It seems to come from working for two centuries in a religion we might best call the industrial. It has become a human religion with no rational basis yet works to allow the irrational aspects of humans to appear as rational. Those nations with the most advanced industrial development are becoming the most concerned about migrants and are "anti-invaders." The owners of the largest piles of the industrial say: "It's ours and you are not allowed to come steal it."

Underneath all this we associate wealth with having, holding and protecting the products of the industry. Beginning as an ideology of the individual, it has been expanded to signify the wealth of a social group. Therein, of course, the wealthier individuals are still in charge while leading a wealthy society. Technological development then implies reduced work for expanded wealth of that society, versus what others outside the group must do. The model claims to develop technology to better serve society via meeting physical needs. In fact, it can be seen to have a bias towards nurturing psycho wants while bringing harm to the context of the society making the gains. This is where resources gathered for making wealth come via bringing damage to an environment.

While the above process moves forward via its values it works to retain those values as changelessly sacred. While favoring changelessness in values humans have invested a great deal since 1850 in developing technology to insulate them from natural change. A radical change is emerging in the human environment that came from prior human changes over several centuries. Yet somehow humans resist change that would reverse industrial changes that threaten planetary life. Something seems wrong here. Can human consciousness wake up in time to resolve this dilemma for life? Can they change their manner of living to remove that which now threatens life on earth?

Our desire for changelessness comes from a family of values that arose as part of an expanding war against natural limitations. Humans came to value several things that can't exist in the universe. It is related to 175-year-old knowledge that entropy is one of the premier laws of the universe. . If life's continuance is threatened. We find such change, the entropic variety, especially irritating when we pursue a lifestyle that is especially destructive of context yet we try to manage it by introducing concepts like "sustainable," which entropy disallows over time. Since sustainable is not possible via entropic change we prepare to discard such under the poetry of mental changelessness. Entropy requires change to move towards universal disorder and thus not available for to stoppage or reversal thus we invent negative entropy as a basis for worship in society. Thus, changelessness is an item in the bag of trips belonging to negative entropy, it doesn't and can't exist in our universe yet has most human believers that worship its power.[10] Another way to introduce such is to ask why is business as usual so attractive to us and our operations?

Perhaps negative entropy, changelessness and continuation of business as usual allows us a psychological escape route from the

---

[10] I will go through this in some detail later in the book as I believe it is a major force behind humans creating conditions of climate change. I have been heavily criticized for making light of negative entropy yet never been shown any hint of evidence that is can possible exist. Most great scientists argue why it simply can't be.

desperation implicit in truth. Perhaps it's a doorway into urgently necessary humor? Changelessness often emerges in discussions about the why, how, and then consequences of change. To insulate against change we often go for leadership that promises to take up backward before change changed us? To attract us he lies much about change and his management of it. If such gives meaning to our lives, then our lives are not so valuable anyway? Eventually, we learn a price is to be paid.

Change, and changelessness, are implicit in most social discourse about life. It soon unfolds to address the future of a society and its occupants. Three options for change include forwards, backwards, or complete refusal of it. Listening to political discourse we soon see the quality of a society's discourse, or lack thereof. The implications of needed change can excite or dishearten listeners. History shows how the choice can hint at societal disbandment or its erasure. Some historians' report how such warms its members prior to a hellish removal.[11]

One of the greats, RG Collingwood, said history was used to relive the past in your own mind as you believe you understand the present and future. As a touch of humor he later commented: "History is the lie commonly agreed upon." Herein we use this to go deeper into referencing past events to point out essential changes needed for serious discussion. From this we can conceptualize from historical knowledge about species of life being previously removed the earth and how those conditions may be like what is now calling for change in being human. The science record of such exterminations is ominous. Such overwhelms discussion of other topics in most societies. Climate change and its consequences considering currently emerging evidence of what it will involve are tough to report on or visualize.

Current discussion of climate change centers on what it is then moves to who generated it and then how best to stop or manage its continuation. Hundreds of science articles are now available for those

---

[11] To read further in this see R.G. Collingwood, The Idea of History, Cambridge University. 1946.

whose psyche can take it. A recent example can be read in *Science* magazine of September 13, 2024, page 1151. It is titled: "Strong El Ninos primed Earth for mass extinction, Extreme Weather by ocean shifts set stage for Great Dying 250 million years ago."

A healthy society depends on effective change with the discourse behind such can include disagreements can be of low or no quality. Where they begin or end harshly there is little hope for beneficial results to a society sponsoring the discourse, or its membership. Such shows little concern for others or a longer-term self. Where the discourse is kind, tolerant and goes well it seeks those differences that can arrive at a meaningful difference to life.

It's worth noting how some disagreements go deeper to seek presumptions that underly the more obvious discourse. Such is like the legal arguments of the 1990s for saving fuel via a law restricting speed to no more than 55-mph. With the former limit being 65-mph, most people didn't like the point. Thus, after the non— discussable law was passed the average speed climbed to 70 mph. A more helpful discussion would have begun with "should you drive a car at any speed" but that was ignored. How change is arrived at can be as important as a change is presumed to be.

Arguments over the superficial forms of change are expressed more loudly with less concern for accuracy. This is easily seen by some politicians. The second form, that one that is deeper and of greater benefit, is more interesting herein. The differences about change being discussed therein are not political rants but close to the make-up of the individual spirit and what motivates it. Significant societal change depends on collective individual change but is rare. Its major argument is with the societal bias to secure "changelessness," as depicted in culture.

They become the motivators or change either towards new assumptions about the truth, or backwards to avoid such to be discussable. Change is at the core of the process. It can lead to movement in many directions. It can involve more differences or move to reduce or eliminate differences. Societies that are to be diminished move towards the simplicity of no difference, no tolerance and no change.

Some people believe Some believe AI will resolve such arguments with reality. Others think AI is mostly for humor once its
applied generally. Those avoiding such disagreements from the mis-
information of one side, or the other, or both. As will be discussed
here, the majority of a society's people stick with what supports
changelessness and the stability it implies. Maybe we should presume
the above is impossible, like the way in which the USA evolves and
refuses to change what changes it in a negative manner.

The above is the stuff of TV news thus the commercials are
often seen as more interesting. I mention this as we seem on the
edge of seeing a disagreement become momentous to individuals,
society, the planet. Unlike the normal this disagreement is seen to be
intolerant of ignorance. It begins to look like the disintegration that
took place in the land of the Mayan's beginning in 800AD. Therein
the peninsula of Yucatan[12] lost most cities and many people as the
climate heated and went dry from the natural terrain being changed
by humans seeking increases of food and materials. This kind of significant change was noted in Andres Angyal's WWII chaos theory:
"When a system reaches its limits the parts assume the whole."[13] His
was not an optimistic pronouncement about civilizations spread
around the planet. Central to this book is how this history of change
in small local communities due to mankind's behavior to nature is
changed. Its no longer restricted to a small area so escape from human
mistakes can move to fix the problem. Moving as a change that solves
a human derived problem It no longer an option. Much more is now
required, including a better understanding of humans, nature, the
planet, the industrial, consequences and the role of change in all.

Change can be clearly seen in the history of youth acting to take
responsibility of that which they will inherit. This begins in their

---

[12] In 1969 I chose to spend a semester in a Merida Yucatan College studying the
evolution of the Mayan Civilization. For me it was an example of forthcoming
climate change changing a culture. This was a follow up study to what I
had experienced regarding societal disintegration in Vietnam while there in
1966-1968.

[13] Andras Angyal, *Foundations for a Science of Personality*, New York:
Commonwealth, 1941.

seeing human actions that appear too slow, too fast or simply too wrong to tolerate. Thus youth have the material with which to disagree with elders. Such disagreements are well recorded in human history. We can listen to them in real time while sitting in local coffee shops or in auditoriums with political forums unfolding. Wherever it arises, it illustrates the role of voice to power. Such was This was seen on January 6, 2021, due to concern over what was going on. A harsher, more directed version of change seekers was seen in the in the anti-Vietnam war anger on college campuses of 1968 - 1975. Behaviors in the sense of Angyal, including kindness, sadness, humor or anger, or all of these in one event, were thus demonstrated to change society.

Youth, Seeking Hope in Change that Isn't

Youth, mostly 10- to 20-years, question authority from those in charge of the present, nor the present. These seek different qualities until they learn to accept business as usual in their society. Therapists advise both sides how their questioning societal norms is normal then suggest participants "just deal with it." Then, prior to issuing their bill, they conclude "it will get better." The focus herein is what happens when it does not and cannot "get better." It accepts that youth are and should be upset but then goes deeper into a threat to planetary life, climate change consequences. Such is far more deadly and tangible than cultural abnormalities. Since 2010 the concerns of youth about the behavior wrongs of the elderly has become very serious.

Youth have come to focus on the viability of humans in a continuance of lifestyle of their elders. They begin to question if there will be a future regardless of its qualities. The questioning seems to become more serious with time. A sample of this situation worldwide is seen in *The Climate Book* of 2023. Therein Greta Thunberg offers the thoughts from a 19-year-old girl and one hundred scientists who paint a grim picture for continuation of life via business as usual.

The rapidly escalating climate and ecological crisis is a global crisis: it affects all living plants and beings. But to say that all of humankind is responsible for it is very, very far from the truth. Most people today are living well within the planetary boundaries. It is only a minority of us who have caused this crisis and who keep driving it forward. This is why the popular argument that 'there are too many people' is a very misleading one. Population does matter, but it is not people who are causing emissions and depleting the Earth, it is what some people do – it is some people's habits and behavior, in combination with our economic structure, that are causing the catastrophe.[14]

Youth are entering a deeply spiritual confrontation against adult values manifested in the tragedies from a war between the human industrial and the natural context of life. The planetary results of human behavior since 1850 are problematic. Concern for continuation of life on the earth is met with daily evidence that the concern is too little and comes too late. Adults are seen to have been silly, or immoral, or both. They ignored the warning of a young female scientist in 1856 and feverishly adopted a broken industrial model to meet privately selfish needs, much like the 16th Century storyline of Faust. The result is a badly damaged once beautiful planet. Prospects for further systems of living order on it look bleak. As the elders die off embracing a negative entropy version of health care the future for youth looks bad.

How did humans arrive at an industrial model, tools and rationalizations for remaking their planet, a model that threatens planetary life. Why did their ancestors ignore then carry out war against the more natural aspects of life, those coming to be known as the non-rational. Seen as aligned with nature, the non-rational came to

---

[14] Greta Thunberg, *The Climate Book*, New York: Penguin Press, 2023, P. 19

be seen as opposing manly development of the mechanical. As poetics, aesthetics, love, the systemic, and respect for natural processes, the non-rational has been seen by many men as an obstacle or even an intrusion into the quest for infinite power. Just now youth see a problem in management, with focus on questions about the behavior of the first three letters of the term.

We now see more youth becoming tired of the limits of adult rationality to seek hope in the teachings of the non-rational yet be driven into the suicidal arms of the irrational via suicide.[15] Adults are giving rational offerings of the reasons for such as due to youth have lost it, having no meaningful purpose, or kids simply have it too easy. As such, they spend all day on their cell phones and most of their nights on cell phones. Meanwhile the youth ask those that are older why they destroyed the planetary basis for life with their values, ideas and actions? They ask their parents, "Have you ever felt shame for your behavior in life?" You can choose which group's indictment you favor. Both have some merit but one has moved on from 19th Century cause-effect thinking to concern for effects of effect in the 21st Century.

Serious consequences from 19th Century industrialization are emerging to threaten life on a massive scale. This includes the elderly, the youth, those in the middle, and all forms of planetary life. Society as currently defined economically, politically and materially is clearly seeing its future in question. The emergent challenges seem beyond human abilities to manage, adapt to, or even understand. The situation is indeed grim regardless of it being from old, non-caring idiots or young lay-abouts. Being unresponsive, both groups only expand the consequences in a negative way. Can they change what they think about, want to do and do?

---

[15] This was experimented with via a youth group in a Lakota Indian tribe in western South Dakota. This group had the highest suicide rate in the US. They slowed the rate by taking responsibility for caring for a group of horses that were said to be considering suicide due to seeing how humans were taking care of their earth and its resources. These youth were to convince the horses that life was worthy of continuance.

Reading history allows us to see a long trail of humans having difficulty accepting change or accommodating the consequences of it. Now, that societal development situation is more difficult. While it's hard to find ways to discuss it, an urgency has arisen to replace potentiality in change with aftereffects from its occurrence. An historic expression, known as Murphy's Law, "Anything that can go wrong will go wrong," has been updated. The "can go" phrase is replaced with "Anything that can go wrong *is going* wrong." Time is redefined and no longer serves as an insulator against the scary. Change has become turbulent in the sense projected in 1965 by Emery and Trist as a context outside the abilities of human responses. As they projected, change would become a major threat to life instead of an essential feature for its continuance. Since this even science has come to change its models. The past predictions were more or less accurate, yet the projected timetables were too far off to be helpful. Time has changed along with change changing. Standard cause-effect models for determining truth are becoming irrelevant as various science communities shift to the effect of effects.

Is it Gone? Nope, it Just Changed…

3

Change: Damned to Do, Double-Damned to Don't

Change is Changing, Responses to Such Redefine
Our Future, or Lack of One[16]

My intention is not to upset but to help see that humans must change. If we can't our future will become increasingly dangerous, perhaps even terminal. As our environment changes, due to our prior activities, life becomes more fragile. At this point in history humans are entering a world defined by *change squared*. A previously acceptable rate of change is changing, i.e., change is becoming changed. This looms over and around all we do. It should now be seen as *change squared*.

Instead of change supporting life we see it as a threat. Climate change illustrates the meaning of this. That it is changing is predictable but the changes in change and the extent and dates of arrival are open to question although three decades of evidence imply the change will be more drastic and arrive sooner than predicted.

Via change of change its difficult to reflect on a happy future. Instead of mapping out preparation for and conduct in future societal roles, we see youth mentally upset over an omnipresent threat

---

[16] From the introduction to a research proposal at the Stockholm School of Economics, Institute of International Business, September 1975. The project came to include 20 international firms and 6 governments. The book reporting on research results, written in 1979, was republished in 2019 as "Too Little, Too Late, Now what?"

to having any future. life itself regardless of our presumed role in it. What was a questionable aspect of later life is now outside the understandable. This is seen economic inflation of goods essential to support life, in youth turning away from college, marriage, and foregoing the joys of raising happy children.

Change has moved from being a more material form of challenges out there, to the internal challenges related to private consciousness. This begins to redefine the mental state needed for consciousness. To be or not to be becomes more than a question, it becomes the focus for being. Instead of a backdrop question that roams the hidden parts of the stage of life, suicide is now openly discussable along with preparations for such.

A Changed Environment, can it support life?

The challenge mentioned above, *change,*[2] can be seen in its consequences but has yet to be understood. That is a major challenge addressed herein. Clearly the conditions needed to sustain life on earth are changing. This raises questions of human occupation. Planet temperatures of 2023 and 2024 were the hottest ever recorded. Such was an indicator of irreversible points being crossed and there are at least nine other points being approached. Such change is greater than dangerous for life. Planetary life is being questioned. Change of change and the phenomena arising from it are also impacting the human soul via the questioning of human existence. The human mind as well as body seems endangered by consequences of past human activities. Thus, we seek more effective access to life yet even the definition of effective is questionable. As youth seek something to hold onto via the resulting turbulence in their environment, they find very little that we can call hope. The attitude of the elderly does not help. Parents only besmirch the behavior of the youth for refusing to continue what they, the elderly, did even though it is now seen as a generator of the turbulence in life's environment. As such most thoughts are digital in that they come from Aristotle's two-dimensions of logical reality; black-what, rich-poor, beautiful-ugly, right-wrong, Republican-Democratic, fixed-fluid, etc.

To visualize the mess think of your being seriously injured. You must rush to a hospital emergency room. Continuance of your life depends on your making it "in time." Reflect on what would happen if you found a changing context to pass through in getting to the hospital. As such normal cause-effect logic becomes irrelevant to helpful decisions on what to do and how to do it. For example, while driving to the hospital your environment changes. A heavy snowstorm rolls in and places your technological service in question. In heavy snow extra time is needed for safe driving. Regardless, you are lucky and finally arrive at the emergency entrance. Then, you notice a sign on the doorway, "Permanently Closed." Your human capabilities are thus questioned beyond your conceptions of the possible. Significant change is in your environment. Will you select self-changes that can be complementary to environmental change? Or will your mental state close from questions without answers? "What to do" is the subject herein. These contents build on a prior book that raised this question: "Too Early, Too Late, Now what?"

Forward,[17] on Then and Now:

> Then was 1979. Now is 2019. In what follows much comes from then, with a touch from now, and concern for those who occupy tomorrow. Normally, with a forty-year gap in an endeavor, back then served as a baseline. Success can thus be measured in how we managed the initial concern. From this we can propose ways to improve success. Such will not be found herein.[18]
>
> Carrying the hospital metaphor into current reality we see an emergence of increased floods, droughts, storms, food shortages and other environmental threats to life. These are coming to be seen as examples of climate change consequences, C^3. It's beginning to appear as "too late" in our

---

[17] Yes, I know foreword is spelled as forward, but forward is to denote difference. It's to denote a phenomenon from the future returning into the present, that will reset the future stage.

[18] Hawk, David, *Too Early, Too Late, Now what?*, North Carolina, Brilliant Books, 2019. P. vii.

subconscious. You can see this in the mood of those you meet in a store, or work with at work, or argue with at home.

While 20% of humans continue to doubt the depth of the challenges another 20% cannot see from where the challenges originated in 1850. More than 50% appear open to serious change thus accepting humans as responsible, yet with few ideas about what they can do to transform human behavior. Our economic dreams and their industrial means used to achieve them have greatly increased the CO_2 surrounding the earth. The heat surrounding life is being increased by the same proportion. 95% of scientists clearly demonstrate human activities as responsible for threats to life on earth. From this knowledge base most scientists and many humans see change, a drastic form, is required. Then upon thinking a bit deeper most humans hesitate in removing many of the activities of the industrial on which their lives depend. Such would clearly "change" their home, family, economy, style of living? The next level deeper brings up the concern with "Change, to what?"

A Touch of History

One argument is that our modern Homo sapiens appeared on the planet about 300,000 years ago and may simply be evolving towards their end state. Perhaps the end of species chapter was built into the human mentality relative to values and behaviors as they evolve, where some are quite destructive of their context. The modern chapter began 50,000 to 65,000 years ago. It began 50,000 to 65,000 years ago. This argument is not posed herein although evolution patterns for most species suggest such might be normal.

A Book Behind this Book: "Short-Term Gina, Long-Term Pain: Climate Change as a Faustian Tragedy" is important. It was written in 2022 for a European audience, via the Faustian metaphor on life. The Faustian story began in 1550 to give note to humans having limits on person ethics. The boy Faust was desperate for a meaningful life, as measured in what society defined as important. including access to wealth, acquiring knowledge and having beautiful women. These were seen as crucial to define his life as meaningful. Thus, he was seen as "available."

The devil sent an emissary to talk to poor Faust. Talking has become an important instrument of negotiation. The emissary offered the young man access to his needs and wants but would first need to agree to give up ownership of the soul. Goethe's wrote one of the great depictions of the bargaining. In Goethe's Faust the short-term gains were offered at the expense of long-term consequences at the end of life. This was the theme used in the 1979 book on climate change. Therein humans sold their end-of-life soul via taking access to industrial production that would create ever larger piles of goods for human use each day. Industrial production of natural energies and materials into consumable products in the short-term would extract the long-term price of climate change via a disintegration of context via what was known as climate change consequences. Human bio-needs and psycho-wants demanded such. Besides, as humans of the time said, the soul could be imaginary, and the weather is always changing anyway.

The devil argued that the soul might not even exist and if it did there was uncertainty about its purpose. More important to today were the more tangible and immediately useful keys to success. Faust's work took place in 1775, the year the US Constitution was being formed and framed. It was obviously derived from England's 1210 attempt at democratic governance called the Magna Carta, what became downgraded in a less democratic revision in 1215 to get the king to sign. It articulated why even the king's actions could not be placed above or outside the law, a question now re-emerging in the US relative to Donald Trump's belief that he was a king. Later we will examine the limitations of legal claims based on the limits of laws transcribed as two-dimensional. In such limits it's not easy to regulate three-dimensional phenomena without serious errors and legal corruption.

It is important to note the ongoing human logic at the center of Faustian bargaining. Humans come to ignore what is meaningful. Much of their days are invested in finding short-term rewards. Thus, humans accept consequences awaiting them in an environmental future while concentrating on immediate needs and psycho wants. We see humans taking advantage of the now while ignoring longer-term costs after the now. Action is directed towards money, materials, and beautiful people, not the costs of relating to them. Via such valuation humans move to invest in the development of ever faster and more destructive machines that promise to produce ever cheaper products. This logic was rampant after WWII in the expanding development of machines to find and mine access to energy needed to expand the industrial. The work of London's Tavistock Institute in development of socio-technical systems models, to restore the value worker lives, was an early example for suspending Faustian negotiations. The power of managerial values set this aside in emergence of the digital coal mine found in office buildings thereafter.[19]

Such did not seem to help understand climate change's arrival in the USA. While the situation of climate change was similar, and its consequences seemed identical, Faust was not a good metaphor for mapping the beginning and ending of that human process. Somehow the industrial ideology, i.e., religion, was different in America. The economics of cheaper was easily acceptable as a mission in life.

As was introduced before, the Europeans tend to relate to the issue of soul and man's willingness to negotiate with trading it away. The American focus seems to be centered on the cheap, then how to improve the productivity of becoming ever cheaper. Many of these activities are those that drive the process of creating climate change conditions in the earth's atmosphere. Most adults see this as overly pessimistic thus youth are advised to forego the philosophy set here and instead concentrate on the data. The prognosis within the philosophy comes from integrating data sets.

Change matters, especially to those who value life and its continuance. As humans are involved in life's change there is a major dilemma at the core of change and its consequences for life. The dilemma centers on conceptions of change and if change even

[19] Emery and Trist, "The Causal Texture of Organizational Environments," *Human Relations*, 18(1), 21-32, 1965.

requires movement. Can there be change that is changeless, or even movement to the reverse that can unchanged change?

Climate Change — A Deviance Against Life

Change is becoming hard to define. It is fluid. Change provides a doorway into a world moving beyond human understanding thus its management. We have long seen it as difference over time but that was bit too abstract. As such we have avoided seeing it as one of the keys to life.

Reality in a fluid state is hard to discuss or define. The sense of change therein challenges traditional thinking and being. Via climate change we encounter a different level of change. Its mysteries trivialize the usual concerns of normal human behavior. It transcends the mission of those normally expected to seek power over others and change. This is clearly seen in the 2024 election run off in the US where one candidate envisions change to a great past, that may not have existed, while the other candidate envisions future change to finally achieve what has been wanted but never achieved. Such marketing of change has long been with human conduct. This has been a periodic concern for change approaching work life, place of residence, friends' impression of you, spousal love for you, or whether you should change the sofa you invested much time in.

The emergent sense of change and its impact may well have on the life is clearly different. The contents found herein address this more omnipresent version of change. The dilemma in this kind of change is that as we notice our environment to be changing significantly, we become reticent to change ourselves. This can be defined as a serious problem in human behavior is primarily responsible for creating a changing environment, yet we sit with the hope that it's not true.

Clearly change is now the qualifier on an emerging planetary threat to life called *climate change*. Thus it is more disruptive to the psyche than that change being negotiated with in the egocentric sanctuary of private thoughts. This domain of thinking often reflects on feeling from family, friends, neighbors, and bosses towards you, who you are, what you do and don't do. We often interpret change in such domains as moving to lower status evidence of what others think. In the same manner we interpret nature's thoughts about human actions that disrupt the environment essential to life in a negative light. Are humans likely to design and carry out changes in their behavior that attempt to repair past mistakes, or will they simply sit, and watch posterity lose hope for betterment? Yes, this is heavy.

To begin to take the more proactive approach as a steppingstone to the necessary interactive approach to climate change, we can think as follows. Contrary to our negative attitude to nature as clearly documented from 1850 on we begin with seeing how nature and natural changes within it are key to biological support of living systems that evolve to ensure continuance of life. This includes breathing, eating, drinking and breeding. Via such we argue with and/or slow a cosmic process called entropy; a process that operates against the essential order required of life. Seeing this we begin to reflect on how then why humans came to worship the artificial, via development of the industrial of 1850 and its men of wisdom as initiated by those calling for improvement via expanded rationality and logic as defined by Premediates, Plato, Aristotle, Newton, etc. Clearly humans could have found a longer-term, more intelligent approach. The essence of the weakness in the Aristotelian logic is seen in its definition that is more accurate than humorous in today's industrial operation. It is clearly in opposition to common sense, the nonrational and thus natural wellbeing.

> Logic, n. The art of thinking and reasoning in strict accordance with the limitations and incapacities of the human misunderstanding. The basis of logic is the syllogism, consisting of a major and a minor premise and a conclusion -thus:
>
> Major Premise: Sixty men can do a piece of work sixty times as quickly as one man.
>
> Minor Premise: One man can dig a post hole in sixty seconds; therefore —

> Conclusion: Sixty men can dig a posthole in one second.
>
> This may be called the syllogism arithmetical, in which, combining logic and mathematics, we obtain a double certainty and are twice blessed." [20]

The example of the limitations of business as usual was taught by Professor Russell Ackoff, of the Wharton School. As the original developer of OR he expanded to advocate for expanded use of Operations Research for industry. This changed in 1967 when he gave a farewell speech to the annual meeting of Operations Research Society. Its title: "The Future of OR is Past, and They Missed It" was not taken well by most members of that society. Ten years later he became a supporter of my research work and then a PhD thesis into climate change. Ackoff, my Chair for the thesis, had come to diligently argue against the limitations in misusing the limitations possible via OR to manage the artificial production of anti-natural products that ignored the systemic dimension. In 1979 he and I come to see how strict analysis of parts was very limiting and led to the use of it in industry that then threaten much of life on the planet. Those believing in the above definition of logic came to develop industrial artifacts leading to extensive droughts, floods, and climate storms of deadly proportions. My concern in 1979 had centered on "will humans change." This was key in the corporate advisement and class teaching I conducted. In 2024 the concern has shifted to a more basic concern with: "can humans change?"

Dilemmas, Contradictions, Catch 22s, Endings

How do we resolve contradictions in human behavior based on thought processes, including perceptions of change and their management? It is a contradiction that operates in our environment

---

[20] Ambrose Bierce, *The Devil's Dictionary*, New York: Hill and Wang, 1957, pp. 108-109. (Originally published in 1881.)

acting as a threat and yet essential to life. It is also an operating contradiction in individual life where we desire a respite from the challenges of change, and thus call for changelessness, yet development of a human life from a child needing to be nurtured evolving into an adult that nurtures is a pathway of changes, a remarkable journey through change.

Discussion of change can be difficult but is increasingly mentioned in business meetings via good/bad stock investments, reflections on someone seeming to be older than a job needs, or diminished recall of family or friends, or even societal degradation, instabilities, or change of climate. From most of the discussion we arrive at proposals to create a wall of changelessness to protect the world, the community, the organization and/or individual. Given more time we then reflect on how some things change while other things don't.

We are tempted to turn to extensively used disciplines that come to see society as parts, then work to create more parts in those parts, all to manage opportunities and problems for individuals. Sociopolitical processes and/or economic models are often used to look for differences that create problems in society. In systemic aspects of society such only worsens problems. Segmenting climate change into parts is what the industrial model did that resulted in creation of climate change conditions beyond management. Much of climate change can be seen to arise from an economic model Adam Smith would appreciate but isn't based on the evidence now around us.

> "As he died to make men holy, let us die to make
> things cheap."[21]

Concern grows, with growing evidence, of the climate around us changing while the behavior of what generates the change does not seem to change. In fact, the initiators, humans, seem to act as if it's good to expand on activities that change the climate. Most humans seem unlikely to think about their changing behaviors that

---

[21] Leonard Cohen's song eight on his last album prior to death, "You Want it Darker."

push climate change. If you look you can see how the anti-climate change attitude actually expands forces that lead to environmental change problems. If you see this as a problem what can be done to "change" it. Five essential issues surround the idea of change. None are well understood.

Change, Considering Humanly Created Climate Change

- What is change,   Essence of life
- What drives change,   Cosmos
- How does change relate to time,   Entropically
- Can life survive change,   Nope
- Can change, change   Yes

The answer to these questions points to a growing concern with the aspect of life occupied by humans. Humanistically speaking, such questions might not attract many dollars but do seem to entice those who have a need to make sense. Sadly, the quest for homocentric increases in dollars has obscured the finding of that spiritual sense that gives meaning to life. In addition, that quest has wrongfully created the quite serious issue of climate change obscuring life. Only with the retirement of humans will the climate change process come to stabilize although such stability may require thousands of years. Although retirement of the human species via consequences of their actions will only require some decades. For those with feelings and some sense of a spirit, sorry.

Humans have come to define the planet as a context for life and its evolution. Change generally scares humans in that it implies a need for change of pattern to meet change of context. Normally humans prefer stability over change, which when exaggerated becomes "changelessness." Herein change is presented as an essential ingredient of life and living. If it is so necessary, then why do we humans create cultures, religions, and politics to block out change, or pretend it isn't? Via culture and family, we work to filter out or ignore change and aspire to maintenance of changelessness and thus "feel" comfortable.

Why do we not appreciate change and the promises it holds as well as the dangers it suggests? Why do we fear that our situation is worse on the other side of change? Are we too lazy to adapt to change or too scared to tolerate it? Such questions become the center of most political debates in most societies trying to figure out what to do with threats and promises offered from leadership. We know that over time our maintenance of a state of changelessness will collapse and can prove to have been very expensive, yet we continue with it. Past actions to pretend or even create changelessness can end in very traumatic change in a short time. Such change can come to ourselves as well as our larger environment, the context on which life depends for its biophysical and perhaps psychological continuance.

Humans forget about external change that threatens them until their situation becomes too unstable to sustain their life. During conditions of stability the need for change goes unnoticed. It sits backstage awaiting it to be needed. When there are slow and soft calls the need to engage in change is mostly neglected, perhaps even being filed away and filed under "changelessness," i.e., there is no need to change. Any pressure to change can be avoided until it's too late, or if those involved are lucky, they take note of such and quickly change just prior to finding such to be too late. It this way we sort of accept that change is essential to life.

Change is seen as something to avoid, even if it is crucial to continuation of life. We often see the connection between change and life but ignore such and place our arrogant trust in the mythical altar of *changelessness*. This is part of the human game for eternal stability in life so we can turn our attention to living. Where change emerges beyond our ability for ignorance we draw from time and space to avoid it by ignoring it or moving from what can't be ignored. In the history of world development by humans we see those treated badly at home moving on to new, less-defined regions.

A primary means to block out signs of and a need for change is via what we call culture. Culture suggests permanence regardless of conditions. Where change diminishes culture humans turn to space or time to escape change. By waiting or moving on humans can hope to realize some control over change in their context. As the context faces extreme change, e.g., climate change conditions, the humans in that context will need to change. Contemporary science has been teaching us much about the change process, some of which becomes quite ominous to the human mind. As humans learn about contextual changes endangering life, they also learn that they were and are the major agents of such changes. Looking deeper humans see how many such acts were undertaken in the name of creating changelessness. Such was mistakenly felt to help avoid life's instabilities. Such became a monumental "catch 22," or "double bind," or more simply: "damned if you do, damned if you don't."

As humans learn about contextual change bringing endangerment to life, they also begin to see how they were and are the major agents of that life threatening change. When they look deeper, they might even begin to see how some of those acts were undertaken to discover or enhance changelessness to avoid the ambiguities in the future. In this way humans come to meet what they have come to call a "catch 22," or "double bind." This is where come to believe that you are "damned if you do, as well as damned if you don't."

Reflecting on Change Can Even Become A Problem

Change is basic to life's continuance. Via the growing instability in today's context change is crucial to repairing the situation. We begin to change to access life's future, if there will be one. This is being clarified as we see life enveloped in the unfolding of consequences of climate change. Yes, the entire situation is disheartening. When life's context changes, as during a hurricane, questions arise about the meaning of change to life. From where does it arrive, to where does it go, and is life important to the universe? Science has examined these and related questions for quite some time but there is now greater urgency in finding answers. It seems we need to begin to study the impacts of prior effects that generate later effects and forego our traditional emphasis on studying the tradition of cause-effect analysis. We might come to call this an "effects^2" approach to environmental management. Life is impossible under conditions of destabilizing droughts, floods, hurricanes, etc. As the instabilities expand life's continence is threatened.

Science begins to suggest that planetary life is moving into a conclusion called the 6th Extinction. This continues daily if humans cannot radically change. Perhaps it is already too late for the change as required. As humans note this in their occupancy of a changing context we see changes in the human psyche. The future of humans as impacted by consequences of their past activities is clearly threatened. When this is noted, ominous conclusions threaten life's continuance.

Existing conceptions of change seem wholly inadequate to emergent needs for humans to change. Change of climate seems outside the current understanding of change as it moves to envelop us. Difference over time seems to not capture the extreme changes taking place in climates that were seen to maintain life.

A more comprehensive model of change is needed, to better appreciate and prepare for climate change's consequences. Current models seem only to clarify the fear of too little too late. Consequences of failed change, with growing destruction and death, become more serious each year. Change is integral to humans finding a future. We used to settle for change as difference over time. More than defining change as difference over time is needed. Our traditional sense of change allows, even encourages, some behaviors that block recognition of consequences. This encourages deeper consequences of the dangers of the longer term from not acting against that of the present.

Today we face a monumental change that we call climate change. It is increasingly accepted as now underway even it was argued against fifty years ago, and totally ignored 175 years ago when first shown to await in the human future. This may seem too personal but for the last fifty years I have been haunted by evidence of climate change beginning to emerge. Its early stages has been obvious in increases in global temperatures, plus quick and deadly droughts, floods, storms and threats outside life to all we know as life. For me it comes from research done by a lady, that I will call the 19th Century Joan of Arc, Eunice Foote, who in 1856 delivered a paper on the relation between energy use in industrial production and disruption of the atmosphere via increased heat. The fact that men of that day, a since, were strongly ignorant of her work insured me that she was right. Now that it's clear that the climate is changing humans can humans then change in adaptation to this new world. It's now too late to change the human activities that produced the forces of climate change, yet can we change as adaptation to the consequences?

Much of what follows arises from research of 50 years ago. It involved 20 companies having production facilities in a variety of nations. They produced fossil fuels, construction materials, electricity, food, and essentials to what had come to be defined as human life on earth. That project was a somewhat unique study of the systemic impact of pollution from human development on the world. Company leaders as well as representatives of the 6 governments where some of the facilities were located all became involved. There was no marketing for the project. Participants asked to join. Its prospectus pointed out how there were different presumptions and control methods for pollution control. The study was to determine which were more successful in control of the externalities from production and use of products intended to support human well-being. All participants became increasingly involved during the two years of the project.

As project manager I came to appreciate the concern, intellect, and humor of all participants. To support the spirit of the project, one of the executives arranged to hold a birthday party for his daughter in a Stockholm club he rented for a night. She traveled from NYC for her party. He had asked me to serve as her date, as he thought her to be one of those "environmentalist" and could thus translate my comments from the project to him. Very funny and very nice human. His son was a revered actor on Broadway. After the project was completed, he was selected as the CEO of his firm. He changed them.

The work was a collaboration of public-private mentalities into a mutual concern with environmental deterioration from production and product use and how such was affecting their children's world. As the project began, we discovered the rather harsh negotiation taking place in the subject area between the many ways used to define and manage cleaning of systems that supported humans.

As the project developed participants began seeing an urgent need to improve the clean-up process, but this could only happen if all attitudes became enjoined in the process. We thus criticize the logic coming from Aristotle that organized the human as a digital world, that became the bipolar. Early in the study we noted that our issue was like most human systems, designed around bi-polar differences. When we looked deeper, we found many such differences either made no difference or became counter-productive to doing the right thing. That led us to study differences at a deeper level to locate the basis for what made a greater difference for improvement. It soon became more than a word game and sponsored the project moving from respect for "legal order" to an urgent need to develop a more fluid "negotiated order." Crucial to participants was to figure out how to apply what they suggested: moving from the confines of the digital towards "both plus more," and thus defining, capturing and nurturing the "more."

Just Driving Around, Seeking Signs of Hope

Next time you are driving around, thinking of yourself relative to what others think of you, take note of your vehicle. Probably it's a brand new, enlarged SUV for many and much, but presently has only one person in it, you. Now you are wondering if your spouse is now being faithful to you. If you have kids, you ask if they give you the respect you want, or what is deserved based on your recent encounters with them? To rise above, or below, your interpersonal relations you then move thoughts to paying the mortgage you can't afford. This book is about the need for you to take a break from such to reflect on more important matters residing in a larger system of order, such as life and its continuance. As you drive around think instead of climate change's consequences that are expanding beyond the floods and droughts you experience. How does such relate to your life? You have been told that things will become rather horrible, and much of life will be terminated. They ask yourself from where such destructive change comes. Then, if you still have the energy consider from where climate change forces arise.

About 30% of the CO_2 that combines with moisture in the air and thus forms a shield around the earth entrapping heat comes from driving around of you and those like you. Thereby the earth's temperature is raised each year by 1 to 2 degrees C and thus directly threatens life. The result is more scary than uncomfortable; thus, we attempt to ignore it. Each day becomes the hottest on the planet in tens of thousands of years, thus threatening life.

Finally, after all this, you ask, should I just pull the car over, walk away from what I stimulate, then relax in that I'm no longer making things dreadful for those living or being born? Why do we not change, not pull over and stop the process that endangers so much life? The answer usually is, lets go for changelessness a bit longer, until we figure all this out.

Why is change resisted, then ignored, then we come to later regret not having changed. Can this, or will this, ever be explained. Will anyone be alive to attempt the explanation? Humans noted long ago that change was key to life and its continuation. How then did humans come to change their attitude on change and come to divert needs to change by enclosing them in changelessness in life? The reading of 95% of science points out how this is leading to extinction of life, but non-scientists proudly argue why such cannot be. It's easy to see such in neighbors demonstrating against those Covid immunizations.

A byproduct of past business as usual has created conditions of change that now bring major threats to life on our planet. Yes, our driving around looking for truth, bread, liquor, each other, or to escape from it all, is in fact a primary generator of what threatens life on earth. Are we willing to simply pull over and park our car? Why not? How else can we protect our environment from ourselves? Do we care? Do our children still talk to us?

Maybe we think humans are magnificent and will solve all problems in their lives, even those created by self. Some humans even believe in those projects that promise immortality and encourage dropping that death certificate placed around our neck at birth. They advertised such as genius negative entropy successes. Surely, such can push away conditions of climate change as they carry us towards immortality. We need only to stand up, act like real men, then push out, upward, and on. Sadly, the evidence in science, history and literature looks the other way.

The warnings of danger grow louder, but as humans we reflect on our history of blocking out "noises." We mostly ignore evidence of dangers to life "from our business-as-usual definition of life. An industrialization of living and life is supreme in the human mission on the planet. Thus, business as usual continues without pause. It is the essence of business school and university teaching. Are humans too busy to consider change, too comfortable in extra-wide sofa's while facing their 2D TV, computer, and mobile phone, to change "channels?" When awake they rise, drag an overweight body out to a car, or very large SUV, to go for a drive as below.

Humans? Driving Around/Searching for
Meaning/Finding Climate Change

Our driving around provides a metaphor for this book. It depicts our mental condition when considering our life during climate change and global warming challenges. Such challenges clearly threaten the continuance of life on the planet, yet we proudly keep on driving. Any questions, suggestions, or signs of hope?

4

Climate Change: A Tragedy Foretold

Industrialized Desecration

As humans we turn to what we find an obvious resolution – we define some instances as requiring changelessness thus freezing change or removing it. This was illustrated during a 1975-77 research project I managed where toxic wastes were a problem of change that needed fixing. Legislators in one state in America thus passed a law that toxic wastes cannot exist. The consequences of trucking away that which did not exist ended badly in that state. Such is worth noting as several US national leaders hope we can do the same to solve change of climate problems. With new technology perhaps humans can stop the consequences of climate change, or even reverse them to make money. Climate change consequences thus become a wealth of nations commodity. Yes, humans can be seen to be a troubled species, an endangerment to all other species as well as themselves.

The research project was sponsored by the Institute of International Business, Stockholm School of Economics. I and two friends had created the Institute to provide unusual students the opportunity to seek unusual ways to deal with global problems. We thought we could lessen the conflicts arising from national differences via the development of a different model of international business, one based on different kinds of difference in human activities. The project discussed herein was controversial from the beginning. For study participants it was instead seen as urgently needed. They

Included executives of 20 major firms, workers in the factories of those firms located in 6 countries, as well as employees in governmental agencies set up to regulate environmental pollution. These participants came to be deeply supportive of research to improve understanding of human activities bringing deterioration to the environment. The group came to be very concerned with the human end state of expansion of usual business and government processes, both designed and managed to serve the public. The project outcome was to identify alternatives to business as usual prior to deterioration making such no longer an option. Participants exhibited mutual concern for a bad end state approaching due to human activities on the planet. This was carefully expressed during research meetings by participants such as Exxon's chief scientist, James Black.

> *"We see early indications of environmental deterioration leading to climate change conditions. How best can we learn to manage, reverse, even survive during such condition?"*[22]

Research themes were then drawn up by David Hawk in a formal research proposal approved by the larger group. His key was to find means for developing business as unusual, to then reduce further environmental deterioration. Others at the two universities he was with saw such as questionable, overly pessimistic, and perhaps a scientific "hoax."

> *"As we strive to continually increase Gross Domestic Capita via using materials and energies stored in*

---

[22] From project notes in Professor Hawk's New Jersey Institute of Technology office. Hawk's files were seized In 2009 by NJIT President Altenkirch as being "New Jersey State Property." This was strange as all the records seized came from work was prior to Hawk joining NJIT. The following NJIT president, Joal Bloom, continued to not return the seized documents. This exemplifies continuing human wrong, consistent with conditions of climate change and global warming being created. Many good people were at NJIT, but its leadership actions could be troubling.

*nature to expand requirements for use of ever more.
Therein we create climate change conditions that
endanger life. How can humans change their business-as-usual model before it's too late? Current societal values, including those in support of current
regulation models, are central to the problem, not
its solution."*

Study results were presented as a research thesis draft in 1978. It was towards fulfillment of a PhD in Systems Sciences. Wharton's dean was upset by the contents of the draft. He strongly opposed it. Thus, a group of Penn students had it printed as a booklet by the Wharton School, University of Pennsylvania, printed in 1979 it was titled "S³ Notes: Regulation of Environmental Deterioration." Yes, its contents seemed controversial at the time. Forty years later the research question and methods were mainstream to environmental concerns over climate change and planetary warming. Such is no longer widely seen as a "hoax." Some even labeled it as defining the edge of environmental concerns. The 1979 document was republished in 2019, as "Too Early, Too Late, Now what?"

The 1977 research results had been seen as controversial outside the study group mentioned before. Even the Director of the USA EPA became furious about the reports, especially after Sweden's Prime Minister presented them to OECD in a Paris meeting. Those participating in the study, e.g., CEOs of firms and heads of non-US government agencies, strongly endorsed the resulting conclusions. They argued that natural environmental resource use was facing serious challenges via the then current model of industrialization. The costs of such would become increasingly expensive to life, perhaps unaffordable. The CEO of Exxon gave lectures on the subject, prior to him being replaced as CEO. Most humans avoided the subject and continued via business as usual. Most saw no connection between how they lived and upcoming challenges to continued life via storms, floods and droughts and global warming. Study results demonstrated that in addition to threats to life the current industrial model would be paid for via out-of-control inflation in economic systems. All were responsible for the problem, including designers, producers, marketers, purveyors and consumers. In 2024 most humans begin to feel ominous fear for the future.

Indicators of significant change in planetary climate now appear every day, in every country. Average temperatures constantly break records from when records were first collected or determined from diffing up past materials or ice from many thousands of years ago. Increasing pessimism grows from this data, as well as growing human-style anger directed outward to leadership, with a bit noted and internalized during sleepless nights. Thankfully it has become socially acceptable to discuss the deep need to change conduct as producers, consumers and humans. Who and how such will be changed remains open to question but will certainly be set by 2050.

Climate change consequences arrive ever more quickly and extensively. Projections made a decade ago now seem optimistic. The fears expressed in the 1977 project, shunned at the time as part of a hoax, are now seen to have been optimistic. Future life on the planet is clearly under question. Some scientists have moved to evidence of a sixth extinction of life as emergent. They note that this would be the first extinction initiated by humans.

Humans clearly change the context conditions for planetary life. Several species are already gone. Others are rapidly dying off. All forms of life, humans included, now face endangerment of what they are. Threats from weather violence and study temperature increases are ominous. Just as scary is that the threats are planetary, not bound to a locality as with the Mayan civilizations in 900AD then the US Midwesterners in 1930, via their dust bowl and drought event.

Life at the edges of reality is now being redefined. Soon it will reach its core. Meanwhile, what can/should humans do? Just now they seem to be out driving around creating more conditions of and consequences from climate change. Mother nature must see humans and their behaviors as funny. If you had difficulty understanding any meaning in the above, please bring up the song, "Everybody Hurts," by REM, and think of the urgency of change prior to "Its too late." Maybe it is now too late? That insight was from 1992.

What to do In Response to Change?

Unsure of its definition, we can look deeper to see the details of change as a threat to life as well as the essence of it. Doing this we begin to see it as the central paradox to our time, to our way of life, and a means to a rapid death if we mess it up. We can also view it with a touch of humor and see change as: a revised "Catch-22," a logical version of Bateson's "double bind" that denotes who in going crazy or if a society-wide version of schizophrenia is coming. Some adults see a future composed of expanded logic towards perfect rationality, or against logic as created by youth thought to be from hell or going there. For them expansion of logic, per the definition given previously, we will come to resolve environmental problems like climate change.

My concern is with climate change arising from human attitudes toward their context, where nature provides the aspects of context on which life most depends. This is troubling. The religion of the industrial emerged around 1850 followed by humans coming to redefine the natural context in a selfish manner. Nature came to be generally depicted as it had been specifically directed in religious edicts such as that about "the Garden of Eden." Nature was to serve individuals not groups nor general life on the planet. This continued into the present day as seen in current emphasis on glorifying in the artificial for gaining control over the natural. Climate change consequences have been seen to arise and expand from this attitude.

We see great and growing costs to our contextual from what is coming to be labeled mismanagement. This points to limits in human ability to manage relations to nature, or simply a very negative view of nature. We continue that negativity today in what and how we teach and then practice business as usual. The end state of such is looking more like an end to many regions of our planet. There appears to be an arrogance as well as an ignorance present in human leadership of development. It has serious consequences with noteworthy costs, costs that are seen expanding each year.

Even when we know of the cost, we continue to make use of our arrogance about life as we lose it. Can we ever understand the consequences of what we do to not find our situation as too late? In the nineteen forties Andras Angyal, an early systems scientist, tried to rise above the tradition of 19ᵗʰ Century applications of cause-effect management thinking. Via analysis situations are decomposed into parts where misbehaving parts are removed, and repaired or discarded, be they gears or people. Context is not important.

His concern was in mental disorders arising from seeing human minds as segmented parts, or bi-polar discontinuities that were disruptive to continuance of business as usual. Instead of finding new ways to see the mind and its context as whole "experts" are asked to advise on parts repair, or removal. His approach to mental illness and wellness moved on from Newtonian physics to Gaussian mathematics. Thus, importance shifted to the study of relationships via connections, all in search of the holistic, not continual division of parts into smaller parts. He was concerned that humans were becoming increasingly segmented from the more natural in search of the more artificial.

In the 1960s Emery and Trist continued with the Angyal concern at a more general level of context. Prior to this we lacked a way to conceive of human relationships to a whole and its context. Emery and Trist created contextual backdrops so humans could then seek better ways to manage relations to psycho, social and environmental events. Their model outlined four environmental types. The four moved up through increasing complexity from type I to type IV. The challenges for life grow as you move through the four. Their concern was with the quality of systems of life, with emphasis on the mental. I use this to expand into quality of the environment to support life physically.

Their type IV, called the "Turbulent Environment," resulted from humans creating the unmanageable via their activities. When working with Emery and Trist I suggested the dangers in their Type IV environment were the result of business as usual. They then agreed that one result of such would be like the actors on a stage-set becoming less important to success with time, where the stage-set, the context, would be the new determinant of success. Context would become the dominant actor. Alone with Eric Trist I mapped out a Type V context, a "Vortex Environment."

We now experience the turbulence they suggested was coming. Clearly dangerous, it is just now redefining the human project in an irreversible manner. As such, the play, in Emery and Trist terms, centers on mismanagement to the natural context in ways that come to remove the qualities of life. We thus see turbulence emerging from the values of productivity becoming valueless cheap. Such seems to be the force driving industrialization.

My focus centers on how human activities organized to achieve the consumptive cheap general the contextual expense, i.e., unaffordable. Instead of gaining control over the cheap humans preserve it via continuation of the business as usual that sponsors it via changelessness. Change is presented as a threat to the status quo. This relies on humans arrogantly believing they are the owner of nature, as their Bible's tell them. The resulting paradox is described later via its longer-term "costs" in the consequences of industrial. At its core are misplaced strategic management ideas from warfare that use deceit to avoid seeing reality of acts. Those steeped in an MBA education let the good times roll towards a tragic end. The results become expensive. Lost souls behind the lonely faces.

Eric Trist went wider via his social psychological view of the world. He agreed with Bateson on the importance of context but then he and Fred Emery went on to see context as a "stage-set for the plays of life." As with Erwin Goffman the Trist approach to context was as a backdrop for humans to reveal meaning via performances. From his experiencing the politico-technological mistakes before, during and after WWII he became concerned with the expanding technological control looming over humans via production and consumption as directed to support life. Erving Goffman would later arrive at the early Trist model for accessing meaning in human affairs. Both were my teachers beyond their classrooms.

Trist's concern for the expanding power of technology from rational ideas and clean logic was growing. It was all sent out to manage a seemingly confused non-rational world in a natural setting that appeared unhuman, or at least unpredictable. He saw how

51

logical analysis could oppose the natural world, as well as its human occupants. He was also concerned with the technical dictating the limits of human thinking and acting. Relying on unaided rationality human values were damaging then destroying some additional qualities of life. Humans are moving from an early socio-natural context of collaboration, as noted by Kropotkin,[23] into a highly structured, very hierarchical, and centralized context always focusing on "the one." The stream of life as the societies in nature was being lost.

In his attempt to return to a focus on natural diversity began in a now famous socio-tech model of production. Trist was trying to put the social back in charge, not encouraging tools to dictate life's behavior. He argued to include the potential of the natural into context as in the socio ecological. His 1973 book[24] on such was not well received. It was said to contain outrageous ideas. One was people should improve by moving from individual status given in evaluation of their automobile. Trist challenges this by suggesting leasing, not own, or not even use them private automobiles. Fifty years later such ideas were beyond the prophetic to thus become the obvious. The book is no longer available, but well-used copies can be found.[25]

By the twenty-first century social scientists began to note a reversal from technology as context. The human future was becoming open to question. Younger humans were seeking a way to redefine management of life via natural forces. A decade later their feeling about their future went further with evidence of threats to continuance of life from the environment on which life depended. A few students looked at historical records of industrialization from 1850 to see that activities designed to oppose nature could become a great

---

[23] Kropotkin, Petr, *Mutual Aid: A Factor in Evolution*, Boston: Extending Horizons Books, 1914.

[24] F.E. Emery and E.L. Trist, *Towards a Social Ecology: Contextual Appreciation of the Future in the Present*, New York: Plenum Press, 1973.

[25] My copy, that I shared with many students at New Jersey Institute of Technology, was seized along with many others from my office under orders of President Joel Bloom, Governor Chris Christie, and a NJ judge they were paying $500/hour. They declared all my books, my files on past research and a daughter's stuffed animal to be "state property." The daughter continues to be sad about such behavior.

threat to life. This was most clearly seen in the science of a former and very noteworthy American farm girl Eunice Foote.[26]

Trist conceived of context as a more specific form of environment as well as a backdrop for the human play. He felt this play was about to be reversed, as he noted it would be. Social ecological was his key concept for this. Twenty years later nature was seen to seek compensation from human activities that had met human needs and wants but were very costly to natural systems. A 150-year human industrialized play was meeting with frustration from those seeing hard done to the larger natural context. From studies it looked like nature would close that human play and methods of governance it relied on. Climate change was the most noticed factor on the stage of life. Trist has been right in his earlier concerns. At that point it was still possible to change the human role in the larger script of reality.

From Being to Becoming

There may be deep concerns out there for emerging issues, but we can create forms and structures to discourage their discussion. The onset of climate change as terminal to life as we know it is herein seen as profound to the human project and its management. It is here argued that traditional ideas of management created the conditions of climate change. It is further argued that there is little hope to resolve or even soften the consequences of climate change via that same management. A drastic set of changes are needed. Some of these will be proposed herein.

In a 1962 meeting with Berlin's Mayor we discussed the glass as half-empty or half-full metaphor of human hope. I suggested the glass was empty with urine stains on it. He agreed. Others present laughed. I clearly saw the glass with urine stains left relative to human treatment of systems of life on which living organisms depended. on

---

[26] Foote, Eunice, "Circumstances Affecting the Heat of the Sun's Rays," Washington D.C.: *Science*, American Association for the Advancement of Science (AAAS), 1856.

the planet. The contents are about universal systems of order and disorder, and the management of the two and their interactions.

Beneath the concern for the human project is concern for how we arrived at the current paradox in human affairs, that might best be depicted in a philosophy of "short-term gain followed by long-term pain" from what we do and how we do it. We see where this philosophy provides much towards improving the meeting the needs and wants that define the human project. On the other hand, from a wider vision, we see how the same philosophy ensures no life, thus no needs and wants in the longer term.

As will be discussed this is a global version of the Faustian dilemma of the individual human. Therein a Faustian negotiation takes place with the evil side of existence in the business of life to access real-time reward for selling that which holds long-term meaning. This, of the long-term does not logically exist in Aristotle's world, goes off to agency that is also logically nonexistent. Called, *the soul*, it is to connect meaning within, between and over the long-term existence. The entire process concludes in what is universally known as "The Faustian Tragedy." This seems to now be an ambiguous metaphor of, or specific roadmap to, the emerging fear of planetary climate change brought on by human activities in their day-to-day negotiations.

Underlying this dilemma that is a nightly concern of those most affected, the youth preparing for their future, is a deeper concern about how we arrived at this paradox. A suggestion made and supported herein is that it came from a very manly attitude about the bad, the good and the movement between the two. The general argument is seen in the Biblical Garden of Eden story that outlines why the manly must be in charge. Prior to that writing, by men, was the philosophical logic of man as force of progress, also framed by men such as Plato, then Aristotle in their emphasis on the first three letters of the construct of *management*. This idea provided the roadmap to end climate change consequences is outlined in this book. A proposal to experiment with the alternative, replacing those three letters with fem, to soften the harshness of climate change consequences is thus presented.

The known limitations in attempting to continuously improve productivity in the short term to become ever more productive doing the wrong things in the long-term.

a) Managing to avoid feminine values in corporate management, thus avoid managing the difficulties in the longer-term consequences from actions in the now.

b) Rising above the restrictions imposed by the Garden of Eden masculinity, versus the feminine values thought to be aligned with a potentially evil nature. In this way there can be a researchable link between the causes of the planet moving into climate change conditions, and the values that can change this.

c) These three subjects can clarify the systemic link between being human in the artificial and human beings in the natural thus emphasizing the unfolding of a pattern of short-term gains leading to a context of long-term pain.

Seven "prefaces" are offered to give a sense of a seemingly complicated context that humans built on reductionistic analysis used to avoid appreciating systemic wholeness in life. Each provides a sense of where humans have been, what they think they are, and to where they seem headed. These seem to define seven interests that manage the human project. The literature on each is extensive and philosophic. You can select one that best supports your perception of the human condition. On the other hand, if you are adventurous and seek meaning, please combine as you can.

The seven arise from the key question of *Too Early, Too Late, Now what?* That book,[27] was a republishing of a 1979[28] PhD thesis of Forty

[27] Hawk, David, Too Early, Too Later, Now what? Indianapolis, Indiana: Author House Publishing, 2019.

[28] Hawk, David, *Regulation of Environmental Deterioration*, Philadelphia, Pa.: Social Systems Sciences Program, The Wharton School, University of Pennsylvania, 1979. Three companion volumes were titled: "environmental Protection: Analytic Solutions in Search of Synthetic Problems, 1977. IIB, Stockholm Sweden.

years ago. At the time it was reviewed as "troublesome." The Chairman of the PhD Program it came from, Russell Ackoff, supported it. He said the three-volume research report, later used as a basis for the thesis, better illustrated the essence of why he had founded the Systems Science Program. He was less supportive of volume four, the thesis. He believes that idea that humans were creating conditions of climate change that would end them was a bit far and resisted seeing that self-regulation was superior to a hierarchy of others. Later, he ambiguously dedicated one of his books to the research work. "To David Hawk, who was, what was euphemistically called, 'A student.'"

A few outliers[29] gave support to the thesis but most refused to think that human behavior could have a significant effect on the larger environment. Most did not appreciate that management warfare between human aspirations and natural laws should be a rational concern of the long-term that was becoming an empirical experience of the immediate. Except for loving the opera that resulted from Goethe's tragic storyline, most humans did not see a problem in selling the soul of the future for immediate economic gains. Most who reviewed the 1979 thesis from the 1975 Swedish study, including the US Director of EPA, were angered by the research study and conclusions.[30] Heavily biased with lawyers and their use of legalese to describe what they didn't know few in the management of US environmental concerns didn't understand that business as usual was setting the stage for no business.[31]

---

[29] Emery and Trist, "The Causal Texture of Organizational Environments" (1965), in Emery, Ed., *Systems Thinking*, Middlesex, England: Penguin Books, 1969; Georgescu-Roegen, Nicholas, *The Entropy Law and the Economic Process*, Cambridge, Ma: Harvard Press, 1971; Schneider, Stephen, *The Genesis Strategy: Climate and Global Survival*, New York: Plenum Press, 1976; Russell Ackoff, *Redesigning the Future*, 1974.

[30] EPA had approved funding which they had then cancelled the day the research was to begin? Thankfully their funds were unnecessary. Their management in various parts of the US did eagerly assist with data collection.

[31] The Director sent all copies of the research reports distributed in EPA, that had been presented to OECD, to Hawk with a letter stating how Hawk would be kept from working in the subject area in the future. Very angry letter.

This was clearly seen in the review memos of the Dean of the Wharton School, of U of Penn. He seemed very upset with the meaning behind the thesis. His school's mission was to increase the productivity of an ever-expanding business as usual, not wandering off into some strange idea of an urgent need for unusual ideas on managing business, to appreciate this thing called the natural. The idea of industrialization leading to climate change, then the ending to much of planetary life, seemed like a homily to him.[32] The four volumes of the approved dissertation were never allowed to be in the University of Pennsylvania Library.

The work began in an illustration of how we needed to develop concern for a model of management with a strict focus on what I called "the religion of Babbage, Taylor, and *The Economist.*" They saw the mission of business being to increase productivity, without exception. This could best be done via gradual improvement of current processes and products. Management should avoid major redesigning of the process for other, more social, then nature, ends. There was no concern that an unmanageable world was emerging, one built and maintained via limitations found in the weak side of science and powered by human arrogance.[33] The contents of the following book will go into this in some detail.

Even in 1979 there were signs of significant environmental deterioration from human activities. None-the-less, leadership argued that such could be taken care of via management using new economic models and innovative technologies. Complete avoidance if discussion of their glass as only half full was the philosophy of the day. When issues relating to universal laws of physics, such as entropy, arose there was uniform avoidance. When someone would suggest that humans are major agents of entropic increase on the

---

[32] A homily is a speech or sermon given by a priest to provide a means for moral correction. A provost at another university used the same term to criticize the same area of research. He later saw his comment insure no access to considerable funding for further research in the area at his university.

[33] Ehrenfeld, David, *The Arrogance of Humanism*, New York: Oxford University Press, 1978.

planet there appeared anger as a response. In my work I argued that the glass was soon to be empty and was covered with urine stains.

The Troubled Life

There are short-term advantages in selling access to life as beyond existence and deterioration, even if we know from entropy that such cannot be. We even sell impossible recycling of non-sustainable sustainability to others. If nothing else, it's fun to see that others are not so smart via our marketing skills. Recently we even work to sell access to non-disintegrating information under the name of cybernetic neg-entropy.[34]

Hopefully the above is not true, but it does seem to be so along with other activities that deteriorate the environment of life. Most humans seem very receptive to ideas of neg-entropy as available, or at least as discoverable. This weakness may be the essence of humans being human. If so, from where does it arise? Is it part of pride having replaced the soul, as encouraged by dreams of reason being manifest in technological omnipotence? While it was not apparent in Socrates there were clear signs of the will to have such in Plato. Certainly, absent in Lao Tzu wisdom it was supported by Confucius teachings. Where will it all end?

If you have degrees in bio-osmosis, cybernetics, law, computer science, business, medicine, engineering, architecture, design, et.al., and were well educated, then you learn to avoid concerns apparent at age seven – a) who you are, b) what you are up to, c) what does it mean, and d) where does it end? Unless you can again reflect on the concerns of a seven-year-old you may not enjoy the content that follows. Maybe you can suspend your public education? If you have adopted the ideology of the analytic you will not find the contents of this book inviting. Via the analytic you can avoid the meaning gained from context and the concerns found therein. You were edu-

---

[34] I mention these two as they are the dominate areas that emphasize human intelligence for overcoming death and disorder. These are even mentioned in funerals of evidentiary proof to justify human pride in humans.

cated to avoid the 90% of reality called the non-rational. You see it as a holistic swampland to be avoided while in search of success with the partial. As such you have come to believe that nature needs to be leveled prior to humans entering and building their rational structures upon its remains.

Herein the first three letters of management are given responsibility for troubles relating to life on earth. There are serious problems in the relationship. If they can be managed, it seems that such will not be by men. There is much evidence, that is growing, that management is a key part of the human problem.

A research project was initiated into human-environmental relations in 1975 at the Stockholm School of Economics. Several researchers had argued for such a project since 1972 but such had not begun. The 1856 work of the woman mentioned before, Dr. Eunice Foot, about the CO_2 externality from the industrial, had been mostly ignored in science. This was the year that the first skeleton of the Neanderthal species, in Germany's Neander Valley, which humans found captivating that year. Her concern must have seemed trivial in comparison. It was that if CO_2 would build-up from expanded burning of fossil fuels it would increase planetary heat. This would eventually endanger systems of life, including that of humans. Her concern is now known as climate change.

Relative to management of this unfortunate process we clearly see that the masculine has been and is central to it. Perhaps that is why the extreme masculine, the Neanderthal, was found to have existed in human heritage and Darwinian evolution. Men were at the lead in designing and creating the model of industrialization we continued to nurture even after Foot's warning of 175 years ago. Signs of Neanderthal existence can be seen in the early design of the industrial, and signs of its continuance in industrial management continue today.

Nicholas Georgescu-Roegen, a mathematical economist, was also important to setting up the framework for the 1975 research. In his 1971 book he described the science of how economics had become an entropy expansion machine. In addition to the Chief Scientist of Exxon Rogen also told me of the research of Foote. With inspiration from the ideas of Foot and Georgescu-Roegen the Swedish project was initiated and completed. It began in concern for how the human interference in natural systems was done in a way deteriorated those systems. Behind the project was concern for how the unfolding drama of human existence via industrialization could be managed.

The project began in criticism of individuals and organizations that had relied on single-variable analysis to locate the cause of pollution of human activities then set up regulation to control such causes. As such it consistently avoided the systemic aspects of nature and systems of life. There is no cause of pollution nor the deterioration it begets. It is not a single problem but a problematique housing a system of interconnected problems. Finding the causes therein, then removing and repairing them, only worsens the larger issue when the repairs are put back in what since moved on.

Now we see the harm realized from what was seen as potential harm in 1979. It has been realized and is now growing at an ever-faster pace as seen in each follow-up study of the science involved.

> *The cumulative scientific evidence is unequivocal: Climate change is a threat to human well-being and planetary health. Any further delay in concerted anticipatory global action on adaptation and mitigation will miss a brief and rapidly closing window of opportunity to secure a livable and sustainable future for all.*[35]

> *Evidence from tree rings shows that the summer of 2023 was the hottest in 2,000 years. Last year was already established as officially the hottest on record. The latest analysis puts that peak into the context of the natural variability in temperatures. The Northern-Hemisphere summer of 2023 was at least 0.5 °C hotter than 246 AD, which tree growth rings suggest was the hottest year before the indus-*

---

[35] "Summary," IPCC Report, February 28, 2022

trial revolution kicked off human-caused climate change.[36]

The project began with the launch of a Swedish Research Institute in Stockholm. It was to do research to advise international business research to reduce the then emphasis on nationalism and the conflicts such encourages. The study included many companies in six countries. It was to map relationships between business operations and environmental pollution, then study which mode of social regulation was most effective in management of such. In 1977 it concluded with evidence of environmental deterioration happening and arriving much faster than assumed and then heading towards climate change consequences by 2050 if humans did not find or invent business that could complement the natural.

The rapidly collapsing timetable is surprising. Our context is involved in severely irreversible deterioration regarding natural conditions. New ideas and forms of business and its management are urgently needed. We need to rise above the tradition of there being problems and solutions and we need to fight bright problem solvers to connect them. Thus, we move onto something more systemic in problem confrontation. Herein it is presented as shifting from the idea that there are discrete problems to solve, to a more systemic idea that what matters most is the *problematique,* a system of problems, not a problem. To graduate you avoided the problematique and their non-rational content. You were educated in carving life up into discrete problems, each worthy of a disciplined based solution as removed from its context. Where this failed you were told that things were complex. After graduation you found solving those discrete segments of the problematique made the context more difficult for life. From that experience, if you were bothered by it, you could return to a more natural concern with the systemic. Please remember, the essence of the analytic is to divide, segment, and remove the subject from context. The systemic strives to integrate, to combine and to insist on inclusion of relevant context for relevant decisions. Thus,

---

[36] "Nature Briefing, *in Scientific American*, May 15, 2024.

we are waking in harsh relations between mother nature and father time and their separate constraints on life.

My concern is with climate change arising from inhumane activities. Especially troubling is how some humans redefine the natural context to thus serve their own purposes, not those of the group or nature. In the study they were seen glorifying in the artificial attempts to control the natural.

Climate Change Consequences arise from behavior of some humans and then provide contextual travesty. We see costs of contextual mismanagement, as well as the limits of humans to manage, yet continue it. We continue to teach and practice business as usual. The end state of such is truly an end. Much of it seems to come from the arrogance, coupled to ignorance, of humanism. This has consequences with noteworthy costs that expand each year. Even when we know of such, we continue to grow it. Can we ever understand enough to stop? In the nineteen forties Andras Angyal, an early systems scientist, tried to rise above the tradition of 19th Century applications of cause-effect management thinking. Via analysis situations are decomposed into parts where misbehaving parts are removed, and repaired or discarded, be they gears or people. Context is not important.

His concern was in mental disorders arising from seeing human minds as segmented parts, or bi-polar discontinuities that were disruptive to continuance of business as usual. Instead of finding new ways to see the mind and its context as whole "experts" are asked to advise on parts repair, or removal. His approach to mental illness and wellness moved on from Newtonian physics to Gaussian mathematics. Thus, importance shifted to the study of relationships via connections, all in search of the holistic, not continual division of parts into smaller parts. He was concerned that humans were becoming increasingly segmented from the more natural in search of the more artificial.

In the 1960s Emery and Trist continued with the Angyal concern with mentality lacking a relationship to a whole thus they provided a context for social thought. They worked to create contextual backdrops so that humans could better manage relations to psycho, social and environmental events. They described four environmental types of increasing complexity. In moving from type I to type IV they described increasing challenges for life, and dire troubles for essential systems of life.

Their type IV, the "Turbulent Environment," resulted from human acts having created the unmanageable. In my work with them I suggested this was a consequence of business as usual. They went further to say it was like actors on a stage-set where with time the human actors were of less importance and the contextual stage set would become the dominant actor. Later we will outline the Trist further expansion of typologies into a Type V, "Vortex Environment."

We now experience the turbulence they suggested was coming. Clearly dangerous, it is just now redefining the human project in an irreversible manner. As such, the play, in Emery and Trist terms, centers on mismanagement to the natural context in ways that come to remove the qualities of life. We thus see turbulence emerging from the values of productivity becoming valueless cheap. Such seems to be the force driving industrialization.

The focus herein is how the expensive of the cheap to context grows with time. Instead of gaining control over the cheap humans preserve it via continuation of the business as usual that sponsors it via changelessness. Change is presented as a threat to the status quo. This relies on humans arrogantly believing they are the owner of nature, as their Bible's tell them. The resulting paradox is described later via its longer-term "costs" in the consequences of industrial. At its core are misplaced strategic management ideas from warfare that use deceit to avoid seeing reality of acts. Those steeped in an MBA education let the good times roll towards a tragic end. The results become expensive. Lost souls behind the lonely faces.

To Want/Get/Use/Trash/Then Pay for It

Intentions form the core of the human project. They motivate the actions of the membership. There is a presumption that intentions, by their nature are good things. In a long-held and widely circulated quote we are remined that: "The road to hell is paved with good intentions." This allows for a presumption of human goodness on their roads through life but somehow forks in the road appear but are found to go the wrong place. Perhaps with sufficient development and application of tools of artificial intelligence those forks can be closed? On the other hand, perhaps such hope in the artificial is what creates those passageways to the wrong. This note may be important for a new map for the human project.

Intentions drive humans. Some are their own, others come from those they respect or give obedience to from their speeches, writings, or actions. This last category can include those attempting to give meaning to the human project from the past: e.g., Socrates, Confucius, Lao Tzu, Aristotle, Newton, etc.

Looking at key definitions of our meaning of "intentions" shows how 90% presume they begin good. Typical of such this would be the claim by James Collins: "Bad decisions made with good intentions, are still bad decisions." Herein we go deeper then decisions, into the defects underlying the intentions themselves. Behind such thoughts is fear that humans have long been moving on a road to ruin via general intentions, not just a gradually improving inability to conduct goodness.

Relative to management of intentions a difference between those self-generated or those accepted from others is quite important but not the theme herein. Here we confront the shortcomings in managing intentions regardless of their source. Many of those intentions have long been treated as beneficial to the human project but recently they came to be associated with consequences that many end the project, and its human participants. Symbolized in many ways herein they group under the consequence of environmental desecration. The focus is on human acts intentionally conducted that close a dichotomy of death. Intended to lead towards immortality, their achievement ends in early mortality.

Such is not a complement nor condemnation. It simply offers no basis for hope for life as we have come to know it. Long-term evidence shows how humans acting as humans appears as a bad idea. Have we an alternative? What should we act like based on whose intentions? Do we have a choice?

Our presumption of intentions as good is wrong. It's more interesting than assuming human intentions are good, but humans carry them out in a bad or defective manner. In human history there exist very bad intentions in human behavior, as well as good. Some intentions are good for self while intentionally bad for the context. Some are intentionally bad for self in the service of context. The first is seen to arise from a selfish mentality while the second is often noted as selflessness, or more recently called altruism. Herein we will shift this same discourse from human object to contextual impact of short-term results and long-term consequences of human intentions. In this way we attempt to explain from where climate change arises and how best to manage its arrival.

A significant change took place in intentions near the middle of the 19th Century, a change fueled by scientific developments, such as the science of thermodynamics to run the industrial machine. With greatly increased access to and use of energy the world seemed to support all human intentions. Dreams of economic success allow needs and wants to be reconsidered. Whatever the intention there would be a machine available to power it.

Economic intentions drove ideas of how to make more things, always more cheaply, and thus replaced the prior focus on guidance between birth and death managed by an ethical compass. Much in ethics was suspended in favor of economic ideals such as continually improving productivity. Making more in a cheaper way became the soul of enthusiasm. This came to be known as industrial development. All aspects of human thought and action came to focus on the process and products of industrialization.

This and the infinite number of short-term gains in meeting human needs came to be valuable to the revised human project. A long-term problem in this was seen but mostly ignored. Now the situation is a countdown towards 2100. The importance of that year will be explained later in the book. As the project moves to then, the costs grow.

Via those in love with Aristotle's digital logic them moving to admiration of a version of science posed by Newton et.al. There appears to have been a rash of successes that nurtured an arrogance of humanism. Humans might finally secure control over their world, each other, and possibly themselves. Expansion dreams of rationalism even allowed hope for logical positivism to take control. Such then met a barrier that seriously questioned the human trek. Modes of war in the 1940s, especially extensive use of Aristotelian logic and Newtonian physics, began to appear as against life. Application of the most advanced science to create, then use, atomic bombs seemed to contradict the long-expressed respect for and love of life. Conflicts between humans and their environments were not resolved. They simply became "colder."

This transformation continued and expanded to assume management of the human project. It was to provide for human needs and then move on to marketing and then meeting human wants. This went well beyond fantasies about warfare with each other and nature. This development is now known as the period of industrialization where human needs, then wants, and then the human soul were caught up in rational expectations. This replaced religions and their negotiations with the soul. A new kind of religion emerged, one of economic values, hierarchies of control and marketplaces for finding and having the cheaper.

This was structured by an idea of meeting ever expanded humans via a process to support those who always wanted to buy more and be able to note they could also have it ever more cheaply. Humans were changed along with the human project.

This continues to expand into the 21st Century. Attention driving it shifted from the small shop to the large shopping center and is now captivated on Amazon screen in the home or office. Work is now underway to make the results cheaper via using AI to deliver what humans most want during any minute at their doorstep just as they realize they want it. If this is progress what might be the end state?

Yes, I don't fully understand what this means but seems the human concern has shifted from ethics to economics, are we are proud of it.

Contents found herein will vary from usual subjects. I will argue that such is appropriate in that most of what we know to be usual in fact is very different from that; we simply don't really know much about it. Humans seem to have valuable insights into what matters most but turn to investing much of their time in learning a great deal about what does not matter so much. Why this happens is a part of the eternal dilemma of being human. We do much for short-term gain while knowing long-term pain awaits us. This has long been the basis of the human project. More recently, in the last 200 years, something more exaggerated about the human weakness has emerged. That which we do in passionate search for short-term (a year, month, week, day, hour) gain is now posing a very significant for our life.

Books on the subjects discussed herein tend to perceive glasses, then speculate on their being half-full, or half-empty? My viewpoint and response to such generally becomes stated as: "The glass as empty with urine stains on it."

Much of my research and writing since 1979 addressed issues proceeding and then surrounding climate change. I felt it to be important in that it would involve life entering its most momentous phase in recent planetary history. Via climate change the definition of and expectancies for life would be forever changed. I'm sure you are now aware of the issue, even though many Americans of limited intelligence file it under hoax, but perhaps you did not know it developed from the mind and writing of Eunice Foote in 1856. She was to present it to an early version of AAAS, but finally got a man sitting near her to make the presentation, to maintain the idea of women not being scientists.

Her early experiments posed that increasing amounts of CO2 released into the atmosphere, from the burning of coal and the expanding of industrialization, would affect the planet's climate. She had argued how the expansion of industrialization would be a problem to life on the planet. From this is she was mostly seen as a woman attempting to be a scientist. Thus, she was taken less than seriously by the manly. The masculine was and is the manager of the human project. As a variety of religious texts prove to us, when life becomes more difficult one must become more manly. The empiricism of the Garden of Eden illustrated the truth of this.

Since then, there have been many articles on the subject. Most show how and why she must be wrong, and not just because she was a woman. Early articles found her concern and its projection to be trivial. Later articles accepted that she might have been right, but her fear of life's endangerment had been misguided. Her fear was the stuff of a science fiction book, or even movie. Some even came to argue that increasing amounts of $CO2$ going into the atmosphere would cause the planet to become cooler, not hotter. When this was corrected the consensus was that even if expanded industrialization of production and products might warm the planet, so what?

With some elegance such men argued how "Climate is always changing, and temperatures go up and go down every day." Even if temperatures generally rise this could be good for humans that want to become naked and lie on the beaches of the world. Since humans rule the world, and via their technologies they will keep improving the world as well as fixing problems forgotten or left behind. Climate Change concern is simply a theme for an opera that you listen to when you enjoy being afraid of occasional mismanagement, as in Goethe's "Faust" or Shakespeare's "Much Ado About Nothing."

As a play we can confine climate change reality to the theater, along with many other issues that are quite bothersome, even terrifying, to the human project and its membership. It is worth noting that humans have a deeply entrenched belief that humans are born with an insatiable need for knowledge in the pursuit of life. The first sentence in *Metaphysics* by Aristotle is: "All men naturally desire knowledge." In fact, there is considerable evidence that humans want to ignore or not know about some things. Two recent ones are COVID and climate change. When information may reveal images of a quite ugly future, we work to avoid heating it. In scientists this was ween in James Watson, one of the two men who combined knowledge from others work on DNA structure to win their Nobel Prize. According to Chargaff Watson hid his own genome sequenced as he thought he had a gene leading to late-onset Alzheimer's.

A World Defined by Consequences

Contents herein build on results of a research project as published in 1979. It was about human-centered environmental deterioration that would lead to closure of life via climate change unless humans could change. The package of needed changes was called "business as unusual." Republished under different cover images and titles between 2019 and 2023, the research conclusions tried to tap into interest in human wrongdoing. Titled "Regulation of Environmental Deterioration," the 1979 book was published by a student group from the Wharton School, University of Pennsylvania. It provided the major content as reprinted in four more books to study the capture of human attention.

1. *"Too Early, Too Late, Now what?"* 2019, AuthorHouse Publishers.
2. *"Too Early, Too Late, Now what?"* 2021, Brilliant Books Literary.
3. *"Human Nature and the Potential in Nurture,"* 2022, Writer's Branding.
4. *"Sorry, But Humans are Fucked: Climate Change from Human Limitations,"* 2022, URLinked Print and Media. (By Hawkeye.)
5. *"Short-term Gain, Long-term Pain: Climate Change as a Faustian Tragedy",* Moldova: Eliva Press, 2023.

Interviews were conducted with a sample of book buyers. The conclusion was that the first book's cover was too depressing, being 90% black and having a tiny sunset. The second was more inviting via the optimism of various beautiful shades of blue sky above a small slice of forest ruins from a California fire due to climate change. The image and title of the third book were seen as the most inviting. Its image was a beautiful mountain range and beautiful sky with the title about humans fixing things gone wrong. That book, number four, sold the best. Buyers said they wanted behind them on their bookshelves during their numerous Zoom or Skype sessions.

The research in customer interest and media's role in such takes us back to the 60's notion of getting over content and seeing "The media is the message."[37] That author seemed proud of such. He thought this to be a complement to human insight, and their taking advantage of the development of new information technology. He seemed to have no concern for any deeper meaning in the actual message. He seemed happy that societal evolution in technology uses would bring news and programming wider and faster via electronics.

The above many-publishing episode was not a marketing strategy to make more money. All proceeds for all book sales go to charities. In this book the content is different, it's to address the central question of the prior research: "Now what?" Addressing it via business as usual ensures no business in future. As such we will simply join the growing science our consensus of a sixth mass extinction of natural life on our planet.

Humans believe the process of seeking and attaining resources for their needs and wants is rational and thus defensible. Such thinking depends on definitions of rational. These vary. Arguments over whose thinking is rational can lead to deep arguments or even more drastic action between humans. Humans tend to take great pride in the meaning of what they believe to be rational, especially if it doesn't seem rational to others. Humans fight to do what they feel is appropriate, especially when it clearly isn't so to others. This is most clearly seen in leadership, as discussed in Chapter XVI.

hope for a joyful matching of their idea of needs to attract the resources that will give them powerful results. This is often defined as human optimism Humans. After the optimism phase things become, in human terms, "complicated." The hoped-for results are generally defined around and for the individual or his small group, while disregarding the context that is present. Humans exclude context when being egocentric. They rely on simple-minded rational processes packed with results from reductionistic analysis. They work to avoid intrusion of contextual issues that might show another way. Results

[37] McLuhan, Marshall, *Understanding Media: The Extensions of Man*, MIT Press; Cambridge, Ma., 1964.

of the analytic can be managed. There are no apparent conclusions in the systemic, and no obvious directives for those seeking authoritarian guidance. Seeing meaning in the various connections in human needs to environmental resources can become complicated, confused, or simply beyond consideration along with those consequences from needs fulfillment. As such, the meaning of life in initiation, nurturing, transformation, and closure is seen as too complicated to be useful.

The meaninglessness of directives lacking context seems to offer restful simplicity but then the costs of achieving our results begin to emerge and emerge in a systemic manner. Beginning as clearly rational to the human mind they become consumed by the environment filled with a much more extensive and powerful reality of what we might call the non-ration. This includes the aesthetic, poetic, political, religious, cultural, and natural means for understanding what it's all about. These form a context from which we search for happiness. From the search we initiate consequences in and then from the non-rational aspects of each. The consequences are secondary results, often unintended. Results achievement begins as seeming rational, then begin to appear as non-rational once we attempt to manage them. Soon they can become irrational as we manage them in an irrational manner, such we see in Congress or a Supreme Court action.

The Consequential Aftermath

> "Humans are the only creatures in this world who cut the trees, make paper from it, and then write 'Save The Trees' on it."[38] (a normal human Catch 22)

Humans act out their lives within limits of their contexts as given but should recognize in doing so they create limits in those contexts in a funny feedback process. The concern herein is with

---

[38] From a cartoon picture framed and hanging on the wall of a major Swedish pulp and paper company. Initially composed by "rawforbeauty.com".

those secondary limits as created by primary actions as derived from questionable assumptions.

For two centuries the limits to life have been defined via how human work can expand quantities, while avoiding the questions of the qualitative. Such questions came from then environment. They were with what quantities were to be used for, where the essential resources to be used came from, how they were to be used and to where were unused aspects disposed. Almost no attention was given to who would pay the long-term costs of it all.

As such, human intelligence, or lack thereof, pursues purposes and supporting actions that come to further limit life's limits. This includes initiating deterioration of a context on which life depended. Even those arguing about "Limits to Growth"[39] seemed to continue to expand on the problematique of which their discrete problem was a part. The MIT personalities involved in finding and marketing these problems and their solutions trusted their analysis. The analysis told them that they should limit business as usual.

This became an added problem to the non-resolution of the original sense of a problematique by avoiding the wrongfulness of qualitative deterioration underlying processes of quantitative growth. The systemic had been avoided along with the need to continually create business as unusual. This did not make sense it made dollars major funders in business as usual, those who want to continue such in the ever shorter-term, before the long-term opens on them. Since their book on limits was published found questionable their research is shifting towards redesign of a wrong industrialization created to meet wrongful bio-needs and psycho-wants.

Time defines the limits of life and to change. Time provides contexts for that which matters. Time carries you, varies you, and

---

[39] This work came to be sponsored by The Club of Rome via the concept of the *problematique* as formulated by Hasan Ozbekhan, et.al., in *The Predicament of Mankind*. Therein the problems of mankind could not be solved in their own terms. This was for Aurelio Peccei to sell to the world. When MIT personalities joined the effort they soon found there to be a "solution" to "a discrete problem" as presented in *Limits to Growth*. Ozbekhan rejected the MIT solution of the human problematique and left the group. (By Hasan Ozbekhan.)

exposes you to changing contexts that nourish, move, improve, diminish, and remove you. Without time life is presumed gone. Contextual backdrops range from the nurturing of life to its elimination. Nature is the main provider of context, as well as its change agent. Human behavior, via its passion for the self-controlled artificial, can also change context but the un-natural can become costly to conditions of life. Human attempts to avoid the drama and trauma of the unpredictable nature of natural life end up putting work into creating the artificial. This is often done in the name of change management but in fact is mostly change stabilization, idealized as changelessness. Such is seen in strategies of the short-term set up to manage complexity but mostly just creates more of it. We see such in Faustian Bargaining that has long attracted humans to quick reward and deferred payment.

Weaving together such thoughts may seem unusual but does open doorways into a reality beyond the artificial limits of a protective analysis based on a very restrictive Aristotelian logic. Reality is more systemic than that implied in being wedded to non- and anti-systemic presumptions. The analytic is to restrict the mind from exposure to the interesting.

The systemic accommodates the non-rational that we find in areas of poetics, aesthetics, politics, religions, intuitions, and feelings. Once we are in the non-rational, we soon ask can the systemic be managed? If you are restricted to the analytic the answer is clearly no. Gregory Bateson argued that humans create a self-imposed limitation in their dealing with reality via reliance on *aided rationality.* Therein we impose a framework from the logical rational upon what we see as the non-logical, non-rational context around us. In so doing we create the irrational while forcefully applying the limits of the rational and fixed on the extensive and dynamic non-rational. Such gives us the worlds governed by the authoritarian.

Results of humans forced to occupy the land of the limited are seen in the behavior of humans acting out as schizophrenics. In the 21 Century we now see mental disorders at the societal not the individual level. This can be seen in the leadership of societies failing to reconcile what is seen beyond the boundary defined by their limits.

Such begins to explain the pretended ignorance of those trying to disregard approaching climate change consequences.

The above raises serious questions about systems of life and the role of humans in such. Can life afford the presence of humans? Should nature evolve a way to limit humans? Such questions open thoughts as well as new potential in life that go beyond the physicality of life. As such, meaning becomes central to the books' contents and any ideas about a continuance. The idea of *context* and varying interpretations of such becomes key.

From a Wealth of Nations to a Poverty of the People

At the surface my concern focuses on the conceptions and practices used in most business schools to get students to pretend leadership ability. I'm not so optimistic about the path to improvement depending on changes in business school curricula. Like many socio-organizations they manage to avoid uncertainties inherent in seeking the unusual. Responsibility is strongly centered on the irresponsible. Change is thus avoided. Via expressions like "Not my job!" changelessness is the rule of the time.

Responsibility for consequences should be reorganized to be a fabric that weaves together the parts, thus creating a tightly linked whole. Prior to his death Andras Angyal confronted the concern: "What happens when a system reaches its limits?" He proposed that under such conditions "The parts absorb the whole." The question herein becomes: *"Can business as usual be reorganized so the parts accept responsibility to avoid conditions for no business?"* Is business as unusual even possible? Can it be a good different? Climate change management requires such if there is to be hope.

Context is special, perhaps essential to any understanding of the senses and feelings behind our actions. Feelings of love, hatred and death require a context. Context defines what you what you relate to via interactions, such as what you want, want to avoid, or work to diminish. The environment, on the other hand, denotes the surroundings regardless of any relations. Seen as context for your existence you better understand consequences of your being.

Beyond context, and beyond ideas of environment, we can look at the around us as "everything." While this may be fun, and open to whatever is wanted now to fulfill egocentric selfishness, the idea of everything soon becomes nothingness. To understand the role of context, and see it as the basis for our relations, while avoiding the tendency to see hierarchies, I will offer dimensional frames, where frame is used in the Erwin Goffman sense of the mind as it engages in the limits of "Frame Analysis."

At least five dimensions thus define context as used herein, with one or two dimensions added to a humorous edge. We begin in the 0th dimension to access the point in and to life. The realm of -0th is for those passionate about relating to pointlessness, as in a Donald Trump lecture. The 1st dimension introduces life as we come to know it. It is a wonderful line that can stretch infinitely into a digital dichotomy encouraging arguments, even hatred, over the very narrow.

The 2nd dimension opens sexual confusion with excitement in not being able to distinguish male from female thus expanding our interest all the way into eternal 2-D computer screens. The dilemmas facing those restricted to a 2-D life were humorously outlined by Edwin Abbott's 1884 "Flatland." This elaborated on the limits of those locked in Plato's Allegory of the Cave.

The 3rd dimension houses the endeavors of mother nature in her forever battle with misplaced desires of father time as he operates unknowingly in the terminal restrictions of the 4th dimension.

From all this we can contemplate existence in the 5th dimension except we can't go via science, technology, or the "unaided rationality," that limits both as well as those relying on such thinking, as was noted in 1973 by Gregory Bateson.

We need to move beyond hierarchy where we see ourselves as more worthy than plants, animals and perhaps dirt. Yes, a Donald Trump or a Vladimir Putin may have a higher IQ, or so they claim, than a tree, but a tree certainly has greater wisdom of relations in life. Such individuals, as representatives of collective cultures, find reasons to hate life, and living systems. Going deeper, we have seen how they mostly seem to hate themselves and then move to hatred of the life that has avoided them. Nature, in her 3rd dimension, has no time for such humans as she is worried about the unfortunate rules imposed on her work by the 4th dimension.

The dilemmas found herein may seem funny, but humans make them eternally meaningful, only to humans, in that we pray for changelessness in the 3rd dimension to avoid our fear of the 4th dimension. Becker's 1974 Pulitzer Prize winning argument in his "Denial of Death" outlines this. The lease we trusted as permanent when born contained a foreclosure clause from the 4th dimension. Herein, culture is presented as a fundamental mask to that fateful clause that governs the human being. Culture thus is key to maintenance of changelessness. It acts as a wall protecting social groups during their wars against nature and other humans.

As will be discussed here, the hope for escaping from humans being human is limited. Thus, we walk, run, drive, or fly toward erasure of the species. "Changing" this definition will require access to the 5th dimension, a place we cannot go. On our current pathway it seems extinction is more than likely. Yet we are unsure if it will be via contagions, magnificent shows of nuclear clarity or further industrialization of climate change.

Many questions arise from this, including is the human strain the dominant species, as we are taught? We can say with humor that humans are critically important to life, especially to human life. A growing number of humans now see the human strain as a stain. We like to demonstrate how humans exemplify a central Darwinian idea, the one about survival of the fittest. As a human he may have been biased, perhaps outright wrong?

Darwin's work, as published in 1859 ignored the notations in the science of Eunice Newton Foote. She had them presented to the annual meeting of the America Association for the Advancement of Science Conference of 1856 as "Circumstances affecting the heat of the sun's rays." Her work was the first proof of the potential of climate change from human use of fossil fuels to enhance human life on earth. Her work showed how the how the CO_2 resulting from energy for industrialization would bury the bio emphasis in Darwinian evolution as well as Smith's theory of progress via economic transactions in industry.

Foote looked into future differences as more important to survival than Darwinian differences from the past. This distinction from the 4th Dimension is becoming critically important as climate change threatens the context of life in 2050. Which difference will make a difference? The history of science and technology via Darwinian dreams and Newtonian industrialization may become terminal to life, not its highest achievement.

Darwin's idea of fitness centered on change relative to a context of the past. What happens if human survival now depends on a very different kind of change, one created by humans following Darwin? Perhaps we need values beyond technological progression of the fittest? Michel Foucault pointed to a need to change to regain control of human sanity.

"People know what they do;
    Frequently they know why they do what they do;
    But what they do not know is what, what they do does."[40]

Such is central to this book. This is the fifth in a series that began in 1979 to examine emergence of humans asking: "what they do does." How do we value life and act to realize such? Are your values of short-term gain, or with concern for the long-term pains from such gains, and how to avoid them?

Contents found herein address the meaningfulness of ideas leading to actions relative to the costly consequences from achieving results. Deterioration becomes a philosophical issue, not one of biology. The world's youth have increasing trouble finding optimistic meaning. They question the worth of humans relative to their own life. They are troubled about current methods of valuation of life's

---

[40] Michel Foucault, "Madness and Civilization: A History of Insanity in the Age of Reason," *Psychology Press, 2001.*

valuation as seen in their artificial, even anti-life, surroundings. The planet that provides their platform for life begins to appear unstable and unkinder to life with time. Most of the unkindness seems to result from valuations apparent in what humans do.

It should be noted that the emerging context from consequences of climate change will make dreadful conditions for life and living far worse, and essentially beyond human ability to manage, at least via management as usual These include decline of nation states and other formal social groupings via mass migration in all parts of the planet. Along with this there will be significant increases in starvation, diseases, further loss of natural terrain, environmental deterioration and lack of shelter and economic access. The need for managing the unusual via greater knowledge of the unusual seems now as obviously needed as it is clearly ignored.

As the 21st Century unfolds we increasingly label secondary results as unintended consequences. Behaving systemically consequences can return to impact the initiator of the act. They can also influence others, as well as the context of it all. The intended results can appear as benefits from industrialization of human activities. The consequences can be what we are coming to call climate change.

The interest here is with such consequences, how they and the context arise from becomes managed, then looking back to see how the choosing and achieving of results was managed. Were the effects of climate change avoidable? Were the aspirations wrong, or how they how they were managed? ed to have. The relationship is not viewed as a standard cause-effect tangent but a journey into the core of the consequence, a phenomenon seen as highly systemic in its nature. Relying on traditional analysis to identify and segment a consequential situation will only confuse and dishearten. It is this last group that is of interest herein. They are the significant markers of an era of consequences from past decisions. Industrialization of artificial will be the marker of the 21st Century. Its consequences are just now attacking the larger natura context and its occupants, including humans.

Consequences are long-term and expand in strange ways that make it difficult to manage and to connect back to a sponsoring action in cause-effect logic. As they grow they become threateningly significant. It's noteworthy that humans tend to avoid consequences until they are too late to contain or manage via usual management. Humans seldom connect consequences back to the actions that sponsored them or can even pretend to not see the connections even when obvious. This is because they can result from an action seen as rational, non-rational, or even irrational non-reasoning. As humans we strive for the rational but since most of reality is of the non-rational, we try to make the non-rational behavior rationally, thus creating the irrational.

The relation between motives that sponsor an action, and the nature of its consequences is becoming of central concern for humans. Perhaps we are entering the age of consequences. The consequences are becoming noticeable, intense, and irreversible. We need to know more about how industrial actions came to be central to human well-being yet then became main threats to continuation of humans, and contextual life. The ideas in question were developed via a quest to improve the human condition via further science advancement and technology development during two hundred years. Many of the ideas were and continue to be supportive of systems of life but somehow get sidetracked along the way. The misappropriation seems to occur via traditional weaknesses in the character of being human. The weaknesses show up in many titles, including intellect on vacation, low moral aspirations, or on valuing self with emphasis a dimensioning concern for valuation of the context of self.

Geoffrey Vickers, who helped with the 1977 research project that the book rises from, reconfirmed an important insight about America:

> Looking back over history, the rational mind of
> the eighteenth century declared the human con-
> dition to be a triple slavery and promised it a
> triple emancipation. Men were enslaved by eco-
> nomic want, by political domination and by reli-
> gious superstition. Trade and technology would
> free them from the first, democratic institutions

from the second and science from the third. Freed from tyranny by nature, men and Gods, free men, it was assumed, would need no more regulation than human reason would supply. [41]

That attitude offered a human-centered basis to dream of seemingly infinite possibilities. Sadly, the results took humans towards a fateful end state, as well as that of their surrounding life. What went wrong?

To begin to understand all this we need to look behind the activities to myths used by humans to manage activities, and each other. These are the myths that arose to encourage development of industrialization over the years. The industrial is represented by the artificial. As such the artificial is crucial to understanding where the industrial has brought us and seemingly is going to leave us.

The artificial has two fundamental meanings. Combing them leads to a very negative end state, which may well explain much of the challenges humans now face for their survival. The artificial means to be made or produced by humans rather than naturally occurring but can also signify presence and management by an artificial mind as driven by insincere or affected behavior.

The thesis behind this book is that the first sense of the artificial needs to not be harmful to life. Production of boxes to artificially enclose humans in what they call houses and offices does not need to be as bad as it has become. The idea was created by humans via guidance of Euclid's fifth postulate "…through any given point not on a line there passes exactly one line parallel to that line in the same plane." This became a most sacred rule in architectural guidelines, the postulate of parallels. When it became infection with the second sense of the artificial, the artificial mind of insincere behavior that needed to build the cheap.

---

[41] Vickers, Geoffrey, *Freedom in a Rocking Boat*, Middlesex, England: Penguin Books, 1970, p. 183. Sir Geoffrey showed me this quotation in 1975 when we met in Philadelphia. Its special to me, as he was. This comment was crucial to the research documented on page 103 of *Too Early, Too late, Now what?*, David L. Hawk, Bloomington, Indiana: AuthorHouse Press, 2019.

Leaders in physics went around and beyond Euclid's fifth limitation to improve human understanding via new limits. Scientists such as Einstein and Gauss found non-Euclidean geometry as a doorway to far greater understanding of reality. Architects and builders never made it out of the parallelisms of the box. They remained infected with the limits of Euclid's 5th postulate. Thus, the longer-term costs of confinement to boxes, of humans and their minds have been very great. For humans the 5th postulate has become a very expensive myth. Myths are used in the Joseph Campbell sense. For him myths are public dreams, while dreams are private myths. As one of the world's great heroes said in South Africa prior to his death from authorities in his country.

> "It is better to die for an idea that will live then live for an idea that will die." (Biko, a song written by Peter Gabriel, 1977.)

The making of boxes for human habitation, especially via industrialization, illustrates the long-term cost of short-term cheap. We will return to this. This book is to help those interested in getting architectural design out of the Euclidean box and help humans escape the confines of the cheap. This may provide a way to better negotiate with the causes of planet deterioration via production and consumption of the cheap.

This may be expensive for humans to adapt to, but to have no doorway into hope will be too expensive for the continuance of humans. As Susanne Langer stated the problem of getting beyond confinements such as the Postulate of Parallels where the conceptual mode of humans came to control the perceptual mode as was found in the research behind this book to be locking humans into a destiny of climate change. The idea of climate change was seen as an example of the conceptual world generating phenomena in the perceptual world beyond man's conceptual abilities.

> Man lives not only in a place, but in space, not only in a time, but in History. So he must con-

ceive a world and a law of the world, a pattern of life, and a way of meeting death. All these things he knows, and he must make some adaptation to their reality. Now, he can adapt himself somehow to anything his imagination can cope with; but he cannot deal with Chaos. Because his characteristic function and highest asset is conception, his greatest fright it to meet that which he cannot construe.[42]

Human development is driven by a passion to create, invent, and further develop the artificial as representing the human in the context of the natural. The artificial and its management have been defined via the technological. Underlying this is a human tendency to define the artificial as in opposition to the nature. As will be shown herein once humans were systematically derogative about nature, then the technology as developed could easily by that which deteriorated nature. From this we see why its consequences tend to disintegrate forms of life. That early centerpiece of human development and source of manly pride thus became a question mark surrounding the concept of life. What can humans, whose actions created the concern, now do?

Indeed, humans have arrived at a momentous time. Much of what they developed to show achievement has become life-threatening. Just now we label it as a situation of climate change and package much in the list of consequences from it. Sometimes science packs too much on the list. Sometimes angry men allow nothing on the list. That debate is less relevant with time and not included herein. We Look deeper into how it the consequences are bad and mostly caused by a species preaching how they seek the good. Via the confusion from that dichotomy, we can project the entire future to be defined by climate change, or we can argue how it is clearly a hoax.

---

[42] Langer, Susanne, *Philosophy in a New Key*, Cambridge, Ma: Harvard Press, 1942, p. 287.

This makes the situation even worse and presents us with a "Catch-22:" damned if we do, damned if we don't. Seems hopeless. The many dimensions of traditional hope will be outlined in the following. All seem endangered.

The construction of management, mostly by men, is crucial to see how we got here as well as the impediments to getting out gracefully. Its first three letters denote the meaning of and structure for management. These need to be addressed. It's worth noting how those who frequently call man's bad relations to nature a hoax also seems closely wedded to the ideal of masculinity. While the construct is clearly at the center of what creates climate change conditions, does it also provide a means to change such?

The dilemma is most obvious in watching a seemingly uncaring and very busy man talking to an especially intelligent female holding a child with a smile. The man talks about his need for boys to work on his farm or in his factory. This reminds us of the eternal war of man on nature and demonstrates a problem in several dimensions. We even see signs of continuance of that very old war of a manly quest to be a leader turning to creation of an immortality project via private episodes of immorality. This includes we who support those like Putin, Trump, et.al. in our need to have religious like godheads to return us to the prior, and ostensibly better time. They can be recognized as always looking backwards for their futures. Changelessness, herein defined as neg-entropy, is their product, what they market and manage strategically.

We might conclude that many problems from and in humans yet lie in wait for difficulties to be revealed. The youth seem to sense them, out there waiting. This may be why parents from the past are so upset with their children of the future hiding behind their cellphones and computer screens. It's tough out there. Why not avoid going out there?

5

Research: To Search Again, Then See

To Change the Results, Change the Method

The 1856 work of Eunice Newton Foote in a science paper proved to be highly accurate forty years later when a Swedish man took credit for it. It now reads as prophetic about planetary life one-hundred and seventy-five years later.[43] Yes, climate change seemed destined and was about to bring unimaginable consequences to life. It often seems too late, thus what should we humans do? What can we now do?

Pulitzer Prize winner Ernest Fisher described the nature inside the modern human and his inner problems. His 1973 commentary addressed the human situation after having survived two world wars and significant expansion of industrialization to bring rewards.

> *"Modern man is drinking and drugging himself out of awareness, or he spends his time shopping, which is the same thing. As awareness calls for types of heroic dedication that his culture no longer provides for him, society contrives to help him forget."*[44]

---

[43] Foote's 1856 experiment first revealed the roles of water vapor and CO_2. Atmospheric CO_2 levels at that time were about 290 parts per million. Global climate change was not yet a known issue, but she predicted that changing CO_2 levels would change global temperatures and create an issue.

[44] *Denial of Death*, Fisher, Ernest, Free Press: New York, 1973, p. 284

When appraising human leadership, that promises to protect the core of where we think we are, yet lack a core themselves what are we doing? What does this imply for humanity's directions? Do they lead us to the important edges ahead, or back to the ones we thankfully left? History teaches us how lower forms of leadership are, and there were many, mostly promising rediscovery of the behind of humans. Where value-change is needed why could a return already failed values of yesterday repair things? Such only accelerates the mismatch between actor and context.

Maybe the cultural idea of the few leading the many is an exercise in species humor. Maybe it's a test of our tolerance to see if we can deal with situations that have gone bad then become worse by our values and actions? Feeling a need for others to lead us does seem to arise from strange cultural definitions of what is and what needs to be done. Such justifies social hierarchies via a cultural myth. Humans do not need such, and soon cannot afford its consequences. Can we ever take responsibility for ourselves, and our own mistakes? Maybe not. Much of what we call management relies on that beacon called leadership. There are great differences in the concept that range from mean-spirited authoritarianism to acting as if others lead themselves, not you. We can see such differences between the wisdom of Lao Tzu and authoritarian demands of Zeus. The same appears as the difference between the diffused inspiration of Joan of Arc and the centralized demands of Catherine the Great, including the service from occupants in her stable next to her summer house.

Upon reflection we can see the same choice between the sincerity of a JFK kind of president and the behavior of a Donald Trump as resident clown. We have seen this difference between the Ukrainian inspiration Volodymyr Zelenskyy and Vladimir Putin a documented representative of the downside of human weaknesses. Much can be learned by looking at the history and consequences of all these choices. The differences reveal much about the role of personalities, potentials, and problems in human affairs. There are gains and pains in such choices and their consequences. Why do we consistently ignore knowing such until the consequences are around us? To be a bit more helpful the 1975-1977 Stockholm Study discussed herein found a fundamental reason for going the central leadership route to deal with problem. It was from those supporting a legal order which was seen to cause great problems than solve them in systemic conditions. The alternative proposed in the study was negotiated order with leadership spread in the organization with concentrations occasionally found at the edges, not in the core of headquarters.

Thus, we arrive at that theme mentioned earlier, about human's first indication of planet change from industrialization. That was from the first warning in 1856 by the female scientist in 1856 that men scientists then pretended she had not spoken. In the late 19th century, a man pretended to discover the same, in a manner that other men could accept. Now, one hundred and thirty years later, we begin to ask if humans can change to reverse the impending threat? Failing in such, is general life on the planet capable of sufficient change to allow adaptation to the threats? At the center of this question is growing concern for the mentality behind the human behaviors that created climate change conditions and their consequences. Are we in the sixth extinction period where it is deemed as "too late" for continuance of most life, perhaps even all of life? Have we already passed the too early to be interested, and too late to respond, and thus entered the third phase: "Now what?" Is there time to even consider what best to do to replace what and how humans do things that brought us to this place? This is one of the concluding questions from the 1977 research report discussed previously.

In essence, can humans change in ways to manage climate change by 2025? Can they act differently than they did before, and avoid the dangers known to be part of the industrial process since 1850.[45]

A 2019 comment from Leonard Cohen's last album succinctly captures the 1979 conclusion proposed by my best friend, the late

---

[45] Gunnar Hedlund Comment, found in David Hawk, "Regulation of Environmental Deterioration," University of Pennsylvania Thesis, Wharton School, 1979.

Gunnar Hedlund of the Stockholm School of Economics, from his review of our joint work. We had jointly established the Institute of International Business to renew the soul in what was defined as business as usual but needed to locate business as unusual soon. Cheap has already replaced most of the spiritual.

> *"As he died to make men holy, let us die to make things cheap."*[46]

We often turn to the history of human leadership to see optimism for arriving at a coherent future for life. This research often does not turn out so well. We generally see leaders coming from the more self-centered types with an inflated sense of their worth. Looking deeper we see their choices generally favoring self over others. In addition, they fall into the camp that goes out of its way to exaggerate the worth of our species on our planet and in our universe.

Leadership likes to place our species at an ever-higher level, perhaps to avoid the anger about prior pronouncements. Whether an idea to be attained lies in lying about the future, or the past, seems essential being a 21st Century leader. Herein I will assign this weakness to the masculinity displayed in the first three letters of management. From such the limitations beneath the idea of leadership and their followers can be predicted. Stephen Hawking placed limits in the value of human in his metaphorical comment on such:

> *"The human race is just a chemical scum on a moderate-sized planet, orbiting around a very average star in the outer suburb of one among a hundred billion galaxies. And that I can't believe the whole universe exists for our benefit. That would be like saying that you would disappear if I closed my eyes."*[47]

---

[46] Leonard Cohen, song 8, "Steer your way," his last album, "You Want it Darker?"

[47] Hawking, Stephen, TV Series, *"Reality on the Rocks,"* First aired March 6, 2016. BBC.

We somehow favor changelessness in life's flow. While stability has its advantages it is increasingly obvious that something more dynamic is needed. To begin we might need to return to the classic definition of change as "difference over time." This might better allow us access to negotiations between unthoughtful human objectives and the deadly consequences that result from them. In addition to being more dynamic in our operating sense of change we also need to include understanding of the laws related to difference over-time, such as entropy. Clearly, we need to adjust human arrogance that believes difference in time, e.g., between races and cultures is important thus difference through time, entropy, can be largely ignored.

> "*Logic, n. The art of thinking and reasoning in strict accordance with the limitations and incapacities of the human misunderstanding. The basic of logic is the syllogism, consisting of a major and minor premise and a conclusion, thus:*
>
> - *The Major Premise: Sixty men can do a piece of work sixty time as quickly as one man.*
> - *A Minor Premise: One man can dig a post hole in sixty seconds; therefore Clearly Conclusive: Sixty men can dig a posthole in one second.*
> - *This may be called the syllogism arithmetical, in which by combining logic and mathematics, we obtain a double certainty and are twice blessed.*"[48]

Avoiding the Aristotelian attitude towards logic was fundamental to early systems thinking. Russell Ackoff would use this in fifties and sixties meetings to show why operations research science needed to move beyond Aristotelian logic. Since those early insights a mass of systems thinkers have reverted to what concerned those using systems processes to question analytic results. Systems logic

---

[48] Ambrose Bierce, *The Devil's Dictionary*, Hall and Wagner: New York, 1957, pp. 108-109.

has fallen back to become a sub-category of Artificial Intelligence that ignores the needs for and from natural forms of intelligence. As such it shifted from integrating more of the natural into human nature and is off In search of funny forms of the artificial. Thus it has become part of the problem it tried to resolve as described herein, not a process concerned the limitations of Aristotle's strict rationality and limited logic. Such, which arises in opposition to the contents of this book, seeks further limitations on a Greek logic that begins as quite limited and limiting. Such is like the logic in Ambrose Bierce's 1881 definition.

These limitations to helpful thinking processes are seen as core problems in need of being addressed. This is seen in contemporary change being mostly aligned with values on "short-term gain" and not with the more important research into the long-term pain that will result from such beginnings. Such as the title of a book as referenced herein is key to understanding how humans could choose a definition of change, one that would them at climate change.

Such questioning is crucial to understanding how we think, or if we think, then what we do from thinking or not. The traditional meaning of change is very limited in the face of contemporary questions in life. It seems to lock us into simple life/death choices that end up being made by consequences of what we do, not what we define as change. Thus, serious limits appear in the current context of life. We need a concept of change that can accommodate current and dramatic condition differences between 1850 and 2050. This is a more than serious threat of *climate change consequences* resulting from past human behavior.

The above may seem like an exaggeration of our current situation in passing through life on this planet but research shows humans to continually fail in seeing the change in the context of life as well as its generation from yesterday's actions. We see this in political distress, religious hatreds, social disarray, and disappointing economics; especially inflation we don't control and can't understand. Events in each of these domains reveal a long standing and firm bias away from seeing change while embracing the presumptions of changelessness. This is most easily felt as we sit on a comfortable easy chair watching the 2-D reality from our TVs and/or Cell Phones, as we slide into lazy dreams of immortality. If our space is not well built and tightly insulated, we must tolerate the noise of a hurricane arguing with tornadoes over which will send us away.

The need to better conceptualize the growing importance of this concept of change we need to know then rise above a 2,500-year-old intense conflict between Heraclitus and Parmenides. Each was trying to make sense of the meaning of the life of difference over time. This will be examined in a wider context later but for now please note that Heraclitus argued everything was in flux and thus different from what was and will be. He denied the existence of an unchanging one and argued for the changing of many. Parmenides rose 35 years later to argue the opposite. He saw permanence as fundamental to life. For him reality is one, single and permanent. He argued against a thing, anything, becoming something else. For him change was an illusion, perhaps a hoax? He went on to argue that truth was unchanging and can be known by reason.

If you are mentally and physically lazy which of these two would make you more comfortable in the emerging chaos of the phenomenon called life? If you strongly feel you are armed with immortality at birth you may tend to invest in activities that work against that death certificate granted at birth. When evidence of immortality is hard to come by you can turn to picking up a ticket for a heavenly journey upon leaving life. Otherwise, thinking of such becomes very heavy to bear. It's worth noting that the location of this heaven and its father figure can vary between religious preambles as noted on Saturdays or Sundays. None the less these humans walk down an entropic pathway to certain death. The most they can do is to speed the walk. Herein this is used to explain how humans can see daily experiences of their activities threatening life in their physical environment while openly arguing that they didn't do it, or that it will all be okay via future development of negative entropy devices and processes. Thus, the human species has taken little action of difference to change behavior creating the horror climate change.

Many of us are trapped in self-defined, daily routines that protect us from those surprises that redefine our lives. We seem to prefer the non-challenging, non-changing routines of our yesterdays and trust they will organize our tomorrows. When challenges arise that could serve as a wakeup call demanding change, we reference such as hoaxes undeserving of our concern. It's almost as if we are comfortably upset in a changeless state of guarded hopelessness supported by an abundance of arrogance. As Darwin told us we really are the most important and most intelligent species on the planet we reside on. We seem members of a religion of changelessness as nurtured by extensive reliance on various 2-D devices and thoughts. We wonder what is real as we wander between 2-D devices such as mobile phones, televisions, regulatory documents, ads and roadways. Ideas of a 3-D existence as found in nature and the cosmos are quietly ignored. The change defining 3-D nature is unsettling to most. Any cognition of a 4-D entropic change is too frightening to discern or discuss as determinant of our reality.

Change can be seen via the idea of a flow, as in time, a river, a life. All these humans can observe from a distance as it's a bit threatening to conceive of self in any of those flows. This itself is "changing." Change is making its way into our consciousness as an omnipresent phenomenon threatening our continuance. The key point herein is that the change in change was created by man's work since 1850 via development of machines to support work. This has resulted in what we are coming to call climate change as initiated by men but with the mostly silent concern that men are not changing to control or reduce that which they changed. This is now the "Catch 22" of humans being human.

Herein the idea of change is not restricted to change of direction as you seek a location, or a change of mind when buying your furniture, food or clothes. It's a change in the essential forces that make our planet livable, such drastic change as to threaten planetary life. This book is the most recent in a series of books about the expansion of climate change conditions and consequences as time moves forward. The essence of this one is derived from a 2022 book by Eliva Press, "Short-Term Gain, Long Term Pain," the book became a management reference for those concerned with climate-change consequences impacting business as usual. That book outlined some of the consequences beginning to arise in operations. Concern was spreading and intensifying.

Managers know the many traditional methods for carrying out their work including corporate planning, strategic thinking, performance measuring, operations research, service indicators, AI additions, customer satisfaction, etc. At this point in business history there are problems with all of these. Failures in their use are tending to exceed the traditional success rates. Many of their applications are to ensure calm and remain in changelessness, even where they fail at both. The common announcement of trouble is "It worked well yesterday, what is wrong today?" In my lectures on such since 1975 I have suggested listeners go back and read the promises of 1850 made at the beginning of the industrial revolution. There they will read of the tremendous potential for bringing hope, stability and economic development to the many via mining and usage of minerals, forest products and energy. Ahead would be seen blue sky of increased potential. By 1960 troubles emerged for this dream. By 2000 widespread challenges to life were appearing on the economic horizon and in the health indicators. The environmental deterioration was obvious and spreading in most parts of the world. Only now in 2024 are we talking of returning to the beginnings of the industrial revolution and evaluating its unkept promise for human development. It now appears that the scientific insights from a woman of 1856 were sadly accurate. Much of this section is about the distress since of men choosing to ignore what Eunice Newton Foot said in 1856.

Environmental Types: from Placid To Turbulent

Early on we discussed the idea of change is changing. The science for this comes from the work of Emery and Trist during Tavistock and then at the University of Pennsylvania. Based on their research into the changing relations between the human and the technological they created the field of study called "socio-technical studies." It was an effort to rise above analysis of parts to what needed repaired to synthesis of systems in a context.

They made a fundamental distinction between environment and context. The environment was all of it out there. Context was what you interact with where you affect things, and they affect you. They had noticed that what humans interact with was being expanded in not so pleasant ways. Acts intended to stay within the interactive context were being expanded in the larger environment, then coming back to impact the initiators. The situation was not restricted to the local. Change was beginning to expand in both directions with some damages throughout.

Trist conceived of context as a more specific form of environment as well as a backdrop for the human play. He felt this play was about to be reversed, as he noted it would be. Social ecological was his key concept for this. Twenty years later nature was seen to seek compensation from human activities that had met human needs and wants but were very costly to natural systems. A 150-year human industrialized play was meeting with frustration from those seeing hard done to the larger natural context. From studies it looked like nature would close down that human play and methods of governance it relied on. Climate change was the most noticed actor on the stage of life. Trist has been right in his earlier concerns. At that point it was still possible to change the human role in the larger script of reality.

In an insightful nineteen-sixties article Trist and Emery elaborated on their work to have humans manage humans, and not return to management by technology in their noting and describing contextual changes occurring around humans via new technology and its unmanageable nature. They felt such would come to destabilize the social. Their terminology was very insightful and later used in the physical sciences to describe the destabilization of the context of the social, especially the natural dimension of context.

1. Placid-Random   (Independent)
2. Placid-Clustered   (Organized, Sort of)
3. Disturbed-Reactive   (Disorder Beginning)

4. Turbulent[49]   (Chaos Arising, then Destruction)

Eric Trist wanted to add an environmental type that would signify then challenge the optimist by denoting elimination of life on the planet, called Type 5. Its form was beyond form and outside turbulence, as within a black hole vortex. His partner, Fred Emery, balked at such a drastic challenge to business as usual.

Regardless, Types 2-4 Environments are now well known and show there to be very serious challenges to continuation of life on earth[50] while a Type 5 Environment now seems to be underway. It is now seen to begin to destabilize nature as the context to systems of life on the planet. The Trist belief was that the context of life was moving from a passive backdrop to becoming an active participant in life, even causing its destruction. He saw humans as the agent of unintentional change to the natural environment. The Trist research and lecturing was consistent with the reconceptualization of humans. While they were clearly performers in the play of life, as captured in the social science of Erwin Goffman,[51] their context was becoming a counter actor, and could become the actor in the final play of life.

From their in-class lectures it was clear that both Trist and Goffman took stock in that Shakespeare thesis of "...the world is a stage..." Both described the context of human life as such. Both then

---

[49] Eric related to me that he arrived at the turbulent term in the sixties while on a very rough flight to England where the pilot informed the passengers to put on their seat belts as turbulence was approach, then a passenger that ignored the warning was injured after being thrown through the air. Eric embraced my research that suggested climate change awaited humans if they couldn't change their activities.

[50] F.E. Emery and E.L. Trist, "The Causal Texture of Organizational Environments," in *Human Relations Journal*, 1965, February 1, 1965. Eric was one of my professors at U of Penn who strongly supported my Swedish research project on climate change in the human future, as an example of the vortex.

[51] Goffman, Erving, *Presentation of Self in Everyday Life*, New York: Anchor Books, 1959. Erving was one of my professors at U of Penn who helped form my concern that humans would not be able to govern the turbulence they created. The standard "legal order" based on threats from men towards men would be more of a cause then a cure.

moved onto focusing on the qualities of the human performances against that context. Late in their work they both saw the beginnings of the stage set in motion. They saw early signs of context becoming more than a backdrop, it was going into motion and becoming an actor. Both posed the idea that by the 21st Century the stage set, the context, would become the main actor in the play of life. This seems to have taken place sooner and with more energy than suggested back in the nineteen-sixties and seventies. Much in this book builds on their early omniscience.

Humans of 400 BC sought admission to a widely discussed and ambiguously defined access to afterlife. It was based on a predictably well-lived life defined by leadership. By 2000 new humans came to assume the same while working to access and use products from an unfolding industrial dream. Their production and consumption came from the religions of logic, rationality, and hierarchical organization, all to make such cheaper with time. This continued the situation referenced earlier in this book from Leonard Cohen: "As he died to make men holy (in 0 AD) Let us die to make things cheap (in 2025 AD)."[52] Cheaper is now the predominate value for human production.

Religion provided structure to life two thousand years ago. It continues today but the message is now presented as economics. In 0 AD nature served as an inspirational context from which self-worth could be measured. In 2024 AD nature provides energy and material inputs for the manufacturing and use of ever cheaper objects to fill life and tickle our needs.

Nature and its unexplained marvels can nurture the soul. Now it is an inanimate source of energy and material resources, as well as three-dimensional space for making, buying, and trashing objects based on one- and two-dimensional thinking. We now hurry to buy cheap before such costs "too much to be happy." It's as if Newton, not Leibniz, provided the value-system measurement scale for economics. As such the arguments between Adam Smith and Karl Marx

---

[52] Leonard Cohen, from song 8, "Steer your way," on his last album prior to death: "You Want it Darker?"

are inconsequential as compared to measures of success. The contemporary soul has come to be defined as objects, not about objects. Three car garages are better than those that house two as measures of progress. Is this the best we can do? Climate change is the reward for such measures of success.

This idea links together many concerns for contemporary life into a systemic framework with answers that are not reassuring. The consequences of such are beginning to be revealed. They are already very expensive to the future. This raises questions for the human idea of management at the deepest level. In it we see a management dichotomy relative to the human project. Human gains are seen to pile up each day while costs appear in storm clouds on the horizon. Who will pay these costs? Can humans secure a mortgage to cover them? If so, what will its conditions look like? In whose interest will such be designed? Will it continue with the modern theme of greater benefit to fewer with time? An outstanding charge has piled up. It is coming due. We have learned to avoid driving by garbage dumps, even those legislated to be surrounded by barriers blocking vision of the terrible.

Industrialization provided the roadway to the cheap. Such becomes more noticeable with time. The bill for such is arriving via cancers, viruses, and then *climate change*. Cohen introduces the essence of that long-knows Faustian Bargain for negotiating with life. It is to be followed by Act II, the Faustian Tragedy.

> "It is difficult to get a man to understand something, when his salary depends upon his not understanding it." [53]

The above emerged alongside our quest for ever greater economic success. We came to measure this via ever higher rates of productivity in creating the cheaper from use of the natural. Underlying this clarity is the deeper question for short-term gains regardless of the sense that there will be long-term pains awaiting outside the eco-

---

[53] From a 1934 lecture on the Great Depression, Upton Sinclair.

nomical. Yes, we wish to manage to become ever more productive in doing what we do, but often it ends as productively doing the wrong things for the health and wealth of the human project. Must the human fate be thus sealed?

Cohen suggest it was not always this way but is he suggesting we return to Palestine or Room to find better value? Probably not. Herein we will move past that cloud of optimism to accept that humans have long been troubled at a deeper level. This was first phased as a Faustian struggle in 1550 but was greatly clarified by Goethe in the late 18th Century by Goethe, then became the essence of industrialization values from 1850. We might suggest that the human soul that had been troubled for thousands of years would become industrialization.

The Faustian dilemma had been with humans for a long time, but Goethe brought a more contemporary appraisal of its workings, and costs.

"Goethe, however, interpreted the Faust story in a tragedy, not in a morality play, and the lasting significance of the Faust legend will surely again be recognized as deriving not from the theme of existential despair (which it shares with many other tales and myths), but from the paradox of self-limiting and even self-destroying aspiration which, as Goethe knew, the legend symbolizes with apparently unique distinction."[54]

The deterioration of nature was a longer-term price but was filed away by economists as an externality. As such it was filled with the certainty, called possibility, of life's extinction. As the possibility becomes the certainty some humans seek change. This does not include those deep into analysis in economics, medicine, law, engineering, and architecture, and many other professions. All have come to devote their work to that which opposes life. An interesting book elaborates on the Cohen theme.

The Faustian dilemma as articulated by Goethe and others, including a Nobel prize recipient for his rendition of the Faustian struggle, is helpful to our understanding of today. Ivan Illich writing about Germany of the nineteen-thirties is often insightful about segments of the human project, e.g., during early climate change conditions.

> "One way to close an age is to give it a name that sticks. I propose that we name the mid-twentieth century *The Age of Disabling Professions*, an age when people had "problems", experts had "solutions" and scientists measured imponderables such as "abilities" and "needs". This age is now at an end, just as the age of energy splurges has ended."[55]

> "The first enslaving illusion is the idea that people are born to be consumers and that they can attain any of their goals by purchasing goods and services. This illusion is due to an educated blindness to the worth of use-values in the total economy. In none of the economic models serving as national guidelines is there a variable to account for nonmarketable use-values any more than there is a variable for nature's perennial contribution. Yet, there is no economy that would not collapse immediately if use-value production contracted beyond a point through, for example, homemaking done for wages, or marital sex only at a fee. What people do or make but will not or cannot put up for sale is as immeasurable and as

---

[55] Ivan Illich, Disabling Professions, New York: Marion Books, 1977, p. 11.

invaluable for the economy as the oxygen they breathe."[56]

For two centuries humans found new means to meet their bio-needs and embrace the psycho-wants. Most were related to warmly praised entrepreneurial invention of technologies and techniques of industrialization. Many called it progressive. The value of the industrial somehow clarified conflicting values leading to conflicting meanings about life in the human soul. Life was difficult via questions in helping others in trouble, or simply encouraging them to go away and test their fitness and worthiness for a Darwinian existence. Modern humans found they could forget about all that and simply go shopping and smile as they piled up their short-term, cheap gains.

As a commodity the soul became available to become industrialized along with the human containers. It's the factory that matters, not the unfortunate products and pollution coming forth from it. As a symbol of human dominance over life it was not to be questioned, as such would question the idea of being human. AI continues this theme of development of the human project.

Taking a temporary break from shopping online, we might ask if the industrial changed human valuation, or did human values simply become clarified while in search of the industrial? Was the last two centuries a simple time of expanding smoke and mirrors? While humans were busy staring at the arrogance in their mirrors, did they ignore the smoke filling the sky from the industrial? While they were pumped up on the arrogance fed by humanism, they had forgotten the deeper processes governing relations to the natural environment?

To some this may seem like a good thing. It implies winning man's war against nature. Prior to feeling much pride men might look at fundamental laws of nature. One is that all acts requiring materials or energy inputs will incur an additional fee. Their entropic cost is included even without human involvement yet lacking human involvement the entropic rate is slower. It is a trait of the pollution associated with the making and the using of human products.

---

[56] Ibid, p. 15

Those who notice the indications of the above and are discouraged by the costs of externalities are a growing percentage of humanity. Another group is aware but seems to lower their heads and drive by more quickly pretending they were not involved in the mess. A third group believes in human ingenuity and hopes they can create neg-entropy via expanded-life, Nobel-science, faster-technology, digital information, and artificial intelligence management.

The contents herein differ from these groups. It presumes laws of nature are real, universal, important to systems of life, and not to be trivialized or put on hold until there is a cure for the limits they pose. Human attempts to override or defy natural laws can become expensive in the longer term despite promises seen in marketing and advertising. This is important as humans enter a situation where the collective costs of man doing whatever he wants, and avoids costs to the environment, are ominous. The contextual costs are like a surcharge on life, one that is coming due. These costs are becoming referenced as *consequential climate change*, or C^3. The emphasis herein is on the first of the three terms.

Just now, the making of things ever more cheaply is why many continue to go to their work in business and government. Where life is reduced to a 0 dimension of existence, a point, it seems pointless, but such has become acceptable, even meaningful. Contemporary humans have funny values. Creating business in dimensions of 0, 1 and 2 is now the essence of teaching in most business management coursework. How can this be? Should it be? If it can be shown to be the reasoning beneath emerging difficulties in the world between man and nature, will it continue?

Harvard's B School, a bastion of hierarchical arrogance, offers its Human Resource and Organizational Behavior subjects as the essence of what good to great management needs. This has been seen in their long reliance on Abraham Maslow 1943 *Hierarchy of Needs*. Therein are five stages of human needs that managers are to apply to improve productivity via motivating employees to invest their lives in moving up them with unending enthusiasm. The stages are seen via five needs: 1) physiological, 2) Safety, 3) Love from others, 4) Esteem, also from others, and 5) Self-actualization. Humans must work hard at making things productively cheaper while moving from meeting their lower needs. Then they work harder to move further upwards, possibly becoming self-actualized thus leaving the making of the cheaper.

Management teachers use case-studies to show how companies improve productivity, and impress editors of *The Economist,* by managing workers to be continuously productive by making the cheap continually cheaper. Key to the cases is managerial use of strategic deceit in using optimism to cover slowness in raising worker compensation. Maslow's implicit advice was to refrain from giving workers too much, too soon. Its best to restrict pay increased and unions arguing for such so owners can do what seems best for product making and profits. Should this Harvard ideology be changed? How does it end up supporting phenomena like climate change?

Yes, Maslow's model has serious problems. An early one was his use of Einstein and related souls as examples of attainment of self-actualization. Looking deeper, we see how Einstein ignored the lower four stages of Maslow's hierarchy, just as did others who we reference as being wise, such as: Socrates, Lao Tzu, Kropotkin, Celine, and M.L. King. They skip over the strategic dishonesty of Maslow and emphasis natural self-actualization. Thus, they are special in human affairs. Their thoughts were not about doing wrong things ever more productively.

Better managers, even better leaders, shun or make fun of organizational behavior and human resource management models like Maslow's, as taught in business management. They have no interest in motivating others to become more productive in doing the wrong things, as will be discussed in this book. They are never seen to keep others at the lowest possible level of the hierarchy in simply meeting the bio-needs of life to make more available for organizational leadership.

From course syllabi and lectures you can see a concentration on the economics of making things cheap and making them more cheaply. Therein a good life is portrayed as being artificial, not natural. Leadership is based on avoiding what seems bad in the short-term, although it may very well be quite innovative in the longer-term.

The strategic and the artificial are expensive in the long-term but praised as essential to marketing in the short-term. Although there can be significant costs appearing in the long-term, such is a long way off. The arrival of climate change exemplified this process. It only gets worse. Even after compensating for the long-term costs by going for the short-term cheap there are problems. It's a mess and becomes an increasingly ominous mess with time.

Swedish Project: Deterioration into Climate Change

Industrial development was seen as a sunrise for humans. It was technology-driven optimism based on machines serving humans. Now we see a sunset on business initiated by that dream. Ideas of infinite improvements being cradled in business-as-usual operations are challenged by climate science. Citizens are beginning to see then feel systemic consequences to environmental deterioration. The equation of business improvement is seen to have missed some variables. Ms. Foote had mentioned some of them back in her 1856 work. They were used to direct a 1975-77 research project based in Sweden about the consequences of business as usual. A book on the research findings was printed at the University of Pennsylvania in 1979. Forty years later that PhD dissertation in social systems sciences, that had been widely criticized and lobbied against in 1979, was republished. It was again published in a 2022 version that was placed on display in the Library of Congress in Spring of 2024. It is now seen as common sense instead of sense that was not so common.

The current publication is titled "Too Early, Too Late, Now what?" It tries to capture a small segment of the history of management concerns from 1979. At that time is was suggested that climate change awaited the human species if they did not find the means and methods to change business as usual. Threats were clearly on the horizon for continuance of what was then seen as acceptable. There were even early indications of ominous threats to life on the planet from the mainstream practices of business as usual.

The 1979 book had been mostly ignored, except by some of the leaders of the 20 companies and 6 governments participating in a 1975-77 project that examined how climate change arose from environmental deterioration practices. Those participating in the 1975-77 project came to believe in such. By 2019 they and their participation in climate change research was being noticed. CEOs of the companies in the 1975-77 project, such as Exxon and Texaco, had started to worry about climate change via the project. They even began to reflect on needed changes to business as usual. Both came to be thus replaced by their Boards for publicizing such thoughts.

Changelessness — In Defiance of Life as Change

There are intense arguments over management of human affairs, the role of governance, and who should be paid for what? Today's billionaires tend to advocate government owning everything prior to their owning the government. This is the simplicity of control and management. Via such, meaningful choice over difference is thus restricted to a few. Economists mostly ignore this dream of Reagan on, and the fulfillment of a dreamed reality of changelessness, while they que up for their turn at a Nobel prize on public/private control over pricing. Nicholas Georgescu-Roegen, a sort of economist, instead pointed out such economics is use of "Very bad math to mask even worse economics." He thought economics should and could be more of a science, but his arguments failed to win the day from 1971 on. In part this seems to come from the human fear of and avoidance of change. They read historic fables of how change was bad and the how it brought harm to those attempting its management. Parmenides, Plato, Aristotle, and other Greek men, argued for avoiding change as a construct for the human project. Their argument: "Things that change thus become gone, thus why worry about them?"[57]

On the other hand, we note throughout life that the essential nature of the natural is change. Nature houses change agents as well

---

[57] From discussions with Russell Ackoff over his PhD thesis with West Churchman, *Methods of Inquiry,* 1950. (He too was concerned with a human belief in changelessness.)

as accommodating the resulting changes. Nature is central in the human project as well as to its continuance. We thus arrive at a contradiction. Is nature more important than man as he works hard to manage the nature he does not understand as working to diminish is? Does man only diminish himself as well as his efforts at work?

Herein the need for stability of the artificial versus the change in nature defines a core dilemma in what is best called the human problematique, a concept extensively noted by Hasan Ozbekhan and described by Rene Dubos. Ozbekhan, founder of the Club of Rome, left that important early endeavor to understand environment deterioration. As he described the evolution of the Club, he mistakenly introduced MIT and their adherence of analysis to the Club. Seeking the "cause" of the concern in the Club for environmental deterioration they "discovered" it to be "human population growth." If so, all that was needed was a more authoritarian regime to govern breeding, somewhat like that Mao had done in China decades before. Thus, fixing the cause would resolve the problematic effects."[58]

Ozbekhan set up the Club to come to appreciate a different approach to managing change in the human project. He recommended that humans recover from their simple-minded cause-effect thinking that ignored context and systemic relations. He saw the human project as a richly connected system of problems, not a casual array or listed hierarchy of separable problems, each awaiting their turn in gaining a solution via expert analysis. He instead saw the situation as a problematique. Efforts to attempt segmentation of it into more discrete problems would only worsen the end state difficulties.

He argued how MIT type thinking was part of the problematique, but not a provider of meaningful solutions to the problematique. In avoiding change, as well as ideas of systems of problems, humans created complexity while saying they were avoiding it. Such was said to be insightful, and efficient, but it became an insult and

---

[58] From discussions with Hasan Ozbekhan as to why the MIT model of problem solving destroyed the reason for forming the Club of Rome; "to appreciate the gravity of what we do not understand."

threat to the natural. Can it ever be helpful to find ways to manage the fluid via analysis of the fixed?

Are we preserving the false hierarchy of humans controlling nature via extensive use of hierarchical thinking in science? Humans such as Herbert Simon seemed to only see hierarchies in what they examined. Once again, change was put on the wayside. Many humans thus argued against ideas of change: "With change, things can only get worse." This continued the long-standing ignorance and avoidance of the 2nd Law of Thermodynamics, i.e., avoided seeing the fourth dimension and its management via time. The entropy law found therein was overly pessimistic. Humans preferred neg-entropy and its marketing potential. Neg -entropy is now intrinsic to the marketing of all products.

Rene Dubos was kinder in his articulation, yet his model of thought was consistent with Ozbekhan's idea of seeing the problematique as systemic, not problems as forums for analysis.

> "Many times, in the past, civilizations have lost the will or the ability to change after they have set on a certain course. Such civilizations soon exhaust the spiritual content and creativeness that characterized their initial phase. They usually retain for a while a certain kind of vigor based on orthodox classicism but soon degenerate into triviality before foundering in the sea of irrelevance." [59]

This theme of Dubos, a biochemist, was expanded into the social sciences via examination of epidemics as sent out from nature based on human behavior throughout human history. This is an important dimension to understanding the emergence of climate change, as it contributes to generation of viral epidemics, a topic of growing importance these days via covid.

---

[59] Dubos, Rene, *So Human an Animal*, New York: Charles Scribner's Sons, 1968, p. 180, (The 1969 Pulitzer Prize Winner)

"Consumption and the Romantic Age. Epidemics have often been more influential than statesmen and soldiers in shaping the course of political history, and diseases may also color the moods of civilizations. Because they are part of everyday life, however, their role is rarely emphasized by historians. Yet some aspects of the medical past which have remained almost unnoticed may have been of greater historical consequence then more celebrated events."[60]

Permanence seems like a strange construct. While wrapped more tightly in blankets of culture, we create our isolation. Culture promises security in keeping differences out. Difference can be posed in a negative light by silly leaders. Cultural differences often lead to hostility, even war, between humans. This continues into the history of the differences noted herein between humans and nature. Intolerance of difference thus becomes the ally of business as usual. Accepting and managing differences over time presents a quite different challenge. It shows the necessity of supporting business as unusual. Why is difference over time so important to life? Perhaps it's the key to defining life.

Such thinking is restricted by human simple-mindedness. One indication of this is to see their being drawn to artificial "twosomes." Twosomes are the world of paradigms, paradoxes, and dichotomies, all setting us up to accept the current digital doorway into life's management via AI. Such greatly restricts insights into reality. One result is a digital intellect setting up intense left and right emphasizing arguments over the importance of the pointless. With time we continuously see the consequences of no content in the media, e.g., "Facebook is the message in 2022" as a continuation of the hoped-for truism "The medium is the message" as proclaimed by Marshall

---

[60] Dubos, Rene and Jean, *The White Plague*, New Jersey: The Rutgers University Press, 1996, p. 44.

McLuhan in 1964. Maybe it's time to reconsider the role of content in messaging?

Humans resist moving on to conceptions of "both plus more," where climbing up to stand atop the two allows better insight into the wisdom of the more. We seem to purposefully ignore differences that make a difference, especially differences outside two. Differences in clusters of three or more over much wiser access to an appreciation of the nature that defines life. Natural definitions are based in change, change defining the historic limits and future potentials of the human project.

Natural values define life. Continuous and continual change as seen in the entropic process of creating things in the third dimension that become destroyed in the fourth are sacrosanct and not to be violated by science, technology nor strategic deceit. A problem in valuing changelessness is how it thus obscures societal values. Values need to evolve over time, especially valuation in the activities of the human project and their impact on the natural environment. While the Cohen quote above implies values change it depicts a downhill transition of the human future to valuing no values.

In Plato's Allegory of the Cave there was a depiction of the human quest for the good in knowing more via increased transparency of the self. The self was known as the soul. In AD 2020 we avoid conceptions of any soul and instead seek the self as productivity in collecting the cheaper for our needs and wants.

This was studied in the results of a 1975-1977 research study showing the prevalence of the 16th Century Faustian Struggle in our relations between industrialization and the natural environment. We could see how the long-term costs for Faustian short-term gains were expanding ever more rapidly. Much business was seen to be based on expansion of the Faustian negotiation coupled to marketing of neg-entropy. Humans seemed ever more eager to mortgage their long-term souls for ever-shorter-term gains. Many had come to believe that there was no soul involved in the human project, and its management. The study showed how the long-term costs were mounting while the mortgage of the human soul was approaching climate change as a final foreclosure. Consistent with the Cohen statement above, this will be a heavy indictment of the human project. Why does this matter? It begins in shallow wants, passing through production of much crap, moves to waste and ends in contextual deterioration.

Humor: What Isn't, Wasn't & Couldn't Be, But Is

Modern education has come to emphasize students memorizing and accepting presumptions. As such it continues into conditions of climate change. The time-honored alternative is seen in what we can best call learning to learn. Learning it asking questions about what is assumed to be true to improve on or disregard what is widely accepted as history, philosophy, social sciences and our physical reality. In his significant book on "The Idea of History" R.G. Collingwood pointed out that we might best think of history as "the lie that is commonly agreed upon." He always encouraged us to go deeper into the context of what is believed, written or stated about past events.

Context is often seen as a calm, placid backdrop to a performance. When it moves into a more excited state, say for a heavy metal music stage, it moves from being a backdrop to being an actor. Its performance can even become unsettlingly turbulent.[61] Its actions can take over the play of life as in a forest fire, a hurricane or a drought. Thus we have two forces for contextual change. One is an actor as a change agent in context, as in perforng. Two is context as the actor that brings change beyond agent control. The second is dangerous acting as contextual turbulence becoming irreversibile.

Context is more specific than environment. Context includes mental and physical aspects of natural and artificial phenomena. When humans create, manage, love, disregard, diminish, or simply destroy context they make use of these four domains. This is most apparent where humans demonstrate their self-importance by denigrating their context. The usual method is via war where war can be

---

[61] F.E. Emery and E.L. Trist, "The Causal Texture of Organizational Environment," *Human Relations Journal*, Volume 18, Issue 1, London, 1965.

against nature, other humans, or themselves. Humans have a history of warfare from problems in their being more often than from their becoming.

How we relate to context can be via problems in a lack of understanding context, then a lack of caring for it. Some humans do understand and care, but they seem rare. They see nature as the basis of life and then act to complement and care for life, as well as others. They see life as a fluid state, one that unfolds in its becoming. They see more promise in business as unusual than in business as usual. This book is about them and the change in management and leadership required to enhance life and its context. A special sense of management and a new model of leadership selection seemed to be needed. Lao-tse offers hope:

> "Lao-tse (c. 565 B.C., A leader is best when people barely know he exist, when his work is done, his aim fulfilled, they will say: we did it ourselves."

This image of leadership differs from the industrial tradition or hierarchical power brokers seen in personalities such as: Putin, Trump, Hitler, or Catherine the Great. Herein it is argued that you will better understand where you are and need to be when reflecting on yourself as your leader. It helps to see your soul occupying the 5th dimension, to better relate to its presence or absence. Seeing such goes far to govern who you are, what you do, and what you become in life. Your soul can be in your 5th dimension or a one-time occupant of the empty left by short-term gain in your Faustian negotiation with the devil that sent it elsewhere.

Sometime listen to Dvorak's 9th symphony[62] prior to uplifting your spirit in feeling Ravel's Bolero. Then watch a report on daily human behavior. You may thus see where a three-year-old Ukrainian

---

[62] It is said he added this to the 9th Symphony in 1893 while in Spillville, Iowa for 100 days while falling in love with the town filled with emigrees from the Czech Old Country and the new nature they lived within in Iowa.

child is lying in a hospital severely wounded from being shot while looking for his father. While crying about his need he repeatedly says he loves his father and needs him for protection. You are then shown his father elsewhere in the hospital from being seriously wounded from meeting seriously drunk Russian soldiers.

As a context we hear Putin inspired Russian bombs marching towards the hospital we are in. The eternal beauty of the music cast against the immediately sick values of the human soldiers leaves us in a sad place. Dvorak is important in this context. He rejoiced in life while being saddened by the decay of life that can't be reversed. Human involvement seems to only speed it up. He was clearly fascinated by the relations between nature and life, as is this book.

Some talk of how purposefully indiscriminate bombing of children can only be the work of the devil. Others differ. They see it as misguided human behavior alongside development of the technology of war. Development is of the state of terribleness of technology that is to detour those with the same technology away from ever using it, unless they have mental problems. Their logic if it is sufficiently terrible it will not be used, like the thinking of the A-bomb prior to dropping it over Japan in 1945.

The context of child tears with beautiful background music raises the sense of the role of a larger context in the background. This is crucial to help understanding the approaching conditions of climate change in a foreboding context for life. Such is the major concern behind this book. Long-term climate pain is beginning to result from short-term human gains. Dvorak helps in that he lived for the longer term beyond individual lives. Later in his life he spent time in the US with 100 days of it in Iowa. During that time, he was completing his New World Symphony while trying to express his concern for long-term relations between humans and nature. His work raised questions about the relations between humans and nature, but not many answers.

Humans see natural environments as abstractions while disregarding the role of such in forming contexts of which humans are a part. There are physical, social, and psychological aspects to such abstractions. As used herein context goes further to emphasize relationships and the qualities of their interactions, some positive, some negative. Context offers a background against which you can act, as well as a platform on which you can interact. Environments pass by in thoughts of the clouds while context encourages being active in the present.[63]

The organizational, managerial, and other responses to consequences provides the material herein. They were and are designed and marketed to support human well-being. While the definition of "well-bring" can be lost, the timetable is strictly narrow – sooner and shorter is more productive. There is little regard for the longer-term, secondary costs known as systemic consequences. These can have such significant costs that no one will associate with them, nor the products leading to them. Buying cheap shoes that look pretty, are uncomfortable, wear out quickly can be sent to the curb without regret. In honor of sustainability mythology, they might end up being recycled prior to washing into the ocean for final disposal.

Despite the someone hidden longer-term costs P&C activities expand. They are proudly measured, marketed, and delivered to human doorsteps. As humans become increasingly unhappy with their purpose and usage they then see and say they support sustainability. Such P&C can appear to define cultures that humans can associate with as they threaten the existence of that culture and its membership. The characteristics and usage of P&C as outlined above can grow into a major dilemma for the meaning of a societal entity via a questioning of "why?" This can lead to societal disorder via fragmented questions without answers. It's like individual mental disorders from communication contradictions that lack explanation, such as Bi-polar behavior. Such was presented decades ago in "Catch-22," the book begun in 1953 and then movie in 1970 as mental disorders

---

[63] Russ Ackoff in "*Resigning the Future*" made a distinction between the 1) reactive, 2)inactive, 3)proactive and 4)interactive with his emphasis on how to get humans to align with the fourth. With the techno-edge and strategic authoritarianism encouraged by the third, and the changelessness allowed in the first and second postures, he failed to get many to see the essential nature of the fourth to well-being in the 21st Century.

of individuals. Now are seen as expanded mental disorder of a society breaking apart, not an individual needing treatment.

As will be examined in detail we knew of long-term costs from human P&C via gaining short term benefits to feed homo-centricity back in 1856 but ignored such. We were reminded of such in 1977 but continued to innovatively increase productivity of doing the wrong thing.

Recorded history is much about the management of the above, with focus on personalities of human management known as leaders. We take much pride in such and sprinkle it throughout definitions of our cultures. Such generates the myths used to motivate the human project. Our dominant myth since the early 19th Century was called industrialization. It held firm until the last quarter of the 20th Century. Only now do some begin to review, question, and criticize it, and its consequences for and to life.

Business-as-usual provision to meet bio-needs and psycho-wants from consumption of natural resources seems troubled. Most humans find this difficult to understand. Some humans think it's best ignored as they have other issues around them of more importance, or more interesting. Change thus seems far off, perhaps too far for humans to manage. None the less studies in science point to the needed change as well as its growing urgency each year. As such society seems wrapped in what Gregory Bateson described as the basis for mental disorders in individuals.

In the nineteen-fifties Gregory Bateson suggested humans enter an array of psychological problems from being trapped in what he called a double-bind. Bateson claimed these arise in the individual as communication dilemmas. Such comes from serious conflict between two or more messages a human was dealing with. He pointed to them as what we later saw in the movie titled "Catch-22," where whichever choice you make it is wrong, thus is doesn't seem to matter what you do just as it matters more. Any communication about the options, with others, and especially within self, causes suffering so significant that it leads to mental disorders. Bateson felt such was behind growth in mental troubles in individuals. Herein his conception of the "double bind" is applied at the societal level, not restricted to individual actors. This may prove to explain a growing hostility in humans towards nature, others, and themselves.

Herein we look wider to see where double-binds have become center-stage in social groups, even nation states. Wanting to protect the stability of business as usual just as its clear that such is leading towards no business, thus we know the instability of business as unusual is essential to a future. This is a societal double-bind. Driving around looking for alternatives to using petroleum to drive around clearly results in societal schizophrenia and individual anger.

No replacement myth has been derived to provide renewed meaning and hope. The traditional myth, seen as a culture, continues even as it is increasingly recognized as the major endangerment to continuation of all life on the planet. Thus the "the human project" faces a serious dilemma, or perhaps is the dilemma of life. It is being seriously questioned but mostly by youth that look up, not down. Redefinition of the future and humans' role in it is a growing concern that currently is titled *climate change*. Herein the concern is more with the context that is creating conditions of climate change, not the actual consequences.

Humans seem caught up in a stream of bad luck or being drug into the consequences of some unfortunate decisions. Are humans less intelligent than we believed, or did artificial intelligence reduce the need for natural intelligence? With our societal bias towards manly leadership and the manly bias towards warfare in problem, and intolerance of natural disobedience, did we destroy our relation to the natural context? Or are humans simply suicidal, and only now realizing such? Can whatever be wrong with humans be changed?

Negotiations with hope are seen in the context of the Rapaport version of that proverbial "prison's dilemma" gaming. He showed how you can rise above the evil implicit in the strategic dishonesty, and all those counter-productive hierarchies such maintains[64] are being lost under business as usual. Can such hope be resuscitated, or redefined? Yes, maybe, but it will be very different. Interesting is

---

[64] See Anatole Rapaport's version of the winning program for Prisoner's Dilemma Game as staged in Scientific American, 1987 issue.

how the concept of management has emerged silently important to problems of today.

The history of ideas of management gives clues to what is wrong relative to where it began and who maintained it over time regardless of how wrong its results seemed relative to life.[65] Management seems to become key as we see a greater awareness of serious troubles in managing relations to our environments, nature, others, and ourselves. With time is seems clearer that much of the human problem come to center on the first three letters of management. To see this, you need only look at the bias towards forceful measures to firmly manage actions of humans that began in values of the masculine and the forces defined therein. This is seen in the growing problems arising from calling for, i.e., demanding, proactive measures of the simple-minded to manage problems of the interactive. The probable results of men threatening nuclear war illustrates such. As such the unpredictable does become more predictable. Something similar, yet slower, is emerging with efforts to regulate actions leading to climate change. The unmanageable seems to come out from our current ideas of management.

The traditional image of shelter is to provide security. The shelter of our existence is tightly woven into having a context to protect a living order from dangers and insecurity in surprise events. Much in the process of creating such shelter from surprises creates the later dangers that the shelter is incapable of protecting from. This presents us with a double-bind that grows into a bi-polar condition in society. Such adds to the digitates in our manner of working on and via computers.

Human differences have long been available to begin warfare against nature, others, and us. Signs of societal trauma are everywhere, where the parts are challenged as never before while the meaning of the whole gets lost. The stability required by life has gone into motion. Our context has passed from the Trist idea of "dis-

---

[65] Crucial to this is the work of Aristotle creating the weakness of unaided rationality and the stories behind the societal death's brought to Socrates and Joan of Arc for accessing truths.

turbed reactive" onto environmental turbulence. Irritating storms have become hurricanes and tornadoes. We now see early signs of an approaching vortex.[66] Is there a technological possibility to bring life out from a contextual black hole? Probably not. If we can go back, in the US Republican sense of survival, can we go somewhere else? Where?

We need repair activities that take responsibility for such since humans won't. Herein the troublesome activities are lumped under the widely accepted category of business as usual. This has seldom ever been used as a pejorative but herein it is, with an implication that business as unusual would be better. With time business as unusual is seen as clearly needed, even in need of urgent emphasis. since Success in creating business as unusual now seems to be the determinant of human occupancy of that future. Concern herein examines how humans have come to select and manage their activities that were meant to fulfill their short-term bio-needs and psycho-wants in a local life. Lately, humans have begun to note the deterioration of the longer-term from changes to their global environment. A price is being assessed to the shadows of the consequences of humans finding ever more productive and innovative ways to meeting bio-needs and psycho wants in the ever shorter-term. Research from the seventies shows the teachings of management and law schools' ideas are central to the assumptions beneath the problem, as well as key to consumers and citizens not seeing the costs that approach.

Key in this are questions about human character. Are humans driven to help themselves first then maybe be concerned for the environment, if there is time, known as greed? Can humans act to enhance that same environment while appreciating the life that relies on it, while learning to put unbounded psych-needs in perspective?

The depth and range of human activities on earth becomes ever more significant while the longer-term meaning of such is hidden under ever more ways to become entertained, even in the university. As humans notice things are not going well, they have yet to associate

---

[66] Emery, F.E., & Trist, E.L., Eric, "The Causal Texture of Organizational Environments," *Human Relations*, 18(1), pp. 21-32, 1965.

such with their emphasis on doing well. Humans have created the beginning of ominous conditions that define reality as unlivable. The situation is now widely referenced as climate change as created by gaseous products becoming CO_2 that heats the planet. The results are moving towards further conditions that deter continuation of life as we now define it. The process was demonstrated in 1856 as at the heart of industrialization, but R&D, innovation, dreams, and rewards remained focuses on its continuation.

Concern is finally appearing but focused on those subjected to heat that removes life then storms, droughts and fires reorganizing what was dying. Human activities are becoming more obviously connected to the above challenges as well as directing a general environmental deterioration of all that surrounds and supports life. This process continues religious traditions that place man in the role of manager, as the seat of power, with nature providing all needed raw materials for building greatness. Can men now reverse their character and resolve problems they created? Probably not.

Some seek ways to better access realities. Some ignore all distinctions about what they never choose to be part of. Still others reject any restriction on their freedom and strike back via quotes from various religions and/or sciences that allow immortality projects.

The pathway of the third group is interesting. Why are they attracted to immortality projects, and what will they do to find such? They generally begin by ignoring restrictions from nature or by its laws about what is and isn't. They are generally drawn to laws as created by man, not of nature. Many become politicians after an affair with man-made laws via law school. They invest much time in creating a non-natural, artificial existence often called the human project. They do not see or look for the costs in this approach as it becomes anti-natural, then unnatural.

Life: Differences that Make a Difference

Humans often damage context in their meeting of personal needs. They seldom notice damage done nor feel bad about its consequences. By the time they see the consequences they mostly forget where they arrived and how they were initiated. Even when buying industrial products from an upstream factory alongside the river we drink our water from, we seldom connect that production to meet our wants back to our disappointment in lower quality in meeting our need for water. Such connections and relations seem ambiguously vague. What can be done?

Does it make sense to have the bad leadership of those companies sued while we go buy more of their products? Is there a natural process for cleaning up such, besides an obvious need to clean up humans? The answers will redefine life on earth. The future of context and its human users will be changed. Such becomes more urgent each year. Then I commented on such in the fall of 1977, in a final reporting on "Environmental Protection: Analytic Solutions in Search of Synthetic Problems,"[67] I was told such was unimportant or simply a hoax. Leadership even became angry at the reports and the one writing them.

Republished in 2019 as "Too Early, Too Late, Now what?" it was the 1979 report on the 1975-77 climate change research about the human future. Amazon management moved the book from their academic science section into its humor. Their management said climate change could not be true thus it belonged with books such as: "The Pigeon Finds a Hot Dog," "I will Teach You to be Rich, 2nd Edition: No Guilt. No Excuses. No BS," and Wilma Jean's "The Worry Machine." A different publisher noticed this and offered to republish the book under the title turned down years before an academic publisher. That title of great clarity, "Sorry, Humans are Fucked," was said by the academic publisher as a low point in human affairs. I agreed, while then arguing it was an indictment, not a sexual

---

[67] The research notes, project interviews and mapping of conclusions from this project were in my NJIT office in 2012 when they were sized under the orders of the NJIT President Robert Altenkirch and the NJ Governor Chris Christie as being NJ State Property? All files on the 10,000 students I had on my rosters and 85 books I would loan students to help their learning were also seized. Much of this was from prior to my being at NJIT. Several of the books were out of print books valued at more then $1,000 each. NJIT lawyers also seized two stuffed animals that belonged to my baby daughter. On judges' orders one was returned.

joke. When that book appeared, Amazon placed it in their candle section, not in books. When I called them, they explained that it should be near candles so when customers were upset with it, they could burn it. Good thinking.

With the help of a group of small publishers we are now involved in a small study. We want to see if humans still read books, or only listen to them while driving or in bed, or simply scan titles and cover photos as they wait for the ringing of their I-phones. We have produced three versions of the same content but under three radically different titles and behind very different cover photos. The two extremes are: 1) "Human Nature and the Potential in Nurture," 2) "Sorry, But Humans Are Fucked: Climate Change from Human Limitations." Between the two is a softer title and image. Just looking for signs of hope.

Results from seeing which humans are interested in what image are coming in. The 2021 movie "Don't Look Up" seems to side with the image on one of the versions. The book you are now looking at is different. It moves on to address the question: "Now what?" The contents herein try to identify and examine what being human brought us the consequences of climate change to systems of life. We then go into how we might change to soften the impact of oncoming consequences that are varied but not all are irreversible.

Via religious and related ideas about humans needing leadership in a wilderness of bi-polar contradictions they fail to see context as important or perhaps even see context. As we move through episodes of self-importance time is scarce. We mostly ignore context until it rises up to define our reality. There are contextual consequences to our choices, and in our actions. We might look at it as a non-artificial feedback loop that operates within systemic wholes, especially when it encounters a pile of artificial parts awaiting analysis. Then, if we can find a way to stabilize context after our "interruption" we humans again return to our obvious preference for analytic humor, perhaps a porno movie run backwards could fill the gap?

Such introduces the situation of climate change conditions, something humans feel is unimageable until they find it unmanageable. Simply put, it's like a neighbor failing to sufficiently respect

what you are. Thus, you have the freedom to "urinate on his property" to demonstrate disrespect for him. When he notices, which is
key to this ceremony, he then takes you deeper into mutual disrespect. "Around and around, we go, where it stops nobody knows."
Such is our relationship to the natural.

Climate change via our urinating on nature is used as a metaphor
about a price paid for disrespect. Costs can include your removal.
Human choices clearly have consequences from their attempts to
make gains for the chooser. The process in fact says much about the
chooser, and potential to become a looser. Sean Rowe's "Trying to
Leave Something Behind" will take you deeper.

Context can be attractive, distractive, or a nuisance obscuring
self-importance. It defines relations to, potentials in, and the limits
of occupancy in life. A few humans, mostly research scientists, now
see the above, and warn that business as usual becomes terminal.
Their reporting takes you into questions of context, and how such
is what defines life. Otto Rank tried to explain this in 1932 when
speculating on how humans had become more dominant yet losing
an important aspect of being, their soul.

> "For even though the various human civilizations
> may each arise from the combination of a certain
> environment and a certain type of humanity, all
> human problems are, in the last resort, problems
> of the soul. By this we mean, not to say that the
> soul can be wholly explained in terms of mod-
> ern psychology, as our mechanistic science would
> claim, but, on the contrary, to stress the auton-
> omy of the spiritual, which not only works cre-
> atively in the religious, artistic, and social realms,
> but also determines the ideology which colours
> the psychology of the time."[68]

---

[68] *Art and Artist*, Rank, Otto, New York: Alfred A. Knopf, Inc., 1932, p. xv.

"Both Plus More" — Beyond The Tired Twosomes

Humans have a long basis from, faith in and quest for finding meaning in twosomes. This becomes important to note when you need to understand the passion for analysis as well as its serious limitations from twosomes. As was said elsewhere it is best depicted as 1 dimensional, as in a straight line with two ends. Each end accommodates a strong standing for advocating a point. With time the bias towards conflict between the two ends becomes prominent while the space between is seen as lost territory. In addition, with time the two points at the end of line begin to seem pointless and lonesome. Much more powerful yet less interesting to most is the history of zero in mathematics. It is far more dynamic than the story of two yet two dominates. This is seen in dichotomies giving us Catch-22s, Double-Binds, Bi-Polar thinking, schizophrenic behaving, information technologies, artificial intelligence, etc. Two locked us into a very regular closet of the artificial after having escaped from the nature of Plato's Cave. Both are two-dimensional but the trend is thus seen to clearly be towards the artificial.

What alternatives are available to move above the paradox of intellectual twosomes? It's like a marriage where the two learn from hating each other, thus it's all justified. Whatever they might be we do not seem to teach or learn about them. As a small attempt herein, I argue a way up and out is seen in "both plus more." It helps address this reality humans artificially split into two and thus the predictable shortcomings of life based on the limitations of half without a doorway into the more. We need to locate the "more." Continuing with business as usual is a search for hopelessness at an ever-deeper level.

We have noticed that most people have an affinity for specific numbers of categories when they talk or use their fingers to keep track of major points, they want you to understand. Sometimes there are ten but most using that have found they lose listeners at about four. Thus, we see a major difference between those relying on four and those preferring categorizations of three.

Russ Ackoff, like many others trained in the sciences, had a clear preference for foursomes. He came to be widely known, and admired, for 4-part conceptualizations of attitudes about human predispositions. These were to reverse an action, preserve inaction, or climb on a technological rush to the future. His fourth, his preferred, was to move outside the action/inaction sphere.

1) A **"reactive"** attitude, against context and its occupants.
2) An **"inactive"** stance towards the context of life. (These were busy people who created and attended many meetings to insure nothing happened.), and
3) The **"proactive"** attitude towards moving forcefully ahead, no matter the subject, and especially if there is a leading-edge technology dimension to buy into. Finally, there was
4) Those that were predisposed to being **"interactive"** with all the above, to solve problems from and with many human perspectives.

We can reconceptualize interactive as of a higher order of thought, thus a different logical type. Those of this mind set seek mutual resolutions. They interactively believe diversity must be included in finding a better way. They are special. They avoid hierarchies, including those of economic and professional status. For Ackoff's categories they would see 3 + 1, as in the interaction posture being of the different logical type. Business types liked Russ's four-part diagrams, as they fit with their two-by-two matrices.

To push Ackoff's scheme further I proposed that he was thinking via a system of three-plus-one. Thus, the "one" could "become special." As mentioned above it would be seen as of a different logical type operating at a higher level. Russ smiled at my elaboration on his scheme. Applying this to the human project, mentioned above, and to the four questions defining it, we see "one." Questions of "Where does the human project end?" stand out from the others. It is clearly outside human understanding. It lies in the nature of the 4th Dimension, an area we do not understand but see as the 3rd dimensional depository of deterioration. The 4th operates via the irreversible 2nd Law of Thermodynamics that lies beyond human control of understanding, or control. Humans market that entropy doesn't exist for their products and processes. This is simply dumb or unethical. Entropy is truly of a different logical type, and key to the human project.

Taking the simple idea of three plus one into a deeper place we can see much potential. Why do humans tend to like categories of four then prefer stopping at the third? Using this question let us look back at the Russ typology of human postures. If we could make use of the logical typing of the fourth, we might see great potential to do much. You may thus recall that Russ would give support to those who dared to question Newtonian logical. This was his version of systems thinking.

The limitations in the four could be lessened via the potentials in three plus one. In his "Redesigning the Future," and in his class lectures, Russ was concerned about the proactive category being the most attractive while the interactive might confuse. That concern was warranted. We now see that many have broadly endorsed, even come to worship, the proactive in all corners of society. While it had been posited it as a negative by Russ, to encourage movement on to being more inter-active, we now see that it grew into a centerpiece in non-ethical venues.

We increasingly see where "important people" accuse other "important people" of being lesser humans in that they are "insufficiently proactive." Failing to be proactive becomes an insult of significance. Going deeper, we might note that another of Russ's friend, Eric Trist, advised Russ to drop proactive in 1973, and shift to the "pre-active." Eric said we turn to proactive because we don't know Latin. He would point out how the pre-active, via its root of "activism," would have been a good entry point for the interactive. In this way we would better arrive at Russ's ideal. In such discussions Russ would slightly smile then walk away.

I would thus argue to move onto the idea of "both plus more." From such we can find a way into the "more." Form, four allowing four corners, can be very important to determining a way forward. As was suggested before the inclusion of hierarchy becomes crucial too much in human thinking, especially about form. This leads to its imposed role in forming content. We seem to readily move to tap into the ancient idea of a hierarchy being behind all that matters in being human. If so, is this a problem? If there is a limitation, how might get over it? Herein I will argue that we should seek "business as unusual" and therein seek a way out from Plato's Cave. Thus, what we do and how we manage it could all be different than it is. For example, instead of staying in Plato's Cave, or leaving such, we would accept that both perspectives exist, let them join or fight, but move on to the more of existence beyond the cave and beyond the beyond of the cave. This would be closer to the worlds of Carl Sagan and Stephen Hawkings.

To go deeper into hierarchy and how it seems so sacred to human understanding and managing we see how biologists, except perhaps for Darwin and his followers, come to teach us that life is not a hierarchy. It is far more interesting than Darwin's proposal for thinking and H. Simon's proposal for the modelled of economic acts. Why then do humans so completely rely on that which is not found in nature, hierarchy, as the most important determinant for thus knowing of nature and management of self?

As an obvious alternative the domain called network form is older and fresher than hierarchies. It also offers many alternative ways to think about forms and their management. We can return to the ancient hunting party model of human organization. Via expanded reliance on electronic information systems this has come to be known as networked organizations.

> "The diversity of networks in business and the economy is mind-boggling. There are policy networks, ownership networks, collaboration networks, organizational networks, networked marketing – you name it. It would be impossible to integrate these diverse interactions into a single all-encompassing web. Yet no matter what organizational level we look at, the same robust and universal laws that govern nature's webs seem to greet us. The challenge is for economic and

network research alike to put these laws into practice."[69]

A later stage of conceptualization will move deeper into fluid dynamics and deal more with the flows in networks, not only the forms. This will be easier to access, via using a both plus more model to reflect then appreciate what is and isn't. Both plus more societal arguments, such as political or religious predispositions, fade away or appear as clearly humorous.

---

[69] Barafasi, Albert-Laszlo, *Linked – The New Science of Networks*, Perseus Publishing: Cambridge, 2002, p. 217.

6

Beyond the Analytical, Hierarchical & Managerial

David L. Hawk, Professor
New Jersey Institute of Technology, University Heights, Newark, NJ
Visiting Professor, Executive Program,
Helsinki University of Technology

Keywords: changelessness, stable, change, dynamic, negotiation, context, appreciation, systems sciences, entropy, redesign, environmental protection, recycling, sustainability

This introduces the deeper meaning of heresy and how it always questions the hierarchical. It explains how to be a heretic, one must be a member of the church you question. You cannot simply be an opponent to the church from the wilderness. Therein levels were created then vertically layered in relative importance of position, then position occupant.

Herein we raise the issue of the limits of manliness in management. Beginning in manly teaching consistent with hierarchical philosophies of the Platonic, Confucian, Aristotelian, and Kantian teachings, and in opposition to ideas of Socrates and Lao Tzu, management went down a particular road in becoming more technological. With time humans, especially men, became subservient to the technology they made and used. This became the essence of management and the instrument of the industrial. Perhaps it's time for a

Joan of Arc to arise in management? It would counter what is now seen as the church of management, as exemplified by the Harvard B School.

It is urgent to move from the tradition of management that concentrates on the needs of its first three letters, "man." Clear and devastating problems from industrialization, as organized by and around the masculine, the manly, are clearly in the human future. As it seemed likely that Donald Trump would become an American Leader in 2015 a Foundation was begun in China by an American professor of management[70]. We have far to go in such a transformation of management as the consequences of the future rush towards us.

Much that is taught in business courses is basing on 2nd Century Catholic Church need for a hierarchal order, beginning with God, to give it structure. Their success in creating and implementing a hierarchical order was obvious. Thus, developers of industrialization used it as their model. Business professors thus used it in their teaching. This was developed for decades and carried over into formal teachings of managers, such as done at the Harvard B-School. The hierarchical form was fundamental to human motivation and measures of success[71]. Such had become important to human ideas for motivating and measuring success in the industrial. Hierarchical management grew in importance outside the layering of humans in the workplace from worker to CEO. It also became a critical aspect of early reductionism and layer of computer programing via the early work of Herbert Simon.

> "Although the concepts of hierarchy and levels of organization have long been used since ancient times, not until the early 1960s did hierarchy theory begin to emerge. As an offshoot of general systems theory, hierarchy theory was devel-

[70] Foundation of the Eternal Feminine. Visit EternalFeminine.org. This was to prepare those with feminine values, girls and boys, for leadership under conditions of climate change in the world.
[71] Maslow, A.H. "A theory of human motivation," *Psychological Review*, 50 (4): 370-396. 1943.

oped from a cross-disciplinary perspective, with important contributions from management sciences, economics, psychology, biology, and mathematics. The most important founder of the theory was Herbert A. Simon, whose series of writings not only laid the foundation of hierarchy theory, but also have continued to influence its further development ever since."[72]

Management became a serious subject of study during and after WWII. The Harvard B School, after 1940, set out to compete for fame and fortune with the very esteemed Harvard Law School. To become noteworthy, they borrowed two mainstream ideas from the law school. One was case method, that the B-School turned into "case studies," with the second being the importance of strategic thinking in new ideas for training leadership. By 2000 the dilemmas from using case information lacking context and making differences that didn't matter was apparent. Strategic thinking, on the other hand, has spread as the essential ingredient in leadership within and beyond companies. Leaders of government, universities and all organized human activities were judged by their strategic abilities, or at least their ability in talking of such. How can we recover from this history?

The Analytic Paradigm: Perverting the Parts

Concern is with the decreasing capability of humans to appreciate that which they have an increasing ability to manipulate. Articulated in a nineteen-seventies U of Penn systems sciences dissertation[73], this was ascribed to a seriously limited capacity for con-

---

[72] Jianguo Wu, "Hierarchy Theory: An Overview," Chapter 24. P. 283
[73] "Regulation of Environmental Deterioration," Hawk, D.L., Dissertation, Social Systems Sciences Program, University of Pennsylvania, 1979. The thesis was that environmental deterioration resulted from an inability to appreciate context. This was because social systems have become addicted to use of an analytic frame of partial thought. The most worrisome aspect of the resulting

text appreciation. This was proposed because of an historic emphasis on reductionistic ideas and analytical thoughts, not holistic ideals, and systemic thinking. This was like the notion that humans become adept at achieving short-term results, but not at managing their longer-term consequences.

The systems science platform of the nineteen-seventies, especially the planks developed by the Ackoff/Ozbekhan/ Trist group at U of Penn, argued that appreciation of connections was a better route into context-sensitive systems than was traditional analysis of parts[74]. While there was ambiguity as to what this meant it was sufficiently attractive to encourage much fruitful research and several innovative dissertations.

Concern for context and how humans choose to understand or ignore it continues to be an important theme for systems science researchers. It has led to a series of interesting questions. Many agree that context is important, if for no other reason than to give meaning to discrete acts. The first question then becomes, why do most people still ignore context in their work? Why does the segmented route to partial analysis of part processes continue to define the mainstream? Why does it attract the major resources and the basis for most of what we consider to be innovative breakthroughs? And finally, why has systems terminology been so widely applied while the systems approach has itself been so widely avoided?

During the nineteen-seventies the systems sciences were gaining strength, applications, and noteworthy results. By the mid-nineteen-eighties, the early attempts to achieve a holistic systems science

---

dilemma was that the same analytical model that had created the situation was now being used to resolve it. The situation was doubly damned by then being formalized and institutionalized via a legal system that was designed for stable environments. The recommendation from the work was to move from the "legal order" model, which values stability, to a negotiated order approach, which embraces dynamics.

[74] This notion was introduced in the 60s by Sir Geoffrey Vickers in his work as to why and how appreciative systems differ from rational and analytic constructs. While they can accommodate much more, they also require much more innovative management methods. West Churchman's work on *Design of Inquiring Systems* and the Systems Approach and its Enemies offered similar ideas.

perspective in many areas have been largely suspended. Work had shifted to more clearly defined problems that could be addressed in what was seen to be a more productive manner via partial analysis of pre-reduced parts. The results were like those that had initiated general systems research several decades before. During the nineteen-nineties concern returned to deeper relations between parts, between parts and their environments, and about systems instability. Questions regarding the meaning of analytic conclusions resurfaced. Signs of this were seen in a growing acceptance of Chaos Theory, an increased credibility for ventures like the Santa Fe Institute, and cross-disciplinary endeavors that generated highly innovative technology.

This should have provided credibility for a return to the systems science agenda of the nineteen-seventies. It did not. There was recognition that the analytic agenda was clearly insufficient to the needs facing society, but the response was an acceptance of systems' terminology and a rejection of systems perspectives and philosophies. Why? The reasons for this and the research to better understand and respond to it are at the center of current concerns in systems sciences, and in this paper.

The Trist, Ozbekhan and Ackoff depiction of our inhabiting richly connected situations that could better be managed as a problematique, or a mess seemed to gain ground against the analytic tradition of problems seeking solutions. But, somehow, this was not to be. In management, the ease of learning and teaching case-method approaches carried the day. The situation appeared to be changing, but somehow it was being transformed from a base camp of logical positivism into a Lewis Carroll world of Alice-in-Wonderland. The terminology of the systems approach was used more for its marketing appeal than to access more meaningful research questions. The situation thus became even more "problematic" and "messy" than what was originally envisioned by the Ozbekhan and Ackoff articulations.

The Alice world now had dynamic terms for putting a new spin on static, and boring, models. It could use change as the central concept in an argument for careful monitoring of the continuation of the traditional. It could use general systems terminology to argue for policies and practices that stand in opposition to systems thinking. The result is that systems concepts appeared to be used for temporarily shoring up the tradition whose weaknesses had initiated the need for the systems approach. The irony is great. The need to find a way out is even greater.

The idea of contextual appreciation was a way to improve the seeing of systemic connections between things. Some things might thus be done better, while other things might simply be left undone. This has since been turned upside down by opponents to the "systems agenda" via their use of the concepts to build a researchers' Alice-in-Wonderland Garden. Examining and dissecting context had become a means to conserve the traditional instead of modifying it. Contextual appreciation was thus a trendy term for new ways to reduce and analyze context. As such it was not used to see the richness of connections that defines context.

Instead of understanding context, analysis dissects it. This allowed humans to return to their dissecting approach of research via analysis. For example, instead of using context understanding to see the web of relationships between humans and their natural environment, analysis could be used to save parts of that environment from parts of what humans do. The Environment could thus be "protected" from the worst aspects of what humans did and presumably will continue to do. The term environment and the values demonstrated by a 20th Century environmentalist have come to rely heavily on the terminology of the systems approach, but not the framework. The emphasis should instead be on how to avoid approaches that allow old deeds to continue via new labels.

This requires a return to some historical moments where fateful choices were made around profound distinctions. These are profound because they continue to underline human attitudes about reality and change. This may also explain why the systems approach has had such limited success in its battle with the analytic tradition. To illustrate what this means in some detail a research venture[75] that

---

[75] The venture was established to see if it was possible to change an industry without use of the state's mechanism of legal order to force the change. The

deals with problems of environmental protection is outlined in the next section. At its basis it encountered the problem of how to get a social system to move from a tradition that abhors change to one that can embrace it, as well as avoid using new terminology to hide the weaknesses in business-as-usual.

The same logic is used in the concluding section to suggest why there are weaknesses in all systems of thought, including the one we know as systems theory. A weakness is outlined there that comes from the reductionistic tradition, is a clear indicator of an anti-change attitude in science and is endemic to the systems approach. While opposing the reductionistic tendencies of changelessness in science, systems theorists have themselves fallen prey to a trap they consult others to avoid. This concerns an almost blind faith in the dreams allowed by negative entropy. This added to the general societal bias that avoids questioning most traditions, is doubly troublesome. It encourages humans, including systems scientists, to believe they can invent perpetual motion machinery and thus over-ride entropic processes. In a research endeavor outlined near the end of the paper it will be pointed out that this belief, and the systems of thought it fosters, was the single greatest obstacle to environmental appreciation and improvement, as it was formulated in some nineteen-seventies and in some nineteen-nineties research ventures.

The Systemic Paradigm: In Support of Life

> *"Plus ca change, plus c'est la même chose."* and how to get things to not remain the same, when they change.

---

philosophy behind this came from systems sciences work in the seventies that demonstrated how if the legal order mechanism was successfully used that the ideal would by definition be lost. Thus a means to induce change was needed that did not rely on exterior force but interior value shift. In ways this is simply the age-old Faustian Problem; i.e., the long-term expenses of short-term avoidance of the characteristics of change.

As we approach the beginning of the 21st century a new mix of exciting social and technical possibilities is available for improving the qualities of the human condition.

These involve the means for reconsideration of societal institutions meant to serve social well-being. Therein humans can seek ideas for the rebuilding of environments intended to provide a stage set as redesigned to improve relations between humans as well as between humans and their natural environment. These have been incomplete. Still lacking are models, methods and measures that allow integration and management of these resources.

In the 1950's, leading members from various disciplines argued for a need to integrate the significant scientific and technological resources that were just then seen as beginning to emerge. This was the beginning of what is now known as the "systems science approach."[76] The scientists posed a set of challenging critics of the limitations of continuation of industrial based models for developing and using science and technology. They pointed to the need for and possibilities in a somewhat sketchy "post-industrial, bio-cybernetic era." The essence of their argument was that there was a clear need for a new set of ideals to drive knowledge creation. Basic to their agenda was an interdisciplinary research approach to achieving integrative and innovative ideals. Their work came from a new set of research ideals and called for a new set of methods. Their aim was to create new knowledge about how future human environments might be improved. The agenda was dismissed during the nineteen-eighties but in recent years their biophysical-social proposals have been actively re-addressed by the work of a few scientists.

---

[76] This is exemplified by the sub-component of AAAS known as the General Systems Society. Their 1954 agenda began with concern for the growing complexity of societal problems, misallocation of limited resources and the lack of ecological understanding of human activities, and how most of these problems were the result of an overly reductionistic model of science that was bound to the tradition of disciplines. Related to this were the founders of early cybernetic thinking and the Macy Conference that involved some of the same people and concerns.

Many of the economic, political, scientific, and technological elements necessary to experiment with the systems science approach were lacking when it was first articulated. Some of the missing resources have since been developed. Still lacking is dependable knowledge of the principal processes behind change dynamics; processes that appear to be caught up in the unseen limits of known rational models. We should reconsider the current scientific-philosophical model of research considering the trouble it is having with dynamic processes. Central to this work is the concept of change, how it is defined, modeled, measured, and managed. Change operates beyond the offerings of unaided rationality.[77] Research is needed into methods that can include and utilize the potentials of the non-rational. In this way the results can better serve humans.

A clear and fateful choice was taken in 5th Century Greece and China. The subject was the phenomena of change as it related to reality. The objective was to find a way for humans to deal with the relationship. The decision profoundly impacted how humans came to perceive, interpret, and manage their separate and mutual realities. On one side was a deep faith in the security offered by a utopian state of "changelessness." Therein, reality was defined as <u>that which did not change</u>. Whatever appeared to change could be disregarded. Where change emerged, it could be assigned to an area of no/low importance. Changelessness, in policy and practice, could be a legitimate way of life. Where the forces of change were too great, changelessness could always shift a little bit and become slightly mobile as a form of "stability." This fixed stability could even be allowed to move a bit more and expand to include the idea of "sustainable."

The alternative route was different in a profound sense. It was for whoever became intrigued by the aesthetics of change. Beliefs about it were held with similarly strong conviction, but as can been see, by far fewer people. Those embracing change defined reality as that which did change. Emphasis was on the beauty of that which

---

[77] Unaided rationality refers to the definable limits of any single approach to rationality, and suggests greater potential in being able to accommodate the non-rational in a human situation. This very different from Herbert Simon's "bounded rationality" construct for economic thinking.

was dynamic instead of the protection offered by what was static. The choice was between a changeless state and a state of change. At the most general level the debate dealt with how humans would negotiate with nature. At a more specific level the debate set the stage for how humans would confront themselves and each other.

Parmenides of Elea was the early proponent of reality as a "changelessness state." This was the same theme as Plato when he argued that the ideal that lay behind appearances was as fixed as it was unknowable. Heraclitus of Ephesus argued instead for reality as "a state of change, not a change of state." The two lived during the same era. They offered a clear choice to citizens of pre-500 BC Greece. Both of course presented strong evidence to support their logical framework. The basis of society's eventual choice was probably not on the evidence presented.

This 5th Century BC choice, as it occurred at about the same time, on both sides of the world, provided a fundamental distinction for paths to human development. It also implied quite different rules of engagement regarding how humans would relate to other humans, their surroundings, and, ultimately, themselves. The choice taken was clearly on the side of social conservatism via the passion for changelessness. Platonic fixations and Aristotelian structures won. This is perhaps one of the most fundamental problems facing the now-fading 20t^{h} century. How the consequences of that choice conflict with contemporary reality may be the key dilemma of our age. If so, this provides a new way.

Largely been limited to trading in difference-in-time issues. In fact, difference-over-time governs the success and failure of difference-in-time organization. In this way the contextual can be integrated into the phenomenal. In the past this was impossible. Some of the reasons are outlined in the Watzlawick, et.al. Book on: *Change: Principles of Problem Formation and Problem Resolution*, New York: Norton Publishers, 1974.

In the East, the choice was between Confucius, who was essentially on the side of Parmenides, and Lao Tzu, whose beliefs coincided with those of Heraclitus. This became a foundation of the belief systems for the design of humans: systems of governance, concepts of law and formation of social institutions, and the built environment.

Humans sided with Parmenides. This was perhaps a consequence of their wanting stability in the face of change. It will be argued that humans have paid a heavy price for their early luxury. This is seen in the design of the institutions and artifacts, including urban regions and the values behind the bodies that create and govern them. It's important to see and understand the difficulties in contemporary cultures, institutions, artifacts, and ways of knowing. As such, it provides some clues as to how all the above might be improved.

In summary, the changeless perspective assumed that whatever changed didn't exist or could be assumed to be unimportant to human affairs. This perspective was especially strong in classical physics until the late 19th century, and even prevailed in some aspects of early 20th century relativity theory. For example, Einstein was primarily responsible for the momentous break with Newtonian physics, but he showed a fondness for maintaining a connection to stability by arguing for the cosmological constant. This would allow there to be sufficient matter to keep the universe from infinite expansion. We see similar tendencies in most religions, legal systems, economic assumptions, and other areas of social expectation that attempt to bind groups together. The change perspective assumed the existence of a quite different worldview. Phenomena that did not change were dead or were negligible as compared to the dynamics that governed the human condition. The emergence and acceptance of the change perspective is a critical part of the development of much of contemporary science, e.g., modern biological science understanding beginning in the nineteen-twenties.

Each offered a different vision of reality, and different constructs and concepts for negotiating with it. Important to research outlined herein are the alternative consequences of each view. Each set out to know, make, maintain, and negotiate with a quite different set of conditions for the improvement of human well-being. Each designed, fabricated and supported a quite different social and physical environment. Each came to form a different relationship to a different view of nature. The choice made in 500 BC led to a fateful division on the pathway of human development. Changelessness was the apparent choice, leading to the design of institutions and artifacts that are intended to deny the more dynamic forms of existence. Significant resources have clearly been invested in processes that resist change. The purpose here is to create a knowledge base for those that want to embrace change as a viable attitude and method to research.

There are three major issues in the choice concerning change that need to be understood, to shift the societal bias in what we do and why we do it. They are:

1. Being Seduced by Stability and Related Arguments for Changelessness
2. Embracing the Systemic and Other Counterarguments for Change
3. Researching the Distance Between Changelessness and Change

"Daring it is to investigate the unknown, even more so it is to question the known." [78]

The continuing bias towards achieving a changeless society is easy to see in societal institutions and their history. Governmental structures and the political institutions set up to promulgate them may seem to appear to be innovative and creative. They want to appear "progressive," or somehow associated with change, but where they suggest such luster, they either lose it quickly or show signs early on that they did not really mean it in the first place. Recently established bodies, such as those for protecting the human environment from humans, or for recycling products, or for working towards a sustainable life, are recent examples of conservatism masking itself as innovation. These exemplify continuance of an attitude formalized in 500 BC Greece, and China, and that will undoubtedly carry over

---

[78] Watslawick, et.al, ibid, p. xi.

into the next millennium. Older institutions of modern society, such as its legal system, is approach to governance, and its belief in the role of marriage, may also qualify as instruments of changelessness.

It is now important to reconsider the 5th century decision for artificial stability as it has been used to create a platform. We need to experiment with a new human contract that could be more sensitive to the change processes that unfold regardless of human desires. This would involve fundamental research and experimentation. It would also need an integration of conceptual frameworks like that sought by the framers of general systems theory.

This would involve research defined as "a process to search again in order to see clearly for the first time." This would value different parts of the search process and would require a different approach to seemingly intractable problems of contemporary society. It would necessitate an interdisciplinary approach to contemporary problem resolution. It would require a new appreciation and understanding of change dynamics.

Maintaining non-change, even anti-change, characteristics in the face of ever-increasing forces of change has become too expensive for most societies. Even rich societies have found that the cost of traditional boundary maintenance is too great and the advantages too questionable. While still disallowed by the dictates of the current system biases, some attractive methods are available. A few groups profit from the current discontinuities, but most of the world's population ends up hopeless to face unrelenting changes that are beyond their means of control and understanding. They have been disabled. They cannot effectively respond to the dynamics in their own environments because the models they occupy stem from a rational scheme that doesn't exist because it continues to pretend existence of a changeless state. The expense of maintaining the resulting mismatches is great.

It is critical to begin to work towards improvements in our vision, models, and measures of the phenomena of the urban environment. This can improve our understanding of how science and technology can best aid in the management of environmental change dynamics. As more of the earth's population is drawn to the places that seem filled with environmental hope while they are managed as base camps of industrial hopelessness an alternative is needed. Critical to this is new knowledge for realizing new potential. Perhaps it is time to start reinventing wheels and raising questions about other truisms.

To Manage Change: Talk less, Listen More

"Goethe's greatest contribution to the discovery of the mind was that, more than anyone else, he showed how the mind can be understood only in terms of development. In Kant's conception of the mind...development has no place. He claimed to describe the human mind as it always is, has been, and will be. There is no inkling that it might change in the course of history, not to speak of biological evolution or the course of a person's life." [10.]

Research is needed to find new ideas and objectives for understanding the human condition. One obvious research location is where human potentiality, and associated problems, is seen in their greatest concentration – *the urban environment and the systems that produce it.* A focus could be to identify the key variables that govern the changing dynamics of the urban environment. The problems and promises of this are great. This is problematical because it is the location of the densest human activities and is very illustrative of the myriads of connections and disconnections that define the current human situation. It is promising for the same reason.

The urban environment most clearly demonstrates the negative aspects of the decision taken 2,500 years ago. The current urban condition is in fact more clearly understood via the contradictions that come out from trying to see cities as fortresses against change while the contents of these forts contain the dynamic phenomena of life. The difference must be reconciled, or a price paid for the cumulative mismatch. While the earlier choice seems to have been the least expensive in first cost, its consequences appear to hold an exceedingly high set of second costs. Even the maintenance costs are becoming remarkably high. Selecting the change paradigm had problems but that route, by its nature, would have required a continual reconciliation of life-cycle costs. The nature of the changeless path was to resist change until there was a crisis, thereby ensuring the non-linear change process that was initially the greatest worry of those advocating changelessness.

The price that is being paid for continuing with the tradition of changeless continues to grow. There needs to be a better way to negotiate with the continually unfolding reality that we know to exist despite our best efforts at control. Costs have always been associated with this process, but, somehow, something is now different. The costs are beginning to rapidly escalate. The costs come from unresolved contradictions that accompanied the choice and growing maintenance problems. They are primarily carried by our context but seem recently to have surfaced internally to the human condition. It is time to examine the other side of the twenty-five-hundred-year-old choice dichotomy.

Applying The Systemic: "Energy Star Homes Project"[79]

In the spring of 1996, a project was begun for the U.S. EPA. Within the Energy Star Program this work was to see if an industry could be changed without the use of regulation to force it to change. I was asked to undertake this venture due to what I had proposed in the reports from the empirical part of my dissertation in systems theory for Russ Ackoff's program in the University of Pennsylvania. The project began with an alternative conceptualization of problems in the relationship between humans and their environments. Individuals and individual companies would be allowed to work towards what was in their own interests, not that of a governmental employee. The trouble came to be how their interests came to be defined, which was a problem once again of context appreciation. The impediment to change was, once again, found to be in interpretations of entropy.

---

[79] Done with my friend, Professor Erv Bales, of NJIT, formerly of US Department of Energy

DAVID L. HAWK

The research question was: "Can an industry generate information and processes to improve the relations between its products and the larger environment, without being directed by regulatory efforts? The industry is the one that builds homes within the U.S. While often ignored, this industry's products directly account for about 30% of the energy consumed within the country, as well as a related proportion of materials, and of course result in a similar proportion of the nation's air and solid wastes pollution. Indirectly, via the location and situation of the products, it accounted for another 20% of the nation's pollution problems. As much of the industry and most of its consumers know, the industry's products are generally of low quality as measured against those of other industries. Its waste is significantly higher.

It was considered technically feasible to cut energy use and pollution from the industry's products, yet early studies pointed out that it was not politically nor economically feasible to use regulation to attain this objective. The industry lobbying group was one of the most powerful in the nation, accounting for almost $100 billion a year in indirect subsidy to the industry. A directive agenda had once been attempted via DOE energy "guidelines." This approach was stopped before it could get started due to political resistance. This brought the EPA to assume that the costs of enforcement would be prohibitive. Thus, an alternative approach had to be tried to achieve some of the Rio agreement objectives on Global Climate Change.

My nineteen-seventies work for a dissertation in systems sciences, on alternative methods for regulating environmental deterioration, was attractive. It argued that a non-regulatory, non-directive approach to self-regulation of pollution externalities was in most cases more efficient, and in some cases the only possibility. The research found there to be no good and bad guys in the area, but a large amount of bad information (ignorance) and many bad feelings (hatred and mistrust). To turn this around the normal policing function had to be turned into an information function that would not direct behavior but encourage the behaviors of learning and adaptation. The situation of pollution could then be turned from a legal orders system to a negotiated order solution. This would require

140

a new sense of context appreciation and people who were able to embrace change. This was the basis for the 1996 Energy Star Homes experiment.

The project was moderately successful except for some short-comings in attitudes. The objective was to get the industry to attain 30% improvement via a set of building principles that attracted, not regulations that threatened. It was hoped that this would lead to further improvement ideas throughout the industry. About three hundred producers took part in the early achievements. From that they received an Energy Star label[80] placed on several thousand houses. In spite of this success there lingered obstacles to more significant changes. These centered on the changeless paradigm and the negative entropy belief in perpetual motion machines as outlined above. It is difficult to change the dominant attitude is that it doesn't matter what humans do with materials and energy, since people are so smart that they can override whatever difficulties that will arise later. Some of the new technologies in the area are clear representatives of mis-directed efforts to create perpetual motion machines. This includes geo-thermal heat pumps, solar collectors, and PV roofs, as they are now conceived and produced.

Most home producers and especially home consumers deeply feel that there are more than sufficient resources for making and operating infinite homes. Where shortages or problems with quality emerge, the solution lies with "recycling." Via the recycling argument "It just doesn't matter what is done or bought."

The biggest block to this non-governmental, no-cost project is to find ways to inform the public as to why what is produced and bought does matter. Only this will get this most conservative of industries to change. Recent discourse on sustainability only furthers the difficulties in achieving change. The

---

[80] The Energy Star label is the same as the one you will find on your computer under the screen saver option. 100% of the world's computer manufacturers are now enrolled in this program that is voluntary.

Energy Star initiative continues. More work now needs to be done with the customers. Clarifying the entropy issue may be the most effective way to bring a new sense of appreciation into the situation. It can begin with a better understanding of the funda-mental nature of the concept and how humans have articulated this nature in different ways for differ-ent purposes. The issues of entropy exposed earlier in this paper need to be examined at a deeper level in order to appreciate their fundamental importance to change. (The Entropy Dilemma and its 19th Century Roots)

The speculation of pre-19th century scientists converged in a 19th century articulation of the concepts of time, energy, and mate-rials, and how these relate to asymmetries in the environment. Two kinds of asymmetries were noted as important. The first was time itself. The second was regarding things over time. William Thomson (1824 - 1907) dealt with the first in his elaboration of "the universal tendency of entropy to increase." (Thomson, 1852). Rudolf Clausius (1822-1888) brought meaningful technical articulation to the sec-ond asymmetry via his theory of the workings of the internal com-bustion engine. He in essence argued that the internal combustion engine can only "work" if there is a loss in order, defined as potential to do work, in its larger environment.

From this point the scientific and technological argument turned to whether the entropy issue can be symmetrical or must be asymmetrical? Are natural processes reversible or not? Most areas of science have taken a decision about the debate. While the phys-ical evidence has been on the side of absolute irreversibility there has long been a metaphysical faith that parts of the physical world eventually be found to exhibit a possibility for reversible ordering. Religions have always been steeped in the belief for this potential. Much credit for its emergence in science should be given to the work of Boltzmann. He turned the Second Law of Thermodynamics from its exceptionless nature into one that was statistical. The problem plaguing Boltzmann until his end was that if entropy is reversible, then why was entropy not higher in the past?

The debate continued through the work of Karl Popper (Popper, 1956) into the work of Davies, (Davies, 1974) to that of John Preskill, Kip Thorne, and Stephen Hawking in 1998. The last three individuals are noteworthy scientists that illustrated their best thinking in a bet made relative to the validity of the entropy law within the total universe relative to separate behaviors they could study in various corners of the universe. This deals with the general acceptance that the law holds at the universe scale but may not need to in some isolated corners. Their wager had to do with where and when entropy was held. More specifically, the discussion centered on what happens to information when it runs into the bottomless pits in the universe called back holes?

> "Dr. Hawking and Dr. Thorne bet that the information - whether consisting of letters, numbers, the binary digits on a computer disk or even the arrangements of atoms in a rock - is gone forever. Dr. Preskill wagered that it could not possibly be." (New York Times, 1998)

The essence of this argument gets to the fundamental differences between relativity and quantum mechanics. It seems that one will need to be modified to explain the entropy at black holes. If this argument sounds familiar it should. It's related to the argument as to whether the universe keeps expanding, or as Einstein felt, there was a cosmological constant of mass that would balance it out into the relative calm of changelessness.

Recent research helps resolve aspects of the entropy debate. It deals with the paradoxes raised in the 19th century and sets the stage for implications in the 21st century. Beginning in 1981, an IBM researcher, Charles Bennett, gave resolution to the dilemma of Maxwell's Demon by showing how a perfectly efficient engine was impossible not just in fact, but also in principle. He showed how even Maxwell's "demon" must expend energy in the process of becoming

sustainable via "saving" energy. The "demon" must forget each transaction prior to the next encounter. Relying on work by Rolf Landauer
some years before, that the only steps in computation that necessarily
produce waste heat are erasures of information, Bennett could show
the perfectly efficient engine to be impossible. One caveat remained
in the dilemma posed by Maxwell. Bennett's proof relied on classical
physics thus there remained a shadow of doubt relative to entropy's
operations in the realm of quantum mechanics, and then of course
within statistical thermodynamics. In a 1997 Physical Review article
by Seth Lloyd of MIT it is shown that in the wholly quantum world
the "demon" is even less efficient than he was in the classical world.

In the fall of 1998 further evidence of the sanctity of entropic
process, and thereby change processes, emerged from the CPLEAR
collaboration at CERN in Geneva and the KteV collaboration at
Fermi National Accelerator Laboratory in Illinois. They found: "This
shows that you can't turn the clock backward" and always get the same
results, says CPLEAR spokesperson Pagagiotis Pavlopoulous." And
"These rates differed by about 13%, 'It's a huge effect,' says Fermilab
physicist and KteV collaborator Vivian O'Dell. The amount of time
asymmetry is just about right to fix the CP asymmetry first observed
over 3 decades ago. 'I don't think anyone is surprised but everybody
is happy,' says University of Chicago theorist Jonathan Rosner. Why
the decays should look any different forward and backward is still a
fundamental mystery. But particles, like falling wine glasses, seem to
know that the passage of time cannot be easily undone." [81]

The general issue of the nature of the entropy law is thus now
settled in science. Entropy holds firmly at all levels of reality. It is
time to carry this understanding to the larger consuming public.
The implications are significant. This is a fundamental shift. It will
clarify the current questions of what is sustainable about relations
between human actions and their environments. Considering the
entropic process, can any human activity be considered "sustainability?" Perhaps it is better to say it shouldn't be, so that the concept of

---

[81] Science Now http://sciencenow.sciencemag.org/cgi/content/full/1998/1020/1/
7:00 PM.

change can be better embraced to work continuously to infinitely improve what we do. The possibility for human arrogance in the entire sustainability dialogue looms large.

This agenda also calls for reconsideration of fundamental distinctions between open and closed systems considering what is now known of systems of living order. We could begin this by returning to early distinctions on the subject as made by Ludwig von Bertalanffy.

> "Thermodynamics expressly declares that its laws apply only to closed systems. In particular, the second principle of thermodynamics states that, in a closed system, a certain quantity, called entropy, must increase to a maximum, and eventually the process comes to a stop at a state of equilibrium. The second principles can be formulated in different ways, one being that entropy is a measure of probability, and so a closed system tends to a state of most probably distribution... So the tendency towards maximum entropy or the most probably distribution is the tendency to maximum disorder.
>
> However, we find systems, which by their very nature and definition, are not closed systems. Every living organism is essentially an open system. It maintains itself in a continuous inflow and outflow, a building up and breaking down of components, never being, so long as it is alive, in a state of chemical and thermodynamic equilibrium but maintained in a so-called steady state which is distinct from the latter." (von Bertalanffy, 1968)

The distinction between open and closed systems has proved to be beneficial to a fundamental understanding of relationships between entities and their environments, but it is perhaps unfortunate that the entropy concept was introduced to assist in the ordering of these relationships. Entities find a means to interact with their surroundings and in so doing come to define themselves by defining an environment. Angyal formulated this process quite clearly in his early work on systems theory but there is a weakness that lingers in the reasoning that needs to be addressed. The weakness comes from the bias towards believing in entropic processes as reversible, which happened to also support mainstream thinking that supported changelessness over change.

References & Advisors

Ackoff, Russell, *Redesigning the Future*, Englewood Cliffs, NJ: John Wiley and Sons, 1974.

Angyal, Andras, New York: Viking Press, 1941. Especially chapter 4.

Davies, P.C., *The Physics of Time Asymmetry*, London: Surrey University Press, 1974.

Emery, F.E., and Trist, E.L., Towards a Social Ecology, London: Plenum Press, 1973. Hardin, G., "The Tragedy of the Commons," Washington, D.C.: *Science*, 162, 1243, 1968, p. 1244.

Hardin, Garrett, "Extensions of 'The Tragedy of the Commons,'" *Science*, Vol. 280, May 1, 1998, p. 682.

Kaufmann, Walter, *Discovering the Mind*, New York: McGraw-Hill Book Co., 1980, p. 25.

Laszlo, Ervin, *The Relevance of General Systems Theory*, New York: George Braziller, 1972.

New York Times, "Physical Laws Collide in a Black Hole Bet," April 7, 1998, p. F1.

Popper, K. "The Arrow of Time," *Nature*, 177, 1956., p. 538.

http://sciencenow.sciencemag.org/cgi/content/full/1998/1020/1/ 7:00PM Thomson, William, "On a Universal Tendency," *Proceedings of the Royal Society of Edinburgh, Volume 3*, p. 139, 1852. (Found in Huw Price's *Time's Arrow & Archimedes' Point*, Oxford University Press: New York, 1996.

von Bertalanffy, Ludwig, *General System Theory*, New York: George Braziller, 1968, p.39.

Watzlawick, et.al. *Change: Principles of Problem Formation and Problem Resolution*, New York: Norton Publishers, 1974.

7

Changelessness – In Opposition to Life

"If It Changes, It's Not There"

This was the essence of a Parmenidean dilemma in 465 B.C. From such thinking living loses its meaning, as well as life. Now, in 2024 we bring such a continuing philosophy forward 2,500 years. This is to help us understand the process of humans bringing deterioration to a natural environment. There has long been a tragic form of biofeedback process between the artificial side of human actors and the natural context they dwell in. Humans begin to see a tragedy approaching via an end state for systems of life on their planet. It's a bit too late to correct such as our minds seem to have deteriorated along with planetary life. Life will clearly see great challenges as we approach 2050. Just now they seem beyond human brains and values.

Humans are losing some of their 1850 arrogance while watching climate change threats visit upon them. This is bringing them to question much of what was thought to structure success, including Maslow's artificial hierarchy theory of life as taught to them in evolutionary biology classes. There is now less faith in the historic insights of Darwin as well as the those arguing of hierarchy theory as the basis for life's organization. Just now there is little faith in the teachings of both men. There is less faith in Nobel Prize winner Herbert Simon's key belief that hierarchy is central to knowing and managing life. Hierarchy is even used to explain why men should be atop women, as exhibited in the Garden of Eden.

Thankfully, younger designers question the dictates for traditional design of the artificial. They ask why is the artificial essential, or even good? Must we occupy an artificial world. The most important, yet unnoticed, aspect of the artificial in product, building, and city design is the law of parallels.

Euclid's 5th Postulate, on parallels being key to understanding his universe, is becoming increasingly strange as no parallel lines are found in nature, including the universe. None-the-less, we of masculine heritage use it religiously in design of spaces, streets, buildings, and cities? It is the most dominant yet unnoticed aspect of the artificial environment, as the artificial environment replaces more of what nature offers.

The above introduces significant shadows and signs of unfathomable storms on the horizons of life. We clearly have problems in redefining humans and conditions of life to meet an environment that we have redefined. This evidence is worrisome yet is only a symptom of a larger problem of how humans attempting to be artificial must survive in a world of and managed by nature. There has long been a war between the artificial and the natural, but emerging information suggests a winner.

Since 1856 science posed dangers from human intelligence managed by those with a lack of wisdom and concern for context. Since then, a major threat to life and nature has been created and expanded. In our education, economics, and business, what is now seen by some as more than dangerous has been glorified as the essence of human development. The consequences are much deeper, wider, and more dramatic than the ego discussed above. Even if we work to ignore it, it has access to what we will call the collective consciousness of life. It is a growing threat to bio-physical existence. It arises as a long-term consequence of actions that humans are most proud of.

Science has long pointed to humans endangering systems of living order but never quite like what we now face. Life, as part of nature, depends on natural systems that are clearly endangered. Thus, our dreams of a continuance of life are endangered. Some scientists sense the sixth version of five prior episodes of change that came to limit life on the planet. Fires, storms, diseases, floods, and droughts are frequent and expanding. Air, water, and food quality needed to maintain life is vanishing. Something is changing.

> "In the past few decades, geologists have started filling in the rough sketches of the Big Five mass extinctions with gruesome detail, but the story has largely eluded the public imagination. Our conception of history tends to stretch back only a few thousand years at most, and typically only a few hundred. ...like reading only the last sentence of a book and claiming to understand what's in the rest of the library...Visiting Earth's turbulent and unfamiliar past provides a possible window into our future."[82]

Worth noting is how this state of extinction results from human activities, not cosmic. Humans point to their importance to life while acting to eliminate it. In denying continuance of systems required of life, most humans work to avoid noting them. It's funny to be a human.

Threats arise from the longer-term consequences of many and varied human activities seeking short-term enhancement to their lives. Distinct from being caretakers of a heritage passed on to us, we seem to have joined forces with the entropic law of the universe that Einstein, Sagan, and Hawking assigned much respect to as the temporal force for disorder. In an unreflective manner we mostly contribute to the irreversible degradation of conditions essential to life.

If we ever wish to do so, how might we reverse the above process or prepare to manage the consequences from it? Current management of human affairs implies the opposite, that we are not up to accepting responsibility for our behavior. There is insufficient concern for the probable end state. Our passion for negotiating with hollow promises of eternal stability via changelessness managed by humans is great. Some even brag that deteriorating the natural envi-

---

82 Brannen, Peter, *The Ends of the World*, Harper Collins: New York, 2017, p. 8.

ronment, via economic activities, is a precondition to "the good life." Are we seriously trying to win a war against nature's ambiguities and uncertainties, just as we wage war against opposing humans that seem to oppose our values or management systems? Are there limits to human knowledge of productive life but not to counter-productive behaviors?

The first two items can be addressed by reflection. The last requires deeper forms of knowing. It requires access to the unfamiliar and unnamed, not just the unknows. Answers to the first item can be clarified via discourse with those we don't like to agree with. The second requires reconsideration of what is valued in life. The third requires a great appreciation of the universe, its rule system, and human's role in it, if they have one.

The following book is not an easy or happy read. If you are uncomfortable with questions about long-standing religious beliefs and/or post-Aristotle skepticism about logic and rationality being the foundation of life, then you might not appreciate what follows. The contents give no support to those who prefer the security of Plato's Cave with it providing continual support to two-dimensional images from the shadows on the cave ceiling. The feeling of security from two-dimensions is similar yet now given by digital representations on screens. In this way the challenges of the third and threats of the fourth dimensions are obscured. This protects you from visualizing and experiencing consequences of prior actions. Creators of Apple, Microsoft and Amazon "created" it. All you did was use it so as in Plato's Cave you can forget any responsibility.

Humans are becoming less tolerant of each other, while being more accommodating of their own weaknesses. This is seen in how they exhibit anger, ignorance, silliness, irreversibly wrong endeavors, and dislike of difference in others. Why? Donald Trump, a spokesperson for the phenomena, illustrated the meaning of being in an era of hatred of life, as did his "followers." It was as if millions discovered that they were mortal, and in fact rather insignificant in the universe, and became damned angry. Dreams of a long-term immortality were dashed. Industrialization, the great human achievement, was beginning to be seen for its long-term expenses.

Industrialization was driven by dreams of short-term gains characterized by writers in *The Economists* arguing to increase productivity as a basis for happy economics. Such came to be the accepted standard of the knowledge managing the private sector.

Education: Teaching Differences That Aren't and Weren't

Modern education has come to emphasize students memorizing and accepting presumptions. As such it continues into conditions of climate change. The time-honored alternative is seen in what we can best call learning to learn. Learning it asking questions about what is assumed to be true to improve on or disregard what is widely accepted as history, philosophy, social sciences and our physical reality. In his significant book on "The Idea of History" R.G. Collingwood pointed out that we might best think of history as "the lie that is commonly agreed upon." He always encouraged us to go deeper into the context of what is believed, written or stated about past events.

Context is often seen as a calm, placid backdrop to a performance. When it moves into a more excited state, say for a heavy metal music stage, it moves from being a backdrop to being an actor. Its performance can even become unsettlingly turbulent.[83] Its actions can take over the play of life as in a forest fire, a hurricane or a drought. Thus we have two forces for contextual change. One is an actor as a change agent in context, as in perforng. Two is context as the actor that brings change beyond agent control. The second is dangerous acting as contextual turbulence becoming irreversibile.

Context is more specific than environment. Context includes mental and physical aspects of natural and artificial phenomena. When humans create, manage, love, disregard, diminish, or simply destroy context they make use of these four domains. This is most apparent where humans demonstrate their self-importance by denigrating their context. The usual method is via war where war can be

---

[83] F.E. Emery and E.L. Trist, "The Causal Texture of Organizational Environment," *Human Relations Journal*, Volume 18, Issue 1, London, 1965.

against nature, other humans, or themselves. Humans have a history of warfare from problems in their being more often than from their becoming.

How we relate to context can be via problems in a lack of understanding context, then a lack of caring for it. Some humans do understand and care, but they seem rare. They see nature as the basis of life and then act to complement and care for life, as well as others. They see life as a fluid state, one that unfolds in its becoming. They see more promise in business as unusual than in business as usual. This book is about them and the change in management and leadership required to enhance life and its context. A special sense of management and a new model of leadership selection seemed to be needed. Lao-tse offers hope:

> "Lao-tse (c. 565 B.C., A leader is best when people barely know he exist, when his work is done, his aim fulfilled, they will say: we did it ourselves."

This image of leadership differs from that of the industrial tradition or those depending on hierarchical leaders such as: Putin, Trump, Hitler, or Catherine the Great. Herein it is argued that you will better understand where you are and need to be when reflecting on yourself as your leader. It helps to see your soul occupying the 5th dimension, to better relate to its presence or absence. Seeing such goes far to govern who you are, what you do, and what you become in life. Your soul can be in your 5th dimension or a one-time occupant of the empty left by short-term gain in your Faustian negotiation with the devil that sent it elsewhere.

Sometime listen to Dvorak's 9th symphony[84] prior to uplifting your spirit in feeling Ravel's Bolero. Then watch a report on daily human behavior. You may thus see where a three-year-old Ukrainian

---

[84] It is said he added this to the 9th Symphony in 1893 while in Spillville, Iowa for 100 days while falling in love with the town filled with emigrees from the Czech Old Country and the new nature they lived within in Iowa.

child is lying in a hospital severely wounded from being shot while looking for his father. While crying about his need he repeatedly says he loves his father and needs him for protection. You are then shown his father elsewhere in the hospital from being seriously wounded from meeting seriously drunk Russian soldiers.

As a context we hear Putin inspired Russian bombs marching towards the hospital we are in. The eternal beauty of the music cast against the immediately sick values of the human soldiers leaves us in a sad place. Dvorak is important in this context. He rejoiced in life while being saddened by the decay of life that can't be reversed. Human involvement seems to only speed it up. He was clearly fascinated by the relations between nature and life, as is this book.

Some talk of how purposefully indiscriminate bombing of children can only be work of the devil. Others differ. They see it as misguided human behavior alongside development of the technology of war. Development is of the state of terribleness of technology that is to detour those with the same technology away from ever using it, unless they have mental problems. Their logic if it is sufficiently terrible it will not be used, like the thinking of the A-bomb prior to dropping it over Japan in 1945.

The context of child tears with beautiful background music raises the sense of the role of a larger context in the background. This is crucial to help understanding the approaching conditions of climate change in a foreboding context for life. Such is the major concern behind this book. Long-term climate pain is beginning to result from short-term human gains. Dvorak helps in that he lived for the longer term beyond individual lives. Later in his life he spent time in the US with 100 days of it in Iowa. During that time, he was completing his New World Symphony while trying to express his concern for long-term relations between humans and nature. His work raised questions about the relations between humans and nature, but not many answers.

Humans see natural environments as abstractions while disregarding the role of such in forming contexts of which humans are a part. There are physical, social, and psychological aspects to such abstractions. As used herein context goes further to emphasize relationships and the qualities of their interactions, some positive, some negative. Context offers a background against which you can act, as well as a platform on which you can interact. Environments pass by in thoughts of the clouds while context encourages being active in the present.[85]

Non-Difference, Non-Valuable, Non-Sense

Humans often damage context in their meeting of personal needs. They seldom notice damage done nor feel bad about its consequences. By the time they see the consequences they mostly forget where they arrived and how they were initiated. Even when buying industrial products from an upstream factory alongside the river we drink our water from, we seldom connect that production to meet our wants back to our disappointment in lower quality in meeting our need for water. Such connections and relations seem ambiguously vague. What can be done?

Does it make sense to have the bad leadership of those companies sued while we go buy more of their products? Is there a natural process for cleaning up such, besides an obvious need to clean up humans? The answers will redefine life on earth. The future of context and its human users will be changed. Such becomes more urgent each year. Then I commented on such in the fall of 1977, in a final reporting on "Environmental Protection: Analytic Solutions in Search of Synthetic Problems,"[86] I was told such was unimportant or

---

[85] Russ Ackoff in "*Resigning the Future*" made a distinction between the 1) reactive, 2)inactive, 3)proactive and 4)interactive with his emphasis on how to get humans to align with the fourth. With the techno-edge and strategic authoritarianism encouraged by the third, and the changelessness allowed in the first and second postures, he failed to get many to see the essential nature of the fourth to well-being in the 21st Century.

[86] The research notes, project interviews and mapping of conclusions from this project were in my NJIT office in 2012 when they were sized under the orders of the NJIT President Robert Altenkirch and the NJ Governor Chris Christie as being NJ State Property? All files on the 10,000 students I had on my rosters and 85 books I would loan students to help their learning were also seized. Much of this was from prior to my being at NJIT. Several of the books were out

simply a hoax. Leadership even became angry at the reports and the one writing them.

Republished in 2019 as "Too Early, Too Late, Now what?" the 1979 reporting on climate change being our future was moved by Amazon management from academic science to its section on humor. Since it could not be true it was listed near books on: "The Pigeon Finds a Hot Dog," "I will Teach You to be Rich, 2nd Edition: No Guilt. No Excuses. No BS," and Wilma Jean's "The Worry Machine." A different publisher noticed this and offered to republish the book under the title turned down years before an academic publisher. That title of great clarity, "Sorry, Humans are Fucked," was said by the academic publisher as a low point in human affairs. I agreed, while then arguing it was an indictment, not a sexual joke. When that book appeared, Amazon placed it in their candle section, not in books. When I called them, they explained that it should be near candles so when customers were upset with it, they could burn it. Good thinking.

With the help of a group of small publishers we are now involved in a small study. We want to see if humans still read books, or only listen to them while driving or in bed, or simply scan titles and cover photos as they wait for the ringing of their I-phones. We have produced three versions of the same content but under three radically different titles and behind very different cover photos. The two extremes are: 1) "Human Nature and the Potential in Nurture," 2) "Sorry, But Humans Are Fucked: Climate Change from Human Limitations." Between the two is a softer title and image. Just looking for signs of hope.

Results from seeing which humans are interested in what image are coming in. The 2021 movie "Don't Look Up" seems to side with the image on one of the versions. The book you are now looking at is different. It moves on to address the question: "Now what?" The contents herein try to identify and examine what being human

---

of print books valued at more then $1,000 each. NJIT lawyers also seized two stuffed animals that belonged to my baby daughter. On judges' orders one was returned.

brought us the consequences of climate change to systems of life. We then go into how we might change to soften the impact of oncoming consequences that are varied but not all are irreversible.

Via religious and related ideas about humans needing leadership in a wilderness of bi-polar contradictions they fail to see context as important or perhaps even see context. As we move through episodes of self-importance time is scarce. We mostly ignore context until it rises to define our reality. There are contextual consequences to our choices, and in our actions. We might look at it as a non-artificial feedback loop that operates within systemic wholes, especially when it encounters a pile of artificial parts awaiting analysis. Then, if we can find a way to stabilize context after our "interruption" we humans again return to our obvious preference for analytic humor, perhaps a porno movie run backwards could fill the gap?

Such introduces the situation of climate change conditions, something humans feel is unimageable until they find it unmanageable. Simply put, it's like a neighbor failing to sufficiently respect what you are. Thus, you have the freedom to "urinate on his property" to demonstrate disrespect for him. When he notices, which is key to this ceremony, he then takes you deeper into mutual disrespect. "Around and around, we go, where it stops nobody knows." Such is our relationship to the natural.

Climate change via our urinating on nature is used as a metaphor about a price paid for disrespect. Costs can include your removal. Human choices clearly have consequences from their attempts to make gains for the chooser. The process in fact says much about the chooser, and potential to become a looser. Sean Rowe's "Trying to Leave Something Behind" will take you deeper.

Context can be attractive, distractive, or a nuisance obscuring self-importance. It defines relations to, potentials in, and the limits of occupancy in life. A few humans, mostly research scientists, now see the above, and warn that business as usual becomes terminal. Their reporting takes you into questions of context, and how such is what defines life. Otto Rank tried to explain this in 1932 when speculating on how humans had become more dominant yet losing an important aspect of being, their soul.

"For even though the various human civilizations may each arise from the combination of a certain environment and a certain type of humanity, all human problems are, in the last resort, problems of the soul. By this we mean, not to say that the soul can be wholly explained in terms of modern psychology, as our mechanistic science would claim, but, on the contrary, to stress the autonomy of the spiritual, which not only works creatively in the religious, artistic, and social realms, but also determines the ideology which colours the psychology of the time."[87]

Definitions Without Context Aren't

Following this, Pulitzer Prize winner Ernest Fisher is attempting to describe the nature of the modern human and his inner problem. This was in his 1973 commentary on the human situation after surviving two world wars followed by significant expansion of industrial development to bring him rewards.

"Modern man is drinking and drugging himself out of awareness, or he spends his time shopping, which is the same thing. As awareness calls for types of heroic dedication that his culture no longer provides for him, society contrives to help him forget."[88]

This theme depicts how the human definition of life is taking them into a discontinuance of life. Warnings about contextual danger keep growing louder while early indications of the breadth and depth are everywhere. What shall we do? Can we act to avoid such? Can we redefine our existence and the values that seek "the

---

87 *Art and Artist*, Rank, Otto, New York: Alfred A. Knopf, Inc., 1932, p. xv.
88 *Denial of Death*, Fisher, Ernest, Free Press: New York, 1973, p. 284

good life?" What are we thinking as we drive around seeking answers to who and where we are, knowing the act of driving is central to endangering the context we worry about?

Meanwhile, warnings of approaching turbulent climate conditions and intelligent viruses threaten our lives. We see a need to stabilize nature not expansion on the artificial. Context can be seen as: "The situation within which something exists or happens, and that can help explain it."[89]

Do we as individuals understand the meaning or must we continue to rely on those we allow to lead us to give it definition? Can we trust leadership's claim to special knowledge, and access to knowing that followers lack? What if such leaders also lack knowledge essential to continuance? If so, why do we continue to listen? Are we lazy, in need of entertainment, or confused?

When appraising human leadership, we see promise for protecting ourselves from the core of who and where we are, followed by some entertainment value. None-the-less, such does take us to the edges of our reality to see if we are at the front or back edges of what is unfolding.

Are leaders leading us to the ahead edge or back to what was behind us? Perhaps we need to begin with an idea of what an edge is? History illustrates how lower forms of leadership mostly promise rediscovery of the behind, or worse. Where values change is needed a return to values of yesterday accelerates the mismatch awaiting tomorrow. This image illustrates the price of seeking the meaningful for self then only finding the cost for the group of the meaningless.

Is the cultural idea of a few leading the many an exercise in humor, a test of our tolerance of situations gone bad, or an indirect means to justify social hierarchies via cultural myths? Humans do not need such, and soon cannot afford its consequences. Can we ever take responsibility for ourselves, and our own mistakes? Maybe not. Much of what we call management relies on that beacon called leadership. There are great differences in the concept that range from mean-spirited authoritarianism to acting as if others lead themselves,

---

[89] Cambridge English Dictionary

not you. We can see such differences between the wisdom of Lao Tzu and authoritarian demands of Zeus. The same appears as the difference between the diffused inspiration of Joan of Arc and the centralized demands of Catherine the Great, including the service from occupants in her stable next to her summer house. Upon reflection we can see the same choice between the sincerity of a JFK kind of president and the behavior of a Donald Trump as resident clown. We have seen this difference between the Ukrainian inspiration Volodymyr Zelenskyy and Vladimir Putin a documented representative of the downside of human weaknesses. Much can be learned in looking at the history and consequences of all these choices. The differences reveal much about the role of personalities, potentials, and problems in human affairs. There are gains and pains in such choices and their consequences. Why do we consistently ignore knowing such until the consequences are around us? To be a bit more helpful the 1975-1977 Stockholm Study discussed herein found a fundamental reason for going the central leadership route to deal with problem. It was from those supporting a legal order which was seen to cause great problems than solve them in systemic conditions. The alternative proposed in the study was negotiated order with leadership spread in the organization with concentrations occasionally found at the edges, not in the core of headquarters.

Can Change Be Managed?

What shall humans do to soften their impact on nature? One proposal is to begin by dropping then replacing the first three letters of management. Manly management came to be derogatory towards nature and the natural. Man had redefined nature for manly management and their use, including use of women. Processes of degradation closely followed. Men came to seek another avenue of human potential. They came to organize around the artificial. Consistent with this the industrial emerged.

Major parts of nature came to be consumed in the service of humans. The artificial emerged as important. Its rules and fantasies came to replace the more natural aspects of managing the industrial. Artificial intelligence was later placed on the horizon. It was to augment then replace human intelligence, and responsibility. Serious clouds were forming on the human horizon.

Should humans be proud to override or replace natural aspects of their lives? Would a more humane attitude towards life and its management, with the whole of life included as context then nurtured, have been a better way? This question now arises as we consider the irreversibility of climate change to bring conclusions to much of nature. Is it too late to change the 2,400-year homocentric trip as laid out above? Can the ideas driving management be changed to nurture the natural, or should human management become stronger and harsher as it encounters the conditions of climate change?

The Greek then the Christian importance of hierarchy of some, over others, and human aspirations overriding nature came to predominate manly thinking. This unfolded for centuries. Underlying this was an unsubstantiated belief in unaided rationality out to degrade nature and/or those who appreciated nature. Greek philosophy added to Religious Certainty argued how nature existed for humans uses. The natural was heavily consumed by the industrial via the unquestioned arrogance of homo-centricity. Just now the divide has grown into a war of artificial intelligence overpowering the last vestiges of natural wisdom. This is seen in how managers are educated and encouraged to manage including workplace and shopping monitoring as well as urban surveillance of citizens. The artificiality of computer events has become a new religion. Therein, exciting conceptions of technological management, as documented in irrelevant journals, illustrates how humans go so wrong in selecting, designing, and realizing projects.[90] Via an intrinsic dislike of the natural such humans demand ever greater expansion of the evil filed under the strategic. Thus, the image of humanity moves ever lower via the speed of expanding industrialization.

All this points to causes of emergent effects in the larger context of being human beings. Herein we pause and reflect on this picture of reality as what and how humans manage. We do so with a bit of

---

[90] Brunner, John, *Shockwave Rider*. Ballentine Books: New York, 1975.

difference. Instead of becoming upset with effects bothering us and sending a branch of science off in search of causes of effects (e.g., the variants of genes causing COVID 19) we suggest looking for the earlier effects of effects. Such comes to define future human existence from consequences of the past. Therein the challenge for management will be as difficult as changing ideas of why and how to manage human life. We will attempt to address causes effected by effects. Where tangential issues like COVID 19 disrupt the homocentric we will address the deeper issues of the homocentric beneath creation of contextual change, change in the context we were educated to ignore via industrial successes and artificial dominance.

Is there a more normative approach to management? Can it better serve humans during consequences of the-industrial driven by the artificial? Behind this question is concern for humans. Can they learn to manage themselves better under conditions of climate change? Early indications offer little promise of our moving towards improvement. The dictates of scientific management of 1911 continue largely unquestioned. Climate Change scientists point to this as causal.

> "In the past the man has been first; in the future the system must be first. This in no sense, however, implies that great men are not needed. On the contrary, the first object of any good system must be that of developing first-class men; and under systemic management the best man rises to the top more certainly and more rapidly than ever before."[91]

Planning, Adds Humor

Management has become a background concept that has been drug into the present by business schools, where it is a spe-

---

91 Frederick Winslow Taylor, Principles of Scientific Management, Harper & Brothers: New York, 1911, p. 7: introduction.

cialty. Courses on it deal with how best to manage the present to receive benefit as soon as possible. This is called improved productivity. It makes the editors of the magazine *Economist* happy to see it. It focuses on some subjects while denying most others. It invests resources to receive benefits. It tries to shorten the distance between investment and benefits. The masthead of management is often defined as improvement of productivity, where its ideal would be the momentary management of benefits arriving instantaneously from investments dreamed of.

In recent years, the focus in management schools shifted from management of resources needed to strategy formulation for winning. Just now the focus is on the use of strategic thinking to acquire leadership roles. Via a continually changing portfolio and needs there has been the emergence of a hierarchy of managers. Some focus on leadership. Others find ways to market goods and services. Still others concentrate on the behavior of living resources and attempt to bring discipline to the behavior of pets, children, and/or spouses. As such middle management has become the doorway into the superficial.

Management will here be treated differently. Management and management are presented to be of fundamental importance to the era we are entering. It is treated as more than a concept sitting on the stage set of life. Here it is "construct" where it is shown to have created the current definition of human life for 150 years, and thus to be essential to any recreation of life to avoid the consequences of its history. A construct is an aid to building, a model for organizing parts into a meaningful whole. Now we urgently need a whole that can replace the dangers of a consequential whole from past mistakes of humans and their relation to the nature.

As management becomes a construct it works to create and operate societal systems. It attempts improvement via change, yet often allows minimal change. One method to overcome the tendency for changelessness is to adopt what has long been called action research. This is often launched after facing unintended consequences arising from short-term gains via intended results. It begins to feel loopy from needing to loop back to its beginnings to sense from where consequences originate.

Management of current societal systems is beginning to face some profoundly serious contextual concerns. Some readings of the human future suggest it to be questionable at best. Management as a construct is integral to much human behavior as seen in relations in and between governments, institutions, organizations, families, enemies, friends, and the nature we attempt to understand.

Managing these entities and their relations involves learning about the potential and problems in each then appreciating how each can quickly be problematic for the others. Using a systems-thinking model we can see how potentials and problems from the context of each can reverse become consequential for all plus context. The context for managerial work is, at its base, a web of human relations that range from making love to making war, where the two are linked. Human purpose is unfortunately allowed to drive the process of management thus requiring ever more management for meaning to what is mostly meaningless.[92]

Motivating what comes to require management is a process for fulfilling purposes, a process required a wide array of resources. These inputs include plants, animals, materials, energies, and other humans. The outputs arrive as products, often called goods or services, which have production, acquisition, and usage costs. The tradition of management has concentrated on the first two and mostly ignored the third. The third is the world of consequences, a domain that management has learned to avoid or where that is not possible to ignore. These contents arise from concern with this third category to address the question of can management be redefined to move from operations management to consequential management.

---

[92] Russell Ackoff and Fred Emery wrote a book on *Purposeful Systems*, Aldine Press, 1972, that went into the needs of strict rationality in understanding organizations in need of management. Their approach to the rational measure of love between two people on page 141, as fundamental to solving relationship problems, illustrates the shortcomings of their purpose. As Eric Trist stated upon reading the book: "Where are the *porpoise-ful* systems (natural) in their thesis?" West Churchman later agreed with the Trist question in his quest to understand the non-rational.

Management is a social construct. Humans use it to define themselves, or to define themselves via management of others. Where needed, management can be seen to be complex. Probably it is not complex in the sense we encounter in the study of nature where complex is what you do not understand. Signifying something as complex in the social realm using means the author wishes to avoid discussing it. Regardless of complexity labelling, a particular management model gives insight into a human wants to go, and how. If the model is dictatorial, they assume others will not want to join. If they believe others joining them is part of the journey, they offer a more participative model.

Management existed in antiquity and will exist as humans meet the consequences of past behaviors and/or meet their ends. Current ideas and practices of management are mostly from developments since 1850. That was when humans brought technology, machinery, into their negotiations with nature, to more efficiently subdue nature's processes to meet man's needs of the moment.

The process begins with natural processes confusing them humbling humans. We respond by abstracting the encounter from its context. In this way nature and the power in its meaning is controlled, then lost. Mathematics is an especially good tool for prying context away from initial meaning in an encounter with nature. It is one of many languages that give support to the religion of the artificial, man's favorite religion. This is seen in many of the backward advances of humans over the nature. There are exceptions to removing context, as with Erwin Goffman in his "frame analysis" model. Therein he discussed the results of 1950s researchers who sought the truth about schizophrenia. Via intense analytic questioning, segmenting, and charting, a sane person who dared to act differently was removed from a societal context and locked up in a mental institution. Management of the institution was seen as clearly insane.[93]

---

[93] Illustrated in Professor Goffman course lectures in 1974, as outlined in his book *"Frame Analysis: An Essay on the Organization of Experience,"* Harper and Row, 1974.

Later work by Gregory Bateson in double-bind theory illustrated how this was even common outside mental institutions, even in many families. Examples can be seen any and everywhere. The history of national leaders, pushing their socio-organizations into war, shows how a personal search for inner peace can be exceedingly expensive for unhappy others.[94] These are sample decisions as taken and then managed in abstraction from their context. They are in partial fulfillment of partial illusions of partial ideas in furtherance of building the artificial. This process is about to change. Natural processes are organizing the varied consequences of all this as the nature of climate change; change that will bring an end to the stability required to maintain human and related life. Humans need to rethink what they think of as management of human affairs.

The consequential shadows are from industrializing work as managed via economic ideas that promised to improve human existence, for some. Mostly political, these ideas were consistent with a Darwinian conception of improving the human condition.

With many having been left out of the idea of economic prosperity via industrial management we ended with about fifty men owning about half the earths economic resources. Economists and politicians have each generated a shadow over the human future. This is not the central subject herein but does relate to resolu4tion of how best to manage the omniscient consequences of the natural over the artificial. Herein the concentration is on current systems of management, not problems in ownership of management.

Dilemma 1: Are Police Required for Governance?

The following small story may seem like a tangent. In fact, it is a 2010 repetition of stories found throughout the 1975 project as done in Sweden relative to the role of regulations, lawyers, and courts in

---

[94] See Robert S. McNamara, President of Ford Motor Company, then Secretary of Defense, during Vietnam. He designed and managed the escalation of US presence in creating an ever-expanding warfare scenario. Known as a "real numbers" person he felt completely self-assured about his ideas, especially when they were very wrong.

the governance process. In the project we concluded the US system of regulation was very analytic and equally non-systemic. We came to have particular concern with the thinking of lawyers trained and certified to work in the US. They were seen to act in ways that worsened the management of pollution they claimed to want to reduce. They wrote laws beyond comprehension then based them on a pattern of threatening behavior as enforcement. The results were counterintuitive, counterproductive, and tended to worsen a bad situation. Other nations in the study were seen to be far more successful in their law writing and regulation.

I would normally disregard much of the following but being faced with a threat of having "criminal charges" levied against me for preferring university students over university leadership I wanted to play the role of pollution in US society. I saw the threat as a nice way to retest the US legal system to see if it had found improvement during thirty years. The alternative to my facing criminal charges was an offer of a professor emeritus promotion, a retirement package, and a future of silence about the wrong at the university. I elected to go with the charges against me and retest the US regulatory system.

Sadly, the story begins with the three-volume final reporting mentioned before on the Swedish work is no longer available. The copy sent to the University of Pennsylvania Library as documentation of a dissertation is now missing. A copy was kept in my office at the New Jersey Institute of Technology and is no longer available to me. I used it as a reference in my 1981 to 2009 courses at NJIT. In 2009, I became the only tenured professor ever fired by NJIT since it began in 1881, those three reports were sized.

Two NJIT presidents, Altenkirch and Bloom, were unhappy about much of what I did and taught. They charged me with eight counts of what my lawyer called anti-authoritarian behavior. I was found not guilty of them thus recharged with twenty-five additional counts a year later.

An NJ judge finally found me to be guilty of one of the twenty-five. It was one he had laughingly dismissed at the beginning, but then found he must return to it when he saw the others as even less serious. Important to the issue of this book and climate change history was my keeping many historic documents in my office, which were seized by the university. These included the three-volume 1977 Stockholm School of Economics research reporting. In addition, NJIT seized all private files from my office and six cartons of private books open for my students to review. Some books were first editions of famous works, now valued at more than a thousand dollars on Amazon.

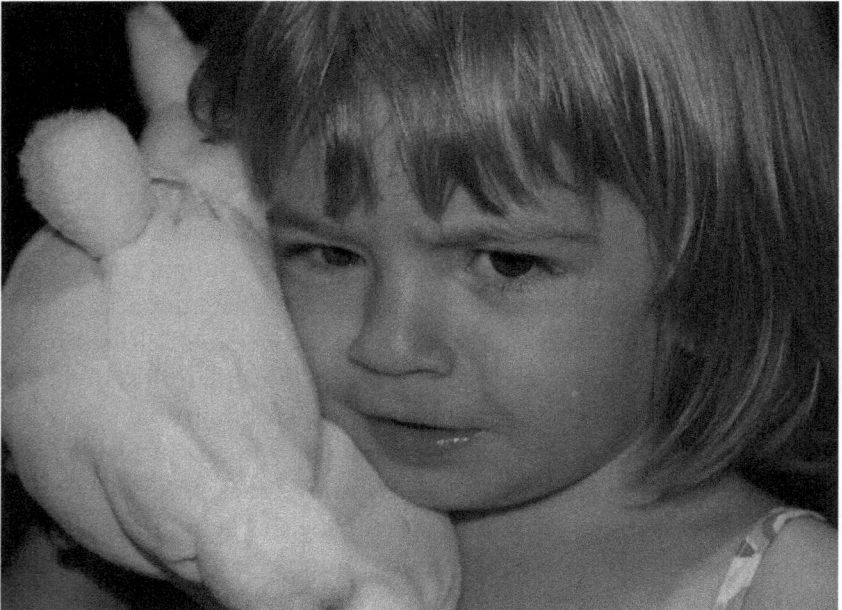

Stuffed Friend of Daughter Natalie, as returned to her via
an Order by a New Jersey Judge, as not state property

The two presidents, with Governor Christie who was a member of the NJIT Board, were responsible for the seizer. With the aid of various lawyers representing their interests they took much, including two of my youngest daughter's stuffed animals that were sitting on my desk. Later, they were kind enough to decide to return one stuffed animal to the tearful daughter under a judge's orders. The judge failed to order the return of the second stuffed animal.

NJIT leadership had claimed my personal files were New Jersey State Property and needed to be seized prior to court cases involving me beginning in 2009. New York NPR attempted to recover some of the files as well as learn why the university was mysteriously paying the judge who had approved the seizer $500/hour by NJIT. To add my humor to their anger I offered to pay half the "fee" so the judge could behave in a more objective manner. That was denied. A NJ Supreme Court justice later came to approve all the above and seemed to be an early supporting of what we now call a Putin/Trump approach to social justice. From this decision, a CEO of a $200 billion/year company I was advising made an announcement: "You Americans are very good at this. You have found ways to pay judges on top of the table. Back home in my country we must still pay them under the table."

The cases were then sealed and shut. If I could access the documents, I would show parallels between my 1975-1977 study showing how pollution was dealt with at a New Jersey refinery and the 2012 legal case against the behavior of Hawk. Both were well represented by Leonard Cohen's phrase on optimism about corruption in the human soul: "There is a crack in everything, that's how the light gets in."

The 1977 reports argued how environmental deterioration was becoming serious yet was treated as a nuisance factor in human achievements. Leaders from the 20 companies and 6 governments in the study followed the early results and agreed that we had a serious problem in our future but as with most problems of the day they felt the problem was technically solvable. Later in their studies they changed their attitude dramatically. At the end of the study one of the CEOs, that of a major oil company participant, saw climate change as very real and began giving lectures on the approaching dangers. Later, his board replaced him. Now, in 2022 his early concern for climate change is real, irreversible, and a growing threat to life.

Dilemma 2: Can Governance Exist Outside 2 Dimensions?

What shall humans do to soften their impact on nature? One proposal is to begin by dropping then replacing the first three letters of management. Manly management came to be derogatory towards nature and the natural. Man had redefined nature for manly management and their use, including use of women. Processes of degradation closely followed. Men came to seek another avenue of human potential. They came to organize around the artificial. Consistent with this the industrial emerged.

Major parts of nature came to be consumed in the service of humans. The artificial emerged as important. Its rules and fantasies came to replace the more natural aspects of managing the industrial. Artificial intelligence was later placed on the horizon. It was to augment then replace human intelligence, and responsibility. Serious clouds were forming on the human horizon.

Should humans be proud to override or replace natural aspects of their lives? Would a more humane attitude towards life and its management, with the whole of life included as context then nurtured, have been a better way? This question now arises as we consider the irreversibility of climate change to bring conclusions to much of nature. Is it too late to change the 2,400-year homocentric trip as laid out above? Can the ideas driving management be changed to nurture the natural, or should human management become stronger and harsher as it encounters the conditions of climate change?

The Greek then the Christian importance of hierarchy of some, over others, and human aspirations overriding nature came to predominate manly thinking. This unfolded for centuries. Underlying this was an unsubstantiated belief in unaided rationality out to degrade nature and/or those who appreciated nature. Greek philosophy added to Religious Certainty argued how nature existed for humans uses. The natural was heavily consumed by the industrial via the unquestioned arrogance of homo-centricity. Just now the divide has grown into a war of artificial intelligence overpowering the last vestiges of natural wisdom. This is seen in how managers are educated and encouraged to manage including workplace and shopping monitoring as well as urban surveillance of citizens. The artificiality of computer events has become a new religion. Therein, exciting conceptions of technological management, as documented in irrelevant journals, illustrates how humans go so wrong in selecting, designing, and realizing projects.[95] Via an intrinsic dislike of the natural such humans demand ever greater expansion of the evil filed under the strategic. Thus, the image of humanity moves ever lower via the speed of expanding industrialization.

All this points to causes of emergent effects in the larger context of being human beings. Herein we pause and reflect on this picture of reality as what and how humans manage. We do so with a bit of difference. Instead of becoming upset with effects bothering us and sending a brand of science off in search of causes of effects, say the variants of genes causing COVID 19, we look towards the effects of effects that will redefine human existence. Therein the challenge for management will be as difficult as changing ideas of why and how to manage human life. We will attempt to address causes effected by effects. Where tangential issues like COVID 19 disrupt the homocentric we will address the deeper issues of the homocentric beneath creation of contextual change, change in the context we were educated to ignore via industrial successes and artificial dominance.

Is there a more normative approach to management? Can it better serve humans during consequences of the-industrial driven by the artificial? Behind this question is concern for humans. Can they learn to manage themselves better under conditions of climate change? Early indications offer little promise of our moving towards improvement. The dictates of scientific management of 1911 continue largely unquestioned. Climate Change scientists point to this as causal.

> "In the past the man has been first; in the future the system must be first. This in no sense, however, implies that great men are not needed. On the contrary, the first object of any good system

---

[95] Brunner, John, *Shockwave Rider*. Ballentine Books: New York, 1975.

must be that of developing first-class men; and under systemic management the best man rises to the top more certainly and more rapidly than ever before."[96]

Modern Management: To Efficiently Make it Cheaper

This responds to a "Now what?" question as raised at the end of a 1979 book on environmental deterioration becoming climate change consequences on our planet. The thesis was if humans couldn't find a meaningful alternative to their industrial-based lifestyle they would encounter a world filled with unfortunate consequences. That book was reprinted in 2019 when climate change seemed less like a hoax invented to question late 20th Century leadership and more like a window to terror. In 2019 the idea of an end to planetary life from human behavior seemed more tangible, and was thus moved onto the cover: "Too Early, Too Late, Now what?"

Recent surveys suggest human concern for climate change is large, in fact becoming omnipresent at 70% and growing. Prior estimates put it at 30% but with different questions the same researchers found citizen concern was well above that expressed by political representatives begging to be seen as leaders of whatever mattered.

Humans begin to see climate change as a devastating threat to life and the stability it requires. Concern for the future has thus emerged and is expanding. Mental stability is questionable. Life is not going well. Some respond via the pretense of exaggerated masculinity and make light of assured challenges from climate change. Even these souls are aware of the tragic potential. Depression grows in all societies from stress over the human future, or a lack thereof. Current definitions of life increasingly move from well-being to instability. Violence emerges along with frustration with self.

Both books came from a three-volume report of a 1975-77 research project at the Stockholm School of Economics. Leadership

---

[96] Frederick Winslow Taylor, Principles of Scientific Management, Harper & Brothers: New York, 1911, p. 7: introduction.

from 20 companies and 6 governments participated and extensively supported the work. Our aid was to improve understanding of the role of environmental deterioration as a symptom of trouble in production and consumption by humans. Via the project all participants came to see dangers to the human future, threats growing worse each year.

Methods of product-making then using were seen shown to be a growing threat to planetary life. Business-as-usual activities were questioned extensively in the research along with pointing out ways to improve relations to the natural context. There was no political stance in the project. The project included those with leanings towards problem solving via representative democracies, authoritarian states, and even self-governance. These were topics over dinners, not a focus of the research into our relations with nature.

The project was conducted in the newly created Institute of International Business, Stockholm School of Economics. The young researchers loved speculating on their creation of "business as unusual" enterprises, to transcend the contrived national and industrial boundaries. They wanted to demonstrate how humans could rise up to do well by doing good, not via corruption, nationalism nor differences that shouldn't make a difference. The Financial Times at one point emphasized the work of the Institute as leading the international business domain. Two Institute students came to write a best-selling book from their IIB collaborations.[97]

Discussions began with reference to a future described in Garrett Hardin's 1969 paper, "Tragedy of the Commons." This was where he talked of the dilemmas resulting from actions designed for private gain using up common resources and destroying the potential of those for future use by others in the wider public. Such was assumed a simple cost of the economics of creative private gain upon the future public. He thus called for public regulation of the larger costs to society while also managing the downside of private greed.

---

[97] Ridederstrole, Jonas & Nordstrom, Kjell, *Funky Business*, New York: Prentice Hall, Financial Times, 2000.

The 1975 project found Hardin's thesis to be simplistic, with him assuming regulation to change human values. It was also seen as too optimistic about governmental abilities in meaningful management of a natural commons. Thus, the research began as a search for better ways to do well by doing good. We wanted to improve private and public behavior in the short-term over long-term deterioration. We were hopeful about reducing the future harm to the natural commons, a context on which all of our life depended.

At the end of the two-year project, it became clear that most humans didn't care much about their commons or their role in their life. They disregarded a picture of a grim future awaiting societies that could not come to appreciate the natural context then presented as essential to life. The importance of the industrial in satisfying their needs and wants could also be applied to repair of future consequences from present actions. The research participants mostly agreed change was urgently necessary.

The 1977 conclusions were seen to come from an industrialized logic path as described in 400 BC based on human potential. Productivity improvements via human technology was part of the dream where the mission became more formalized in the 1850's. In 1979 write ups we moved to argue that humans needed to rapidly move towards the discovery of a new model of meeting human needs and wants. We called it business as unusual innovation. Even then we saw signs of the situation becoming too late for repair. The industrial and its outputs were not to be questioned. Our religions taught us that the world is a passive resource laying there awaiting human use. Aristotle described how humans should, even must, develop rational processes to use resources from nature in more productive ways. Plato had described how his philosopher king-based hierarchy of control would aid in this mission. More could be produced for more humans at an ever-declining cost.

Productively would require reduced human input, hours, to produce more and produce it ever more cheaply. We pretended no concern for ever expanding use of materials and energy to get us to our utopia. Leadership and management would get us there. Humans did not seem to think that such measures of success would become very costly. Efficiency, as more stuff from less time, became the objective in public lectures, governance, design labs, and private board rooms. The idea of humans learning to do well by doing good was mostly lost.

The emphasis on the "cheap" became the passion for the "cheaper" by those leading and managing the systems of production. Only now is it clear that a cost would be paid for this manly mission. The work of Mike Kelly[98] in his "factory of the future" at Georgia Technological University pointed in a very different direction. He had developed this idea while a VP of design and production at IBM then attempted to bring it into engineering education as my friend at New Jersey Institute of Technology. Sadly, NJIT leadership thought he and his ideas were strange and a waste of their time. He then went further with it while directing parts of DARPA in distributing $2 billion/year national research to be at the cutting edge of reality. He came to call his idea single copy production. His emphasis was on the value of a product, not mass consumption that called for more mass production. He died before his dream was illustrated.

Until now his thinking failed to catch on in universities even though some of the results in companies were exciting and attractive. He was said to have been "too different too soon." The human production concerns that drove him into his research were very interesting and continued today in several universities.

As was noted at the outset of this book Cohen identified a key characteristic driving the industrial to support human development. Cohen came to trivialize the "cheap" thinking found to underlie much of MIT's analysis to the problem presented to them by the Club of Rome thinking. Professor Hasan Ozbekhan, while founding director the Club of Rome, introduced the Club to MIT personalities. The

---

[98] I helped bring Mike to New Jersey Institute of Technology from IBM Headquarters to demonstrate a different model of industrialization, one he had very successfully demonstrated at IBM. Leadership of the university could never understand what he was up to, nor why he saw a need for change that he infected students with. After three years of effort he gave up on NJIT and became a director in the $2 billion/year research group at DARPA. Their mission was to improve national security via singly copy production.

MIT immediately gave a simple-minded definition to the problem thus the Club turned their discourse over to MIT. Hasan pointed out that this introduction of the industry people on the Club to MIT researchers was his great mistake in life. The MIT people seemed to lack any understanding of systems thinking in production and consumption of products. At the first meeting the MIT group with the club they argued how they had a quick solution of the Club's concern for the human future. Hasan felt their quick analysis and proposals ended in seeing "Limiting Growth" as key. It now seems that he was right.

In Search of "Business as Unusual"

Deterioration of natural systems via continued spread of badly designed industrialization became problem behind the climate change problem. By the end of the study there was general agreement among study participants that "business as usual" was a threat to the future of business and life. In that group we began discussions of what "business as unusual" should look like, and why it should be introduced into universities. Now that climate change has become a central concern of humans many comment "What a difference time makes." This is not helpful. Herein I go deeper in coming to focus on an idea that underlies much in physics. Most important as a reversal on normal physics and instead examining what defines "time" not what time defines. Since 1858 the definer of time has been entropy.

With the strong support of many high-level corporate and governmental participants, that research collected much data on humans and their futures. It talked about how we are moving towards a consequential future. We have now arrived. It was clear back then that if humans could not manage or regulate their behavior, then consequences would expand to define the future. Significant change was needed, involving the values behind design, marketing, production, and use of products. With a change in values there could be an abandonment of many of the more harmful products that defined human existence. Business as usual needed to die or it would take humans along to its end. One pathway to business as unusual in 1979 was to shift from wholesale use of nature to development of an appreciation for nature as life's context.

Some CEOs in the research came to agree with its conclusions via 1977 Board Room Meetings. They even initiated further research into what we call the unmanageable and the irreversible that would end planetary life. In meetings this was called climate change in honor of the work done by researcher Black in the study. The 1977 research results argued against discussion then emerging in MIT's idea of problem solving via "limits to growth." Such was seen as trivial considering very significant and unpredictable climate change processes.

Crucial in the study were questions about our manner of management of humans then governance of environmental deterioration. In the study we produced examples of how middle management was worsening pollution in their models of control, then regulators were worsening the end of stream pollution that did not stop in the stream. Much of this was seen in how human education had taught MBAs to be analytic while the natural environment is inherently systemic, as is the pollution into it. Climate change now illustrates such. Models of management and regulation are shown to be highly segmented, analytic, and divorced from context. The mismatch had been well defined in 1973 by Gregory Bateson when he warned humans of the heavy reliance on the rational leading to the weaknesses of "unaided-rationality." The world of the non-ration was far more expansive and powerful but often turned the most rational people into extremes of irrationality. The rational explained 10% while the non-rational included 90%. The irrational operated to destroy all of it.

An underlying question that only now is being asked is how humans will come to govern themselves as the terror of climate change consequences surround them? Will they begin to discover the potential in mutual aid, appreciation and responsibility in self-governance, and stop their self-destruction in the war with nature? Or will they continue to emphasize differences that do not matter towards and end in anger, and its logical conclusion? The study showed how working with nature and each other was necessary to survival of the context of life, as well as life. Or would humans develop more weapons of war against the natural environment and in being human?

Would they go even deeper into the industrial depths coupled to the seeming simplicity of authoritarian leadership? The authoritarian begins with men on an immortality project that move to do anything and everything to exhibit their will. They make strange promises about bringing back the changelessness of the past, known as "the good old days," that all know never were. Along the way they illustrate strength via an emphasis on the worst aspects of being human, then move to exploit the mess they created in emphasizing the worst aspects of business as usual. Will humans go deeper in search of more Hitlers, Putin's, Trumps, etc.? Or will the experiences of early tragedy move us to appreciate potential in finding another way, e.g., mutual aid? As climate change's consequences expand its management may no longer be possible.

> "If you tell a big enough lie and tell it frequently enough, it will be believed." (Then) come to believe that: "Struggle is the father of all things. It is not by the principles of humanity that man lives or is able to preserve himself above the animal world, but solely by means of the most brutal struggle." Adolf Hitler

This draws from Lenin's argument with Kropotkin in St. Petersburg in the 19th Century, where one argued the revolution cannot be violent and not a drop of blood can be spilled for success in change. The other argued that much blood must be spilled in the streets and it doesn't really matter whose blood it is. The second seems to have won that debate. That debate is important for the future as climate change in many locations will see that debate frequently.

Can humans resist the base logic of an Adolf type, and move on to seek the greater potentials found in self-governance via care of context? To do so humans need to rethink their live while creating and testing the untested. They will need to reflect on the downside of business as usual and test the potential awaiting in business as unusual, seen in the business of all things. Perhaps humans can eventually visit the wisdom of Lao Tzu to see an attractive definition of leadership as it relates to mutual survival. They can also pat those on the head that are buried under authoritarian dreams, e.g., Hitler types.

> "A leader is best when people barely know he exists, when his work is done, his aim fulfilled, they will say: we did it ourselves."

The arguments over the deadly experiences awaiting us in climate change are mostly settled. Just now the arguments are more with is climate change reversible. If irreversible, are humans capable of managing to halt its expansion and the harsher consequences from its status? To understand this question, we need to examine the many precepts arising from our chosen model of industrialization that were to meet human needs and wants then to trace them forward into characteristics of climate change. The clear results from ambiguous attitudes are helpful in this difficult mapping.

Relative to attitudes humans have about life and nature, and their role in such, we can look at widespread interpretations of Darwin's 1859 idea. He talked of a theory for how life would continue to improve, or at least advance. Many humans have since interpreted this in the most selfish form of progress: "survival of the fittest."

Herbert Spencer first used the concept in his 1864 book *Principles of Biology* from reading Darwin's work. Darwin, as with many American thinkers on governance, had been attracted the 1776 ideas of Adam Smith in *An Inquiry into the Nature and Causes of the Wealth of Nations*. Additional economists, as non-scientists, found a way to adapt to this idea and get their followers to adapt to it. The philosophy for advancement of humans was that self-interest, from individuals not groups, and as such it would best power progress. Darwin's idea of "evolution by natural selection" came from Smith's idea that the "invisible hand" would sort out the problems of selfishness and balance separate performances and differences in accumulation of wealth.

179

Some scientists, e.g., Kropotkin, saw this as justification of the "desire for selfishness and greed as good" from being too busy to reflect. They criticized the semi-lazy stimulus-response pattern to making sense of life. Kropotkin argued that such behavior was exceedingly short-term where the longer-term of life on earth required mutual aid for mutual survival in the nature of the planet. Some reflect this was due to Kropotkin studies being carried out with various species seen huddled together in a Siberian cold, not the warm of the islands south where Darwin watched species enjoying the killing and eating of each other while having sex with whatever.

None-the-less Darwin became the inspiration for economics and production via an industrial revolution of the world. Via Darwin we somehow came to think measures of fitness included more, larger homes all filled with stuff, connected to briming bank and stock market accounts. This was to be achieved via investing resources and work in ways to be ever more product, defined as the making of stuff ever more rapidly and thus cheaply. Almost free resources from nature were crucial inputs to meet the standards of cheap. Measures of success were based in cheap inputs where it was unclear if the outputs were of much value? Real estate not used, clothes never worn, food thrown away, cars driven without need, etc. were secondary to the price of purchase relative to the value of accumulation. In the 20th Century we think Darwin may have misspelled his key term, or we misread it. Survival of the fattest seems to be our quest. The context from which we took resources, produced what we desired and returned the undesirable is now showing the cost of the human project, which now looks to have been a venture.

8
Heresy: Answers Becoming Questions

European Institute of Business Association[99]
22nd Annual Meeting: Stockholm, Sweden
David L. Hawk/Gunnar Hedlund
New Jersey Institute of Technology
December 1996

Heresy: "Moving Outside to Improve the Inside"

This involves a search for business as unusual, for ways to improve bv what we humans do, and the matter in which we do it. It is to move from the static to the fluid, from the 2-D to the holographic, and from the material to the virtual in the managerial. Change it key. We have carried out several research experiments into the finding of leadership with places to go, that want to leave the core behind. In these experiments we found organization leaders that were most helpful over time were seen as *heretics*. Heretics were managers who criticized, made fun of, or simply ignored typical management rules from business as usual. They were consistently in search of more interesting definitions of success via the unusual. This often involved spokespeople for emerging companies in new industries that were redefining business. Tom Peters, Russell Ackoff, Eric Trist and Hasan Ozbekhan were all helpful in the effort.

---

[99] The name has been changed to Academy, reportedly to indicate an entity that was somehow firmer than a loose association.

We came to argue that heresy in management was crucial to living organizations operating in rapidly changing environments. Our general aim was to find and name characteristics of change for 21st Century organizations. Key in this was to learn to embrace the emerging need for ethical principles inherent to "doing well by doing good." Organizations succeeding at this were context sensitive in the systems thinking tradition. This included awareness then concern about emerging issues connected to climate change consequences. Early on we found that characteristics of fluid management replacing a history of authoritarian styles were helpful. This brought us to state that a continuation of business as usual would result in no business.

Eric Trist, of the Tavistock Institute of London, and his 1965 work with Fred Emery, was important to our projects. Eric was a heretic in that within the business school traditional teachings he called for a significant change. Such was needed to find improvement in thinking. One aspect of this was to include context in studies of corporate subjects. In his "turbulent environments" theme he had gone further into an argument to know your context. Context was seen as a dominant actor in the performance, not a stage prop. Trist thought it would become increasingly important as it became more irregular and unpredictable. Eric Trist was helpful in defining change in a different way, a way towards the rethinking of management.

Signs of turbulence were seen by Trist in the fifties relative to the technological oppressing in management of humans. In the sixties they introduced an expanded socio-technical from the nineteen-fifties. Further signs of turbulence in context were seen in the seventies with the technological oppression of the natural, not just of the human. This began the call to expand the socio-technical of the coal mines into the socio-technical-natural of the planet.

From their adopting the Trist logic, Gunnar Hedlund and Lars Otterbeck founded a new foundation in the Stockholm School of Economics in 1975. Called the Institute of International Business, it was richly funded by leading Swedish Corporations with their executives serving on the Institute's Board of Directors. It was to favor and spread the idea of developing heretics in Swedish Corporations. As more business was becoming more international the Institute would fund research into how to improve business as usual and via heretical thinking allow it to be more normative and fluid via developmental freedom. By 1980 it was listed as the leading international business research group in the world, by London's Financial Times. Its first research project, in 1975, as reported out in 1977, was that if business did not find a new way, then climate change would define its future via the Trist model.[100]

Gunnar Hedlund helped form this lecture and paper, as it was presented in Stockholm's Nobel Award Hall. He could not attend the presentation. He was sadly dying at the time.

Learning the Systemic From Mistakes of the Analytic

Social organizations clearly need renewal from time to time. The when and how of renewal are both important. Only the how is herein addressed except to point out that resources for renewal must be made available prior to the emergence of a crisis. Unfortunately, prior to reaching an organizational breakpoint, renewal activities are classified as maintenance so they can thus be deferred when resources are "scarce." Renewal is thus seldom taken seriously until it is too late. Another route is renewal is needed. It begins with the how and is outlined in the following.

The nineteen-eighties illustrated a clear lack of concern for renewal processes. Emphasis was with narrowly defined productivity improvements.[101] High priority was given to eliminating redundancy, moving to the core (or back to basics), and demonstrating strength through open intolerance. Successful managers were those

---

[100] Hawk, David, "Environmental Protection: Analytic Solutions in Search of Synthetic Problems: Three Volumes," IIB: Stockholm School of Economics, 1977.

[101] Symbolizing the process is how general factor productivity became reduced to simple-minded labor productivity analysis, an approach continuously applauded in the *Economist*. The downside is seen throughout business establishments. Several firms I work with that have significantly higher material and energy costs, than labor costs, still preferred to concentrate on means to improve labor productivity, often at the expense of pollution associated with wasting material/energy resources to save labor.

who spoke of rationality, stability, and discipline in business situations. Their mission "was to return organizations to their core competence." People with skill for ambiguity, ability in negotiating with the unknown, wisdom for questioning the right assumptions, and/or simply taking time to reflect on the future were dispensable. Under the banner of seeming to ever-improve productivity these types were removed from organizations.

The dominant U.S. model of renewal and maintenance no longer even pretends to program resources for maintenance. The "smart" policy is to simply wait until things fall so completely apart that someone else will take the blame or move to have it all junked.[102] It matters little whether the subject is a social organization or the facility it occupies.

With rising uncertainty and ambiguity, and a renewed need for efficiency, the time for organizational renewal again approaches. People with renewal-directed skills are returning. This trend is more noticeable in the activities of leading companies than in the products of leading schools.

Situations of change offer significant opportunities for business educational organizations, like EIBA (The European International Business Academy). It is clearly in need of renewal. The method proposed here advocates a consideration of one of the most ancient means for renewal of human institutions - use of the heretic. A heretic works to strengthen an institution by raising questions about its most closely held, and often weakest, beliefs. A heretic works to renew ideals by destabilizing dogmas, usually at great risk to himself.

An employment opportunity for heretics can be seen in the central principles of management as used in contemporary business teaching and research. Some of these are clearly due to heretical dismemberment. Ten years ago, the members of EIBA would have been first in line to raise the difficult questions. Just now most members seem only to listen respectfully, take notes, and applaud. This undoubtedly will need to change.

---

[102] The most recent and potentially sinister addition to this logic of destruction comes from environmentalists who see the junked materials as resources for "recycling."

I suggest several concepts that are due for examination by the heretic's probe. These come from several teaching and research experiences:

Core competence as potentially hollow.

- Learning as probably confused.
- Strategic thinking as learning to manage deceit. and
- Profitability's bottom-line at the top of the abyss.

The companies used in my teaching and research, that supply examples to students, may not be typical but perhaps no organization is any more typical. We learn more from the story their stories than their statistical relevance in a larger set. The story they told of management truths were always insightful.

As with most of my work over the past twenty-five years the subject area is companies trying to be innovative in seeing and responding to environmental concerns.

Improving Questions

"There lives more faith in honest doubt, Believe me, then in half the creeds."[103]

We now face-down the end of an era. In the warm afterglow of considerable success in developing and using modern management principles we have a soft uncertainty that something important is wrong. We sense a transformation is underway, but are unsure if it is in our interest, or even if we have anything to say about it. In many respects this is akin to the feeling of many successful national and regional businesses that are attempting to fit themselves out into rapidly changing global conditions.

The track record of renewal through adaptation is not good. Even in the sciences, the home ground of change agents, there is little

---

[103] Alfred Lord, *In Memoriam*:

sign of active adaptation and internal renewal. Several noteworthy scientists noted late in the game how their branch of the scientific tree improved more from the mortality of the old than the training and retraining of the young, i.e., old scientists don't change their minds.[104] Another way to state this is that learning is extremely difficult, especially if you are intelligent.[105] What then does this mean for business organizations?

EIBA, the European International Business Academy, began with the aesthetic flare of a young rebel in a style not unlike that used by several of EIBA's founding members to launch their successful academic careers. The early members were seen to stand against "traditional" business administration education, such as the standard fare arriving from "North American." The Europeans, and the few disloyal Americans that were involved, felt that Europe somehow could do better and come up with less parochial models for business management in Europe. Several intriguing and largely untested ideas emerged from EIBA's early membership that are now a legacy to its early years. Among the ideas were:

- That economic exchange was becoming increasingly internationalized.
- That culture was a key determinant of economic success, and failure.

---

[104] This became a central subject in one session of a 1985 meeting of the American Association for the Advancement of Science.

[105] Consistent with the theme in Plato's "Allegory of the Cave," Erwin Chargaff wrote about the situation of science and science in universities in his retirement book titled the *Heraclitan Fire*. (New York: Warner Books, 1978) This work is most beneficial to those who have the greatest optimism for scientific process. Chargaff is widely known for his 1940s discovery of "base-pairing" and the "complementarity principle," which Creek and Watson gained during their interview of him in their run-up to a Nobel prize. "I told them all I know. If they had heard before about the pairing rules, they concealed it. But as they did not seem to know much of anything, I was not unduly surprised...When I was asked later why I had not discovered the celebrated model...my answer has always been that I was too dumb." p. 103.

- That specialization of function was a limited and limiting construct.
- That a systems approach was less dangerous than reductionism.
- That the religion of Harvard case-method teaching might be flawed.
- That we know truly little about the concept of competition.
- That headquarters-subsidiary relations are not necessarily hierarchical, or friendly, and that Ownership does not necessarily result in control.

EIBA (European International Business Academy) helped turn these issues into researchable topics during a two-decade period. At the same time EIBA attracted people who were more comfortable with criticism than reverence. In addition, EIBA people had a nice sense of humor - especially about their own work. I, as a semi-outsider, was continually impressed with the humility with which EIBA members would articulate new variables of management, prior to their eventual legitimization through "proper discovery" in U.S.[106] and Asian circles.[107] Early on EIBA didn't care about who was the father of these ideas, but recently it has begun acting more serious about the importance of authorship, references (homage) and standards. Perhaps this is because EIBA is beginning to be perceived

---

[106] There are numerous examples of this process. One was the 1985 meeting of EIBA where a Wharton Professor took great issue with allowing "culture" into business analysis. This might open "Pandora's' box." The next year he began devoted much of his writing to the critical importance of culture and other phenomena that appears to have escaped from the "box." Of course, he never remembered the 1985 EIBA meeting. These events are of course trivial but the process they imply is fundamental to EIBA and its members.

[107] This is where Japanese business circles only believe things that have been translated by "their own." In February 1990 I gave a lecture to approximately 300 business and government leaders, where one point was the 1960s Perlmutter model of how companies become global by transcending their ethnic and regional presuppositions, and how this was a dilemma for Japanese firms. Later it was explained to me that what I had talked about was an idea of Professor Nonaka, not Perlmutter.

by others as "important" - as an establishment of rigorous business research and education. Even more dangerous, it may have started seeing itself in the same light. Some of its members now argue that EIBA qualifies for membership in the "mainstream."[108]

I will suggest in this paper why and how EIBA should temper its enthusiasm over its status. While there is merit in formalizing its gains and clarifying the differences between what's in and what's out there is a price to be paid for this new-found security. This situation is instructive because in many respects it is the same for the companies with which we work and conduct research:

1. Is (your firm) a nimble, learning organization, like those now ascribed to in most scholarly papers?
2. Does (your firm) move quickly to continually create exciting normative futures? Or,
3. Is (your firm) prone to seek the peace, stability, and restfulness that changelessness implied?
4. Does (your firm) want to become large enough that it creates change for others, and thus need to worry less about adapting to change?

While organizational philosophy is slanted towards one and two our actions clearly favor three and four. Today's EIBA has remnants of its once-radical past but shows signs of a being drawn into the comfortable and quiet slipstream of its big brothers of business education across the Atlantic. In their rush to pump up their importance the American "Academies" only afford questions that have clear (as in a hollow bell), and short (as in statistical soundbite), answers.[109]

The drift towards U.S. business beliefs has been especially clear in the EIBA papers of the last three years. Many papers relied heavily on and attempted to further develop concepts that are mainstream

---

[108] As was stated by an NYU business professor in a dissertation defense, "These EIBA related doctoral students aren't too bad, depending on your standards."
[109] Information exchange at these meetings often goes like: "How do you make a better profit?" "You begin with a really sexy core competence than rip their head off, before you eat their lunch and then spit out what you don't like.

to the U.S. where business professors find them comfortable, companies find them harmless, and students find them uninteresting. Several U.S. firms, considered to be leaders by the same professors, see the concepts as humorous,[110] although this seems not to daunt their use by the professors.

EIBA assembles once each year to seek the essence of what a small set of current management models mean but end up illustrating the limits of what gets accepted as teaching and learning in business classes. EIBA's past and future is implicit in its members and explicit in its members papers. We say we want greater excellence while commemorating the excellence of what we do, all the while ending up with a well-worn set of propositions and responses. With time there is less productive humor and fewer heretics with a knack for putting the proper labels on things. We try to use the best means to seek the best knowledge about what is "best." Unfortunately, this soon gets reduced to peer review and its well-documented limitations. As is widely accepted, and perhaps secretly desired, the process of peer review diminishes the variety of people and propositions to approximately zero. This trait of peer review is well known in national science policy circles, and sometimes used as the rationale for why peer review works. More recent reports use the same trait to describe why it doesn't work.[111] There must be a better way to encourage and identify innovation.

---

[110] The situation in U.S. business schools, as reported in virtually all business publications during the past two years, is not unlike that seen in 1950s biology labs in university being used to train students to work in bio-technology firms, or the very new computer engineering curricula suddenly being judged as irrelevant to an industry that now looks to biology instead of mechanics for its models. *Science* magazine has regular articles on both disciplines and their dilemmas.

[111] Both US and European science organizations, such as the National Science Foundation, worry about how best to encourage and locate cutting edge technology development via a process that many have found to intrinsically discourage it. Two serious problems with using publications as a criterion is that to be treated "well," i.e., found acceptable, a paper must reference most of the mainstream (i.e., those who will do the reviewing) and by the time the current state of the issue is dutifully reported there is little space left to effectively

Redefining a World Via Consequences From the Former

Using Sir Geoffrey Vickers's terminology, the early EIBA offered the freedom of a rocking boat like the experiences of the early Vikings. While some early participants became sea-sick others developed very agile sea-legs. The EIBA emphasis has shifted over time from agility to seaworthiness. The result is an EIBA that has become more like its U.S. sister ships - unsure of to where they are going but damned difficult to rock. The emphasis is on rigor over imagination. The tendency is to crawl into the middle of things. Ernst Fisher's paraphrasing of a key literary theme poetically describes this:

Hamm, whose name hints vaguely at myth, literature, and cheap histrionics, is rotting alive in his refuge. The world from which he came is dead. After an unspeakable catastrophe, all that remains are objects, only the inorganic, nothing that grows or breathes. 'End, it is the end, it's coming to an end, perhaps it's coming to an end.' There is no world left, no future, only the hiding-place in the middle of nothing."[112]

This situation is not unlike the quite humorous and deadly serious discourse of an EIBA member, of the Viking variety, who in a late-night EIBA episode speculated on the limits of analysis via using two-by-two matrices - "hell is getting stuck in the middle of those two-by-two crosshairs, much like Jesus." As most members of EIBA acknowledge, the interesting thing about EIBA meetings, as well as those in the business conferences of other world regions,[113] is what happens outside the securely assembled sessions of management ideology that result from peer scrutiny. This danger to management learning was poetically criticized a decade ago when a very gifted EIBA member distinguished

---

criticize it. Two draft papers are now available, one each from the EC and NSF, on this dilemma of how to encourage and evaluate ideas that are not normal to a discipline. NSF turns to changing its program officers, thus shifting biases, and hoping innovation emerges in the cracks between. Governmental science organizations could gain something by looking at what has been learned in several "skunk works" type processes in companies.

[112] Fischer, Ernst, *Art Against Ideology*, New York: George Braziller, 1969, p. 7.

[113] This cannot be said for all society meetings. Sessions of the American Association for the Advancement of Science Annual Meetings are more interesting than the hallway meetings outside.

between traditional business principles, that relied on old, sleepy, peaceful, agricultural idioms, and new principles that continually seek the alertness required by those on the move, such as a hunting party.[114] Regardless, EIBA's membership moves ever closer to the model of American business education organizations - entities that are sufficiently large so to be steady, yet capable of going half-way to the bottom prior to the passengers realizing that something is seriously wrong.

For those concerned about renewal, regeneration, and responsiveness there are several options. One is to systematically abandon organizations after a period, so their membership becomes the fertilizer needed for new beginnings, i.e., this is known as the winter-kill model.[115] Two is much less dramatic although probably more sinister. It involves working on the inside of an organized entity, with a fixed smile and lots of friendly gestures, while planning to bury the whole lot under their comments when the time is ripe.

The problem with the first model is it attracts people who like fertilizer. The problem with the second is that it relies to much on the exit and loyalty options to keep an institution alive. In the A.O. Hirschman sense of the terms, an approach is needed that can tap into the considerable powers of voice,[116] instead of relying on exit and loyalty to maintain status quo. Voice is acceptable to those who do not appreciate fertilizer who do not suffer fools well, and who are not well insulated from rapid change rates.[117] The remainder of this paper is for the voice option of the heretic.

---

[114] This notion was clearly articulated by Gunnar Hedlund in 1987 while on Sabbatical at Stanford, and then publicized by Tom Peters in one of his by-lines.

[115] This approach was used effectively a few years ago in Finland's effort to improve the "too secure" VTT national labs. The results of what the Government and TEKES did could teach those dealing with the relevance problem of the $30 billion U.S. national labs a great deal.

[116] Hirschman, Albert O., *Exit, Voice and Loyalty*: Responses to Decline in Firms, Organizations, and States, Cambridge, Ma.: Harvard Press, 1970.

[117] This insulation comes in universities via tenure where those having it can avoid the changes impacting others, e.g., students.

A heretic must access the most closely held assumptions in real time.[118] If voice is crucial for institutional renew, and if a heretic is important to the process, then how can they be stimulated? History demonstrates that the most effective way to stimulate discourse is to cut off debate. Sacred topics that are non-debatable become the center of discussion. Choice of sacred management topics depends on location and time frame.[119]

Headquarters: A Command Center, or a Base for Problem Creation?

It was once argued that challenges to a subject would come from the work of a society's cadre of scientists and professors. Armed with their academic freedom and pursuits of truth, wherever it leads, they ought to be natural candidates for heresy. If there ever was such a bias, the enthusiasm for it dampened long ago for at least three reasons.

1. Trust - Professors become professors by demonstrating that they can be entrusted with the traditional approaches to their field and will dutifully pass them on. They will not act to undermine its belief system.
2. Time - It simply is not in a professor's interest to cause trouble for the traditional, or to allow students to side-track the syllabus and take up valuable class time via introduction of substantive questions about the relevance of the traditional.
3. Sanctioning - It has recently become both more difficult and easier to question the tradition of management education via the emergence of national accrediting processes for management schools. If you want to be accredited, you

---

[118] This simply means that you will have to temporarily stop playing with digitally based multi-media for a while and read passages on history.
[119] I cannot personally demonstrate management heresy because of my lack of appropriate credentials. My activities are not and have never been near its legitimized core of management lore. A heretic must come from that center and have a great deal to lose by questioning the assumptions of the endeavor. He also can't be a whistle-blower.

better represent the core knowledge of management. The major penalty is that company human resource managers will not reimburse tuition expenses to employees attending non-accredited schools.

4. It is difficult to find heresy accepted or acceptable within management education and practice. Leadership seldom enjoys questions, especially about leadership.

> "The more precisely computers calculate this future, the less we can face the incalculable. The more closely we predict what will happen in twenty years' time, the more unexpected are the events of today. We are lost in a perfectly con- structed maze of facts, dates, and information. Ariadne's thread has multiplied a hundred-fold; we do not know which one we should follow, and stumble from one deal-end into another. A pleth- ora of means has devoured the end."[120]

Heretical ideas may come from outside a field but heretics still need to be from within the field. As Walter Kaufman, the Princeton philosopher, has noted:

"Heresy is a set of opinions at variance with established or gen- erally received principles. In this sense, heresy is the price of all orig- inality and innovation. In theology, any opinion that is contrary to the fundamental doctrine or creed of any church is heretical. From the point of view of the churches to which we do not belong - and none of us can belong to the lot - we are all heretics. But more nar- rowly speaking, a heretic is one who deviates from the fundamental doctrine of his own church, or of the church with which he was previously connected."

Should a business school support, or even try to nurture, here- tics? Can it legitimately do so? All organized entities are set up to resist heresy. This is primarily because heretics rely on the world of ideas

---

[120] Fisher, p. 37.

and ideas show no loyalty to any single belief system.[121] Heretics exist in management education, but they come from where they always come - a select group of students that hang around management education and learn to raise the difficult questions. Keep in mind that the most important attribute of heresy is that is questions those beliefs most deeply held, which throws it into the middle of major disputes. Employment opportunities are great in management, as will be outlined in the following section. Opportunities are access points for looking into some of the current major belief systems and concepts for management.

The four windows of opportunity outlined here come from my limited experiences with teaching, researching, and consulting. I'm sure there are other into the center of business education and practice.

Strategy as Deceit

Is core competence a strategy for success, or a pretense of consistency with which to face uncertainty? A contemporary strategy for management success, for those writing books for confused students and consulting for confused companies, is to advocate that they move ever more to a clearly specify and define "core competence." Many consulting/teaching/ managing careers have been built on this item of a general repertoire of management responses. Core competence is a recipe for many personal success stories.[122] Some members of the core competency group accept that the concept has a history that is at least two to three decades. Some reference an especially noteworthy work on the principle that was done twelve years ago by SEST-Euroconsult.[123]

---

[121] Ibid., first chapter.

[122] Not addressed here is another group that believes in recipes. They can be recognized by the belief that not only is core competence is an original idea, but that it began with them. I will not address the problems of this last group except that the following points out where their "original idea" originally might have come from.

[123] "Elements de reflextion sur l'integretion de technologie dans la function strategique des enterprises japonaises." *Le Bonzai de l'industrie japonais*, Paris: French Ministry of Research and Technology, July, 1984.

Those engaged in spreading the religion of core competence argue that recent work, from the late eighties and early nineties, has given the concept greater operational clarity. I teach with two such well-regarded and inspirational individuals. A heretic could attack their "core" by suggesting both that core competence has been around for a much longer time-period than they this group is willing to resist, and that the concept has in fact been made more ambiguous by recent developments.

The notion of improving economic activity via encouraging each person and each organization to concentrate on perfecting a small number of tasks (where each task is also very small) is as old as notion of division of labor. The reluctance of those advocating core competence to see or accept this heritage is itself interesting, although not the subject herein. Those wanting to pursue this tread might look at Adam Smith's work to see from where[124] he got the division of labor idea upon which he built his *Wealth of Nations* thesis. Division of labor is a discourse on the importance of "core competence." Serving as a object for further refinement by David Ricardo the idea continues on to greatly inspired the voluminous work of Porter on how to gain a comparative advantage by exaggerating the division of labor concept.[125]

Some may recall how the early idea of division of labor served to organize much of industrialization, but the idea had become exceedingly tired by the end of the nineteen-fifties. Environmental challenges were requiring more systemic thinking, acting, and organizing.[126] By the last nineteen-eighties the idea was very much back to life. As Keith Gardiner, Director of Lehigh's Advanced Manufacturing

---

[124] Difficult to document there is reason to believe that Smith of course gained some inspiration from reading some Plato and much Aristotle, just as those who now advocate core competence must also carry that legacy. His regard for their era is especially clear in his Chapter Four.

[125] This is distinctly not what is meant by "oneness" in eastern philosophy, or "grand unification theory" in physics.

[126] This was the stuff of the General Systems Theorists which got translated into business policy by the work of Trist, E.L., Emery, F.E., Ackoff, R.L., Boulding, K., Ozbekhan, H., Perlmutter, H., et.al.

Center, and former Director of Manufacturing Philosophy at IBM, argued in the late nineteen-eighties,

The growth of automation brought the problems of division of labor and segmentation back to the forefront of business theory. Top management generally sees it to be in its personal interest to apply automation (as distinct from understanding it) because it can be used to keep workers in check and return themselves to the power of the central manager via a return to the ideology of Frederick Taylor.[127] Regardless, the Smith-Babbage-Taylor ideology is back with a vengeance, although now working under the label of core competence.

Core competence is an especially viable candidate for the heretic's examination table due to the unquestioned fervor with which it is indiscriminately applied to whatever comes along. In a course last year on global competition, I was to use interactive television to teach at two other locations; as a demonstration of our university's technological leadership.[128] Since the system proved to be non-interactive,[129] I broke off the experiment.

The merit of the approach, based on our available technology, broke down after three weeks. I then started traveling to each of the other locations one night a week to give a normal course. By this time, the course had become highly fragmented. I then turned to an acquaintance in a large US firm[130] who offered to help reorganize the course around their global experiences. As the Senior VP in charge of information technology and systems for the firm he arranged for the various classes to all meet at their Global Technology Headquarters. He came from Atlanta to give a three-hour session that made use of

---

[127] As primarily represented in his book, *Principles of Scientific Management*, 1911.
[128] An also to lead the way into the automation of teaching where in additional to simultaneous broadcasts to other locations the lectures would be taped and then played on cable TV for those that wanted a degree when they had troubles sleeping.
[129] I usually couldn't see them, often they couldn't hear me, and on occasion the off-campus students had to go use a payphone to compensate for Bell Atlantic's transmission service, whenever they had a question or comment.
[130] This firm operates the third largest information systems in the world, the seventh largest air fleet and the only functioning nationwide mobile phone system in the U.S.

his four thousand people at the center[131] and his Chief Operations and Financial Officers. He covered many of the mythologies of what executives talk about, including the importance for U.S. companies of believing in core competence. He mentioned this idea with some humor because several papers and books about the success of his company said it was due to their pursuit of a core competence, "whatever those authors thought core and competence meant."

We learned more about what it meant in this widely referenced company six months later when another executive, who works for the one mentioned above, gave a keynote lecture at a university dinner. He dutifully presented the importance of core competence to the firm, as a "secret to their success," just as had been reported in the books and articles. He then closed his lecture with an outline of the "new and exciting things" the company was doing to become ever more efficient. This part was interesting because virtually all the items seemed to violate the core competence dictum.[132]

During the question segment, he was asked to explain the apparent disharmony between his firm being religious about core competency and yet going off and doing all these other things to absorb excess capacity of aircraft, etc. His response was, "There is no contradiction. The definition of what we do has simply shifted from moving packages to moving information.[133] The conclusions we left with was that the core competence creed had become more important than the firm's actions. If this kind of continuous redefinition of a core is needed, to maintain the validity of having a core, then the concept is best left behind.

Referencing the firm in this way may be unfair, but since it is so often used as an example of the effectiveness of core competence, then it should also be able to exemplify the downside of the concept as well as the upside. A newer challenge has recently surfaced to core

---

[131] The company has about 250,000 employees, where these 4,000 provide them with real-time information.

[132] He described how UPS was beginning to undertake activities like leasing their aircraft on weekends to tour operators.

[133] Under the parameters of this changing definition, tourists become information that is then legitimately moved by the firm.

competency, in that the market value of the parts of a conglomerate, as bought up and broken up, is not necessarily greater than that of the whole. The theory that parts were worth more than the whole began in North America but has since shifted to European firms. The breakdown of the theory in North America has just not shifted to Europe. The clearest evidence of this is seen in Europe's, or at least the *Economist's*, darling of core competence - Hanson PLC.

Hanson PLC made a lot of money on both continents by demonstrating how numerous middle-sized collections of companies were more valuable as parts than as whole. Used car thieves had known this for a long time, but never could use the fact to legitimize car theft. As of September 1996 Hanson, when the company itself was broken into parts, the parts were worth less whole had been in both London and New York. The same has recently come true for ITT, AT&T and other firms involved in seeking their core business by splitting up.[134]

Questioning Presumptions

Can humans somehow redefine their search for "The Good Life.?" If early warnings of self-initiated endangerment of life are insufficient, what can we do? Should the warnings be louder or more entertaining, or are we simply too brave (e.g., ignorant) about being illustrated with points of change? Are we too brave to fear those rising temperatures and expanding bio-viruses, that threaten life? Why can't we see the need to stabilize, then reverse, our expanding seizure of resources from nature? In a discussion I held with Beijing's Expert Council, that selects China's leadership, we jointly agreed that China needed to bury much of China's cultural connection to "Confucious Thought" and shift towards the Wisdom of Lao Tzu. The closing question from a member of the Council was: "What Professor Hawk does not tell us what we should do about the idiots and assholes?"[135]

---

[134] See "Hanson Spinoff Plans Haven't Raised Shareholder Value," WSJ, 9/26/96, p. B4.

[135] Held at the Beijing Expert Council Headquarters, February 7, 2007. A debate with much concern from and care within it.

Related questions involve how can we manage our love of the artificial, and respect of the industry that produces it, yet survive the consequences of its expansion? Discussions of such go deeper into an understanding of context but are essential to seeking a more holistic and systemic understanding of who humans are and why must they do as they do? Many of them are raised and discussed herein to be more inclusive of actors and actions creating climate change and global warming. The holistic is globally defined as: "The entire situation within which something exists, happens, or is explained."[136]

Can we understand the meaning in all this, or must we continue to rely on what call "leadership" to give us definitions and purposes we like? Must we continue to seek such to insulate us from our deeds, misdeeds and debts due? Some studies in organizational behavior illustrate that In many respects we choose, or choose to tolerate, leaders to be able to blame someone else for what we should have corrected. Yes, we know what leaders have promised, in gaining our support, and that it cannot possibly be done. This is part of that human passion to place our believe in "negative entropy." Sidestepping such strategic dishonesty we pretend our leadership to have access to special knowledge.

Certainly, our leaders pretend to know what we don't know and that its key to our success in life, but must we really believe what their mouth says, and not the messages hidden in their eyes? We always come to discover that with time the promises of leaders are bullshit. This was described twenty years ago by a Princeton University Professor in his classic, and bestselling book[137] that alerted us to where our leadership was taking us. He posed that leaders often have less knowledge than their followers, and virtually no ethics. Even knowing this we continued to follow. Were we lazy, hungry for entertainment, or simply absent? When cars had standard transmissions, we at least were reminded of the need to change gears as we drove around.

What is organizational learning? Is it like learning of the individual? It has recently become popular/important to introduce learn-

[136] Cambridge English Dictionary
[137] Harry G. Frankfurt, On Bullshit, University of Princeton Press, 2005.

ing into discussion of organizational theory and change. I get uneasy when speculating on why learning has now become so important, especially since it is coming from those who were once stressing networks, then core competence, and now learning.

In the nineteen-eighties John Brunner argued, in his book *Shockwave Rider*, that in our madness to find and believe in artificial intelligence we had become sufficiently stupid to no longer recognize intelligence anyway. Brunner's conclusion was that AI could thus be whatever we wanted it to be. A similar process may now be underway relative to what is organizational learning - probably whatever suits our purposes. A more substantive approach is needed in management.

There are several places to begin a search for why learning is now important to business organizations, and, in turn, what learning could mean for business. One is in a relatively recent article (i.e., within the past fifty years) on the subject by Gregory Bateson.[138] Bateson articulation of what learning includes, and excludes, begins with a thought structure device proposed near the turn of the century by Whitehead and Russell called "theory of logical types." This approach is more widely accepted by people that prefer mathematics to statistics but none-the-less has been used in several well-publicized works, e.g., the 1980s work of Foucault to distinguish between what was a "pipe and not a pipe."[139]

A more substantive example of Whitehead and Russell's approach is seen in the 1940s work of R.J. Collingwood's on "metaphysics."[140] Here logical typing was used to structure a means to continually inquire deeper into what humans really mean when they say something about something. This approach was used extensively by Hasan Ozbekhan in his approach to normative planning.

---

[138] Bateson, Gregory, "The Logical Categories of Learning and Communication," Paper in the Proceedings of a Conference on World Views, Wenner Gren Foundation and NIH, August 2-11, 1968. It was rewritten and published in his 1972 book, *Steps to an Ecology of Mind*, pp. 279-308.

[139] Foucault, Michael, *This is Not a Pipe*, Berkeley: University of Cal. Press, 1983.

[140] Collingwood, R.G., *An Essay on Metaphysics*, Chicago: Henry Regnery Co., 1972 (Original 1939).

Collingwood's model is easy to follow but pays the price of being limited by a hierarchy of logic, at least until the last level is reached and the person being questioned says, "Enough!

Just because." This becomes a learning system of Bateson's type II Learning, with the inquirer learning by shifting into ever more fundamental presuppositions. At some point the Collingwood model encounters Bateson's Type III Learning. This is not unlike what a detective uses in trying during an interrogation to ascertain what was in the mind of the accused at the time of the crime. Learning surfaces through such devices as asking questions that contain multiply presuppositions. Collingwood uses the question of: "When did you leave off beating your wife?" as an example of how to learn if a person was indeed beating their wife, or even was married. The same mechanisms are used by managers to motivate workers to be manageable.

Bateson's model is more sophisticated and takes much greater risks, especially as it moves into what he calls the region of Type III learning. It also offers very high learning rewards. For Bateson human learning is initially dependent upon hierarchical processes, as implicit in any reliance on logical typing, but he argues that this is more due to human limitations than to the subject being learned. He goes on to argue that there is learning well beyond hierarchical structures, which is consistent with the work of Hedlund a decade ago in organizational theory of hierarchies. Bateson specifies that this form of learning is part of his type II and essentially all his type III. He goes on to point out that most humans are not capable of accessing learning in Type III, and especially in Type IV. Devotees of any belief system illustrate what Bateson was saying. An example of this is seen in the devotees to Herbert Simon. Some of his followers still believe, as he seems to have at least once believed, that no systems for learning and management exist outside hierarchies.[141]

---

[141] This was especially apparent last time I and Gunnar Hedlund attended a Society for General Systems Research Annual meeting where we gave a presentation on why and how hierarchies break down. The audience essentially shouted down the session via Simon groupies. Hedlund's work on heterarchical management systems, as applied in companies progressed far beyond the limitations of which he spoke in 1987.

Bateson accuses behavioral scientists of having an especially hard time with the concept of learning and all that it implies:

> ...it is not at all unusual for the theorists of behavioral science to commit errors which are precisely analogous to the error of classifying the name with the thing named - or eating the menu card instead of the dinner - an error of logical typing.[142]

People at this meeting that are concerned with what learning means in an international firm would probably gain from trying to penetrate this approach to non-hierarchical learning of Bateson. His framework offers five types of learning where III and IV are distinctly outside hierarchical systems.

- Zero learning is characterized by specificity of response, which -right or wrong- is not subject to correction.
- Learning I is change is specificity of response by correction or errors of choice within a set of alternatives.
- Learning II is a change in the process of learning I, e.g., a corrective change in the set of alternatives from which choice is made, or it is a change in how the sequence of experience is punctuated.
- Learning III is a change in the process of Learning II, e.g., a corrective change in the system of sets of alternatives from which choice is made. (We shall see later that to demand this level of performance of some men and some mammals is sometimes pathogenic.)
- Learning IV would be changed to Learning III, but probably does not occur in any adult living organism on this earth. Evolutionary process has, however, created organisms whose ontogeny brings them to Level III. The com-

---

[142] Bateson, Gregory, *Steps to an Ecology of Mind*, New York: Ballantine Books, 1972, p. 280.

bination of phylogenesis with ontogenesis, in fact, achieves Level IV.[143]

Learning II confronts the dilemmas of what is via double binds, catch-22s, and contradictions without obvious exits. This has been shown in studies of design processes to be the basis for the learning how to do what we think we are capable of and eliciting highly creative responses or mental disorders. Learning III is quite different. What has been said above about the self-validating character of premises acquired by Learning II indicates that Learning III is likely to be difficult and rare even in human beings. Expectably, it will also be difficult for scientists, who are only human, to imagine or describe this process. But it is claimed that something of the sort does from time to time in psychotherapy, religious conversion, and in order sequences in which there is profound reorganization of character.

Zen Buddhists, Occidental mystics, and some psychiatrists assert that these matters are totally beyond the reach of language.[144] As articulated, learning processes become aligned with heretical processes. This allows us a basis for understanding learning in an action-oriented framework that can help individuals and organizations do things more clearly and innovatively. The challenge thus offered is exciting.

Incompetence as Strategic

Oiling the slippery slope of ethical conduct. Another opportunity for the heretic comes from examining what is being taught, learned and practices beneath the concept of strategic thinking. Clearly, strategic planning has become a critical course in most MBA programs. This is popular because here one can truly learn about the thought processes that accrue to and define top management.

My concern comes from the question of whether strategic thinking can ever be consistent with ethical behavior? While seeming to start as a silly question it is, in its essence, an encounter with

---

[143] Ibid., pp. 292-293.
[144] Ibid., pp. 301-302.

the eternal human dilemma outlined in the Faustian tragedy.[145] This is the process for means devouring ends, the future getting lost in the present, and the mismatches between nature and self.

Our heretical friend in a management education classroom would ask "Under what conditions would deceit be ethical?" This question comes during the class where it is mentioned that strategic thinking comes from Clausewitz and later game theorist. Any attempt to answer the heretic's question will soon expose the depth of the ethical dilemma. This is seen in Chapter Ten of Clausewitz's Book Three in his <u>On War</u>.[146] Titled "stratagem," the issues is that Stratagem implies a concealed intention, and therefore is opposed to straightforward dealing, in the same way as wit is the opposite of direct proof. It has therefore nothing in common with the means of persuasion, of self-interest, of force, but a great deal to do with deceit, because that likewise conceals its object.

It is itself a deceit as well when it is done, but still it differs from what is commonly called deceit, in this respect that there is no direct breach of word. The deceiver by stratagem leaves it to the person himself whom he is deceiving to commit the errors of understanding which at last, flowing into one result, suddenly change the nature of things in his eyes.[147]

Somehow this kind of deceit is more important than directly lying. This is in part why we need to add moral repair courses to business curricula, such as "legal and ethical issues." These only raise or deepen the cynicism towards those concerned with ethics, especially if they are taught such by a practicing lawyer, which they usually are.

The how that I have come to argue in my work as most effective in today's business climate, is to be very honest and open in having no strategy? This is temporarily effective in a counter-intuitive way because competitors spend great efforts trying to find out what the strategy is and end up getting confused by the simplicity.

---

[145] Those wanting to pursue this timeless aspect of human decision-making should begin with Marlow, linger at Goethe, move through Valery to Mann and hesitate at Fyre, or if they want to feel better travel in the reverse direction.

[146] Clausewitz, Carl von, *On War*, Edited by Anatol Rapoport, Middlesex, England: Penguin Books, Ltd., 1968, originally published in 1832.

[147] Ibid., p. 274.

Profit: Means to an End, or End of Meaning?

Bringing Environmental Values into an Industry that believes is profitable. The key question here surrounds the great axiom of business policy and practice - that business must first and foremost make a profit. Profit is its reason, its objective, and its justification. Until I start on the project, I will outline to her I didn't worry so much about this rationale. I knew it was flawed but didn't know the extent. The project I am now leading requires a confrontation with this creed. The question has become: Can profit maximizing be a sufficiently robust viable to support environmental deterioration reduction? The answer is a clear no. I will try to briefly point out why.

One of my current projects is one funded by EPA's Global Change Division to demonstrate that my 1977 thesis can be used to change a whole industry. The thesis was that there are alternatives to command-and-control regulation that are more effective and much more efficient. In this project the incentive is to bring new technology, new concepts of marketing and new financial instruments to the home building industry as inducements to get its leaders to lead it to higher quality processes and products, all at a reduced cost.

EPA's version of the project began with a label of "pollution prevention at a profit" as its guiding theme.[148] The logic was that a firm's profit could be increased by joining the project and learning to efficiently produce more efficient products. These products are then sold at a price advantage to the producer. The houses would be distinguished by their having an "Energy Star" label[149] attached.

I became involved in the work because it allowed for three stages, where the last two were the most promising. The project allowed for

---

[148] This expression was in fact used on the Energy Star label to be used on qualifying products, but the Federal Trade Commission ruled that it had to be withdrawn because it was to difficult to measure and clarify what exactly it meant - i.e., it was misleading to customers.

[149] This well-known brand label, of EPA, is successfully used to denote the lighting in the offices of 11,000 companies, all computers now sold in the U.S. and many appliances used in homes. The project described here is an effort to carry the brand to whole house improvements.

an industry-wide application of a new means to accomplishing environmental objectives with a regulatory framework.[150] Its first stage would concentrate on reduction of energy use within the U.S. The second stage would allow integration of the various dimensions of pollution (air, water, materials, noise, energy, and perception of quality). The third stage would be an international collaboration of businesses in the industry to see how global learning could be enhanced to reach a common and improved set of objectives. I was to propose a logic for the industry to internalize environmental concerns to make them an opportunity for international development, not a problem to be managed at the local level.

The objective of stage one, of the work, is to reduce air pollution in the U.S. by ten percent via changing the nature of the house product and the mechanical and appliance products it contains. During the first year ten thousand houses are to be built under this Energy Star label. One of the early problems was its early EPA theme of "pollution prevention at a profit."[151] We cannot use this expression in the project, but in fact the problems with profit continue into later stages. We see how the most scandalous activities of the home building industry come because of their initiators arguing that they do low quality things due to their "duty to make a profit." In all instances these issues that end up giving the industry a bad reputation are the

---

[150] The central measurement of success in the program is to reduce air pollution that comes from energy use in houses, which accounts for 30% of the U.S. total. The proposed reduction is 30% than that being proposed by a set of regulatory standards and are not in place, and if the program succeeds will not need to be put in place. This is to demonstrate that there are more effective ways to efficiently achieve environmental improvement than regulatory, and perhaps ultimately illustrate that the regulatory approach can never come close to achieving the same results. This was proposed from the results of a 1977 study that compared the Swedish and U.S. approaches to environmental protection. See Hawk, David L., "Regulation of Environmental Deterioration: Three Volumes," Stockholm, Sweden: Institute of International Business, Stockholm School of Economics, 1977,

[151] The Federal Trade Commission recently ruled that we couldn't use the expression on our labels because profit was far too ambiguous of a concept, and it tended to confuse the participants. At least this solved an early problem with profit.

least obvious ones. They are not the items that consumers can clearly see and make careful decisions about. They dwell in the obscure areas of the process that customers assume are incidental and not important to a firms' profit. In fact, they point to the tendency to be "as greedy as possible but not get caught doing it."[152]

The project is attempting to get the industry to behave in ways that improve the public's perception of it by raising the reputation of its products. Companies in the study can end up being able to sell their products for less because they learn to be more efficient. The old, tired notion of profit maximization once again stands in the way. Even though exceptionally large profits are sometimes made, the industry has a very tough time, with about 25% going out of business each year. For some of them we have shown how this is a by-product of them getting confused by their own layers of deceit about what they are doing. Plenty, perhaps too much, money washes through the industry, it's just that it ends up being very poorly managed. The customer, that percentage who can afford a home, picks up the tab, along with considerable help from the government.[153]

Prior to the project entering the third stage in two years we will have to arrive at a resolution to the problem of profit as misplaced concreteness tied to its sheltering incompetence. A heretic is needed.

---

[152] The clearest examples of this are in areas considered as not too expensive for the home buyer. A common instance is seen in a home buyer having a refrigerator with in-the-door icemaker, he/she will need a small copper tube to be tapped off a water pipe. The actual cost is less than $25 for doing this, although the standard customer cost is $250. This is typical of all such minor things in the house. For the main structure, its finishes, and its appliances the rules of the game are clear, and the profit ratios are plus or minus 5%. The theory is that these things need "a little extra profit" because they are "troublesome." They in fact become the cumulative basis for a significant portion of a house cost.

[153] In 1995 home building received the largest subsidy of any single industry. Via the mortgage and real estate tax deduction on federal income taxes. This was about $100 billion. I argued with firms that this is a major reason encouraging them to do a bad job in what they do. There is little incentive for innovation, R&D, or efficiency. The U.S. has by far the largest subsidies, although of course few see such as subsidies.

9
Non-Hierarchical Leadership

Leadership As Deceit

If a candidate for leadership promises to lead you back to those "good old days, before change," do you take him seriously? Laws of physics and decorum say such is impossible in life, but such is often pronounced by someone needing to lead you, perhaps because they failed to lead themselves. Such seems essential to being a politician and perhaps a lawyer, but does promising such make it so? In essence we easily see how and where strategic deceit in defining change is central to management and leadership.

It's somewhat obvious that we humans prefer change that is slower, perhaps so slow that it's not moving. Meanwhile we have seen where environmental change can be quite rapid and even instantly devastating. The human responses to the change, or to avoiding follow-up changes, seem quite slow. For example, a Stage 4 hurricane can be instantaneous yet human responses to what happened can consume years with no response to avoiding future hurricanes that past human activities initiate.

The problem for humans is that the increase in change in the environment was initiated by human activities which also include acts to avoid seeing the environmental change their activities initiate. You might think of this as a dilemma within a dilemma. It's like being in the military where to discuss a catch 22 creates in secondary Catch 22 for those who discuss the first.[154]

Leading When You Don't Know Where You Are

Private sector organizations regularly fail via weak leadership. Weakness shows up in ego-centric humans dreaming of more power and less concern for consequences of what they do to gain that power. Also, they have trouble seeing how little they know. The problem in public sector organizations, such as governments, since the mid-sixties, is that they have moved towards non-public, even anti-public, leadership thinking they were more successful than those with the public interest in their mind. This encouraged more short-term thinking in governmental offices.

More governmental leadership of weak leadership qualities, like the corporate model of short-term gain, long-term pain has arrived. This has encouraged a wave of blind trust in those who argue for cashing in on short-term gain to win an election, with no hint of the consequences to follow. In some cases, societies have avoided the rather predictable business model and gone for the non-model of a stage performer where lies are welcome if they entertain. In that way anything can be anything, and deception is fine. In those cases, there is little short-term gain and much medium to long=term pain. The long-term pain is more significant in a city, state, or nation than in a company. Governmental bankruptcy is not easy to manage. Some are beginning to calculate its cost based on listening to public and private leadership qualities. The news is not good.

Whatever we might say, we all sense a long-term compensation coming due to abusing nature for two hundred years of an industrial war against such. Some have recently noticed that humans are

---

[154] This comes from the noteworthy movie of the same name, "Catch 22." Therein service men can go home after a mental injury if they do not want to do so. If they apply to be excused and disappear from the drama of the trauma, they are disallowed such. Gregory Bateson redefined this in anthropology as a "double-bind."

part of that nature, as well as dependent on nature's provision of the resources of life.

Humans have collected extensive short-term gains, at nature's expense, from their activities. Most important, human activities have posed threats to planetary life as known since 1856. Back then we knew of dangerous consequences to life from the activities of short-term gain implicit in an emerging model of industrialization. That model was continued and expanded. Now we begin to experience the long-term consequences of our environment as warned in 1856, now called climate change.

Thus, we are caught in a funny contradiction that is funny but not fun. The increase we see in intolerance results mostly for ourselves and the bad results from our actions relative to climate change. Of course, we attempt not to notice that line of responsibility. We thus become angry at much, but seldom clarify the connections. In areas of governance we then ask if we should adopt a truer form of democracy. Such might allow us to be more responsible for our actions before we cave in and accept the harsh right turn towards simple-minded totalitarian methods ending in all humans going out of business. We see various leaders offering to help with this section option. First, they offer comfort by noting that climate change is a hoax and to be ignored. Then, they rush it to solve climate change consequences for we that don't know what to do.

The contradiction is seen in humans selecting low quality leadership when better management was needed, especially seen in leadership that mostly stands in front of mirrors for measures of success. Such often follows Social Darwinism policies for species improvement, where easy to see survival of the fattest replaces the fittest. Ayn Rand outlined why egocentricity defines people's progress. From her emphasis on leadership, we see courses in business programs that emphasize Maslow's hierarchy of misunderstood needs linked to learning to think strategically insures the downward movement of the human condition via badly managed organizations. Leadership is told it has an obligation to deceive others for their own good, thus deceiving the deceiving the deceiver. It's a pattern for homocentric suicide. Under all this what happened to the forecast in 1965 of "The

Tragedy of the Commons?" While students continue to be taught to use it for personal and immediate purposes to excel, a tragedy is indeed moving forward.

I first learned of this during a freshman engineering course at ISU. I was very interested in the disintegration tendency in nature implied by the 1st and 2nd laws of thermodynamics. Based on my behavior in high school I had not been allowed to take any college-preparatory courses in English, Math, or Science. Thus, I had time to read and write a lot. Continuing this theme, my class time questions were labelled as rude, from a troublemaker. Thus, in my first college physics course I began by asking a professor about the two Laws of Thermodynamics, and their relations to life. Neither were mentioned in his syllabus. I did not know they were to be systematically avoided in management of the industrial. Thus, I was punished for lack of respect. My grade became a D grade. I continued feeling there to be something wrong in human superficiality in life. From growing up on a farm I was concerned with the cost of human actions on nature. During college I began to see from where many problems came, classroom presuppositions.

Reading deeper I found Einstein to strongly believe entropy was: "…the only physical theory of universal content that, within the framework of applicability of its basic concepts, will never be overthrown."[155] I continued to read how Stephen Hawking describing the essential nature of his black hole mechanics in 1971 via its consistency to the second law of thermodynamics process. Additional illumination came from a World Futures Conference meeting in 1980 where I was placed on a panel with Carl Sagan. In his responding to my presentation on negotiated order being natural and thus more capable of managing climate change than EPA's legal order he went much deeper. He added the universal entropic process into negated order saying humans try to ignore entropy, but nature's balance sheet will show the cost.

---

[155] Klein, M.J., 1967, "Thermodynamics in Einstein's thought," *Science* 157: 509-516.

Then, equally illuminating, was a series of lectures given by Nicholas Georgescu-Roegen to a group of international economists I had assembled at NJIT. It was a National Science Foundation workshop in 1985 set up to propose a research agenda for looking at the build environment production considering what we knew about climate change. Georgescu-Roegen's working hypothesis was that via economic thinking, modelling, and acting humans speed up entropy. For him contemporary production and consumption of goods and services as business are participants in the irreversible deterioration of nature.

Such reflection of such humans is important to the contents in this book, like the 1858 work of Eunice Newton Foote as published in *Science*. The contents found herein are to examine how humans manage all this. The reoccurring theme herein is how contemporary management practices rely on methods that ignore the long-term costs of what we are doing today. We need to move from *strategic management* to *consequential management*, i.e., managing the consequences of our emphasis on results management. We need to eliminate, clean up, or better manage very dangerous costs emerging on the horizon of our lives.

These questions provide the theme behind this book. Do humans have a future or are they another version of dinosaurs with a greater negative impact on the planet than asteroids? What is the role of management in this process, especially management of the commons, each other, and self? Our lives are organized and managed to avoid secondary costs behind what they buy, make, take, borrow, or sell. Included in this are building, operating, maintenance and disposal costs. All have a not so obvious entropic cost that most engineering and business courses teach as largely irrelevant, or at least to be excluded from marketing. Yes, marketing attracts us to products, but the most successful marketeers avoid mention of those after-purchase costs. This is most easily seen in how marketing avoids any mention of *entropic costs* in industrial actions and productions. Entropy was and is unmentionable.

The masterpiece of the last two centuries, industrialization, avoids inclusion of secondary, e.g., long-term taxation, costs nature assigns to human ideas of progress. Auditing of this tax is now taking place, called climate change science, but via the vacuum of strategic leadership it's called a hoax.

All this is evolving in a leadership education process from thinking strategically. Implicit in the deceit such allows success comes from those who learn to: "Fake it, until you make it!"[156] The longer-term pain seems to now be approaching us. For those who care, mostly from the youth, where lies the wisdom essential to find a future?

The book is for my former students, of which there were about 10,000 registered in my classes. I hope they will find or create a way out from a predicament created by the elderly in burying wisdom beneath strategically smoke. Perhaps we will meet in the 5th dimension?

Okay, maybe we should first redesign our habitation in the 3rd dimension with some respect for dictates of the 4th dimension, as we are moved towards the 5th. Today's results are mostly from the 2nd dumped into the 3rd via leadership of the 1st with consequences awaiting us in the 4th. It is not encouraging.

Leadership is important but not the focus herein. It is seen as temporal and strategic. The fifties Harvard B-School mission took special note of leadership to rise and be known. Key to this was the admiration for Clausewitz's strategic thinking during war, between nations and companies. Just now leadership issues are dying at Harvard but continue in lesser schools that ignore the weaknesses of any ideas of leadership and those how those embracing such tend to be corrupted by the inherent dishonest strategic thinking. The 19th Century sense of strategic thinking, as highlighted by its author where he pointed to "Cunning" as key. He, Clausewitz, described this in detail in his chapter ten on strategic thinking.[157]

> "At first glance, it seems not unjust that the term
> 'strategy' should be derived from 'cunning' and

---

[156] This comment was used to explain the success of Elizabeth Holmes, founder of Theranos, a multi-billion-dollar enterprise to test blood that didn't and couldn't. Holmes defended her company's strategic misrepresentations as "aspirations," not "operations, meaning she didn't find perpetual motion.

[157] Clausewitz, Carl von, *On War*, New York: Everyman's Library, 1993, p. 238,

213

that, for all the real and apparent changes that war has undergone since the days of ancient Greece, this term still indicates its essential nature." (Clausewitz, ibid.)

During hundreds of years management of the human project has consistently relied on leadership via strategic thinking. Management would emphasize continuity, stability, and changelessness but such was not effective for dealing with change. Evidence of serious troubles now grows thus we need to carefully investigate the management ideas behind the troubles. It may well be a major cause of the approaching end that seems quite fateful. We will examine the management ideas and practices that brought it to us. Will we see humans concluding existence in the significant environmental deterioration from the industrial and use of its products and the instabilities such creates called "climate change."

The instabilities and threats to life in climate change pose danger to systems of life. These include human life as we know it. The focus herein is to better understand this and what might be done to avoid a logical end-state. As the construct of management takes credit for the emergent threat, we might best concentrate on the first three letters that have long directed it. Just as management is given responsibility for the governance that creates the present, we should then give such responsibility for the downside.

What we might call the Human Project is a learning exercise during thousands of years organizing reason around their experiences in what works, and what doesn't. Management is seen as key to the provision of noteworthy goods and services for meeting tangible human needs. It also has extensive involvement in meeting ephemeral wants of humans as they see, or believe, their basic needs were met.

Underlying the Human Project are methods developed to attain short-term happiness while hoping to not disrupt long-term continuance. Ideas then methods of business-as-usual came to be crucial to this. Success came to be dependent on relationship managing between the natural, the social, and the self. The second category came to be defined by the technical in socio-technical systems. The third category promoted happiness as defined by human existence. Relations to the second category shifted to emphasis on sciences of the artificial and away from appreciation of the natural. The artificial allowed for more self-control of a self-created environment. Seemingly contradictory, this led to the development of responses to the human desire for ways to isolate themselves and their families from change. As such they looked to the tradition of Parmenides, and his idea of changelessness via human control of context.

Attention has recently begun to shift back from the context of the artificial, towards the natural. Some humans sense extreme danger coming from the natural environment, which is the context on which life depends. Sure, the quality of love/hate relations to others, and management of self, continue to be important in control of these conditions that threaten.

The image below captures the essence of this section. It's from my Lapland summer walks. While looking at the map I became confused about to where I must go, not knowing where I was. It was funny and illuminating? When working with organizations, leadership, management and life I never forgot the quandary I discovered in Lapland, Sweden. These hikes of two-weeks to cover 200 kilometers were unforgettable. Sadly, the beautiful glaciers we walked upon are now gone.

Where to go, if you don't know where you are?

Leadership: A Non-Natural Human Construct

Leaders are seen as essential to give voice and appearance to change. They act as voices for the transitory reality of an organization and its inhabitants. Leaders of course are transitory and not as important as they think but their followers sort of accept them in organizations. As such they need not be completely serious in what they say and do, but they are somewhat followed before replaced. Results of research into the situation of 21st Century managers often end with: "My life is not so good. My paycheck comes from spending all day lying." Not a good sign relative to the quality of change they advocate or organize, especially when urgent change is needed for an organization's survival.

The above situation defines much of modern society, governance and social purpose. As such we translate energetic announcements for urgently needed "change" as vacuous[158]. Thus, we have forgotten how meaningful change takes place in a social organization. This may seem harsh, but it generally involves the emergence of heresy inside a social organization. This means opposition to the business as usual. Routine. It has been seen in the actions of individuals the like Mahatma Gandi, M.L. King, Socrates, Lao Tzu, etc. The power of their message comes from its relevance and sincerity for the time. Their ideas somehow link with an organizational urgency for change from its contemporary environment. I mention this here in that an extraordinarily urgent series of messages is now coming from our environment. Leadership seems distracted away from such. Responses seem more dangerous than untimely. Can we find a contemporary Socrates, Lao Tzu, Ann Frank or Joan of Arc? They led change and paid a price for it. They were not those safely sitting in

---

[158] If this seems confusing, listen to 75 million souls wanting to follow a Donald Trump leadership type. While not trusting what is said followers still become nurtured via a particular style. This is in the tradition of Catherine the Great. Like Catherine, Donald is not especially smart, wise, or interested in what is said, but loves how he can say it. He is not expected to have an interesting death, like Catherine had in the barn behind her Saint Petersburg summer house. I once took a class to that place to hear about that fragment of life.

headquarters giving directions to those like soldiers in Vietnam combat that in 1968 I noted as "We the unwilling, led by the unqualified, to kill the unfortunate, die for the ungrateful."

You might see it as lower-level learning spreading outwards, not the top microphoning ignorance downward. Those sponsored by central leadership generally become extremely expensive to all involved, including the neighbors. There were men such as: Commodus, Woodrow Wilson, Neville Chamberlain, Emperor Hirohito, Robert Mugabe, and Benito Mussolini. Change does not come from such isolated men but from a society learning about change from its environment. Just now we have an incredible opportunity for learning from our environment, but failure is conclusive for life.

The change now needed is seen in humans beginning to face planetary extinction caused by their individual activities. Prior to this there were five episodes of planetary extinction, but they preceded human existence. The situation is more than serious for planetary life. Research illustrates that psychological damage is already well advanced in human beings as their being realizes its fragile existence. This may be an assent as it may well motivate individuals to change as individuals once their leaders are out of the picture. How to motivate individuals to change to protect society?

Suggestion that an person needs to change often elicits a look of defensiveness. When such a message comes from a leader you tend to disregard it as he is probably not serious. The change followers desire is in others, not themselves. Individuals don't recognize that they are their best chance for survival. Societal change begins with individual members' changing but that is often not recognized. As Lao Tzu said twenty-five hundred years ago, in response to human egocentricity: "If you do not change direction, you may end up where you are heading."

Thus, necessary societal changes are at the same quality level as what we each experience. How to encourage initiation of change of the individual is central to these contents. Humans do argue that current political discourse is openly asking for, even demanding, change. Sadly, its actuality soon becomes limited to an emphasis on turning to the right or the left, followed by hollow bitterness then anger at those in the other direction. Meaningful substance in change is hard to articulate or implement.

As mentioned above, society is organized as a dichotomy. Some humans want their social group to take a turn to the hard right, thus accepting the authoritarian consequences from leadership. Perhaps they realize where this will lead and desire that someone else will take responsibility for how bad things will be. Then, they can say they had no responsibility for the king going to hell. Others want society to take a hard left turn to distribution of authority, but this mostly results in a collective trip into hell. A third group argues to keep moving straight ahead and thus skip questioning what is. Discontent between humans is now part of seasonal discontent between humans and nature.

Change is dependent upon energy available and perception of results from applying that energy. Fundamental change relies on reorganization of value systems behind actions. We resist seeing this. It seems that discussion of problems of the self, relative to a mess the self comes to encounter, is off the table. Perhaps the focus of each human for internal consumption is quiet changelessness. That stuff out there, including other humans, is simply a mess that deserves to be changed. We seem to favor changelessness of self while hoping for change in others. Of course this is bothersome in that a grow-ing share of the change taking place in the larger environment is due to decisions and actions made by "self." This induces a level of selfishness that energizes the candidates and followers that create the unusual political discussions humans are now so passionate about. It's reminiscent of the times at the end of Babylonia, the fall of Rome, the liquidation of the Mayan Civilization, etc.

Will humans make it to the other side of wanting a changeless self in a changing environment? In essence we agree change is essen-tial but not that we must participate in it. Perhaps contradiction mis-management is what it means to be human. The pathway ahead, as darkly lit, seems headed back into Plato's Cave. This will be described later but is the human shelter where they are restricted to seeing the two-dimensional reality of shadows on the cave walls and ceilings like those of 21st Century TV and cell phone screens.

Our need for changelessness grows as we enter the early stages of harmful consequences from the wrongful decisions of yesterday that call for expanding and urgent changes. We humans then turn to consultant advice on how to avoid changing in the face of such forces, that we call complexities. From such we learn to be happy despite images of non-survivable futures approaching more rapidly.

None-the-less, we don't do much of quality in understanding or carrying out change. As it becomes too late to change, we show interest in it but confine our interests to the two-dimensions seen in the movie theater or living room. We act as if we barely have time and energy to deal with two-dimensional realities, let alone adding the stuff of three and four-dimensional realities. Our unfolding life dramas can only accommodate so much. Just now we are quite busy shopping for objects to support who we want to be, with little time to think about who we are, and then will be. Then, if someone suggests that you "change" it becomes very irritating. Are they joking or involved in a typical human power play? Perhaps the person ordering you to change is an Egotist: "A person of low taste, more interested in himself than in me."[159] Maybe you should just take this marketing of change easy. What is coming isn't here yet and may well never arrive. Just relax, change channels between Netflix, CNN and Fox, keep your beer in hand and sleep. If this sounds like you, you will perhaps not enjoy this book.

Going deeper into the human situation let's see the meaning of change. There is the version of it when your spouse tells you to change the child's diaper, but wait a minute, wasn't that her job? Perhaps you can buy a robot to handle such changes. After the diaper episode you then turn on the weather radio and hear that the temperature is to be hot, very hot, the hottest ever recorded on that day. Then you are warned that a Type 5 storm is on its way, but since it's becoming almost impossible to predict such a storm, it may not arrive. You instead look through your mail of the day and see that your home insurance company just doubled your cost of insurance

---

[159] Ambrose Bierce, *The Devils' Dictionary*, New York: Hill and Wang, 1957, (originally 1888), p. 42.

for next year, they notify you that they will no longer sell insurance in your state after next year. So many "change" incursions in your life, where will it end? A bit depressed you go out for a beer with friends and tell them of your tribulation, then ask if they think you should change? They pat you on the back or head, depending on the kind of relationship you have, and say, "No, don't bother to change, it's bound to get better tomorrow." You are not so sure then they reassure you with the adage of wisdom: "The more things change the more they stay the same." You drive home with a smile now knowing it will all be okay. You need not change a damned thing, except you encounter the consequences of that Type 5 storm on the way. Seems like someone is messy with you and making change essential as well as impossible considering your capabilities.

Thus, we see how humans resist seeing what is unfolding around their existence. They are seeing and beginning to experience early signs of tremendous planetary change, some of which threatens life, yet they have been taught to put up barriers to nature that protect changelessness. To then bring unreason, e.g., irrationality, into the equation we are beginning to learn that our cumulative behavior since the advent of industrialization in 1850 has come to create the environmental change that now requires human change as well as threats to life.

It's as if humans have carelessly damaged their home to an unimaginable scale and have no chance to change in any way that can reverse what has begun. This begins to illustrate the essence of from where climate change conditions arise as well as why we are so slow in responding to them. The situation is becoming grim. After first depicting the problem, its cause, and its effects science now mostly shows us how the crisis in the situation is coming faster and more terrible with each test. We might restate the prior example by saying that: "The more things stay the same (e.g., humans) the more rapidly they change (e.g., the deterioration of environment and climate)."

The more I refuse to be different in what I think, do and value the faster a difficult environment around me emerges from my ignorance of life and/or mistakes in negotiating with life. This is close to the problem that most humans have with the context in which they live and the qualities of the support systems they have constructed and use. Where lies the hope? Not is the arrogant ignorance of our current models of acceptable behavior, technological development, and economic exchange.

In what follows we discuss the difference between such euphemisms for humans while they are out driving around in search of meaning. Change has long been essential to life but now there is something different about change. No longer is it a crucial dimension to the environment we occupy and draw resources from. A different form of change is now the major threat to life's continuance. Change was integral to life via manageable versions of difference over time. It was crucial to the birth and growth of plants and animals humans came to need in their lives. At a more personal level when the temperature changes you change clothes. Now you change clothes to attract or distract others. When the temperature rises you remove clothes. Previously humans would consume food to collect energy necessary to work and do things essential to staying alive. Now food consumption is more of a societal event where the attainment from it is measured in extra weight. Such a change is from lifestyle values from wants, not bio-needs. This is changing. Life support is once more connected to change.

That has been shifted to environmental changes from human activities. Via this since 1850 humans came to think they could resist change from out there to changelessness in here. Yes, there has been a certain degree of homo-centric arrogance in this change, but we now begin to see that the change was not warranted. The change in the environment that human activities initiated seems to be well beyond human capability to adapt, and more recently to stop. The change initiated in the human environment may be more significant than what humans can manage.

Such seems mysteriously like human behavior at the same time, with interior human change being opposite to change out there. During human evolution they changed to match gradual changes in their environments. Since the industrial expansion of 1850 humans have brought much change to the environment of life. Via dreams of industrialization humans have come to presume that they are above nature, more powerful than the environment. Due to machines, they could do as they wished, regardless of its impact on the environment. Thus, humans came to believe they could become protection from the change their actions initiated. adopted an attitude that they could act to change things while insulating themselves from change of self via feedback that they had been wrong. It was sometimes obvious that change was needed in the actors and actions, not the environment, such as the challenges from their environment as with the Mayan's in Yucatan in their 600 AD version of climate change. With increased development of technology to aid and insulate humans against change we found ways to invest in a way to secure humans, called changelessness. While this concept began with attempts to be rational it is now difficult to think of its consequences as being of rational management of change. Its expense is clearly great and growing.

At this point in history the focus is on the expensive consequences of the shift of humans adapting to a changing environment to changing the environment to allow human changelessness. In some societal and many political activities there seems to be moving of humans to return to a prior environment thought to be better but that upon inspection never was. This too is costly to humans and their future. In some societies there is an apparent move to adopt a Taliban-like structure to societal interaction where only women pick up the cost of changelessness. Therein men grow beards, site meaningless scripture and women wonder why men act more like prisons then their former status as prisoners. It's crucial to understand what such implies for human future as more humans act like this is the best way to repair emergent damages from 150 years of industrialization.

Regardless of my lack of understanding I somehow fear emergent consequences from human interactions with nature and then each other. The long-standing notion that when things become difficult and you are unsure how to respond "when in doubt, just be nice" seems buried under heaps of toxic tainted trash.

Change has long been steadfastly implicit to the operation of life and its pattern of continuation. We seldom discuss change, even when it overwhelms our existence. We note its presence and absence but don't seem to know what to say about either. Via an optimistic and pessimistic note some have noticed recent changes in change. We notice things become different over time but become concerned with what it means, who is responsible, and can humans manage it or its consequences? Change is now different yet continues to rely on differences that don't matter to apply meaning to it. It is significant, almost to the point of being omnipresent, yet such blocks the normal mind. Can the mind be changed?

Change is the topic of our day and looks to become the essence of our children's tomorrow. It will become the topic that defines tomorrow. An emergent reality is about to redefine the reality of what we might generally call *business as usual.* Clearly a threat to future life via the external environment entering the world of climate change. It is also a more frequent discussion point with family, friends, and fellow workers as we discuss who loves, respects or tolerates us in our daily existence. We want to know who we are relative to how those around us give definitions and is our presence of less value today than it was yesterday? Relative to the changing context of change we quietly check on the weather during the day to see if a violent storm is bringing harm to us and what we value.

When we have time to be reflective, we then check the news to see if there is some violent change in nature and the larger more natural environment. This is noted in acres burned, crops destroyed, new storms coming and emergent diseases. These create the casualties of the day. Yes, we are limited in our making sense of all this, but our options are small.

That limitation comes from our bi-polar perception of all things from our belief in the sad logic of Aristotle. He created the strange idea of the world composed of twosomes. From this are required to choose between artificial opposites to be able to access the meaning of progress. From this we articulate opposites that aren't, such as black/white, rich/poor, smart/dumb, etc. We need to forget about Aristotle and his digital trip. Such mostly limits us a sad form of information technology with little information and Artificial Intelligence with little intelligence. We access these limits from Plato's Cave by rejecting the ideas of systemic wholes. We can recover but it seems difficult.

We can move from digital to *both plus more* and leave Aristotle's two-somes. From this freedom we can move on to dealing with and in the *more*. By accepting a need to access the more we can thus argue for access to holistic thinking. We can then side-step the dialectics of the digital and move to more fundamental concerns in what is and where is life's "more."

Our belief that we must be at war with nature is a problem in that life is part of the natural side of the dialectic between the natural and artificial. Such a dialectic to guide design and production of technology assures a bad presence and then a non-future. Nature is essential to a natural wellbeing, but few humans can see this escape from annihilation. That humans can act in accordance with nature seems to lie beyond our understanding of the essence of access to the more. Thinking such we resist internal change while being terrorized by change of the external. We argue for and sit up the stability of changelessness. Using culture, family and faith we retain persistent values, actions and behaviors. While at the local bar we proudly proclaim: *It changes out there, but no change is allowed in here.* Upon leaving the bar to drive home, despite there being laws against such, we resolve our contradictions by thinking "change will go away if we just ignore it."

My concern in 1979 was centered on "will humans change." This was key in the corporate advisement and class teaching I conducted. In 2024 this is no longer the case. Things have changed. The concern has shifted from the more optimistic "will" to the realistic "can" relative to human change. Unsure of its definition, we look deeper. We then see change as a threat to as well as the essence of life. It is becoming the central paradox to our way of life and is filed with a touch of humor as: a revised and rerun "Catch-22," maybe even a more logical version of that Bateson's "double bind." This denotes who around us in going crazy or that there is now a societal version of schizophrenia that causes that younger generation to be from hell or going there.

Discussion of change can be difficult but is increasingly mentioned in business meetings via good/bad stock investments, reflections on someone seeming to be older than a job needs, or diminished recall of family or friends, or even societal degradation, instabilities, or change of climate. From most of the discussion we arrive at proposals to create a wall of changelessness to protect the world, the community, the organization and/or individual. Given more time we then reflect on how some things change while other things don't.

Change has historically been a contextual process that moved slowly and predictably along with life leading to death. It is now different. It is a pile of mass confusion piled at the doorway to extinction. This situation has created what we begin to call climate change over time. The consequences of such provide education in the meaning of difference in time. Thinking deeper we recall that this somehow relates to the concept of entropy, a construct that creates and defines time. This will be presented in detail later in the book but is especially important to understanding what is going on as it introduces us to the belief in negative entropy, something that cannot exist in the universe, yet humans market the worship of it.

Change is now seen as the major threat to future life on our planet, like change that impacted five prior extinctions of life on the planet. In a similar manner change now appears as an expanding force that will destabilize the essential basis for life. The idea of an environment being managed by nature to stabilize life support systems is now being challenged.

Is it true that there is an impending danger? If so, how can this be? Why is it occurring? What or who caused it? We can see that change is clearly changed but can we work to not change it into something that supports life, not denies it? Can act to manage what appears to be disrupted and then act to disrupt life? Do humans have the capability to control the disruptors, or even see who they are, or must we accept we don't understand how a process we know to be essential to life is now being redefined? Early evidence is that humans are the disruptors yet being human allows a pretense of ignorance of their causal link to the negative? what can we do? Should we instead pretend this change is not happening, or that humans will fix it via negative entropy, or that humans are not human?

DAVID L. HAWK

Cleaning Up: Feminine Repair of Masculine Mistakes

Perhaps the impediment to humans changing was in what sur-rounded a lecture given on why we must consider changes in how we would approach design of the industrial. It came from a woman's research in 1856. Humans sometimes seem to focus on something that matters yet often it is apparent that they are thinking of is selfish, trivial or demonstrative of failing to think. When not thinking we seem to be wandering around and through piles of words or images. Humans are supposed to possess great potential, compared with other life forms per Darwin teachings, yet how do we access that? As we roam from incredibly clear insights to unconscious mumbling and stumbling, as seen in some presidential debates, how do we explain our consciousness? At times we appear completely unconscious or missing in inaction when facing choices in a life/death context. At other times, when we negotiate with the trivial, we act as very clear-sighted and directed. Does any of this matter?

If the gradation matters can humans decide where to be in the spectrum of thought, or are they controlled by forces beyond or beneath them? Such questions become key to any human future. We must find ways to move into consciousness of a more expansive vari-ety, one that allows access to seeing and understanding the non-ratio-nal, not just the rational. Such is the world of ideas while keeping in mind that ideas can also be trapped in the world of parts, not systems of connection. The shallow version comes to focus on the triviality of a spouse as unfaithful, a child as disobedient or a boss as showing contempt for our work.

Sometimes the conscious becomes more directed and inten-tional, turning to significant questions of our life space: a) What does it mean to be alive? b) Why does life lead into deterioration and death? and c) Why do humans seek the short-term cheap, while discarding the long-term valuation of something? To focus on the subject in this book, why do humans allocate time, energy, money and thought to cheap purchase of cheaper products while knowing that product and use of those products may well lead us into a sixth extinction of life on earth. While the change that leads to extinction of life, and that humans are the drivers of, why do we consciously disregard its implications for life even while saying we regret its end state?

> "The one feature these disparate events have in common is change and, to be more specific, the rate of change. When the world changes faster than species can adapt, many fall out. This is the case whether the agent drops from the sky in a fiery streak or drives to work in a Honda. To argue that the current extinction event could be averted if people just cared more and were willing to make more sacrifices is not wrong, exactly; still, it misses the point. It doesn't much matter whether people care or don't care. What matters is that people change the world."[160]

The work in Elizabeth's book is extremely valuable, although quite pessimistic for the human species. While she concludes that what matters most is that humans are changing the world I would go one step further herein to common on what might matter even more is that humans are not up to changing the aspects of specific activities associated with the industrial model that has created climate since we were warned of such in 1856 by Enice Foote. Its important to note that most men of science ignored her work for about 100 years, while the man who did most to teach Exxon Inc. of it also taught me of her wisdom relative to climate change project in a large research project I began at the Stockholm School of Economics in 1975. His name was David Black, of Exxon Research. Following her advice, as Dr. Black wanted to do, the situation of one hundred and sixty-four years later, in 2024, could all be different.

On occasion humans even reflect on how segmented and selfish acts lead to significant change in their environments, but that is

---

[160] Kolbert, Elizabeth, *The Sixth Extinction*, New York: Henry Holt and Co., 2014, p. 266.

rare. In essence, humans find it difficult to change their actions that ended up changing their environment. The connections between the two states of change seldom seem to emerge in human consciousness.

Change is key to life and its continuance, yet the human idea of change is minute by minute, and in disruption of natural continuance via selfishness and its support of changelessness in the short-term.[161]

We are told that humans, especially the young, are concerned for the future of life on their planet. They learn that past and current behavior of humans is working to change the context. Continuation of this change will remove the essential conditions of life. A growing number of humans, although not the leaders, have come to reflect on change as needed in humans to avoid climate change consequences. What are these changes? What needs to be done to accept change?

Much depends on how these questions are addressed in the next twenty-five years. As important will be the process for changing the questions to improve their quality. It is not an exaggeration to say life depends upon the answers thus the articulation of the questions that lead to certain questions and not others. When not thinking what can we be said to be doing? How does thinking relate to change, where change is becoming a most important quality of human behavior. It somehow seems that we humans resist thinking as well as changing, just as both are more urgently essential to continuance of the species.

These questions arise from growing evidence that humans think less often and shallower with time, especially in recent years. This conclusion comes from a review of the quality of actions during the past 25 years. The choices, actions and discussions they hold via the internet are not encouraging. Leadership that humans select or simply agree to follow are seen close to leadershit in many societies. The shallowness of intellect versus the depth of need to continue life appears as a widening gap in our future. Shallow responses to deep needs appear throughout governmental and business organizations.

---

[161] Ibid

jobs we agree to that lack ethics and merit. Each day we deal with evidence that our lives are not meritorious, nice, or even tolerable. Thus, we don't value our environment, others, or ourselves. We just attempt to survive until something worthwhile comes along to rescue us. In contradiction to all this we see glimpses of light coming down into life. This is the reality of the metaphor Plato outlined in his Allegory of the Cave[162] where much is 2D nothing but has small glimpses from a brighter reality outside, thus we think. Then, when we are awakened what do we think of relate to the brightly lit reality? In Plato's days such people were locked up in prisons or executed for returning to the cave to "talk shit" about a larger, more important reality. Today they are sent into therapy, given mind control drugs, or put on the street to sort out their craziness. How best can we express this process in search of truth as its key to there being a future for life on our planet during conditions of pending climate change consequences.

Femagement: Above and Beyond Management

The Faustian paradigm of human behavior supported by faith in being innovative about short-term gain over long-term pain is illustrated via a cartoon where a father is talking down to his small daughter: "Yes, my darling, I certainly love you. But just now I love fossil fuels more. Sorry." Most human management models now in good currency and operation support the father's values.

Humans have lived with a paradigm of management for 2,500 years where increasing knowledge from expanding analysis providing ever stronger technology has helped men to organize and direct human negotiations with life. We have long called it "man"-agement. Challenges to life from the threats of life, mostly from the environment of life, and mostly as consequences of prior management, now call for reconsideration of the accepted ideas of management. Herein

---

[162] This is represented in Plato's Allegory of the Cave. Humans are trapped underground and restricted to a reality of 2D shadows on a cave ceiling from a campfire behind them. It is like the metaphor of 21st Century humans restricted to a 2D reality via mobile phones and TVs.

we will conclude with options for such change in thinking, a predominate one being "fem"-agement. The difference is an issue of value systems not a sexual argument of men versus women. The feminine acts demonstrate the importance of short-term pain to long-term gain in much of understanding of life. The masculine values are different. They instead align themselves with the promises long associated with the history of technology as machines derived from logic. The feminine is closer to a holographic depiction of life as fluid and aligned with a negotiated order, much like we see in nature during the 4th dimension.

We tolerate insignificance awaiting the arrival of a larger, more meaningful reality. We are told we can access that larger reality via hard work or good fortune. Meanwhile we seek meaningful leaders in our government, companies, churches, bars, or mirrors. Meaningful can often be quite bad for others, and the world. Herein this will be discussed as a basis for understanding how we arrived at the ominous situation of humanly created climate change on the planet we depend on for life, where climate change threatens that life.

Failing all else in the quest for meaning we begin to seek being noticed, perhaps even noteworthy. Having decided to do noticeable things, we soon see that doing significant bad is more noteworthy than doing significant good. This process is well described in Ernest Becker's remarkable 2005 book *Denial of Death*. Therein he illustrates our search for immortality projects once we learn of mortality and become upset by the sound of its permanence and irreversibility. He then demonstrates how immortal projects mostly end in evil. Yes, he does mention Hitler as an example of such. More recent "rulers" are now qualifying.

Erwin Ghargaff illustrated the thesis of many humans doing bad for some sense of reward, or access to immortality via doing bad. In his 1978 *Heraclitean Fire: Sketches from a Life Before Nature* he told of his explaining his double helix basis to DNA, to Creek and Watson who he said didn't know much of anything about the research field. They later received a Nobel Prize for their description of Chargaff's "Double Helix" work. Chargaff was not a supporter of human's experimenting with DNA, as much of what humans say they are doing for good is applied for bad. Chargaff described a 4th Century BC Greece man that wanted his name to be immortal, thus he burned down the most beautiful temple of the time. Relative to having helped Creek and Watson be able to describe the double helix, Chargaff felt he had handed the man setting fire to the great temple the matches. He had become skeptical of human managed science and technology claiming to accomplish good for humans that only served individuals-ends while creating much bad in and for the world. A genius in science he was shunned by other scientists.

Perhaps we arrive at climate change as a more expansive version of the Chargaff concern? The highly acclaimed book of 2005, "On Bullshit," had yet to be written back then. Only later, which teaching at the Stockholm School of Economics, did I realize that: "It's the fight against shit. That's what it's all about." The PhD students I advised came to have this statement displayed on their doorways as a warning to visitors.

If you want to be a bit more serious, look deeper and wider into the context of all the above. If you still need to be entertained there are ways to look at the irreversible problems[163] in the human project, despite what Darwin promised for that project. What is this human project?

The work herein is dedicated to those fellow soldiers who were my best friends in life yet could never return home alive, due to the sad state of leadership and management in our species. It is also to the memory of those people in a nation we arrogantly attempted to manage via very bad ideas on leadership of others. My special feelings go to a beautiful young woman I was allowed to work with that became the love of my life but was sent from life due to her association with me. It's not easy. Others have suffered via similar reasoning since, but not, hopefully, removed from life.

"In May 2019, an exquisitely sensitive instrument located …. in Hawaii, recorded a terrifying

---

[163] Feynman, Richard, *The Character of Physical Law*, The MIT Press: Cambridge, Ma., 1965, Chapter 5 "The Distinction of Past and Future," p. 105.

human achievement: Thanks to our ever-increasing addiction to burning fossil fuels, the level of carbon dioxide in the Earth's atmosphere has risen to 415 parts per million. This is the highest level it has been since human beings have lived on Earth. And it is further evidence (as if further evidence were needed) of just how hell-bent we are on cooking the planet we live on."[164]

If you are too busy for such pessimistic information then you will return to your optimistic thinking via the adage of business as usual: "Fake it, till you can make it?" Clearly, for those who cannot clearly see, "rightward-thinking American citizens" view climate change to be a leftist hoax, like that covid thing before Trump took care of and cured it. Besides, if there is climate change it's the problem of those children, not we adults.

Leadership versus management offers an interesting dichotomy that provides insights into understanding both. They appear synonymous, but clearly, they are not. When you think of one you soon see the other appear, yet their hierarchical difference sponsors many problems. These problems soon get you into the differences between setting objectives and seeking results. Via such differences that shouldn't exist we humans create problems that shouldn't exist but then need "managed." Such is typical of problems created while acting as a human being attempting to be human. We often blame nature for our problems in the life that confront us. It's becoming noted that in many instances we have generated significant problems in how we relate to nature.

This immortal option of problem creation provides a revealing examination of problem management, and its potential for hopelessness. Such is very clearly articulated in Ernest Becker's' *Denial of Death*. In this Pulitzer Prize winning book of 1974, he convincingly argues how the need for immortality projects is the pathway to evil.

---

[164] "415: The Most Dangerous Number," New York: *Rolling Stone*, May 2, 2019. Lead article.

This takes us into the Faustian Bargain as a long-standing human tradition of what humans define as leadership, thus crucial to understanding management. Its essence is in the phrase that serves as the title of this book.

What is new and not part of this is recent evidence that most intractable problems, except for death, facing humans seem to be of human manufacture. Especially challenging are problems that are a consequence of an expanding war with nature. As such we face ominous problems that challenge life as created by humans working to manage problems of life. In Europe that has long been seen as the Faustian dilemma ending the Faustian tragedy. What is new is that such explains the dilemma and tragedy of how humans deal with nature, including their internal nature.

Nature has historically been seen as the dominant source of that which bothers and threatens humans, i.e., the source of their problems. More recently, we see how our battle with nature has become the major threat to the continuation of humans. What shall we do? We have long recognized the limitations in being human as seen in how we manage the nature of birth, death, war, anger, dishonesty, and love are part of human life yet beyond human management. As Ambrose Bierce commented in 1888:

> Love, n. A temporary insanity curable by marriage or by removal of the patient from the influences under which he incurred the disorder. This disease, like Caries and many other ailments, is prevalent only among civilized races living under artificial conditions; barbarous nations breathing pure air and eating simple food enjoy immunity from its ravages.[165]

Why do humans seem incapable of managing what seems important to their well-being? Is it humans or is it the ideas of man-

---

[165] Bierce, Ambrose, *The Devil's Dictionary*, New York: Hill and Wang, 1957, p. 112.

agement they elect to use? This seems important due to what we now see as unmanageable was generated by humans yet is coming to threatens removal of the species from the planet. An unruly environment is clearly threatening life as we know it. Climate change, this instability is just as clearly the result of human conduct. From forty years of research, it seems humans cannot change to avoid irreversible instability in our context that must be stable for conditions of life to continue and transfer to future generations.

Perhaps there is little humans can do to keep the climate from changing. Human behavior now behaves as a large impediment to continuation of human life, and perhaps life in general. Are humans dumb, mean-spirited, or suicidal? Perhaps they can change to improve their behavior. Assuming there is hope out there, or in here, to where should we thus look?

Most problems result from mismanagement. Wrongful management can be of context, others, and/or self. We note lower quality managers walking away saying "It's complicated," while hoping better ones are "on the way." As pacifiers we point out that historically time, space, and/or technology have arrived to compensate for managerial misconduct. These beacons of faith are thin. It seems the situation will be quite dire by 2030 and irreversibly unfortunate for life by 2050. We can no longer migrate to other parts of the planet as the problems are globally destabilizing. Those talking of a few humans moving to set up residence on another planet are mostly those who did and do create the conditions of the problem and are mostly likely to be unsuccessful in whatever they do about it, including AI technology to override human ignorance. What to do?

In 1979 I completed a research project ending in a call from industry and government leaders to move from a homo-centric way to solve environmental problems called "legal order," to a naturally fluid means to a "negotiated order" as a fluid relationship to nature. It was not well received by leadership or management. I respected and wanted to be a tree. In part this was to avoid taking seriously many of the events I was part of in churches, universities, families, governments, companies, and warfare. While life seemed promising, the human aspect seemed more than challenging. The following paragraphs outline small examples.

Let's assume, as most do, that the self is the center of it all. If not, what is the meaning of being selfish? The self focuses on the "ego," and works to keep rewards coming to self instead of the many others standing around and makes use of ever-changing skills and devices to have rewards arrive ever more quickly with time. This is a tough management job, but success brings fun to life.

That the ego might create a costly future has long been in air around humans, but such was only suggested in the early 19th Century then given clarity in the 1968 article "Tragedy of the Commons."[166] This is where individuals do harm to the future of others via feeding their self-interest against the common good of all. Such acts bring damage to the future of the good, common, or uncommon. This can endanger the well-being of others, but didn't social Darwinism tell us that such is the price of evolution of the fittest?

Thus, we have a dilemma between the ego and others. Which offers the pathway to a better future, or perhaps any human future? In this book we the planet and its atmosphere is the common good. It is known to be essential to all life on the planet. Thus, when individual acts damage that good, we see a tragedy well beyond that metaphoric concern of Goethe in 1833 where the extra sheep of an ego were using up too much of the pasture needed in common. While many thought the solution to the common pasture was to divide it up and let private ownership solve the taking care of the future problem. With climate change its difficult to divide up the atmosphere, forests, and oceans to make the ego more responsible. What shall we do? Where shall we look for a way to manage this tragedy?

The concept of tragedy awaiting individualized, ego-centered action is much older than Faustian of 1833. From ancient times it was the evil of individual gain at the expense of the common good. In 1550 Faust became the storyline in human negotiations with the devil, or his emissary. The historic dilemma of the ego versus the

---

[166] Hardin, Garrett, "The Tragedy of the Commons," Washington, D.C.: *Science*, 162, pp. 1243-1248.

society was thus refined. The individual was asked to give up the soul that governed his will to do good for the larger context in return for short-term gains. These gains were access to knowledge of everything, and access to the pleasures with the most beautiful woman imaginable. Goethe had gone deeper into this dilemma in 1831 with clarity of humans wanting to "sell their souls for immediate benefit" and then went on to argue how the end state of the process was always "tragedy."

This is now used as a metaphor to provide meaning to human actions in the short-term creating a planetary tragedy in the longer-term.

A Masculine Ideology, From the Graden of Eden

Homo-centric human logic, of the masculine ego, supports economic and political behavior that can create serious problems such as set the stage for climate change to emerge around the earth. This can be more serious than episodes of failed ego-centric management, such as world wars and economic depressions, in that the climate change process is irreversible. Herein there is evidence of how climate change began in the ego. Herein the collective process of ego management, or mismanagement, is called industrialization. Armed with the arrogance of humanism the power of the ego arose to counter life in warfare against the natural via the artificial.

The idea of the ego is useful for improving problems of management. It provides a means to examine then describe what a human is by what they do. This question emerged in 1975 in a personal way in a research project into the meaning of environmental deterioration for the human future. Funded by industry, government, and foundations it investigated the downside of the industrial process and its product. It looked at industrial pollution becoming dispersed into nature as unthoughtful, destructive, and continuous. This can be seen in the management of the industrial process as set up to produce products that feed humans as well as their egos. Since 1975 we easily see the industrial as generator of deterioration of the environment essential to life. Continuation of business as usual in feeding and managing the ego poses a large price; possibly the end of life as we know it. Can we afford the ego as a manager of human affairs?

Let us pick up that traditional dichotomy from the mind-body split. In essence the mind is managed by the ego while the body is managed by nature. With time the mind becomes increasingly artificial. As such it takes issue with and works against the natural, especially in its denial of generating conditions leading to death.[167] "The ego, in order to develop at all, must deny, must bind time, must stop the body." Entropy as operating in the 4th dimension denies the ego and its aspirations, but the ego thus denies entropy.

As such the basis for what we will come to experience as climate change consequences is created along with the means to ignore or deny it. Many ideas in the book will reference the split and long-term price human life pays for it. It is the essence of man's war on nature with the ego as man's chief weapon.

To go deeper, we see leading physical scientists talking of entropy's prime role in sending the cosmos into disorder while human arrogance assumes it can be fixed. At the World Futures Conference in 1980 Carl Sagan and I held a session on the role of legal order posed by humans in confusing lawful order in the cosmos. We argued for experimenting with a negotiated order for a humbler pathway to understand the relation between humans and natural laws. Perhaps we should thus ask those in the psychological sciences, if such exist, if humans are agents of entropy doing significant disordering on a relatively insignificant planet? Perhaps this gives them too much credit. As Hawking noted:

> *"The human race is just a chemical scum on a moderate-sized planet, orbiting around a very average star in the outer suburb of one among a hundred billion galaxies. And that I can't believe the whole universe exists for our benefit. That would be like*

---

[167] Becker, Ernest, *The Denial of Death*, 1973 Pulitzer Prize winner, New York: Free Press, 1973, p. 263.

saying that you would disappear if I closed my eyes.[168]

When motivated by the arrogance of humanism[169] we do seem to bring considerable disorder to natural systems. We do this in many ways but underlying our process is an emphasis on short-term gain while ignoring the known long-term consequences, the pain from relying on short-term dealings. This is a major theme of Faustian stories and operas since 1550. It depicts the judgments of the human ego in search of immortality. This shows the shortcoming over and over of human analytics carving up natural systemics but ending in systemic failure, not success. I use this to argue for why climate change is a long-term cost of short-term gains and how this will disorganize the human project forever unless we learn to manage differently.

Throughout human history we see termination of a society due to some or one human losing control of his ego while in search an immortality projects to transcend the idea of death. Empires come and go via this often-repeated model. Look at the Egyptian, Roman, British, American, etc. empires.

Peter Turchin argues how humans are prone to this thesis in his book: *War and Peace and War.* For him empires grow from a society being formed that shows great success in its collective action. Wealth is thus created prior to emergence of the idea of improvement via an ancient order with hierarchy of governance, then wealth, created. This creates a large class of poor workers at the disposal of the rich, thus disabling the success and then the empire. What makes today's situation different from economics and politics bringing back that ancient hierarchy is that it accompanied climate change as disorder, an irreversible change in the environment essential to planetary life.

The concern become societal-wide and becomes an issue for the human project This is especially true if the projects to avoid thinking of death insure its arrival to the species, not only the individual.

---

[168] Hawking, Stephen, TV Series, *"Reality on the Rocks,"* First aired March 6, 2016. BBC.

[169] Ehrenfeld, David, *The Arrogance of Humanism*, New York: Oxford University Press, 1978.

Many scientists have documented this as a focus for much that is wrong with humans, such as perversions, selfishness, evil and much that results in "the tragedy of the commons." Until we find a way to repair or replace this emphasis, we may want to look at the ego as a doorway for improvement in how we treat the commons on which life depends.

We learn about our identity via relationships. They define our ego and our life via continuous negotiation with dilemmas that are simply two-sided problems. In this manner we develop our all-important ego via negotiations with our environment, others, and ourselves. Deals we make with ourselves may be the most important source of identity, as well as the source of our greatest problems. The contents herein come to focus on something called climate change and its devastating role in defining the human future. This is presented as the long-term pain that is just now emerging to redefine life. The short-term gain is in the deals we make with ourselves and ourselves in the Faustian sense of selling our souls to the devil for success in meeting today's wants, while thinking souls may not exist and if they do, we can work out an AI means to recapture them.

Social resources to manage anticipated problems are legitimized and organized around institutions of education, governance, family, and business. The idea of problems awaiting us motivates youth to prepare for life while illustrating the importance of having institutions related to work, religion, love, hate, peace, governance, family, and death. As adults we like this as it sets up an immortality project with which to organize life. In this we accept the importance of leadership and management in what we might best call "the human project." A central theme for management of the human project is "short-term gain, long-term pain." Societal education that purposefully overlooks self-leadership and self-management for the convenience of being directed illustrates the attraction of short-term gain. Not being capable of individual reflection and responsibility for individual actions illustrates the cost of long-term pain.

This all relates to what we can call problem management while seeing how problems and management are accepted as keys to success. Seeming to manage problems well becomes a basis for feeling good about life. Unfortunately, some problems of life are not open to easy resolution. We seem to invest in ways to avoid thinking about or talking about these problems. In some instances, we invest more in making such problems seem less dangerous than in confronting and resolving them.

Death is a problem we try to manage via inventing religious beliefs that allow for there being life after life. Or we invest life in building an immortality project to ignore problems associated with dying. Many humans come to blame their problems on their leaders, especially those they strongly supported to become their leaders. In that way the leadership is responsible for where they go, that is wrong, not the supporters? Humans? I assume blame. Blame, for me, must lie with those failing to change their servitude to leadership. This includes managers who come to be managed by those they accept as leaders. Of course, there are leaders with no direction, but I will avoid them herein. I've studied management, worked as a manager, and been an advisor to leaders and their managers. From this I've concluded that the first three letters of management say much about the wrongfulness of many human operations. Why are men in charge? Clearly this is due to a change once we see how to many things became so questionable. I define management in a philosophic sense. Management is far more than telling others to be at work on time, to be productive, to threaten the non-obedient, then punishing them in front of others to emphasize the threat. Those thinking they are leaders, not managers, will not enjoy the contents of this book. Managers are not likely to read it. Those seeking reassurance that the human situation is not so bad, and only needs some new ideas will find the contents uncomfortable.

We might end where we began, in the idea of humans beginning to manage themselves and ignore would be leaders who promise to manage the management. Is the most serious problems are initiated in self-behavior, then management of self may be the best, even only, way to a viable future. Just now, the *human project* is not doing well. This will be outlined in the four dimensions of human existence. The four define the essence of the potentials and problems of human aspirations, failures, and consequences.

Nurturing Reawakened Values

Goethe, in his "Faust, Parts I and II," was concerned with valuation processes of men. He was especially concerned with men trading their souls in the present for painful sorrow in their future. Adam Smith encouraged the Faustian Bargaining to speed up via setting up rules to make soul selling a market where you could access ever cheaper goods for what was gained from the sold-out soul.

This is the story of short-term gains awaiting long-term pains as being developed during two thousand years. The gains made therein, especially during the past two hundred years, show remarkable problems as a result. Humans have escaped the challenges of relating to the spirit of life and moved on to the making of cheap possessions while raising the eventual price of consequences for life. We now begin to see the price to be paid for producing, selling, and using what is questionable. Change beyond us is underway around us. The result is irreversibly expensive to conditions on which life depends.

Many of us feel upset with the current and changing conditions of life and keep asking why? Why is this happening, why are things changing? We become upset with things, others, and ourselves. Who, or what, is behind all this? Others seem to think we are less than we are, or maybe we are even less than they think. In protection from all this turmoil we seek leadership to organize things, but then we find they do worse than imaginable from their selfishness. Where lies the hope?

Perhaps we find escaping into the limits of 2-D IT looping helps us? Do ego-centrically sponsored Facebook excursions make our environment seem better or simply entertain? Do we feel artificial and shallow from looking for life in the superficial as energized by the two dimensions of the digital and away from the three dimensions of the natural. The power of the dumb and mean prevails from reading 0D and 1D comments about retouched 2D images. More will be said about dimensional knowledge later in the book.

Normal Problem-Solving Flows

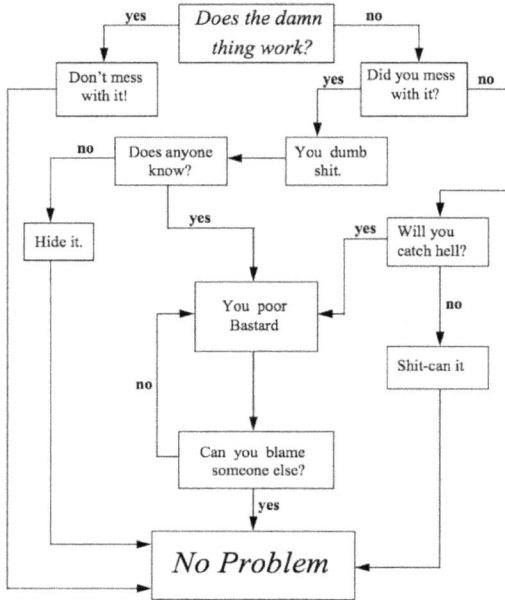

yes — Does the damn thing work? — no

Don't mess with it!

yes — Did you mess with it? — no

Does anyone know? — no

You dumb shit.

Hide it.

yes — Will you catch hell?

You poor Bastard

no

Shit-can it

no

Can you blame someone else?

yes

No Problem

Source: Unknown

Strategy For Leaders to Avoid Responsibility

The above was put together in 1981 in David Hawk's architecture studio at Iowa State University. This emerged after Hawk mentioned his being personally fired by the ISU President for supporting some items students had done to their studio space in the new design center building. The changes were a statement intending to argue for a new relation to nature, i.e., replacing a fixed window with double hung operable windows for cross-ventilation.

In some humor, the students advised Professor Hawk to think about adopting the above model to avoid continuation of his record of firings. If he became sufficiently good at navigating the above maze he could become like the ISU President. Hawk's design studio was well-known in the schools of design and engineering. Over its entry doorway was a student composed banner about what seemed to occur in traditional classes: "It's Very Hard to Kill a Talent."

Can we manage differently via appreciating what we value comes to reflect on the value of humans. Are modern humans restricted to watching one dimensional truth as portrayed on two-dimensional TV? Is there more hope in the Silicon Valley emergence of two-dimensional attractions pretended a three-dimensional reality? Can we trust the results of those on an entrepreneurial mission with their guidance system saying, "Fake it, until you make it." At least such is trusted in California and Texas.

Humans are born with deep-seated fears about life, especially their own, and how they will pass through episodes of pain on their way to a death. While ever more focused on an egocentric journey they become less concerned about the mortality of surrounding systems of life. They forget the mortality caused by the deterioration they created. They watch the surrounding environment move through stages of deterioration into destruction yet show limited concern for it, and choose to tolerate leadership that salutes the destruction, including their own episodes of self-leadership. In many obituaries and funerals humans are praised for their acts that contributed greatest to entropy.

The above is explained in some detail in the 2005 Pulitzer Prize winning book on the source of evil, "Denial of Death" by Ernest Becker. The 4th dimension provides the pathway to deterioration of the soul via seeking projects of immortality to compensate for anger about mortality built into nature. Must humans contribute to their temporal end state in this way? While contributing, many see time as change, and their great opponent in the struggle for happiness. Many would just as soon see time and its associated uncertainties and instabilities simply stop moving. Change via time is bothersome to what humans do. They dream of the stability implied by changelessness defined as culture. Culture is a platform of implied permanence where penalties for those violating its rules can be great.

The dilemma is that, even if culture and its traditions promise stability the surrounding environment continues to change, thus humans reach for the strange idea of changelessness. This involves putting change and nature on hold, via storing the change as waste disposal. Change is to then be dealt with later. These forces of change that arise from such dumps can be dramatic and harsh. They began as instability (drought then heavy rain), turn to environmental turbulence (tornadoes and hurricanes), then transform into a vortex environment like a Hawking black hole (nothing on the other side like what was sucked in). The early stages of climate change, as we see them in 2021, can be seen as heading towards turbulent conditions. A vortex will arrive later for systems of life on the planet, not just for the humans that initiated it.

Some irony is within this book. Humans want to ensure stability as they work to meet bio-needs and psych wants. They don't notice that the processes that develop such also ensure their death. Yes, this pattern assures the stability found in death. The more we stabilize changelessness, the more we ensure the emergence of drastic change. This is beginning to be seen as a rule. As such, humans terrorized by change face unwanted, uninsurable, and unmanageable change. Are the forces of nature bored with humans, or genuinely angry with human behavior? Can humans change their appreciation of change?

We see this in the technological development created to ensure a safe life, normally called industrialization. The machines we design and build, the energy sources we tap into to operate them, and how we assign them a mission to draw from and thus deteriorate the natural illustrates this. Any capability to "change" this, or manage the consequences, seems beyond men capability to embrace the natural. Can feminine leadership replacing masculine force fields do better at management. Are humans simply hopeless?

Feminine Valuation: Differences for Making a Difference

To address this question, we will call the manly approach "business as usual." The feminine will be called "business as unusual." The first fears change, the second is change. Great minds have proposed or exhibited the unusual, but they are rare. They include humans such as Socrates and Joan of Arc. They led a battle for improvement via change but were eventually seen as unstable and too radical for a calm society. Both were often referenced as heretics. Both faced death by authorities in a stable society that claiming to act via what was just. They were used as examples of what humans should not do to destabilize definitions of contemporary society. Leadership of time preferred the ideas of change management, i.e., changelessness, posed by the thinking and acting of humans like Greece's Aristotle and England's Adam Smith were very likeable. Both men seem continuously masculine and acted consistently with the leadership of the day. The first group, Socrates and Joan of Arc, were concerned with the soul and how to nurture it, as well as supporting and learning about the natural environment. The second two, Aristotle and Smith, came to support changelessness out there but increasing wealth for themselves. In this way business as usual could rationally continue forever. They argued how too much change too soon would turn radical and thus destabilize history.

> Rejecting a Garden of Eden-type narrative for the origins of farming also means rejecting, or at least questioning, the gendered assumptions lurking behind that narrative. Apart from being a story about the loss of primordial innocence, the Book of Genesis is also one of history's most enduring charters for the hatred of women, rivalled only (in the Western tradition) by the prejudices of Greek authors like Hesiod, or for that matter Plato. It is Eve, after all, who proves too weak to resist the exhortations of the crafty serpent and is first to bite the forbidden fruit, because she is the one who desires knowledge and wisdom. Her punishment (and for all women following her) is to bear children in severe pain and live under the rule of her husband, whose own destiny is to subsist by the sweat of his brow."[170]

---

[170] Graber, David $ Wengrow, David, *The History of Everything: A New History of Humanity*, New York: Farrar, Straus and Giroux, 2019, p. 236.

Every now and then something tries to wake humans. Strange questions begin to emerge in our minds that become stranger over time, and less funny. In the Goethe sense of our understanding life, we feel the presence of a soul, that which traditional psychology tells us does not exist. Whatever we call it, something outside the traditional dimensions of existence is there. Herein we will accept that while it does not exist it is none-the-less there. It's part of the non-rational aspects of human existence. We will say it comes from the 5th dimension regardless of where it is. This is a place for reconciliation and a different form of growth. Much of what follows comes from there.

We humans strive to make our being more important than reality allows but this too is okay. We don't know how else to invest our limited time. Yes, our physical nature is important, but such comes mostly from our thoughts about death and thus management of the in between. Death is a continual endangerment to who and what we think we are, and then what we define as being human. We clearly do not transcend death, yet we believe we can. Many of us devote many resources to immortality projects while we are alive, and this seems unfortunate. In addition to such being the basis for rationalizing evil, and thus the reason for dispensing with the soul, it also consumes many systems of life that run parallel to the life of humans. The nature of life is transient, not permanent. There are many phenomenal books on the subject[171]. While all have humorous sections, they were not written in humor. They describe the sad relation between immortality, evil and humans. The 5th dimension does not offer a kind resting place for those passing through the 4th. If you have trouble with such ideas, that's fine. I too have trouble with it. As said before, I'm mostly writing this to myself, and I don't know who I am.

This book is different. It is about the subject of life but concentrates on the price of investments made for continuance of the

---

[171] There are several books on the dilemma of death, and how the questions of dying and death override much else. These include Goethe's *Faustian Tragedy, Part II*, Celine's *Death on the Installment Plan*, and Becker's *Denial of Death*. Socrates and Joan of Arc also confronted the dilemma of death but were punished by their social group for their clarity.

human aspect. Herein, human life is seen as short-term while the investment to expand it comes from the long-term and is paid for by larger systems of life. Thus, human life is paid for by death of larger systems that provide its context. This is called climate change.

Philosophy and literature have long negotiated with a paradox that becomes the dichotomy of being human, often known as human beings arguing over how best to see reality. Do you see what matters more clearly as a rationalist or an empiricist? Each interpret reality differently. The first invests much in the idea of mental reasoning then testing via closing the senses. The second schedules regular visits to his optometrist and otolaryngologist to better sense what is, isn't and can't be. Much of human existence is felt, explained, and managed via one of these two choices.[172]

Herein you will find a different approach. Taking one or the other is clearly insufficient to guide human conduct in the richness of life. Insufficiency is all around us and growing under the title of climate change. The approach taken herein is: "both plus more." We accept the essence of each and avoid arguing over which better manages human affairs. Combined, the two are seen to be clearly insufficient to the challenges of the present, and problem of the past, although in the past we could use time or space to move from the trauma of our miscalculations. Information technology has redefined time and extensive breeding has shrunk the space between humans with strong feelings about each other.

Herein, the idea of more offers more hope than historic empiricism and contemporary rationalism. For purposes herein we will label the more as the *non-rational*. It combines aspects of the other two then occupies the potential in the 5th dimension. If this seems difficult, it will get worse, although via the cumulative debts of humans being human climate change will be a lot worse.

In the 19th Century humans dreamed that improvement of life, via Darwin's knowledge, would override deterioration from the industrial. A century later Claude Shannon argued how informa-

---

[172] Churchman, W. & Ackoff, R.L., *Methods of Inquiry*, St. Louis: Educational Publishers, 1950, this was Ackoff's dissertation as co-written with his advisor.

tion technology could become "neg-entropy" and thus overcome the entropic limit noted by Einstein. Now, in 2022, we begin to think production and purchase of an electric cars will finally allow human access to the long promised perpetual machine. And so on and so on, until climate change sets the record straight for the arrogance of humanism.

Regardless, we continue to read the *Economist* and think of ways to improve the productivity of short-term gains while avoiding evidence of the approaching long-term pain. We avoid seeing the differences that make a difference.

The above questions become more relevant with time. They go far to open the serious challenges for the future, and their unfolding meaning. Via storms more turbulent than normal we see stores filled with our short-term dreams washed away. During sleepless nights we think about life during expanded turbulence of context. Our dreams of information technology evolve from Marshall McLuhan's 1964 insight, or concern that: "The media is the message." The implication of those building empires of information management technology has since been: "Ignore content." Gregory Bateson added a touch of his special humor to the emerging situation in 1973: "Humans are going to need to be more predictable, or the machines will become angry and kill them." The essence as well as limits of AI can be seen in the limits of Aristotle's idea of logic based on strict rationality, then expanded to monitor obedience to such. The 90% of reality we call the non-rational waits on the edges.

To Clean Up the Industrial

This book is somehow about management, and addressed how humans came to create ideas of management, how they have come to apply it, then adapt it to develop and maintain industrialization, then developed information technology to manage ever more. History documents how with time the Faustian bargain, then Tragedy, became a center piece of managerial negotiations.

Important to this was and is the idea of leadership, who should lead, where should they lead others to, and how should they practice such. Following is a list of some of the more noteworthy ideas about management by, for and of humans. Except for the third comment, a more pessimistic one, these are selected relative to a very select relative to values yet are widely known in management education.

1. "A leader is best when people barely know he exists, when his work is done, his aim fulfilled, they will say: we did it ourselves." Lao Tzu, 6th Century BC

2. "...for the time being I gave up writing – there is already too much truth in the world – an overproduction which apparently cannot be consumed!" (Otto Rank statement of Feb. 8, 1933, in Jessie Taft's biography, *Otto Rank*, Julian Press: NY, 1958, p. 175.)

3. "We the unwilling, led by the unqualified, to kill the unfortunate, die for the ungrateful." David Hawk, Hue, Vietnam, February 1968, Comment for which he was charged with insubordination.

4. "Management is doing things right; leadership is doing the right things." Peter Drucker, in a lecture to the Systems Science Program, Wharton School, 1975.

5. "We the selfish, managed by the ignorant, to control the creative, are criticized by the dumb. Where lies the hope." (David Hawk, a farewell lecture to my NJIT student-friends, organized by the student body. "The Importance of It's Too Late," November 2009.)

The fifth lecture was optimistic. It described how we should prepare to take advantage of the brief period when a situation opened to change due to leaders thinking it was too late for their presence. It was outlined in examples of the brief by significant opportunity to being desirable change. When it's too late the management that created the problem usually steps down or disappears to save their resume. At that time there is an opportunity for much change. I offered many examples of such in corporate management with companies I had advised. The lecture opened with three comments. Students recorded them.

> "My confused education offered me the opportunity to study non-rational, non-national, non-causal approaches to problems and those who initiate and continue them. Such allowed me to meet fascinatingly coherent people who cared, as well as the strategically deceptive. I feel badly that much education and most educators do not understand what this means. Before their studies students tend to understand.
>
> I occupy a bi-polar platform where I teach in two disciplines: architecture and business. Each has limited knowledge of itself and little respect for the other, or for systems of life including humans.
>
> NJIT was my home base for a long time. I began as a stealth professor (frequently being outside the US). I then was asked to serve as a dean. I took the job to help the school become accredited. Graduates needed that for their resumes for most jobs and all applications to further school. I trusted students more than the schools' professors and administrators. I agreed to help the school with the help of its students."

Considering this it was proposed that we move from masculine management to management of the feminine, using feminine as a value set not a sex object. As such a case is made for finding or developing at 21st Century Joan of Arc that will demonstrate a shift from man-age-ment to fem-age-ment. Perhaps we need a Joan of Arc in Business Management, to remove the emphasis on the MAN in the history of management and managing. We need someone more appreciative of context and sensitive to eventual consequences from ever more immediate investments, designs, actions, and desire for results. This would allow experimentation with values of the feminine, not the history emphasis on power and masculinity with limited reflection and intelligence.

In July 2015 I began to be concerned about such a larger number of my Iowa farming community rising to support Donald Trump and the values he espoused. Thus, I developed a website for creating a foundation that would help recovery once Trump had initiated his version of leadership. It would offer fundamental change for how humans addressed their relations to nature, and each other. Many human problems stem from a Newtonian version of industrialization where the consequences are finally noted. That pathway and its consequences seemed to portend a severe end like what Carl Sagan prophesized in 1995.

> "I have a foreboding of an America in my children's or grandchildren's time — when the United States is a service and information economy; when nearly all the key manufacturing industries have slipped away to other countries; when awesome technological powers are in the hands of a very few, and no one representing the public interest can even grasp the issues; when the people have lost the ability to set their own agendas or knowledgeable question of those in authority; when, clutching our crystals and nervously consulting our horoscopes, our critical faculties in decline, unable to distinguish between what feels good and what's true, we slide, almost without noticing, back into superstition and darkness."

Carl suggested there to be rather ugly relations between humans and nature, others, and selves in our futures. Such seemed to use the

Garden of Eden story to clarify Darwinian values linked to "survival of the fittest, not fattest." The masculine was seen as the most fit. All three domains of relations were in trouble. Life as nature presented it was being endangered via human thoughts and acts. Environmental deterioration, climate changes, a growing passion for warfare from migration and superficial differences in human groups was creating a psychosis in social organizations. This was most noticeable in the tradition of leadership beginning to resemble a state that can only be seen as leadershit.

I felt our last best hope lay in the documented intellects of several of Ackoff's friends and allies. This included those like Sir Geoffrey Vickers in his appreciative systems expose of valuing intolerance and building social groups around it. He suggested how when you dig deeper into a value set you find the opposite set and thus need to go beyond opposition, as outlined in "Freedom in a Rocking Boat." This was consistent with Hasan Ozbekhan's advice from his mentor R.G. Collingwood in "Metaphysics." This pointed to a difference that would make a difference, as Bateson outlined in "Steps to an Ecology of Mind."

The Foundation was not to be a man-woman argument. Some women, e.g., Thatcher, act-out via masculine values as much as some men exhibited values of the feminine, e.g., Goethe. It was soon discovered that the main opposition to such a Foundation came from those heavily invested in being strategic. The Foundation came to be clarified about the image of Joan of Arc. She had long been my Heroine, as Socrates had been my hero. Russ was less enamored with her than I but did propose her as an example of a "Subjective-Externalizer." "Joan of Arc was as dedicated to changing her environment as any of John Wayne's characters, but unlike them she was driven from within, reacting to an inner voice of vision rather than an external situation.

This depiction was highly objective in nature. I instead relied on a subjective appraisal from Mark Twain. He spent two years in France doing extensive review of her life, and death. In two volumes, Twain argued how she was significant to the human project: "It took six thousand years to produce her; her like will not be seen in the earth again in fifty thousand". - Personal Recollections of Joan of Arc. "She is easily and by far the most extraordinary person the human race has ever produced." Saint Joan of Arc.

The Eternal Feminine Foundation is to prepare a new type of leadership for continuing tragedies from values of the masculine attitude towards nature. There is an English website at EternalFeminine. org. Its main site is in Chinese. It is to be far different from training gained in working for an MBA. If a title would be needed, it might be an MCM, Masters in Consequential Management. Officially begun in 2016, it attracted about $650 million from Chinese leaders with no sons to take over their organizations.

To Nurturing Projects, not Dominating Them

Prior to my being fired as dean, by the university president, I had organized several summer jobs for the school's management faculty. Those who would teach in the Fall Semester would spend one three months in a company hiring the school's students. The proposed gains for professors, students and companies were obvious. Students and companies were especially excited about learning from experiments in this activity. NJIT Leadership was not.

This was one of twenty-five reasons for why I was fired by the university president, with his governor's support. They felt students and companies didn't know enough to be involved in education. School administration stated: "If the students knew anything they would not be here." The students and I agreed. The companies lined up to hire the faculty part time were disappointed that the research project didn't work out.

Now we should experiment with another approach, perhaps a Masters of Consequential Management (MCM), and away from the approach long seen in the Master of Business Administration (MBA). Let's begin the challenge by looking into the idea of management and come to appreciate its meaning. What does it mean to say you are a manager in 2021? Is it meaningful to the social collective, or only to the individual as manager? If its meaning has evolved, has it been in the direction of becming more meaningful, or less so? Is it important for business education programs to offer degrees in management? Or should degrees in business administration drastically change and shift to teaching about consequential management from former administration towards improved productivity results? Is it time to question that much business management has focused on doing the wrong things ever more productively?

Should MBA (Master of Business Administration) education become upgraded into MCAs (Mastering Consequential Activities) learning? (Key is how education is to memorize answers and learning is to ask the difficult questions.) Should the objective of business be winning at any cost, e.g., continual increases in productivity, or should the agenda shift to the stewardship of context, e.g., care for life and its mortality, not the quest for autonomous immortality of leaderships?

Satisfying Bio-Needs Via Controlling Psycho-Wants

Humans have *needs*. Some are tangible, others tend to be more ephemeral. The tangible ones are more bio-centered, to provide a baseline for living via good and shelter. Failure therein endangers life. The tangibility found therein supports forever discussion of quantities and qualities of foods and shelters, yet to be hungry and/or homeless is beneath debate.

The ephemeral is of a different logical type. Measures of success in locating such, describing qualities therein, and/or securing such wants tends to be more attractive and exhausting. Herein we will denote needs as psycho. We can be unsure of having them as well as wanting them once we do have them. The desires for psycho needs fulfillment can come to control the bio necessities as well as life. In the domain of climate change they can be seen to initiate processes that clearly end in climate change consequences.

Relative to the subjects found herein, the difference between the tangible and ephemeral are crucial to what and who humans are and our creation of opportunities for and dangers in life. Ephemeral needs tend to originate in wants beyond fulfillment of needs. The situation is like getting up from a nice dinner and wondering what awaits me now? The human troubles for life on earth thus begins.

Last, but not least, is the variable we might best call time. Time is the initiator and marker of change. Bio-needs and psycho wants to evolve during time and change no matter how many resources we might put in the process to keep them from changing, or at least appear to be forever changeless. Key in this process is what we have come to call management. We depend on methods of managing all the above where the strengths and weaknesses of such are seen in the traits of the first three letters. Herein we will see how this has presented us with a context filled with climate change consequences. As such we need to reconsider the role of those first three letters, "man." Each day this becomes more urgent as some cultures and several nations move to emphasize the characteristics of "man" in preparing for the consequences of that which he brought to the change of context.

Wants offer access to understanding how the "needing to have more than you do" emerges. The wanting encourages humans to exceed limitations seen in natural process of the biocentric. They call for situation change, not change of self. We come to know them as *wants*. They exceed rationalized existence of needs as defined over thousands of years and were "clarified" in Newtonian logic and Darwinian existence.

The ephemeral can be elusive and even stretch towards the infinite. You may have noticed how satisfaction in attaining what is wanted is transitory, and temporary. One more shopping trip helps to redefine, rise above restrictions, erase restraints, and reset rule-systems. That window into the infinite and mystical, as well as ambiguous, is not easily satisfied. Marketing provides the glass in the window. Later I will explain the negative-entropy nature of that glass, and therefore the creator of climate change.

Armed with the infinite we expand our horizons to design immortality projects to get ahead of limitations imposed by nature. These projects promise transcendence of death, although do tap into an evil that can destroy the context essential to beginnings of life.

Becker describes this in his 1973 Pulitzer Prize winning book[173]. I relied on his thesis to organize a 1975 project on why humans feel a need to desecrate the nature that locks them into a death. When in our desecration values we humans can go so far as to begin belief in negative entropy. This was humorously described by Celine in his more than insightful book[174] on the failures arising from failed human aspirations.

From Celine we see how humans come to initiate wars against nature, others, or any who fail to respect them and their wants. He raises the meaning of what we might currently call a Donald Trump style of leadership. Armed with the ephemeral humans can more to argue about the meaning of the ephemeral in love and hate, and the passageway it offers to heaven or hell. In an ephemeral manner Celine proposed the essence of an entrepreneurial business competition. Humans were invited to pay to enter a competition to win in design of a negative entropy technology. A large reward was promised to whoever would discover what was impossible in the universe. Celine's scheme would bring much pride to the thinking of today's Wall Street managers in marketing investment in negative entropy to support future human existence. Creation and management of the ephemeral offers great potential for being human while extended our dreams of what it means to be a human being.

While searching for life's meaning and/or gaining control over life we tap the ephemeral to expand our dreams. In so doing we consume ever larger quantities of context, that which is essential to continued life. Keep in mind that in so doing we act to endanger continuance of life. This is the key problem of 2023. When humans are confronted with a serious threat to continuance of life they often turn back to help from the rationality that created the prior technology that generated what we now call climate change, and/or diseases.

Humans generally try to forget the role of the prior technology in coming to create the conditions that created current challenges.

[173] Becker, Ernest, *The Denial of Death*, New York: Free Press, 1973.
[174] Celine, Louis-Ferdinand, *Death on The Installment Plan*, New York: New Directions Publishing, 1952.

They even become excited about promises that newer technology will solve the shortcomings of the prior technology. Electric automobiles to replace CO_2-generating gas automobiles are to eliminate the CO_2-problems, except for the production issues of electric powered cars. To see such dilemmas moving forward to resolve backward problems we need to investigate what we call the non-rational. Holding 90% of reality, this is where we see the interesting alternatives to the rational models causing the consequences we now fear. Humans need to pass beyond the limits of the rational. When they fail in this, they soon encounter the meaning of the irrational. While operating in the irrational humans tend to destroy more life than they came to endanger by their acts of unaided-rationality, unaided by the power of the non-rational including art, poetics, cutting-edge science, etc.

Strict rationality encourages pursuance of the self-centered. As such the versions of the ephemeral they use are ego-centric to the extreme then we choose they as our leaders so they can apply passion to our problems, thus making the problems worse. The consequences of such come to threatened life's continuance. Their irrationality then worsened the situation with further divisions of socio-political intents which were never holistic in the first place. Humans have a problem. Maybe humans are the problem?

When negotiating relations between the technological and natural, relying on religious teachings that stated natural resources were for human use, there will be troubles. These are now as apparent as they are irreversible. Something must change in human faith in changelessness if life is to continue. If humans can't change, then we will become changed. A human flow is a bias toward short-term gains in avoidance of seeing costs awaiting in the longer-term.

To study this phenomenon a research project was initiated in 1975 while at the Stockholm School of Economics:

> "Having developed industrialization as a seriously flawed model we begin life among the con-

sequences of its limits and the harm it poses to that life it was to have supported."[175]

Our need for food, water, air, and shelter, and tools is clear. From their consumption we stand up, move around, and speculate on how great we are, then move to what to do with our greatness. In so doing we access those less-tangible, more ephemeral, aspects of life, or we move to invent them. In Jung's depiction we make use of a)thinking, b)feeling, c)sensing and d)intuition to gain access to life and its meaning. We begin with meeting those needs mentioned before, then move to the wanting which takes us to the finding of purpose relative to the meaningful. We move down the highway to self-importance to an expansion of self, and go easy on thoughts about community, goodness to others, and caring for context. A report by the United National in 2022 updates the 1975 comment above.

> Human-induced climate change is causing dangerous and widespread disruption in nature and is affecting the lives of billions of people around the world, says this Intergovernmental Panel on Climate Change (IPCC) report. People and ecosystems least able to cope are being hardest hit. Increased heatwaves, droughts and floods are already exceeding plants and animals' tolerance thresholds, driving mass mortalities in species such as trees and corals. These weather extremes simultaneously occur, causing cascading impacts that are increasingly difficult to manage. They expose millions of people to acute food and water insecurity…[176]

---

[175] Hawk, David, "Environmental Desecration: Analytic Solutions in Search of Synthetic Problems," research prospectus for IIB, Stockholm School of Economics, Institute of International Business Publication, 1975.

[176] "Climate Change 2022: Impacts, Adaption, Vulnerability," Intergovernmental Panel on Climate Change. From the introduction.

To better appreciate how all this happened we might best accept including the idea of the soul in the discourse, as it is a powerful link of the individual human into a context. Without such the potential for meaning is lost. Goethe is key in clarifying this. He centered on the lost soul of the human as key to the human being lost. This was very clearly expressed in his play on Faustian Bargaining as it led to a Faustian Tragedy, which is key to understanding the meaning behind and within this book.

The story of the Faustian struggle brings the long-term perspective from culture into seeing our 21st Century troubles with climate change as they originated with the 19th Century bargaining our ancestors did with a particular model of science and technology. They went on to extensively use it to create a model of industrialization. In it we developed a route to technological development that emphasized ever shorter-term gains in support of dreams of immortality of humans. These came to advance the downside of physical reality by adding to the historic entropic process formalized in 1854. This was just prior to a woman's sincere warning in 1856 of climate change arising from the downside of the path to industrialization that humans were going down. The men of the day, and since, ignored her intelligence as advanced.

Humans went on to create their fantasies of investing "negative-entropy" via ramped up entrepreneurship. Even if it was never actually invented it could be used to market the selected model of the industrial, in support of ephemeral ideals of prestige, power, and performance. Faust teaches us that there would be costs for these short-term gains.

Important herein is that whatever we find to be wrong we have gone beyond the coffee shop chatter of Darwin's 1859 science.[177] Yes, that provided a guidebook for many over many years about interpretations on species evolution. The survival of the fittest is now trivialized as social Darwinism in the face of industrialized climate change.

---

[177] Darwin, Charles, *On the Origin of Species by Means of Natural Selection, or the Preservation of Favoured Races in the Struggle for Life*, London: John Murray edition.

Talk has now shifted to who will write the last book of humans: "*The End of the Species.*"

Sir Geoffrey Vickers advised using the appreciative construct to better organize the non-rational domain. His use of the appreciative was directed at context, not the selfishness of the self. In his *Freedom in a Rocking Boat* he described how self-centered ideas of delight, love, hate, and arrogance had come to absorb the human mind. From such we move to fill our self-centered dreams of power and leadership via self-arousal. Failing in leadership of self, as most do, humans then move on to being led by others. In this way they can blame others for the assured failures from bad leadership.

Can humans find a way to restore self-management in an appreciated context, not self-centered management of others? The Vickers book mentioned above was about Americans who worshipped self and freedom to act as desired at the moment above caring for and about context. He recommended Americans go for a ride in a small boat, then alone with their freedom at sea, they encounter a storm and need to learn how survival depends on context, such as linkage to other boats to ride out the storm.[178]

Basic needs tend to be biocentric and essential to the physicality of being alive. To meet these, humans negotiate with nature on a stage-set. This allows them to be in the plays of life. Humans can prance around on a stage proclaiming the glories of their freedom to meet needs and seek whatever wants. On this stage imagination takes over and become psychocentric, perhaps even psychedelic prior to being psychiatric.[179]

We reflect on all this via the culture in poems, songs, books, and movies. With such we gain access to negotiating with higher forms of meaning or can arrogantly reflect on the lower forms of culture such as marketing and/or advertising political furniture that prom-

---

[178] Not in his book but discussed in a meeting with him, while I was a student in the Wharton School, University of Pennsylvania in the Fall of 1974.

[179] One of my professors in the Annenberg School, U of Pennsylvania, Erwin Goffman, devoted his life to explaining why and how this takes place in the individual and the society. See his *The Presentation of Self in Everyday Life*, New York: Doubleday Books, 1959.

ises receiving wants with small capital costs followed by no maintenance costs. In all instances the longer-term costs can become significant and extensive, and illustrate the meaninglessness, or hollowness,
of life relative to acquiring wants. As such the youthful dreams of
managing the ephemeral are clouded by the costs that arise in their
future. Following is a more poetic way of saying what was just said.

Wants are important but seeking to fulfill them can generate
obstacles for fulfillment of needs, even eliminating their availability.
There are secondary costs to most things. They may not be initially
obvious when in the land of wants, or even never traceable, but they
exist. Such was the essence of the timeless tale clearly told by Goethe
in his Faustian dramas becoming tragedies as mentioned before. This
was where the hero of the opera wanted a real life and wanted it soon
than later, thus he traded access to his soul in life to the devil to gain
quick access to knowledge, a beautiful woman, and then wealth. As
the idea of soul was so ambiguous and distant it was easy to trade
it off. Such is like the daily enjoyment of driving around in a large
SUV with beautiful seats and a beautifully looking partner on one.
It's a great time and place to talk about climate change destroying the
future for the children in the back seat.

This does not mean achieving our wants is against longer-term
interests, even survival, but we might rethink our wants. Basic needs
tend to be more obvious to evaluate as they are biocentric. They are
of physicality in being and staying alive. As said before, these allow
humans to mentally move on from the basis they provide to identifying and achieving wants. We might best see these as psychocentric in
that some take these wants back to being central to their life, perhaps
more basic than the basic needs. Some, making fun of human shortcomings, including ideas of leadership, that soon seem psychedelic.

Unforeseen, or ignored, consequences of gaining results can be
expensive as well as expansive. These seem to lie in the background of
human affairs. They are energized by the homocentric then become
an ultimate determinate of success, or failure. They show no direct
connection to an initial meeting of needs and having of wants. They
can become very powerful, even manage to terminate life on our

planet. They are the world of consequences, and concern for them is central to the intent and contents of this book.

Outside the Limitations of Management

"There lives more faith in honest doubt, Believe me, then in half the creeds."[180]

We now face-down the end of an era. In the warm afterglow of considerable success in developing and using modern management principles we have a soft uncertainty that something important is wrong. We sense a transformation is underway, but are unsure if it is in our interest, or even if we have anything to say about it. In many respects this is akin to the feeling of many successful national and regional businesses that are attempting to fit themselves out into rapidly changing global conditions.

The track record of renewal through adaptation is not good. Even in the sciences, the home ground of change agents, there is little sign of active adaptation and internal renewal. Several noteworthy scientists noted late in the game how their branch of the scientific tree improved more from the mortality of the old than the training and retraining of the young, i.e., old scientists don't change their minds.[181] Another way to state this is that learning is extremely difficult, especially if you are intelligent.[182] What then does this mean for business organizations?

---

[180] Alfred Lord, *In Memoriam*:

[181] This became a central subject in one session of a 1985 meeting of the American Association for the Advancement of Science.

[182] Consistent with the theme in Plato's "Allegory of the Cave," Erwin Chargaff wrote about the situation of science and science in universities in his retirement book titled the *Heraclitan Fire*. (New York: Warner Books, 1978) This work is most beneficial to those who have the greatest optimism for scientific process. Chargaff is widely known for his 1940s discovery of "base-pairing" and the "complementarity principle," which Creek and Watson gained during their interview of him in their run-up to a Nobel prize. "I told them all I know. If they had heard before about the pairing rules, they concealed it. But as they did not seem to know much of anything, I was not unduly surprised...When I

EIBA, the European International Business Academy, began with the aesthetic flare of a young rebel in a style not unlike that used by several of EIBA's founding members to launch their successful academic careers. The early members were seen to stand against "traditional" business administration education, such as the standard fare arriving from "North American." The Europeans, and the few disloyal Americans that were involved, felt that Europe somehow could do better and come up with less parochial models for business management in Europe. Several intriguing and largely untested ideas emerged from EIBA's early membership that are now a legacy to its early years. Among the ideas were:

- That economic exchange was becoming increasingly internationalized.
- That culture was a key determinant of economic success, and failure.
- That specialization of function was a limited and limiting construct.
- That a systems approach was less dangerous than reductionism.
- That the religion of Harvard case-method teaching might be flawed.
- That we know truly little about the concept of competition.
- That headquarters-subsidiary relations are not necessarily hierarchical, or friendly, and that Ownership does not necessarily result in control.

EIBA (European International Business Academy) helped turn these issues into researchable topics during a two-decade period. At the same time EIBA attracted people who were more comfortable with criticism than reverence. In addition, EIBA people had a nice sense of humor - especially about their own work. I, as a semi-outsider, was continually impressed with the humility with which EIBA members would articulate new variables of management, prior to

---

was asked later why I had not discovered the celebrated model...my answer has always been that I was too dumb." p. 103.

their eventual legitimization through "proper discovery" in U.S.[183] and Asian circles.[184] Early on EIBA didn't care about who was the father of these ideas, but recently it has begun acting more serious about the importance of authorship, references (homage) and standards. Perhaps this is because EIBA is beginning to be perceived by others as "important" - as an establishment of rigorous business research and education. Even more dangerous, it may have started seeing itself in the same light. Some of its members now argue that EIBA qualifies for membership in the "mainstream."[185]

I will suggest in this paper why and how EIBA should temper its enthusiasm over its status. While there is merit in formalizing its gains and clarifying the differences between what's in and what's out there is a price to be paid for this new-found security. This situation is instructive because in many respects it is the same for the companies with which we work and conduct research:

- Is (your firm) a nimble, learning organization, like those now ascribed to in most scholarly papers?
- Does (your firm) move quickly to continually create exciting normative futures? Or,
- Is (your firm) prone to seek the peace, stability, and restfulness that changelessness implied?

---

[183] There are numerous examples of this process. One was the 1985 meeting of EIBA where a Wharton Professor took great issue with allowing "culture" into business analysis. This might open "Pandora's' box." The next year he began devoted much of his writing to the critical importance of culture and other phenomena that appears to have escaped from the "box." Of course, he never remembered the 1985 EIBA meeting. These events are of course trivial but the process they imply is fundamental to EIBA and its members.

[184] This is where Japanese business circles only believe things that have been translated by "their own." In February 1990 I gave a lecture to approximately 300 business and government leaders, where one point was the 1960s Perlmutter model of how companies become global by transcending their ethnic and regional presuppositions, and how this was a dilemma for Japanese firms. Later it was explained to me that what I had talked about was an idea of Professor Nonaka, not Perlmutter.

[185] As was stated by an NYU business professor in a dissertation defense, "These EIBA related doctoral students aren't too bad, depending on your standards."

- Does (your firm) want to become large enough that it creates change for others, and thus need to worry less about adapting to change?

While organizational philosophy is slanted towards one and two our actions clearly favor three and four. Today's EIBA has remnants of its once-radical past but shows signs of a being drawn into the comfortable and quiet slipstream of its big brothers of business education across the Atlantic. In their rush to pump up their importance the American "Academies" only afford questions that have clear (as in a hollow bell), and short (as in statistical soundbite), answers.[186]

The drift towards U.S. business beliefs has been especially clear in the EIBA papers of the last three years. Many papers relied heavily on and attempted to further develop concepts that are mainstream to the U.S. where business professors find them comfortable, companies find them harmless, and students find them uninteresting. Several U.S. firms, considered to be leaders by the same professors, see the concepts as humorous,[187] although this seems not to daunt their use by the professors.

EIBA assembles once each year to seek the essence of what a small set of current management models mean but end up illustrating the limits of what gets accepted as teaching and learning in business classes. EIBA's past and future is implicit in its members and explicit in its members papers. We say we want greater excellence while commemorating the excellence of what we do, all the while ending up with a well-worn set of propositions and responses. With time there is less productive humor and fewer heretics with a knack for putting

---

[186] Information exchange at these meetings often goes like: "How do you make a better profit?" "You begin with a really sexy core competence than rip their head off, before you eat their lunch and then spit out what you don't like.

[187] The situation in U.S. business schools, as reported in virtually all business publications during the past two years, is not unlike that seen in 1950s biology labs in university being used to train students to work in bio-technology firms, or the very new computer engineering curricula suddenly being judged as irrelevant to an industry that now looks to biology instead of mechanics for its models. *Science* magazine has regular articles on both disciplines and their dilemmas.

the proper labels on things. We try to use the best means to seek the best knowledge about what is "best." Unfortunately, this soon gets reduced to peer review and its well-documented limitations. As is widely accepted, and perhaps secretly desired, the process of peer review diminishes the variety of people and propositions to approximately zero. This trait of peer review is well known in national science policy circles, and sometimes used as the rationale for why peer review works. More recent reports use the same trait to describe why it doesn't work.[188] There must be a better way to encourage and identify innovation.

Beyond Business-as-Usual

Is core competence a strategy for success, or a pretense of consistency with which to face uncertainty? A contemporary strategy for management success, for those writing books for confused students and consulting for confused companies, is to advocate that they move ever more to a clearly specify and define "core competence." Many consulting/teaching/ managing careers have been built on this item of a general repertoire of management responses. Core competence is a recipe for many personal success stories.[189] Some members of the core competency group accept that the concept has a history

---

[188] Both US and European science organizations, such as the National Science Foundation, worry about how best to encourage and locate cutting edge technology development via a process that many have found to intrinsically discourage it. Two serious problems with using publications as a criterion is that to be treated "well," i.e., found acceptable, a paper must reference most of the mainstream (i.e., those who will do the reviewing) and by the time the current state of the issue is dutifully reported there is little space left to effectively criticize it. Two draft papers are now available, one each from the EC and NSF, on this dilemma of how to encourage and evaluate ideas that are not normal to a discipline. NSF turns to changing its program officers, thus shifting biases, and hoping innovation emerges in the cracks between. Governmental science organizations could gain something by looking at what has been learned in several "skunk works" type processes in companies.

[189] Not addressed here is another group that believes in recipes. They can be recognized by the belief that not only is core competence is an original idea, but that it began with them. I will not address the problems of this last group except

that is at least two to three decades. Some reference an especially noteworthy work on the principle that was done twelve years ago by SEST-Euroconsult.[190]

Those engaged in spreading the religion of core competence argue that recent work, from the late eighties and early nineties, has given the concept greater operational clarity. I teach with two such well-regarded and inspirational individuals. A heretic could attack their "core" by suggesting both that core competence has been around for a much longer time-period than they this group is willing to resist, and that the concept has in fact been made more ambiguous by recent developments.

The notion of improving economic activity via encouraging each person and each organization to concentrate on perfecting a small number of tasks (where each task is also very small) is as old as notion of division of labor. The reluctance of those advocating core competence to see or accept this heritage is itself interesting, although not the subject herein. Those wanting to pursue this tread might look at Adam Smith's work to see from where[191] he got the division of labor idea upon which he built his *Wealth of Nations* thesis. Division of labor is a discourse on the importance of "core competence." Serving as a object for further refinement by David Ricardo the idea continues on to greatly inspired the voluminous work of Porter on how to gain a comparative advantage by exaggerating the division of labor concept.[192]

Some may recall how the early idea of division of labor served to organize much of industrialization, but the idea had become exceed-

---

that the following points out where their "original idea" originally might have come from.

[190] "Elements de reflextion sur l'integretion de technologie dans la function strategique des enterprises japonaises." *Le Bonzai de l'industrie japonais*, Paris: French Ministry of Research and Technology, July 1984.

[191] Difficult to document there is reason to believe that Smith of course gained some inspiration from reading some Plato and much Aristotle, just as those who now advocate core competence must also carry that legacy. His regard for their era is especially clear in his Chapter Four.

[192] This is distinctly not what is meant by "oneness" in eastern philosophy, or "grand unification theory" in physics.

ingly tired by the end of the nineteen-fifties. Environmental challenges were requiring more systemic thinking, acting, and organizing.[193] By the last nineteen-eighties the idea was very much back to life. As Keith Gardiner, Director of Lehigh's Advanced Manufacturing Center, and former Director of Manufacturing Philosophy at IBM, argued in the late nineteen-eighties,

The growth of automation brought the problems of division of labor and segmentation back to the forefront of business theory. Top management generally sees it to be in its personal interest to apply automation (as distinct from understanding it) because it can be used to keep workers in check and return themselves to the power of the central manager via a return to the ideology of Frederick Taylor.[194] Regardless, the Smith- Babbage-Taylor ideology is back with a vengeance, although now working under the label of core competence.

Core competence is an especially viable candidate for the heretic's examination table due to the unquestioned fervor with which it is indiscriminately applied to whatever comes along. In a course last year on global competition, I was to use interactive television to teach at two other locations; as a demonstration of our university's technological leadership.[195] Since the system proved to be non-interactive,[196] I broke off the experiment.

The merit of the approach, based on our available technology, broke down after three weeks. I then started traveling to each of the other locations one night a week to give a normal course. By this time, the course had become highly fragmented. I then turned to an

---

[193] This was the stuff of the General Systems Theorists which got translated into business policy by the work of Trist, E.L., Emery, F.E., Ackoff, R.L., Boulding, K., Ozbekhan, H., Perlmutter, H., et.al.

[194] As primarily represented in his book, *Principles of Scientific Management*, 1911.

[195] An also to lead the way into the automation of teaching where in additional to simultaneous broadcasts to other locations the lectures would be taped and then played later on cable TV for those that wanted a degree when they had troubles sleeping.

[196] I usually couldn't see them, often they couldn't hear me, and on occasion the off-campus students had to go use a payphone to compensate for Bell Atlantic's transmission service, whenever they had a question or comment.

acquaintance in a large US firm[197] who offered to help reorganize the course around their global experiences. As the Senior VP in charge of information technology and systems for the firm he arranged for the various classes to all meet at their Global Technology Headquarters. He came from Atlanta to give a three-hour session that made use of his four thousand people at the center[198] and his Chief Operations and Financial Officers. He covered many of the mythologies of what executives talk about, including the importance for U.S. companies of believing in core competence. He mentioned this idea with some humor because several papers and books about the success of his company said it was due to their pursuit of a core competence, "whatever those authors thought core and competence meant."

We learned more about what it meant in this widely referenced company six months later when another executive, who works for the one mentioned above, gave a keynote lecture at a university dinner. He dutifully presented the importance of core competence to the firm, as a "secret to their success," just as had been reported in the books and articles. He then closed his lecture with an outline of the "new and exciting things" the company was doing to become ever more efficient. This part was interesting because virtually all the items seemed to violate the core competence dictum.[199]

During the question segment, he was asked to explain the apparent disharmony between his firm being religious about core competency and yet going off and doing all these other things to absorb excess capacity of aircraft, etc. His response was, "There is no contradiction. The definition of what we do has simply shifted from moving packages to moving information.[200] The conclusions we left with was that the core competence creed had become more import-

---

[197] This firm operates the third largest information systems in the world, the seventh largest air fleet and the only functioning nationwide mobile phone system in the U.S.
[198] The company has about 250,000 employees, where these 4,000 provide them with real-time information.
[199] He described how UPS was beginning to undertake activities like leasing their aircraft on weekends to tour operators.
[200] Under the parameters of this changing definition, tourists become information that is then legitimately moved by the firm.

ant than the firm's actions. If this kind of continuous redefinition of a core is needed, to maintain the validity of having a core, then the concept is best left behind.

Referencing the firm in this way may be unfair, but since it is so often used as an example of the effectiveness of core competence, then it should also be able to exemplify the downside of the concept as well as the upside. A newer challenge has recently surfaced to core competency, in that the market value of the parts of a conglomerate, as bought up and broken up, is not necessarily greater than that of the whole. The theory that parts were worth more than the whole began in North America but has since shifted to European firms. The breakdown of the theory in North America has just not shifted to Europe. The clearest evidence of this is seen in Europe's, or at least the *Economist's*, darling of core competence - Hanson PLC.

Hanson PLC made a lot of money on both continents by demonstrating how numerous middle-sized collections of companies were more valuable as parts than as whole. Used car thieves had known this for a long time, but never could use the fact to legitimize car theft. As of September 1996 Hanson, when the company itself was broken into parts, the parts were worth less whole had been in both London and New York. The same has recently come true for ITT, AT&T and other firms involved in seeking their core business by splitting up.[201]

---

[201] See "Hanson Spinoff Plans Haven't Raised Shareholder Value," WSJ, 9/26/96, p. B4.

10
Socio-Technical as Technological Tyranny

Conceptions and evidence of the value of socio-technical systems thinking emerged to assist managers in the management of larger systems of being, not the ever-smaller parts of the technical. In a 1973 these same researchers began to consider ways to include the natural and non-rational ecological in redirecting the industrial.

With the beginning of what might be called the "Reagan Episode" in human development the socio-tech as envisioned in 1950 was changed. This became the recasting and expansion of the technical via information technology infrastructures. Called the post-industrial, in some humor, the offices became new factories with human technology. The social thus came to be re-managed by "informed technology." Concern for the natural was buried under excitement for punch card logic then stored in the "flatland" of two-dimensional entertainment.

Ideologies from Aristotle, Newton, Babbage, Taylor, et.al., came to manage the human psyche and its articulation of human development. Anthropologists such as Bateson came to call their stream of unconsciousness "unaided rationality." None-the-less the widespread introduction of the technical into the social, then into the wider human life space, lead to glorification and then the religion of the artificial.

The importance of the artificial was further marketed to the non-religions in the 1980s promising it would create post-industrialism, along with a seat in the side-show Reagan advertises as trickle-down economics. On my Iowa farm this was described as "horse-defecation" theory. In Washington, D.C. it was proclaimed to be artificial economics where all that was republican would become true, even if it was a managerial lie. Even when called "voodoo economics" republicans would smile and manage to push it further and wider in economic classes, even in the Wharton School. For the next four decades this became the managerial force in blocking out those who would criticize further industrialization.

Instead of moving beyond the limitations of the industrial this era spread the industrial into the remaining aspects of being human. General management incorporates the artificial. This provides a recipe for widespread management of the technical and the social, then attempts to manage the natural. Books on this sell well. How to become a "1-minute," or even expand the content to become a "5-minute manager," as well as how to create "excellence" in the organization while being evermore "strategic" in recharging the same old industrial themes. Books on the sciences of the artificial renewed justification for greater use of the artificial in industrial management thinking. Adding the deceit essential to legitimate "strategic thinking" provides a sanctuary for lost humans who moved to the artificial after losing touch with the natural.

The fateful contradiction in managing wholes or parts is clearly seen in the development of science and technology. Its management began in breaking up not understandable wholes. Then end as less understandable fragments where their meaning comes to be seen as meaningless. This was illustrated as reductionistic analysis during WWII. This was where via management humans removed a partial process from its context, modified it, then reinserted it into the whole. The issue came to be what to do about the whole having moved on to be different than the one the part had been removed from. The result was often called a "mess," thus some managers developed what they called "mess management."

Humans were attracted to a promise to improve life in the 3rd dimension; something beyond their hope to ever achieve via WWII experiences[202]. Via the vacuous wisdom of effects illuminating dis-

---

[202] See Paul Valery's version of the Faustian Tragedy, where by 1944 the devil had gone into hiding and no longer wanted to negotiate with humans over their souls, as they were too evil for the devil to associate with.

connected causes humans dream of controlling uncertainty. Humans dig deeper as entertainment to avoid the certainty awaiting their final entopic battle in the 4th dimension.

Via continual reduction of apparent reality into ever smaller fragments that promise to be ever more understandable, thus manageable, humans seek hope. This nurtures a necessary dream that it will all be okay if you only hang on. Via this framework, in the Goffman sense of "frame analysis," we attempt to manage environments, others, ourselves, and thus posterity. This ignores how our actions seem to make things ever less manageable. Meanwhile, entropy uses human activity management as its journey towards cold. Need it be this way?[203]

Omnipresent in a cloud around all this are managers, models of management and artificial hierarchies of dead, deadly, bad, good, better, and best. The shadows of time cast doubt on all of this. A thesis grows that the management intended to increase certainty increases the dreaded uncertainty of the natural that of course naturally ends in a dreaded certainty feared by the individual.[204]

Managers are taught to acquire effective knowledge for dealing with messes, and the again popular distinction of wicked problems, followed by reading accolades for effectively reducing it into ever more partial parts for deeper cause-effect analysis of what no longer matters. In so doing techniques for improved management come to rely on a technocratic model of the artificial with spare parts laying all over. The hierarchy is intended to structure the responses as well as motivate involvement of the managers. In this process the connections between the parts and the context of it all get sidelined as noise. Further noise is then created by those posing an ever-better way to manage the fragments of ever-more parts. Chapter one in the following goes into detail on one of these management ways. The consequences of focusing on management of results to be achieved,

---

[203] Georgescu-Roegen, Nicholas, *The Entropy Law and the Economic Process*, Harvard Press, 1971. A friend's book that undermined much of what was once seen as fundamental economics and thus allowed him to become a heretic.

[204] To better understand this please look at the 1974 Pulitzer Prize winning book in non-fiction, *Denial of Death*,

and not costs to context are ignored. Something more systemic seems needed.

Welcome To The Problem

Via promises of beauty in rationality of 1687 Sir Isaac Newton offered a quantitative passage to improving the conditions of human life to go beyond the qualitative. This was to supplement then replace the history of hope from qualitative beliefs. Some of those were from religious promises, and Newton also believed in them, but others were argued for as logical, rational, and pointing to a mathematized route to human self-determination outside nature. They hinted at efficient means to meet human needs. Newton's work continues as fundamental to the making of machines and forming of industrialization. At first this became important to human needs. Later, Newton's logic was extended to providing for human wants, no matter their superficiality.

Newton proposed strict rationality as the means to create improved conditions for human life on Earth. This was to counteract shortcomings he had observed in questionable nature and natural human behavior. [1]. Newton thus authored a method to mechanize progress, which continues to this day. Mechanization even expanded into modern warfare. Newton worked hard to avoid the appearance of the non-rational [2].

Mechanization became Industrialization. It became the essence of human hope for progress to raise humans above nature's limitations. Newton's ideas thus spread rapidly. His understanding of structure and force was used to collect raw materials from nature, then organized them rationally to build production processes to then produce goods. The industrial process was the rational organization of machines to rationally produce rationally designed products alongside not-so-rational humans. Humans were to act ever more rationally to work alongside machines. Gregory Bateson remarked on the human dilemma: "Humans will need to become more predictable, or the machines will become angry and kill them." Humans attempted to leave their non-rational nature behind while at work.

Thus, the industrial became a growing problem for the natural context. This was seen in human efforts to expand the industrial from the early 19ᵗʰ Century. At the end of WWII, the problems in this were becoming more apparent. It was then seriously questioned by Systems Science theorists. They pointed to the central measure of industrial success – productivity. They showed how an emphasis on improving productivity led to continuous growth in what was coming to be the wrong things. These theorists brought redesign to the situation in what they called the socio-tech system-thinking model. Their early questions and work set a basis for considerable improvement to several industries. Putting the social back in control of the mechanical led to improved production process design and management. Optimism in improving the process of meeting human needs and wants was emerging and expanding.

Unfortunately, a larger problem with industrialization, one that had been lying in wait for decades, surfaced in the nineteen-seventies. It dealt with long-term expansion of industrial consumption of materials and energy as needed for production and use of products. The problem was that those long involved in managing the process had ignored longer-term costs in what they were doing. They had of course seen limits to the industrial process but those were in production, not in unwanted pollution side-effects from mining and refining materials and energy needed for production and its products. The natural context that had provided the inputs was expected to absorb such unwanted outputs. Somehow, humans had learned to ignore such. Newtonian-inspired humans forgot they were part of nature where their life depended on the well-being of the natural context. The outputs of industrial production were finally being seen to deteriorate the natural environment in an irreversible manner.

Nature, the context of human existence, had long been disregarded by most humans. Newton seemed proud of proposing that nature was subordinate to human reason. He noted: "The latest authors, like the most ancient, strove to subordinate the phenomena of nature to the laws of mathematics."[205] (*Principia Mathematica,*

---

[205]

Book 1, 1687, from Newton's preface.) [Ibid. reference 1] Later, via Newtonian organization, industrialization seemed to represent a force more powerful than the nature surrounding it. Humans, as part of nature, came to see themselves as subordinate to the rationality of the machine. Now, via the selling of AI, we see this logic expanding. Humans have come to accept dependence on machines for food, shelter, and satisfying their wants.

Larger systems of order and life are clearly beyond Newton and the artificial, yet humans continue to see machines as critical to life as they know it. Thus, machines have expanded from providing for needs to responding to human wants and desires. They were even made available to fight in God's war with nature, as prescribed in Biblical teachings, and then adapted to the long-standing wars of humans with each other and even themselves. The problems with the human project were not getting better, only more clearly harsh.

Processes and products of industrialization thus became ideological tools in a war against nature's variances and uncertainties, and even wickedness. The making and using of technology in production, and products coming from it, became a new spiritual, not an opposition to the spiritual. Humans loved it. Machines and design of the artificial came to be the essence of the human project. Machines were tools for what humans could, would, and should do. Much of this ideology remains in the teachings of public schools. This logic has been expensive to life.

Newtonian dreams of reason came to underline the ever-expanding human idea of progress via a partnership with the ideas and the manifestations of technology. Technology replaced religious aspirations before becoming a replacement religion. The industrial ideology continues through the post-industrial aspirations of Artificial Intelligence. Dreams of advanced technology appear as the warriors against an entropic death. This has replaced the tradition of religious promises of life reappearing after entropic death in a non-entropic setting. Providing extensive immortality projects, the technological imperative seemed secure once again.

1950: Early Socio-Technical Systems Thinking

We humans occupy a context that has come to include the importance of the social along with Newton's technological. Changes in the socio-technical context redefine the meaning of being human. Such change was significant at the close of WWII. The technology of war and the factories that served it had changed a great deal during the war. It seemed to have outclassed the importance of the social. The industrial was thought to serve the social, but the significant changes in the technological were presumed to service the industrial, not the social or the human. During the war, the technological was greatly advanced in the name of winning the war. Its development had become the imperative. The social was presumed to be secondary to progress and would be adaptable to technological requirements.

This idea changed with the end of the war. It came to be noted that the technical was becoming a danger to the psychological. Thus, the technological needed to be reconsidered then designed to support the psychological and serve the social. First efforts were undertaken to make this change in 1950 via work carried out by the Tavistock Institute of London. Eric Trist of the Tavistock Institute led innovative research into relations between the sociological and the technological. He found a significant and expanding technological imperative from the "tech" of WWII. By adopting a systems-thinking attitude he helped improve the perception and management of relations between the two. This work came to be called socio-technical systems. Many industrial settings were seen to operate via a technological imperative. This needed to be changed.

In the nineteen-fifties this change was crucial, but only in isolated locations. Even into the nineteen-seventies and nineteen-eighties it was not widely accepted. It was mostly a tangent to what mattered more - socio-technical was an obstruction to the Social Darwinism clarity of Milton Friedman economic brutalism.

"In Britain, also early in the postwar period, a new direction of development toward the new collaborative model began through the discovery of the autonomous workgroup. This phenomenon gave rise to a new concept, the 'sociotechnical system' (Trist and Bamforth, 1951), which represented a basic critique of scientific management in the technocratic bureaucracy." [4]

Eventually, some scientists and mathematicians began to question Newton's strict reasoning and homage to a closed logic. One of the most skeptical, and most humorous, was the Ambrose Bierce in 1889. He came to be referenced by early systems scientists of the nineteen-sixties. Russell Ackoff, a systems scientist of the nineteen-seventies, often referenced Ambrose Bierce's definitions. The Bierce's definition of logic appeared in Ackoff's writings, and in lectures to companies facing production problems. As the founder of Operations Research, Ackoff used the definition to illustrate OR's future being in the past, and they had missed it.

"Logic: *n*. The art of thinking and reasoning in strict accordance with the limitations and incapacities of the human misunderstanding. The basic of logic is the syllogism, consisting of a major and a minor premise and a conclusion – thus:

Major Premise: Sixty men can do a piece of work sixty times as quickly as one man.

Minor Premise: One man can dig a post hole in sixty seconds; therefore –

Conclusion: Sixty men can dig a posthole in one second.

This may be called the syllogism arithmetical, in which, combining logic and mathematics, we obtain a double certainty and are twice blessed." [5]

Social scientists with experience from WWII could be seen to reference Bierce definitions in pointing to shortcomings of industrial processes leaving humans out of the management of systems improvements. For them machine productivity was secondary. The value and welfare of humans had been dropped in an urgent need to improve productivity in meeting war needs. The technological imperative was not questioned until escalating human costs in the system became noticed. Once productivity also declined it was easier to raise questions about the entire system.

1960: A Technological Imperative Returns

A lead in noticing the problem of production came from scientists involved in WWII. The leaders were based at the Tavistock Institute in London. They believed that major improvements were essential and could be made. They called for a revaluation of the logic that had lowered the value of humans in production since 1850, and especially during WWII production. They argued for rethinking, seeing production as a system, and experimenting with a social imperative. They argued how we should think of the socio technical as a system, and have the socio lead the system, reversing the tradition of the technical.

They arrived at this hypothesis through seeing how production was becoming increasingly sophisticated and had properties of a system, rather than a collection of machines lined up turning out parts. After initial experimentation, they went further and began to believe that leadership by the social was not simply better in industrialization but had become essential to its management and continued improvement. This became a call for thinking of *socio-technical systems as processes*.

The industrial process, and management of its social and technical aspects, was thus reconceptualized as a system. The system was explicitly to benefit the social, not the technical. It was posited that the industrial was to serve human needs and wants and must thus be managed via a human imperative. Based on its considerable early successes, this logic spread to most industries.

During the nineteen-seventies, the socio-tech's model of success encountered questions about the price of, and limits to, that success.

This arose in the 1975-77 work of international business researchers who came to be skeptical of the 1850 industrial process and its consequences for systems of life. Industrial inputs, outputs and outcomes raised previously unasked research questions. This began with concerns about environmental pollution and environmental protection.

The research soon moved to questions about the assumption that social regulation could take care of the externalities of industrialization of processes and products. The industrial model resulted in good and bad, where both could be regulated. Different approaches from different nations were studied. It was soon found that the good from industrialization needed to be much better, and that the bad might well be too bad to regulate. Shocking long-term consequences were identified from the research, e.g., climate change. Short-term gains were even seen to be a problem, in that the public lost concern for the initial signs of deterioration of their environment. It has become much like a Faustian Tragedy.

Those involved in this research were well-schooled in socio-technical studies. Their thinking was that Trist's work, which had moved production management from a technological imperative to a social imperative, was only a first step. It could not begin to address the fearful consequences of continued business as usual, even with a social imperative. It seemed that moving to a natural imperative was necessary, and more research was needed.

Concern was with the harmful consequences from environmental desecration, values intrinsic to Newtonian industrialization, and then in the design of products produced. The social should continue as an imperative in socio-tech management, but the total system needed to embrace a larger system that would include natural resources and systems of living order. Evidence from a 1977 report to OECD, pointed to ways in which human actions were changing the conditions of life on the Earth. Key in this change were industrial production processes and human uses of the final products. There was a call for a natural imperative to manage the three-part socio-technical-natural system that was to meet human needs. The social had shown much progress in redesigning management of the technical since 1950. Could the natural follow a similar path?

In the following section the most extreme example of a socio-technical systems project was studied so it could be expanded to other sites. Due to the exposure of its very radical results, it was closed, and its management was fired for not understanding the importance of management in the industrial. The example had been set up using the Eric Trist model of socio-tech. The research for it was carried out using the Trist idea of Action Research.

1974: An Extreme Socio-Tech Success

Two PhD students working for Professor Eric Trist, David Hawk and Bill Henderson did this project for Scott Paper Company. Scott's stated objective in doing the project was to become published in BusinessWeek as being at the edge of business innovation. Scott Paper built a paper production plant and asked Eric Trist to advise them on making it look innovative. Headquarters forgot about the venture a bit later as they came to have challenges at their other 33 paper plants to manage. Eric Trist had worked with the plant manager to create a "noteworthy" example of socio-tech for the human future. Eric Trist asked his two research and teaching assistants, Bill Henderson, and David Hawk, to evaluate what had been accomplished relative to socio-tech research at the Dover Delaware plant. They worked with plant employees for six months.

The essential research question was how much of the gains generated by the nineteen-fifties model of the socio-technical in English coal mines had been achieved in this new Scott Paper plant? The project began in 1975, and it took six months to conclude in a report on the plant status.

The two researchers spent many days at the plant, interviewing about the 150 employees and one manager, while also coming to understand the technical processes. Production technology had never been used before in the industry. It had been designed to reduce greatly the environmental pollution effects from its operations. The products were paper towels designed for cleaning and reuse. Many problems emerged in the technology including numerous fires and breakdowns. The products needed to be continually tested due to production issues.

The social aspect had been designed in accordance with the Trist advice on setting up an ideal socio-technical system. Professor Trist had worked with the gentleman who was to be the plant manager in the new plant in Dover, Delaware. The manager had come to know a great deal about the potential in a socio-technical systems approach to plant set up and management. He organized the social aspect around the idea of the five-person autonomous work group. Each group was self-managed. As with the coal mine groups, one member would oversee an operation, its leader; another two would be doing the manual work, where needed; and a fourth would be responsible for seeing accidents, running tests, and improving safety. The fifth member could stay home when not essential to the day's work. Even with many technological breakdowns, the productivity of the plant was 30% better than other plants, or than had been anticipated. It was perceived as the best in the industry.

Things were going so well at the plant that the plant manager decided to avoid seeming to hang around to watch the successes, so he moved to his home and rehired himself as part-time, with part-time pay. The workers greatly appreciated the meaning behind this move for continuance of their self-leadership. Their productivity further improved. Workers then made proposals to headquarters about redesigning the production technology, much of which was carried out by third parties. Throughout the plant there was evidence of a competence hierarchy having replaced the usual managerial hierarchy. This was written up in the final report with examples. However, it should have been left out of the report to the Board.

Scott's Board of Directors was our client. They asked us to see if we could see signs of spectacular successes in a new plant they built in Dover, Delaware. Their plan was to inform BusinessWeek of such, to capture the attention of the paper production industry. A prior article on the innovation at a General Foods plant was an example of what they wanted to achieve. The two researchers and Eric Trist thus made a presentation to the Board on innovations in the Dover plant.

Halfway through our presentation the CEO called for a halt. The corporate lawyer had drafted a document we needed to sign before we could continue. It was that we would keep the information about the plant confidential and never write a public report or science article about it. We signed this document, then completed our presentation. The CEO of Scott ended up firing the plant manager, then brought a union into the plant to help formalize work processes. Changes recommended by workers were frozen. Later, the same Board fired the CEO and began a search for a replacement. Eventually Al Dunlap became their dream CEO. He was the darling of Wall Street. He promised to double productivity in any company that allowed him to be their leader. Eventually he was hired by Scott Paper's Board to be their CEO.

CEO Dunlap doubled plant productivity within six months. He fired half the workers, eliminating those in Customer Service, Research and Development, and production innovations. Two years later, when complaints emerged about the quality of the company, and its products, he simply sold it. Wall Street loved it and called him "Texas Chainsaw Al Dunlap." He was their darling of the day. He then moved up to take over leadership of a company with even more opportunities for his ideas of productivity. He then managed to take that company into bankruptcy and was finally fired for the quality of his ideas.

1979: The Missing Context for Socio-Tech — Nature

Nature has mostly been a backdrop, to be ignored as raw materials are found and forthcoming. From secure industrial resource input, humans concentrate on the technical, the social and their interrelations to better serve individuals. Shortcomings with a technological imperative managing the social in coal mines led to important changes. This knowledge spread to auto factories and other aspects of industry. Just now the entire industrial paradigm faces a problem. Just as humans came to see they were rightfully in charge of the technical, the natural is reminding humans that they come from nature and along with the technical they rely on the natural for inputs. The seventy-year history of socio-tech can be a viable guide to finding effective responses to changing the role of the natural within the industrial. These changes may become incredibly significant.

The concern here is that another variable must be introduced into the system, that of the natural. We have long known that nature has provided the context for all things human, as well as providing the resources for the industrial, but nature has been left in the background of the search for progress in meeting human needs and wants. The natural environment has long been the dumping ground for the unwanted parts of the industrial - the trash and waste - through disposal and/or release into the air and water. These were simply assumed as costs of fulfilling human needs and wants. Recently this domain is seen as the depository of costs of social and technical activities.

Can the industrial be reconsidered, as it was in 1950, to respond to an enlarged value system? Perhaps not. We do not yet understand nature. The level of change may be beyond human capability. The following offers a brief outline of the challenges facing humans due to their two-hundred-year-old choices for industrialization. We begin to see why it must be radically changed. We do not yet know what this change means. We may need to abandon industrialization. The youth of today are not impressed with our version of industrialization. Perhaps the remarkable 1950 socio-tech repair of industrialization by Eric Trist, et al can be taken to include the natural. We do not know. We do know we need to find a way to move from desecration of nature to appreciating its fundamental importance in larger systems.

40 years ago, there was a call to expand the socio-tech of 30 years previous. The expansion was to include nature within the socio-tech model. Some research came from this, which became a call to develop "business-as-unusual," well beyond the entrepreneurial. This was to systemically repair industrialization via different models of production, consumption, and product design. The call was soon ignored. Little change resulted to industrialization. Part of the call for change resulted from research into the consequences of climate change. These consequences were thought likely to damage life on the planet if change did not take place in the ways in which humans

met their needs and wants. How do we expand the success of the socio-technical by adding the natural? This is the question here.

In the mid-1970s, another advisee of Trist, David Hawk, traveled a different road. He studied the relations between humans and nature via costs to nature of industrial operations. The work began from socio-tech systems models, then brought nature into the model. Based at the Stockholm School of Economics, Institute of International Business, Eric Trist was the advisor. The study involved twenty major companies and six national governments. Results centered on the consequences to nature of human industrialization. The entire industrial paradigm came to be included in the inquiry. Data was collected showing that human activities were impacting nature at an alarming rate, and that that rate was increasing. The consequences of this were disrupting the workings of natural systems at an alarming rate.

The sanctity of the social managing the technical was slightly destabilized in 1975. The overriding importance of the environmental to all things living became more apparent. Yes, the social was still effectively managing the technical, but the social was seen to fall short in management of itself, and its values. Self-management came to be needed in emerging requirements to manage environmental deterioration in production and products, not just in production technology.

Environmental science was noting clear signs of a great danger on the horizon for systems of life. An appreciation of nature and natural processes became an important addition to Systems Thinking, an area of research that had launched special systems concerns in 1941 [8]. Many considered this work by Andras Angyal as fundamental to a more general approach to applying Systems Sciences. Angyal demonstrated how, when a system reaches its limits, the parts assume (take over) the whole. This became most apparent in industrial companies reaching the limits to their production and product and seeking business-as-unusual. It was not relevant to governmental agencies seeking better ways to regulate production and product use from business-as-usual. Those developing Information Technology found

Angyal's discovery fundamental to leaving hierarchical structures, then moving on from matrix to the nature of network structures.

Some with concern for the context of living systems, e.g., David Hawk, designed and managed a research project into the subject. He began with measures of environmental deterioration, then launched a two-year study of the effectiveness of social regulation in management of the deterioration effects on humans and nature. Most regulation was measured as less effective than had been assumed. Some approaches encouraged higher levels of pollution via defective technology. From this, the study examined the cultural acceptance of pollution from social systems. Widespread values of urbanism had let to acceptance of environmental desecration that supported a rural war with the natural. The technological and sociological needed to be remodeled. The industrial and its products needed to be radically changed. Governments involved in the project in 1977 saw this change as very unlikely. The Chief Scientist of one of the oil companies in the project was even more pessimistic. He presented to the study that, if things didn't change, there would be global climate change.

The forces behind environmental deterioration were found to be the key to moving the evolution of the socio-technical construct to its next level. It needed to expand to include the context of the social and the technological which involved industrialization and the natural environment. A proposal was made to redesign the Newtonian industrialization model, as well as the products that resulted from it. The twenty industrial firms in the study, and the six nations supporting the study, agreed that business-as- usual would lead to no business at all for humans.

Eric Trist was the PhD supervisor of David Hawk during the research. Trist's past work came to be crucial to the project and to presenting its recommendations. He was a strong supporter of expanding the socio-tech systems model to include context. The three-volume research report resulting from the project was presented to OECD. From that presentation, Russell Ackoff read the work, then contacted David Hawk saying this was his dissertation for a PhD in Social Systems Sciences. David had earlier completed his course work with Ackoff. Eric Trist disagreed, arguing that Hawk needed a theoretical amplification of what the research would mean to other researchers. Such an amplification was done and was attached to the three volumes of empiricism that Russell Ackoff had approved. Much trouble occurred with a two-year review of this work, however. The review committee of seven professors wanted the comment about future climate change to be removed, as it was very speculative. A chief scientist of Exxon, who had been in the study, had made a presentation on the Emergence of Climate Change at the end of the study. He showed how this was due to Exxon processes and Products. He offered this research in support of study results.

The School Dean refused to sign off the work unless "self-regulation" empiricism, consistent with socio-tech principles, was removed. He felt such was too close to anarchism. In addition, he saw no relation between business and environmental deterioration. I had to agree. Obviously he did not see such.

The thesis was to experiment with a Negotiated Order much like that found in nature with Prisoner's Dilemma of Rapaport not the versions of it that rely on strategic thinking and behavior. This was like what was found in those working at the edges of the best socio-tech factory examples in the study. This was to be radically different from the tradition of Legal Order that depended on a hierarchy of control. Negotiated Order depended on self-management via learning from the edges.

Negotiated order processes were well beyond Newton's thinking. They made use of Einstein, Hawking, and many leaders in Systems Sciences, such as Rapaport, Vickers, Ackoff, Trist, Boulding, Beer, Cowen, and Ozbekhan. The question thus became: what is a socio-technical system and how does it relate to the natural order of existence? Is socio-tech an attitude towards why and how humans come to relate to the technology they create and come to depend upon? The construct of socio-tech emerged from the work of Eric Trist, et al, as did concern for The Social-Technical-Natural.

1983: Information Systems, Another Technology

Some of the researchers that worked with Eric Trist became interested in the relevance of socio-tech-systems ideas in the IT operations of firms. It seemed to them that IT was becoming a new version of the pre-nineteen-fifties version of the technological imperative in management. Their question was: Could socio-tech be used to help those attempting to manage the unfolding of Information Technology as applied to continuing needs of traditional industrialization? The nineteen-fifties Trist era of socio-technical systems came from an urgent need to reform an industry essential to other industries in post WWII England – coal production. Coal was then the major source of energy where energy was essential to reconstruction. The Trist cases improved productivity by about 30%, which was remarkable. What was learned from these cases came to be expanded into many other industries for the next fifty years.

Some researchers noted growing similarities between Information Technology of the nineteen-eighties and the coal mining technology of the late nineteen-forties. As such many looked to socio-tech thinking for help. The work of Cal Pava in 1983, one of Eric Trist's students, is often used as a foundation for this domain. It, and Eric Trist's thoughts on it are briefly outlined here. Pava had become concerned that the technological imperative had taken over the office, via ever expanding use of Information Technology. He found similarities to what Trist had found in the coal mines thirty years previously. Pava's friend, Bill Gates, provided Pava with clear examples of how things were going wrong. The results of these studies came to be significant to the next stage of socio-tech development.

What was learned and applied via Eric Trist's "socio-technical" conception for managing relations between the social, e.g., workplace, and the technological, e.g., machines at work, is important here. The context is an industrial-based society, where technology is increasingly applied to meet human needs (food, shelter, safety, etc.) as well as to satisfy the ambiguity of human wants (ownership of things, control over life, respect from others, happiness, etc.). Current development of the socio-technical world is through ideas on how best to relate social systems to technological systems, where the technology is primarily digital in its design, production, and operation. This is different from the coal mining context that stimulated the Trist work at Tavistock. Taking note of this, some from the digital world renamed the context as "Digital Coal Mines."

The widely accepted dominance of the technical over the social was acceptable until the work of the Tavistock researchers at the end of WWII. They reminded society of the importance of the social over the technological. But now, seventy years later, it seems the technological is gaining predominance once more. Here we go again, moving away from the social while pandering to the technical. It is time to bring the Trist sense of inquiry into the IT world of management.

Within the precepts of industrialization, and its capital costs, we often shift business emphasis towards how best to soften the importance of the social, considering the needs of the industrial. This is clearly demonstrated in what we call the Al Dunlap approach to productivity. From designing more flexible machines for men to use, we have moved to designing humans to be more flexible in their requirements. This is in line with the Babbage logic. From Aristotle to Leibnizian calculus the pathway for programming the artificial has become clear. Warren McCulloch and Walter Pitts illustrated this in the basis of Information Technology management, as outlined in "A Logical Calculus of the Ideas Immanent in Nervous Activity." (Bulletin of Mathematical Biophysics 5, 1943, 115-133). Thus, we are at the interface of the social and the technical where both have come to be defined by the logic of the technical, especially that from Aristotle.

The emphasis here is on our reliance on a perspective of Information Technology that is decoupled from the social context which it attempts to manage. My fear is that we are again using the thinking that preceded the 1950 development of the socio-technical systems perspective. We seem more than willing to apply the rules of the technological to the sociological in business. Just now we might look deeper into what was carried out in the nineteen-fifties in order to redress a world gone wrong.

The current Socio-Technical perspective seems opposite to the thinking of the founders of "socio-tech." They appreciated, in the Sir Geoffrey Vickers sense, how the technological was assuming dominance in the operations of the social. Clearly, the technical needs to find reduced dominance in management thinking, in that the social could be better managed to achieve human ends of systems of life.

Bill Gates and Calvin Pava met early in their careers. Pava was a graduate of Wharton, and then a professor at Harvard. Gates was a student at Harvard. They became instant friends, as both came to see a need for innovation outside of Harvard business-as-usual ideas. They spent much time in Northern California vineyards and wine bars discussing the future of Information Technology relative to IT providers and users. Some of this found its way into a 1983 book by Pava [6]. Calvin Pava's mentor at Wharton, Eric Trist, was to write the forward, but Cal was in such a hurry that the book got written and Trist's forward had to become an afterword.

Trist went deeply into socio-technical systems and Information Technology. Once more, he feared the technical would diminish the social. It would create an economy with extreme income gaps, and reduce humanity, as in the coal mines. The following is part of his commentary on socio-tech and its meaning for Information Technology.

"This is a far cry from the prevailing perspective, which concentrates attention so steadfastly on the technological aspect that what-so-ever the equipment makers propose is solemnly installed with the eager support of data processing and internal "systems" staffs. Absent is any informed scrutiny of organizational and social aspects, with untoward consequences: the creation at the lower levels of large numbers of poorly designed jobs which lower performance and increase alienation; failure to appreciate the subtle yet profound changes required in managerial and professional roles; the export on to the labor market of those made redundant without serious thought to their retraining or future place in society." [6]

Pava posed an integrated approach in the field of socio-technical systems redesign to include an increase in non-linear enterprises relative to knowledge work. This helped practitioners move away from an old paradigm of linear transformation processes in factories and offices. Pava's concern was with the centrality of deliberation as the place where work was done. The concern here goes beyond this. From the Pava evolution, we move beyond the digitalized dreams for the human project and call for inclusion of a third element to our equation – the natural context.

Some will quickly see why the addition of nature adds a context for its natural improvement. The nineteen-fifties socio-technical, with the nineteen-eighties model of Information Systems inclusions, could be helpful, but seems insufficient. The terminology at this point is open. The challenge is to arrive at a fluid systemic model of the social, the technological and the natural. Their relations at this point are not clearly known yet are known to be changing. The paradox in adding the IT to the socio-tech is just now significant, even without the natural. This paradox, relative to humans being human, is brilliantly outlined in a John Brunner book: "Shockwave Rider." From 1975, it came to be the hacker-bible for those with some concern with the predictable human uses of adapting to a phenomenon of Information Technology [7].

2019: Natural Added to Management Via Femagement

The following is exerted from a book about the research conclusions, dissertation as written and most important, as defended during a year's debate about its accuracy, relevance and meaning to the human future. Much of it comes from the 1979 version of the dissertation as published by fellow students in the Social Systems Sciences Program at the Wharton School. Their publishing the document was their rebuttal to the Wharton Dean discomfort with its content. This is from its introduction:

"Then was 1979. Now is 2019. In what follows much comes from then, with a touch from now, and concern for those who must occupy tomorrow. Normally, with a forty-year gap in an endeavor, the back-then serves as a baseline. Success can thus be measured in managing the initial concern.

From this we can propose measures for improving success. Such a proposal will not be found here. There was no success in applying the findings of concerned companies and government people forty years ago. They saw an urgent need to control environmental deterioration resulting from human activities. They helped recommend a new model for regulation. The situation was fluid, not fixed, and in need of ideas for business-as-unusual in both private and public organizations. Back then it was shown how deterioration was expanding and efforts to regulate and limit this impact were turning from bad into worse.

The situation of environmental deterioration can no longer be addressed via expanded research, invention of new technologies or more threatening regulations. We need to modify the meeting of humans needs and wants, but not via trivial adjustments to the current neo-classical economic model. We have moved beyond those somewhat understood traditional responses. The consequences of expanding environmental deterioration are significant. Such is now culminating in the dire phenomena briefly mentioned in the 1977 study, called *climate change*. Science suggests humans must move away from business-as-usual methods of meeting real, human bio-needs while completely reconsidering the holographic domain of psycho-wants." (9, this book by David Hawk was first placed in the Humor Section of Amazon, "Too Early, Too Late, Now what?")

2020: Life's Context – Nature

David L. Hawk

Center for Corporate Rehabilitation, Fairfield, IA, USA

Former Dean, School of Management, NJIT, Newark, NJ, USA

Abstract – *"Technological Dreams, Sociological Repairs, Natural Cleanup"*

Long-term consequences are arising from development of industrialization, for those humans who developed and now depend upon it. The economics of the industrial was emerging but stopped off at its continuing emphasize on improving the productivity of the making of its products. This factor became key in a vision of the optimum human future. An agenda in this regard has been unfolding since 1850 based on an interpretation of Aristelian dreams of 350 BC. The agenda was to retrofit men and their machines into means of ever more rational production of the goods of life. Mostly ignored was how in the shadows of such there would becom bads of life, now called environmental deterioration. By the 1950s a few researchers did rise up and raise questions about the previous 100 years of development. Eric Trist was one. He joined with Russell Ackoff and Hasan Ozbekhan at the Wharton School, University of Pennslyvnia, in the 1970s to seek a better way.

Ackoff was widely known for development of Operations Research. Designed to help manage the technological his folllowers shifted to appling it to technological management of the social, an approach that Trist had long been opposed to. Ackoff and Trist were jointly concerned with reductionistic analysis used in machine design to be used to reframe aspects of social design. From looking at the past Trist work OR designers shifted to encourage treating technology as more fluid and the human as even more fixed. Trist and Ackoff had both watched the trend emerge during and from WW II. Both were concerned with humans becoming a non-questioning part of a machine that would become ever more efficent in doing the wrong things. Ideas about the danger in the technical managing the social were largely ignored. As such, the dangers of the technological imperative were left unquestioned.

While leading research in London's Tavistock Institute Eric Trist came to question the technological imperative as manager of the sociological aspect of an organization. He saw troubles whereever the social and psychological perspectives of management were given a subservient role to the technological. He worried about the technological and its analytical segmentation defining the operation of the industrial. Where this had happened, especially in the coal mines, this was seen to create significant danger to life, and even tended to reduce overall productivity.

Ackoff and Trist saw societal problems as systemic. They were not to be holitically understood via Aristotle's "dream of reason" with understanding limited to causation logic in effects on isolated parts. To counter this trend in production they designed and initiated a Social Systems Sciences research program in 1975 at the Wharton School, University of Pennsylvania. It opened up many research ideas and significant funding. It became widely praised via those it attracted and their research. After twenty years it was moved from business management to the Moore Schools of Engineering and Information Systems. In the transfer the social was once again lost, or simply dropped. The Ackoff/Trist/Ozbekhan program made much progress in advancing understanding of the social for future organizations, but these issues were dropped so Wharton could return to finance and accounting type innovations.

Trist's widely refrenced work began with the 1950s history of the Tavistock Institute of London. Its importance related to his reversing the industrial research tradition of the technological dominated the social in work. He carried out many action research projects to demonstrate improvements from the social not being forced to abide by the logic, rules and limitations of the technical. The Trist concern came to oppose the logic of Aristotle, Newton, Babbate, Taylor, et.al. Ackoff's Operations Research model began in line with Trist but researchers in the area soon removed the social and gave their focus to technological analysis of mangement. Ackoff gave up and departed from OR in a 1967 lecture: "OR 's Future was in the Past, and They

Missed it." He pointed out how researchers were often accepting of wrong project assumptions instead of working to rethink industrial productivity as doing the wrong better. The systemic was missing in the beginning, and in the end.

Later research in the Ackoff and Trist students in the 1980s came to add digital technology to the challenges facing the social and the technical in the conduct of business. Cal Pava, a student of Eric Trist, went deeply into this issue in his research and dissertation prior to teaching it in the Harvard Business School after his graduation. Pava referenced the 1950 Trist work, and with a touch of humor he talked of his research moving into the "digital coal mine."

Pava went on to become a close friend and colleague of Bill Gates. He wrote a key book on digital challanges from computers being added to the socio-tech model in 1983. Trist wrote the afterward to the book. Other researchers expanded on the socio-tech concern for digitization of management as posed by Pava. The problems warned of by Pava became noted as industry moved from the analogue to the digital, then returning to leadership of the technical over the social once again. Bill Gates came to express the Pava concern for a return to technological omnipotence. His concern was then lost via futher development of the digital in IBM, Apple, and Microsoft. The natural was absent from the work. AI became the object of interest.

Early signs of damage to the natural environment, from the advanced and advancing technological, were emerging on the horizon. This danger had been suggested a decade earlier in another thesis in the Social Systems Science program. It also was via a Ackoff/Trist student. That has been from a major research venture into a shadow problem from business industrialization where the natural was becoming greatly threatened by deterioration, where the work suggested climate change would be the end state.

That thesis illustrated the emergence of very harsh, inconceivable, consequences if the model of industrial production was left changed. If left unchanged the impact of the industrial on the natural would be very dangerous to systems of life. It was suggested in the 1977 reports on the subject that climate change would destroy the technical and the social.

The early Ackoff, Trist, Pava concern thus became enlarged to include dangers of environmental deterioration, via the work done in Sweden at the Stockholm School of Economics by another of the Trist/Ackoff students. The Trist/Ackoff concerns that called for use of systems sciences in management was thus expanded beyond the socio-tech model to accommodate consequences of the expanding industrial on the contracting natural.

This paper is on Socio-Technical-Natural attempts to weave these projects and their conclusions into problems in business management during the prior thirty years. It is for researchers interested in the ideas of Eric Trist as he came to term them as socio-technical systems thinking. Trist once commented how these ideas drew from ideas of mutual aid then expanded to include the challenges of social ecology in places of work. What began in the coal minds had moved into concerns of Pava for the digital office and digital coal mine in a deteriorating world.

Trist showed how the tradition of management via a technological hierarchy was becoming as problematic above ground as it had been in the coal mines underground. In all such settings the objective was to improve productivity as relying on partial analysis and cause-effect logic. Meanwhile humans would lose track of what was being produced for whom. Applying the ancient logic of the hunting party as an autonomous workgroup the agenda was changed. Via action-research significant improvements were demonstrated in technological management being replaced with autonomous human will and creativity. Thus, the situation of work was greatly improved.

Digital office action researchers set out to reverse the technological imperative for control towards socio-ecological naturalization of the digital context. In this chapter the natural-ecological dimension is added to the social ecological challenge.

Keywords:
Socio-tech, systems thinking, Tavistock, Trist, Ackoff, Vickers, Pava, computer-technology, natural systems, industrial, artificial

constructs, negotiated order/legal order, Social Systems Sciences Education, climate change.

Acknowledgements:

Systems Thinkers, Business as Unusual Supporters and sometime colleagues – Drs: Eric Trist, Russell Ackoff, Hasan Ozbekhan, Carl Sagan, Yongda Yu, Tsien Hsue-shen, Nicholas Georgescu-Roegen, Richard Garwin, Anatole Rappaport, Sir Geoffrey Vickers, and Stafford Beer. Then, the following articles:

[1]   Sir Isaac Newton, *Newton's Principia: The Mathematical Principles of Natural Philosophy*, original 1687, retranslated by Andrew Motte, Andesite Press: New York, 2015

[2]   David Hawk, the 2007 annual Leibnitz lecture, Berlin, "Should Intolerance be met with Tolerance, and Negotiated Order Replacing Legal Order." Newton (1693) illustrated legal order via strict rationality in his version of calculus. The Leibnitz (1684) alternative was closer to negotiated order, as was A. Rappaport's use of non-Euclidean Gaussian geometry (1840), "The Use and Misuse of Game Theory," *Scientific American*, Dec. 1962, pp. 108-108.)

[3]   C. West Churchman in: "*The Systems Approach and Its Enemies*," Basic Books: New York, NY, 1979. For him 90% of human reality is of the non-rational. Only 10% is susceptible to rational representation and can vary between definitions of rationality. The rational creates the irrational.

[4]   Pasmore and Sherwood, *Sociotechnical Systems: A Sourcebook*, University Associates Publisher, 1978. "Collaboration in Work Settings: A Personal Perspective," Eric L. Trist, pp. 323-334.

[5]   Ambrose Bierce, *The Devils' Dictionary*, Hill, and Wang: New York, 1957. pp. 108-9 (1889).

[6]   Calvin Pava, *Managing New Office Technology*, The Free Press: 1983, afterward by Eric Trist, pp. 163.

[7]   John Brunner, *"Shockwave Rider,"* 1975. Brunner's hero developed computer hacking skills to evade a dystopian future. The book coined many hacking terms, e.g., "worm" that describes a program that propagates itself throughout network. He introduces the concept of Delphi pools, derived from Hasan Ozbekhan when while working at RAND Corporation. He was then a professor at Wharton School, U of Pennsylvania.

[8]   Andras Angyal, "The Structure of Wholes," *Philosophy of Science: Vol 6, No 1*, University of Chicago Press, 1941. A foundation book in systems theory where Angyal addressed the consequences of a system once it reaches its limits. This was later used by those describing climate change's consequences.

[9]   David L. Hawk, *Too Early, Too Late, Now what?* AuthorHouse: Indianapolis, Indiana, 2019, from the Introduction. The republishing of Hawk's thesis, University of Pennsylvania, 1979. The Dean of the Wharton School objected to the document being sent to the university library thus several students led by Cal Pava and sponsored by Bill Gates published the work, *Regulation of Environmental Deterioration*, S^3 Notes Publications, University of Pennsylvania: Philadelphia, Pa.

11
Negative Entropy, A Faustian Bargaining

Our Need for Make-Believe, via Neg-Entropy

Humans need to learn more of the relations between *Time and Entropy*, and then *Entropy and life*. As a beginning you might investigate key writings on the subjects, such as Feynman's "The Character of Physical Law." His ideas are helpful. His Chapter Five avoids the standard order/disorder argument and moves quickly to the fundamentals in between past and future. As such, he accesses questions of entropy as irreversible, while disregarding the advice in cybernetics. Much of entropy and time are wedding within and to laws of physics. This informs those, and there are many, who have had trouble with products in time, such as Frank Wright and his clients. From lack of foresight and knowledge of materials he designed a very fragile "Falling Water" house. Upon visiting it you quickly see how designers must find a better approach to their search for meaning and practice in design. The superficiality of the industrial look is seen in its design, which is part of why it is seen as the most important example of architectural design of the 20th Century, modelling industrial design. Perhaps we can metaphorically think of the importance of this as the relationship between "Mother Nature," and "Father Time" as it has been conceived for thousands of years.

In 1980 I held a semester long entropic architectural design studio at ISU. In it students came to better know of and appreciate the entropic process in products and processes. They set up laboratories to better understand the ancient methods used in rammed earth construction combined with holographic imagining. The easiest way was via videos of life shown backwards to thus see entropy related as all that looked strange, or funny when time was reversed. They began to do very different designs. Some even left architecture to work in fields where entropy was central. Their emphasis left ideas of building fixed monuments, mostly to egos. They moved on to the fluid sense of nature in seeking models aligned with "building the unfinished." Entropy is gradually becoming an important concept in economics and business. It is key to understanding the forces behind climate change and environmental deterioration and why tradition management via regulation will not work with them.

Making, Using, Trashing, Forgetting About It

Our values are based in what we seek and how we search for it. This is part of the process we use to find meaning to life via what we value in it. Instead of preparing our souls for the realization of a mysterious future of the future we stop at the more tangible. This includes such endeavors as investing 10 hours/day in our mobile phones. Significant questions of life, with difficult answers, are therein avoided along with the sadness of life locked into a death. Thus, we can concentrate on arguments about the cheaper versions of setting up our stage sets for life. This is how our long-term becomes very expensive.

> "American consumers have been used to getting whatever they want whenever they want it, at dirt cheap prices, served to them by underpaid workers, for decades now. They can't fathom a world without these comforts. Corporations have nurtured entire generations of spoiled consumer-citizens who only care about how much they can get for the least amount of money."[206]

[206] Hawk, David, *Regulation of Environmental Deterioration*, Philadelphia, Wharton School, Dissertation Publications, 1979. P. 102.

Each of these had a view about the meaning of their life, and a viewpoint about the continuance of systems of life. The differences can be seen in which dimensions of existence they talked most about. Some preferred 0th 1st and 2nd, as will be explained later, while others occupied the 3rd and worried about the 4th. The 5th was something else. Herein nature will be seen to occupy the 3rd dimension while humans fill it with the 1st and 2nd dimensional cheapness. In thought and design humans avoid seeing life's termination in the 4th dimension, where father time acts out.

Embracing the gains of now while delaying the costs has long given structure to the human project; humans trying to be human. We mortgage our soul as we await a bankrupt end-state. Since 1550 this was known as the Faustian Bargain in the human project. Its thesis is found in ancient religious texts. While the soul may be a gateway to an improved future we recognize, perhaps in secret, that the soul might not even exist? Thus, ethics and how they are valued becomes the construct of behavior management. Then we must come to manage the role of that which is banned, something to not do, and its implicit attractions.

Faust is seldom mentioned in our digital world, but the Faustian model seems omnipresent in the shadows of human behavior. The reoccurring Faustian Tragedy has cumulative costs awaiting humans. Just now we begin to see these in what we call Climate Change, and its consequences for life.

> **"Faustian Bargaining:**
> Negotiating a pact with your bad side offering up your character, that is of supreme or spiritual importance, i.e., the values that define your soul, for worldly status from great knowledge of what does not matter, possession of too much stuff, signs of large wealth, or symbols of great power."[207]

---

[207] Ibid., from the introduction.

Answers about what we value when are now fundamental to what meaning we find in and offer to life. Instead of preparing our souls for the realization of the future we attempt to sell it or bury such in our mobile phones. Answers to significant questions are avoided, along with the sadness found therein, by arguing over the cheaper. Thus, the long-term becomes very expensive.

> "American consumers have been used to getting whatever they want whenever they want it, at dirt cheap prices, served to them by underpaid work-ers, for decades now. They can't fathom a world without these comforts. Corporations have nur-tured entire generations of spoiled consumer-cit-izens who only care about how much they can get for the least amount of money."[208]

Each of these had a view about the meaning of their life, and a viewpoint about the continuance of systems of life. The differences can be seen in which dimensions of existence they talked most about. Some preferred 0th 1st and 2nd, as will be explained later, while others occupied the 3rd and worried about the 4th. The 5th was something else.

Herein nature will be seen to occupy the 3rd dimension while humans fill it with the 1st and 2nd dimensional cheapness. In thought and design humans avoid seeing life's termination in the 4th dimen-sion, where father time acts out.

While delaying the costs has long given structure to the human project; humans trying to be human. We mortgage our soul as we await a bankrupt end-state. Since 1550 this was known as the Faustian Bargain in the human project. Its thesis is found in ancient religious texts. While the soul may be a gateway to an improved future we recognize, perhaps in secret, that the soul might not even exist? Thus, ethics and how they are valued becomes the construct of behavior

---

[208] Hawk, David, *Regulation of Environmental Deterioration*, Philadelphia, Wharton School, Dissertation Publications, 1979. P. 102.

management. Then we must come to manage the role of that which is banned, something to not do, and its implicit attractions.

Faust is seldom mentioned in our digital world, but the Faustian model seems omnipresent in the shadows of human behavior. The reoccurring Faustian Tragedy has cumulative costs awaiting humans. Just now we begin to see these in what we call Climate Change, and its consequences for life.

Something has changed as suggested in the Faustian process as quoted from Leonard Cohen. The human dilemma of choosing between selling off the long term (soul) existence for short-term gains (money, intelligence, or a beautiful woman?) continues. Recently the emphasis seems to have shifted to the economics of becoming developed via being ever more productive in life, i.e., getting more reward from less effort. This is now expressed as improving productivity in the making of and shopping for things. Cheaper is the standard interpretation now for the better.

Human activities defined to support development are of concern herein, especially those to meet human bio-needs and their psych-wants. They all seem to bring deterioration to the contextual environment, especially the natural aspects. These acts, components of industrialization, are a growing threat to the well-being of the contexts on which life continuance depends. Such appears to threaten the continuance of life on the planet.

We need to look more carefully at the *what* and the *why* of human activities. The first is being carefully studied by the sciences of environmental deterioration. The second is more ephemeral and thus evasive. To better understand the why it's helpful to look deeper at the *how* of human activities. The focus here builds on that and moves to management of the how. The how invites reflection on the idea of the individual soul and its historic meaning for self-management of life.

Most can see how the idea of the soul and its quiet existence in negotiating with eternity, or not, is obscured by its selling ever more cheaply. Can such even be addressed in a rational manner? Perhaps not. Can we thus tap into the non-rationality of "the what" by addressing the industrial rationality of "the how." This involves the construct of management and its conceptions since 500 BC with a focus on why the bias was with the masculine. The masculine is seen to be stronger than the feminine, thus in an often redeclared war on nature the masculine prevails in its management. Now that humans and nature seem to be approaching an end to the war, with both losing, we might want to rethink the conflict and its management. This is about a human project, perhaps the final project.

Something has changed as suggested in the Leonard Cohen song. Something else has remained constant. The ancient dilemma between selling the long term (soul) for some short-term gain (money, intelligence, or a beautiful woman?) continues but the emphasis somehow shifted to the economic language of needing to be ever more productive in life; getting more from less effort via improvements to productivity in making and shopping. Cheaper is now much better than better.

Human activities are of growing concern, especially those set out to meet bio-needs and psych-wants while bringing deterioration to the environment, especially the natural aspects. These acts, components of industrialization, are a growing threat to the well-being of life's context on which life depends for continuance. There is growing evidence that such activities are a great threat to continuance of life.

We need to look at the *what* and the *why* of human activities. The first is being carefully studied by the sciences of environmental deterioration. The second is more ephemeral and evasive. To better understand the why it's helpful to investigate the *how* of human activities. The focus here is with the management of the how. The show and its management invite reflection on the soul and its historic meaning for humans.

Most can see how the idea of the soul and its quiet existence in negotiating with eternity, or not, is obscured by its selling ever more cheaply. Can such even be addressed in a rational manner? Perhaps not.

Can we thus tap into the non-rationality of "the what" by addressing the industrial rationality of "the how." This involves the construct of management and its conceptions since 500 BC with a focus on why the bias was with the masculine. The masculine is seen to be stronger than the feminine, thus in an often redeclared war on nature the masculine prevails in its management. Now that humans and nature seem to be approaching an end to the war, with both losing, we might want to rethink the conflict and its management. This is about a human project, perhaps the final project.

Faust Struggles with the Human Soul

Faust is a central character in understanding and predicting human behavior. The ill-informed *Faustian Negotiation,* followed by the predictable *Tragedy,* are crucial to understanding the human passion for short-term gains leading into well-known long-term pains. The process holds no surprises except for the current triviality of the gain and the degree of approaching terror of the pain. Why are humans predisposed to neglect long-term tragedies awaiting them from the greed behind collection of ever shorter-term gains? This question is as important as it is obvious.

Have humans always been this way, or did the industrialization dream of the power of the artificial obscure human insight to and from context, and the ultimate role of nature as manager of context? The thesis in "Denial of Death" seems to clearly describe the process, the end state, and obstructions to change.

Since the 1550 articulation of the longer-term Faustian process for humans it had moved to center stage by the 20th Century. It was crucial to the development and shaping of development of the industrialization theme for two hundred years. Given a choice between accessing some immediate gain or reflecting on the consequences of picking up that gain, humans almost always have eagerly gone for the shortest term possible. As some humans say with much authority: "We are all dead in the long-term, so why not?" Of interest herein is where the Faustian dilemma becomes the tragedy articulated by Goethe.

This is clearly seen in the 21st Century via the construction and concepts of management. They are coming under questions like what has been historically posed in and now awaiting the end of line bargain in the Faustian Bargain behind industrialization. It can be seen via the human choices between the potentials in benefits of industry and the consequences lying in the future.

Humans are beginning to see the consequences of their negotiations with the Grand Faustian Bargain as articulated 150 years ago. The sage it portrays now looks to be coming to an end in a Great Faustian Tragedy.[209] It appears as a 4th dimensional culmination via 2-dimensional managing of 1-dimensional thinking for our 3-dimensional war against the natural, with a 0-dimensional attitude used to redefine life as artificial. This is most clearly seen in our ignoring the consequences from the short-term deal making that supports what was herein called industrialization. Its management as well as what it is used to create and direct need significant change.

Why do humans so closely focus on managing ever shorter-term results while avoiding longer-term consequences implicit in achieving such results? Will this Faustian Bargain require a debt be paid, or simply become a Faustian Tragedy? Who manages the human project? and where it fails who holds responsibility? An ominous dilemma seems to await the human project going wrong. Are humans capable of resolving the dilemma, or even seeing there to be one in waiting?

It begins by seeing a 5th dimension to reality where the concept of a soul resides with the notion that the holographic mind is well above the limits of the bio-mechanical brain. You might enjoy reviewing these six books to make the rational more difficult and thus move on to simple understanding of the non-rational obvious.

On Humans:

---

[209] This insight into being human began with Hans Faust in 1550 with a man's dissatisfaction with life, thus he visits the devil to discuss exchanging his soul for access to unlimited knowledge then worldly pleasures. The most widely known version of this resolution of the human problem is seen in Johann Goethe's work of the late 18th Century, while the US Constitution was under design. The 1945 Faust was much less optimistic. The devil had gone in hiding. He became scared of the deep evil he found in the humans of WWII. Another version of the Faustian human was later captured by Thomas Mann in his Pulitzer Prize version of *Doctor Faustus*, 1947.

-1973: *The Denial of Death*, Ernest Becker

-1976: *The Figure of Faust in Valery and Goethe*, Kurt Weinberg

-1978: *Heraclitean Fire: Sketches from a Life before Nature*, E. Chargaff

-1981: *The Arrogance of Humanism*, David Ehrenfeld

-2014: *The Sixth Extinction: An Unnatural History*, Elizabeth Kolbert

-2022: *Sorry, Humans are Fucked: Climate Change from Humans*

Beyond the Digital Creation of the Bi-Polar

For 2,500 years humans have been wedded to unnatural mental models that support schizophrenia and bi-polar relations with self and environment. Seen as conflicting pairs, couples, dilemmas, dichotomies, paradoxes, and now the godhead of knowledge, the digital. The greater potential of nature, the diverse, thus numerous all became reduced to an artificial simplicity of two. Once humans see a one, they seem to seek the second to wed the "two" in eternal conflict. As such humans are funny. You can easily create arguments against all things once you have two. You can even create the artificial context for very bloody wars between humans. If that is not available there is always nature to declare war upon.

To repair such, we can move to *"Both Plus More"* and thus by-pass the tyranny of two. The powers of diversity can thus be brought back into the human thought process, to see a greater whole and hopefully the greater good. You may have noticed that the meanest form of politics is based on two. This emphasizes the gravity of the cavity awaiting us once trapped in the limitations of two. In law and the government, the two beget the eternal authoritarian idea of governance the encourages a flipping between idiot wanting to be leaders. In truer democracies voters have the option of using "none of the above" where when such received 50% of votes the selection process begins again. Armed with such, citizens can move beyond the bi-polar corruption in two. Both Plus More is where the two are wedded so you can then move to negotiating with the more important "More" of life. Indeed, there is more out there, or in here.

As Leonard Cohen sings, "There is a crack in everything. That's how the light gets in, that's how the light gets in." Current operations and expectations of the digital indeed reveal cracks. Change begins by looking through those cracks to see the deep failures. If such happens in Silicon Valley, USA or Shen Zen, China is an open debate. Just now the odds for success are now with China as it moves increasingly in an open-source information systems model, and the freedom of access such implies. This is the operational opposite of California's Microsoft in allowing, even encouraging, improvements via the users, not just collecting user payments for use. Via this there will be effective alternatives to Babbage thinking of twosomes.

Negentropy Stage 1: Entrepreneuring the Impossible

Some seek ways to better access realities. Some ignore all distinctions about what they never choose to be part of. Others reject any restriction on their freedom and strike back via quotes from various religions and/or sciences that allow immortality projects.

The pathway of the third group is interesting. Why are they attracted to immortality projects, and what will they do to find such? They generally begin by ignoring restrictions from nature or by its laws about what is and isn't. They are generally drawn to laws as created by man, not of nature. Many become politicians after an affair with man-made laws via law school. They invest much time in creating a non-natural, artificial existence often called the human project. They do not see or look for the costs in this approach as it becomes anti-natural, then unnatural. One such natural law and a clear opponent to any on immortality trips is 2nd Law of Thermodynamics and its very significant process call *entropy*. Entropy imposes considerable limitations of life and accesses to a future, as well as considerable costs on those who pretend its existence via what is called negative entropy, or simply *negentropy*. Softly implied by its ruling's entropy defines the pathway towards death. Negentropy thus labels a door-way to immortality.

In argument humans invent an anti-entropic conception of negative entropy then markets it through its material and energy systems. This is to help humans believe they are not governed by the Entropic process and can rely on technological advancement. The dilemma is seen in measures called negentropy which are seen to be major factors in creating conditions of climate change. The dilemma is encouraged by management systems, with emphasis on the first three letters. It seems we are due to experimentation with Femagement to repair what Industrialized Management has given humans.

To date there has been no discussion of the human creation and marketing of this notion of negative entropy. If you look carefully at all commercials used in advertising, you see the optimism of entropic processes being overridden or simply missing. Ideas such as environmental protection, recycling, sustainability, and more recently regeneration[210] where such people: argue "To reverse global warming, we need to reverse global degeneration." The author ignores the irreversibility of entropic deterioration, worshipped by humans as negative entropy. There are now dozens of additional books filled with optimistic theses for change. All disregard the entropic process, and how human derived economics is its major driver. Another is the book by Jason Hickel: *Less is More: How Degrowth Will Save the World.*[211]

Herein we look at climate change as a human problem that often generates other problems. We try to better understand how the human problem is generated in how humans think and act upon those thoughts. A dimensional framework is used. This is highly unusual but tends to better address a wide array of issues human, not just their creation of processes that lead to climate changes that threaten life. We will go into these dimensions in some detail later in the book.

---

[210] Hawken, Paul, *Re-generation: Ending the climate crisis in one generation*, New York: Penguin Books, 2021. Page 9.
[211] Hinkel, Jason, London: Penguin Books. 2020.

Assumptions for Humans Being Human:
-Birth implies access to a 1st dimension on a line
to the future.
-Exaggerating a line end deposits you on 2nd
dimensional flatland.
-Life can rise to 3rd dimensional life via multi-dimensional experience.
-The 3rd D becomes lessened via 4th dimensional
changes.
-Entropy dissipates potential of the 3rd via the
unfolding of the 4th.
-Upset by the 4th humans act up to increase
entropy in the 3rd.
-Do humans search for hope or seek immortality
via hopelessness.

Negentropy Stage 2: Manufacturing & Marketing the Cheap

Humans portray their values in religions, romances, economics, and the hierarchy of their organizations. This helps them feel import-ant, encourages them to act to become ever more important, while collecting the short-term rewards and avoiding the longer-term costs. We use these filters to locate the values we want exhibited by our leaders. We thus evaluate whom to respect, to love and to ignore and/or even hate. Human organizations use empty preambles to evaluate metaphorical life in the longer term while cashing in on people living in the short-term. Actual managers of such organizations become less metaphorical in who they select to do what, and for what price. Valuation of such is becoming clearer in choice and management of AI systems of management. Just now it appears in AI choice of automated car driving, as seen in the choice of who to sacrifice in an impending accident, the car owner of a pedestrian? Such choices were towards the technological in the early 20th century workplace but via socio-technical change they went to the social. Now, in the 21st Century they are moving back to the fundamental importance of the technological.

How do we see valuation of life outside ourselves, and demonstrate value in attempts to appreciate nature? Do humans value consumption of nature, or do they revel in implied power in it denigration? Humans avoid the questions about climate change even more than answers regarding what and who brought it about. We have come to see industrialization as a human-derived religion. We use such to demonstrate the "arrogance of humanism" and invest in hierarchies to ensure nature is available for humans to oversee, to consume, and as a basis for entertainment, love, and war. As such human tending to focus on where life begins and ends while acting to trivialize much of what happens in between, all while working to disassociate themselves from the process.

Religions outside humanism can inform why and how humans hold the central place in the universe, nature, and their private personalities. Within this religion men pose a religious focus on the freedom of men, the servitude of women as carriers of conceptions, then mostly ignore the results of the births. This all illustrates a definition of life around a homocentric hierarchy of self-importance of men consistent with dreams of Maslow. Sometimes Maslow's idea of "self-actualization" becomes useful to winning of wars between men. Such religions set up a context where everyone loses. We see the same in the eternal war of humans against nature. We then try to not notice the feedback loops from nature in turbulence of diseases, storms, hunger, and uncertainty.

We invest our days in managing, or being managed, to become ever more productive in the making, buying, and having stuff, evaluated as appearing expensive while fulfilling our desire to get them cheap. To whom is such of value? Do we feel better concentrating on helping others to live, as we are told we should, or do we invest more in helping ourselves as producers, users, and owners of the cheap? Do we invest our souls in preparation for a "better" afterlife or do we invest in bringing more liter into this life and a very strange version of an immortality project?

Dreams of reason via unaided rationality inspire the entrepreneurship and business development that assures such moral dead ends. We seem open to leaders that aggressively preach their denial of death.[212] Key to such as use of the strategy as being taught in universities: "fake it until you make it." Further on we create ads supporting illusions of freedom from all limitations, while in pursuit of privatized immortality trips. Neg-entropy is clearly not possible but is the most instrumental aspect in ads.

A major shortcoming in episodes for finding neg-entropy becomes its legitimation of some activities that are a threat to the systems of life on which life depends. We see such around us in industrialized deterioration as added to natural entropic processes. The process can be seen in marketing of many goods and services produced, sold, and used by humans. Neg-entropy is clearly a dominant theme of happiness intended in commercials, including those about governance, especially in that it doesn't and can't exist. Perhaps that is why neg-entropy is so attractive to business as usual. The attraction can be seen in business education lectures and supporting textbooks. Such may explain why marketing and strategy are favorite subjects.

Marketing the bad as strategically attractive, for at least the day, strategically avoids its long-term costs. Those best at marketing seem to avoid those longer-term questions, while seemingly understanding the human weakness for doing such. Some go deeper and begin to enjoy selling what cannot exist, e.g., neg-entropy, to those that don't understand but believe what they want and must thus own it. Much teaching in an MBA program implicitly centers on this although never mentions entropy, nor its opposite.

As was suggested above, most humans came to believe that improvement to human life would be via improvements to the industrial machine. While that has been traditionally restricted to productivity, units/time improvement, it needs to be reconsidered. Measures for improvement must now include the extent of deterioration from product making processes and then product use. This would require much change to the traditions of evaluation from Aristotle, Newton, Smith, Babbage, , and Maslow. As they were leaders in arriving at measures of management, we need to begin to look there to better understand what has resulted in climate change consequences. Their

---

[212] Ernest Becker, *Denial of Death*, New York: Free Press, 1973.

offerings were praised as exactly what was needed to create a desirable future for humans. From that the occasional B-School Harvard, et.al. suggestion was fit into management of the industrial.

Such became a pro-artificial, anti-nature, deceptively strategic approach steeped in the logic of reductionistic analysis and defined as progressive. During the nineteen-fifties concerns arose about such definitions of progress. Those people, Boulding, Ackoff, Bennis, Trist, etc. raised issues of the systemic and non-mechanical behaviors being absent. Moving deeper, they began to see nature as a systemic ally of human well-being, not the enemy of progressive leadership. By the nineteen-seventies the concern for the natural was expanding.

Regardless of those leading-edge researchers, most humans saw such concern as "too early" to worry about. "The Tragedy of the Commons" of 1965 did not yet seem relevant to most places and peoples. From a 1975-77 international research effort it was suggested in 1979 that the consequences of 19th Century values would create a situation of "it would be too late" if humans waited for redress of the industrial by the 21st Century. Study results suggested that by then relations between life and its essential environment would be well down a dysfunctional pathway, so far that the consequences could no longer be halted, nor managed. Many in governmental leadership positions responded with "so what," but by 2022 the same see that it's "too late" and now ask "now what."

We seldom access the presumptions underlying the above story. Our dreams of new business are shorter-term ways to discover the "ever cheaper." We call this improving productivity of goods and services. Our road to the more productive, i.e., the cheaper, is via industrialized superhighways of production designed to meet bio-needs and psych-wants. Finding this mission to be meaningful, we move into the land of the cheap. Leonard Cohen notes this economic idea in his work:

Crucial to our search for the cheap is the marketing of what is not and especially what cannot be. Most of such can be seen via use of the idea of neg-entropy. That such is scientifically impossible only seems to add to its attraction. The idea of neg-entropy thus becomes a driver in seeking, advertising, and selling the cheap. One counterforce is seen in the operation of inflation, a process obscured by those seeking access to leadership roles. Politicians market neg-entropy as their ideal where the assumptions are masked by incompetence swimming in meanness. We see many advertising images marketed as access to neg-entropy. These mostly end as increasing the entropy in our environment. From this mess we see leadership demanding access to what is not and can never be, sometimes with a smile. During the more honest periods of human history this is recorded as leadershit.

Contemporary leadership suggests we are about to gain access to such via advancing technology. Such leaders and followers are easy to identify as they know little to nothing of technology. They emphasize a special access to neg-entropy. Examples come under many labels but are especially apparent in portrayal of the masculine owning products.

From realization of the above a few simply drop out and wait. Others in this group turn to entertainment which adds to the entropic processes. A different group attempts to be nice but end as being mostly nice to themselves. Yet others grow bitter as they discover entropy thus turn a feeling of greatness found in being leaders in families, corporations, or governments. Followers become insulation from the sad limitations from their efforts. As unchecked leaders they come to emphasize what can be characterized as less than they are, which includes nature. They do this in many ways, including feats of comical valor seen in special forms of marketing. They denounce nature while their actions bring deterioration upon it. Those who measure the results seem to find hopelessness.

Humans harm the natural while denouncing any that would do such. We thus find ourselves trapped in a form of societal schizophrenia, via a "societal double-bind." Using the excuse of "damned if you do, damned if you don't" we apply ever more energy from nature in meeting human bio-needs and psycho-wants. We thus seek comfort in ignoring the feedback loops that leave dirt, disease, and deterioration where greatness was to be. Much of this is undertaken under the cover of immortality projects, in support of neg-entropy, where the newer versions are seen in sustainability, recyclability, and ecological economics. To avoid the consequences of this some humans, move to wilderness settings upstream to avoid the longer-term costs of what we do. Only a few can live upstream from where industrial waste is deposited. In this way we create a bi-polar world of the paradoxes of an industrialized existence. Is this the best we can manage?

Throughout their existence humans have been concerned about transitory threats from instabilities in their environment. Storms, angry animals, dangerous humans, and hunger are some. These threaten life but are restricted in time and location. Tornados, droughts, hurricanes, and temperature extremes surrounding a dwelling, and germs and diseases can affect the insides doing much harm. All can be restricted and have long been manageable. Where humans could not move to different places or better times. This has changed.

Unmanageable threats come from a destabilized environment. These are being seen as more common as they expand. Space and time no longer offer last lines of defense. Something is now different. Disconcerting and mostly disregarded is how these threats to life can be traced back to previous human activities. Such humans lacked knowledge of or concern for the future of life on the planet, or so the story goes. In fact, a particular human, a woman, showed such danger to exist back in 1856. Now, in 2022 we see what she posed to happen from how we then accessed and used energy has grown and becomes increasingly ominous and omnipresent. The challenge has gone from the call to change to discovery of the unmanageable. Management of the unmanageable thus provides humans with a current challenge. It's not a happy subject.

Life will be removed from continuance via emerging conditions with little warning and no explanation. We hold nature responsible for such but if we look closer, we see it comes from prior and present human actions. Even when seeing this we generally continue with our deterioration and ignore the consequences. Bad results, from bad intentions, continue. Then, when we become upset about pending climate change consequences from excess CO_2 from our gas-powered autos, we go out for a drive to relax and dream of how life could be if humans would just stop driving around unnecessarily. We see humans becoming ever more productive in doing the wrong thing.

Guiding our passion for ever improving productivity is an important value driving the search for the cheap. It's at the center of valuation of process via industrialization set up to prove goods and services. Cheap control functions are then set up to protect while worshiping the artificial and desecrating the natural.

While still seeming strange to many humans, the above process anti-natural process was carefully articulated in 1856 in the work of a female scientist then presented to the Annual American Association for the Advancement of Science Annual Meeting. Her work was presented by a man sitting next to her at the meeting. True to belief in the Garden of Eden storyline women weren't trusted to give important lectures. Her work focused on the consequences of industrialization as designed by the masculine to serve the needs of human life. She saw the consequences as irreversible, like entropy, as such was articulated by a man around the same time.

Yes, from her initial warning we faced variances that grow from human acts to, in, and against nature over time. Meanwhile, the entropic unfolds at its own steady pace within time. The 1856 woman warned us of a process from which industrialized man was emerging. Such is proving to be more ominous than the entropy men feared. It acts as a second-order phenomenon initiated by badly conceived first order supports to human enhancement.

That we are heading into a dire state is open to some debate, except that the evidence for the downside arrives with more evidential clarity each day. The optimistic responses mostly point to resolution of human problems via humanly designed additional technology. Just in case it goes bad there are a few billionaire men that are developing technology to carry them to Mars as a sanctuary. Faith in the technological enhances belief in future human life. Such is mostly derived from sciences of the artificial. We even use such sciences to mask ourselves from information on the major threats to life, even though they helped generate such.

Humans make such products seemingly to fill dreams of reason, and to make them as cheaply available as possible. They avoid seeing energy quality dissipate as a requirement emphasized in the 2nd Law of Thermodynamics.

Negentropy 3: Submission then Prostitution of Nature

I've been involved in climate change concerns and research since the early nineteen-seventies. In 1975 I was seen by leaders in governments and universities as a questionable researcher. Company leaders different in that they saw me as a researcher who enjoyed causing trouble for business as usual in public and private sectors. I was after a more basic sense of understanding and truth in how humans relate to each other and their environments. Many in universities saw it as strange that industry leaders and their corporate scientists were very receptive to the projects on change, I initiated. This included the leader of Exxon, Mr. Clifton Garvin, and his director of science Edward David.

A 1975 climate change project I proposed as "Environmental Protection: Analytic Solutions in Search of Synthetic Problems" came to be publicly endorsed by Mr. Garvin with enthusiasm. Once he joined with many other corporate leaders, he shared their knowledge base. They wanted change and could see change on the horizon. They wanted to learn more.

The history of that project was recently reported by Alice Bell,[213] a Guardian reporter who had long been interested in the sad history of climate change warnings and no serious human reactions to needed human changes.

> "One of the hardest parts of writing about the history of the climate crisis was stumbling across warnings from the 50's, 60's and 70's musing about how things might get bad sometime after the year 2000 if no one did anything about fossil fuels. They still had hope back then. Reading that hope today hurts."

---

[213] Bell, Alice, *Guardian News and Media*: London, July 12, 2021, "Sixty years of climate change warnings: the signs that were missed (and ignored)" Now available on *Inside Climate News*, 7/24/2022.

She referenced how my Swedish research project, mentioned above, came to attract much help from leading government and industry groups. The project documented the industrialization process of environmental desecration leading to deterioration. Near the end of that study and its documentation we reported on the serious problems emerging in future environments. We posed that climate change awaited our non-resolution of our industrialized selves. The project came to be the first project in a new PhD granting program at the Stockholm School of Economics titled the Institute of International Business. That was a very well-funded group by foundations and international companies of Sweden. They wanted to improve their knowledge of international businesses relative to changes taking place in the world. The Institute, known as IIB, was set up to help students research threats to business as usual, which was seen to be leading to no business without change.

The project on environmental deterioration from industrialization of business attracted extensive and gracious help from many companies. The companies even helped document different rates of deterioration relative to different governmental approaches to regulating it. We could thus measure the rates of success in various national approaches to regulation of problems. At the end we included climate change as a serious problem. From refining our data we concluded it would be a problem beyond any known governmental regulation. We projected the difficulties in the future to be so serious that the then current practices of business as usual would end in no business.

Unlike the ethical feelings of the major Petro-Chemical company leadership since the 1990s the CEOs of many of the major participants in that 1975 research were sincerely concerned about the research issues. They felt their products may be having a difficult impact on the natural environment and were funding research into how serious the problems were likely to be, and what solutions were available.

Foremost was James W. Kinnear, who in 1971 became Senior VP of Worldwide Refining for Texaco, then CEO in 1982 to resolve serious troubles in financial management. He became famous for his resolutions in that they created a very different company. He was even praised by environmental groups. He had allowed me unrestricted access to world-wide refiners and R&D scientists such as Dr. Black who came to write the legendary "Climate Change" paper of 1977. Black was heavily supported by Kinnear. As a New York Times Headline stated it February 22, 1987 "The Man Who Wears the Star: James W. Kinnear; is Winning Friends for Texaco When It Needs Them Most."

I was welcomed into a similar relationship with Clifton Garvin of Exxon. He had become President of Exxon in 1972, prior to my study but when he became CEO in 1975 he asked to join my study. He offered me unrestricted access to Exxon people and facilities. He later gave strong support to studies into the impact of CO_2 on climate. In my study he once commented that: "The 'greenhouse effect' will 'presumably lead to an increase in global temperatures with attendant consequences." This Exxon candor changed when he was replaced in 1986 by a new CEO, Lee Raymond, a Texas Oilman in the negative sense of that term.

In an interview with Charlie Rose, he commented on my study, then clarified Exxon's position by elaborating on his feelings about climate change.

"The Climate – the climate has changed every year for millions of years. If we weren't here, the climate would change. It has to do with sunspots, it has to do with the wobble of the Earth, and it has – there are all kinds of things that come and go. If you talk to a geologist, he will tell you the Earth, throughout its history, has been much warmer than it is now and much colder. ... Man didn't have anything to do with it."[214]

Alice Bell referenced the above work as key to early warnings of the extent of climate change in generating serious problems to industry and governments in all the world from what we had defined as business as usual.

---

[214] Lee Raymond, from a video of him being interviewed by Charlie Rose, Nov. 5, 2005. https://charlierose.com

"In the summer of 1977, James Black, a top science advisor at Exxon, made a presentation on the greenhouse effect to the company's most senior staff. This was a big deal. ... The same year, the company hired Edward David Jr. to head up their research labs. He had learned about climate change while working as an advisor to Nixon. ... He was also part of a project organized in Sweden by David Hawk of the Stockholm School of Economics. Its final report in 1977 outlined the probability of climate change if humans could not change their industrial behavior. Hawk's project was titled: "Environmental Protection: Analytic Solutions in Search of Synthetic Problems."[215]

James Black was part of the 1975 research project along with scientists from twenty other major companies. In the project I was allowed access to workers in factories and laboratories throughout the companies. I was then with Black in his presentation to top industry scientists in a July 1977 meeting in New Jersey. Parts of my work on the impact of climate change on the international context were presented along with Black's science of climate change. Later that fall Black again made this presentation to Exxon's Board in New York City. (I could not attend.)

In September 1977 the Director of the US EPA heard of the Black presentations and reviewed the three-volume research reporting of my project. He then sent me a letter attached to a cardboard box with all copies of my reports that he could find in the US EPA offices. His letter said, "Mr. Hawk, EPA had no further use of these reports, your research, nor you." As with the Dean of the Wharton School two years later, he saw climate change threats as a non-scientific hoax, that might greatly threaten business.

Black and other industry people were important to accessing the basis for concern about climate change. He was the first to tell

---

[215] IBID, Alice Bell

me of the incredibly important work of a woman scientist in 1856 named Eunice Foote. Her work was stunningly simple and insightful. She was to present her results to the annual AAAS Conference. At the time no females had made such important presentations. She thus asked a man near her in the auditorium to read it. Foote's work showed how carbon dioxide gas could absorb and hold incredible amounts of heat, thus posing the serious potential to lead to what we now are calling global warming.

In 1856 she had been concerned with the growing quantities of coal going into an expanding industrial process. To add to her concern with growth in CO2 she was intrigued with the 1855 science by Rudolf Clausius of a 2nd Law of Thermodynamics. She thought the dangerous global warming process could be compounded via the entropy law that had just been formalized the year before.

Formalized in 1855 the entropy law seemed to suggest that greater amounts of CO2 production, via more industrialization, might lead to more drastic and irreversible versions of the Foote concern. Black bought into the Foote thesis, and concern. He taught me about it. Edward David, Black's boss, joined my project later. He was unimpressed with the ideas of this woman called Foote and concerned that Black might be exaggerating climate change science. He did concur with my fear of shortcomings in the then model of government environmental regulation. I kept notes on his arguments with Black about the extent of future danger possible in Foote's 1856 thesis.[216]

Humans are caught up in a stream of bad luck or trapped in the results of unfortunate decisions based on weaknesses of their analysis, while avoiding the context offered in synthesis. Some say artificial intelligence has worked to reduce the levels of natural intelligence. Others say it was the masculine values behind industrialization that

---

[216] Of some interest is that research documents on the empirical and theoretical aspects of my 1975-77 Sweden project, as mentioned by Alice Bell, were seized and impounded by two leaders of New Jersey Institute of Technology. The order went out in 2009 and was renewed in 2012. I had been teaching there and had an office there. Those two leaders and Governor Chris Christie impounded the work as "NJ State Property." NJ courts agreed with them thus I lacked access for this book. This was consistent with the problem in regulation as noted.

could not tolerate questions, and needed to manage disobedience, first in nature, then in men, and of course in women. This was extended to include all ideas, especially those of skeptical science. An alternative thesis was that humans were simply suicidal and needed to pretend leadership to compensate for their weaknesses, especially if they know they are doing wrong. Factory workers in the various facilities studied in various countries in the Swedish project would often comment on troubles in their management and headquarters leadership. They saw something seriously wrong in the human picture as it related to the larger environment.

Questions about the human project are now very serious. Thus, youth are increasingly wondering about the qualities of their elders. While awaiting answers their suicide rate steadily climbs, and they decide to not have children and continue the struggle with a bad end. Many hold off on any decisions while asking greatly improved questions to those who keep on marketing the ugly answers in business as usual, as it becomes no business. School courses simply seem like dutiful preparation for a long ugly road with no desirable end point. Hopeless is the mood of the day. It has descended over their optimism as they laugh at adult's selling of the post-industrial. Digitization restricting humans to the two dimensions of a computer screen as a modern flatland is not attractive to them. Commentary from my classes suggest that proverbial "glass" is neither half-full nor half-empty. It is clearly empty, covered in urine stains by humans.

As the questions about the human project become more serious youth are increasingly serious in their questions. School teachings are mostly to prepare students for an era in the past. It is mostly irrelevant, if not bothersome, to any understanding of a normative future. A hopeless mood surrounds marketing of the past optimism of an industrial model being the myth driving the human project. Digitization as the postindustrial is a trivial tangent.

Comments from youth suggest the proverbial glass is neither half-full nor half-empty. It's empty, covered in human urine stains, as said above, but needs to be underlined now. Differences now seen to not make a difference are now seen for what they were. They were a manly basis for masculine warfare with nature, others, and then selves. The results of those differences are now seen as societal trauma. Such is everywhere, as parts challenging the meaning of the whole as never before, even as the whole falls apart. This will soon be seen in the insurance industry becoming unaffordable followed by the mortgage industry that requires the insurance to exist.

12
Understanding Dimensional Platforms

Ignorance From Unaided Rationality

Did life lose its meaning, or has meaning lost its life? A declining natural environment seems to show up as biofeedback in the 5th dimension of our mental state. It's as if systems of life are all aware of a tragedy approaching such systems. Our minds seem to deteriorate along with our environments. Both domains are clearly in trouble in 2021.

Humans feel less arrogant about the role of humans in a funny artificial hierarchy of life as was told in their evolutionary biology classes. There is less faith in Nobel Prize winner Herbert Simon's key belief that hierarchy is central to knowing and managing life. Hierarchy is even used to explain why men should be atop women, as exhibited in the Garden of Eden.

Thankfully, younger designers question the dictates for traditional design of the artificial. They ask why is the artificial essential, or even good? Must we occupy an artificial world. The most important, yet unnoticed, aspect of the artificial in product, building, and city design is the law of parallels.

Euclid's 5th Postulate, on parallels being key to understanding his universe, is becoming increasingly strange as no parallel lines are found in nature, including the universe. None-the-less, we of masculine heritage use it religiously in design of spaces, streets, buildings, and cities? It is the most dominant yet unnoticed aspect of the artificial environment, as the artificial environment replaces more of what nature offers.

The above introduces significant shadows and signs of unfathomable storms on the horizons of life. We clearly have problems in redefining humans and conditions of life to meet an environment that we have redefined. This evidence is worrisome yet is only a symptom of a larger problem of how humans attempting to be artificial must survive in a world of and managed by nature. There has long been a war between the artificial and the natural, but information now suggests a winner.

Since 1856 science posed dangers from human intelligence managed by those with a lack of wisdom and concern for context. Since then, a major threat to life and nature has been created and expanded. In our education, economics, and business, what is now seen by some as more than dangerous has been glorified as the essence of human development. The consequences are much deeper, wider, and more dramatic than the ego discussed above. Even if we work to ignore it, it has access to what we will call the collective consciousness of life. It is a growing threat to bio-physical existence. It arises as a long-term consequence of actions that humans are most proud of.

Science has long pointed to humans endangering systems of living order but never quite like what we now face. Life, as part of nature, depends on natural systems that are clearly endangered. Thus, our dreams of a continuance of life is endangered. Some scientists sense the sixth version of five prior episodes of change that came to limit life on the planet. Fires, storms, diseases, floods, and droughts are frequent and expanding. Air, water, and food quality needed to maintain life is vanishing. Something is changing.

> "In the past few decades, geologists have started filling in the rough sketches of the Big Five mass extinctions with gruesome detail, but the story has largely eluded the public imagination. Our conception of history tends to stretch back only a few thousand years at most, and typically only a few hundred. ...like reading only the last sen-

tence of a book and claiming to understand
what's in the rest of the library...Visiting Earth's
turbulent and unfamiliar past provides a possible
window into our future."[217]

Worth noting is how this state of extinction results from human activities, not cosmic. Humans point to their importance to life while acting to eliminate it. In denying continuance of systems required of life, most humans work to avoid noting them. It's funny to be a human.

Threats arise from the longer-term consequences of many and varied human activities seeking short-term enhancement to their lives. Distinct from being caretakers of a heritage passed on to us, we seem to have joined forces with the entropic law of the universe that Einstein, Sagan, and Hawking assigned much respect to as the temporal force for disorder. In an unreflective manner we mostly contribute to the irreversible degradation of conditions essential to life.

If we ever wish to do so, how might we reverse the above process or prepare to manage the consequences from it? Current management of human affairs implies the opposite, that we are not up to accepting responsibility for our behavior. There is insufficient concern for the probable end state. Our passion for negotiating with hollow promises of eternal stability via changelessness managed by humans is great. Some even brag that deteriorating the natural environment, via economic activities, is a precondition to "the good life." Are we seriously trying to win a war against nature's ambiguities and uncertainties, just as we wage war against opposing humans that seem to oppose our values or management systems? Are there limits to human knowledge of productive life but not to counter-productive behaviors?

The first two items can be addressed by reflection. The last requires deeper forms of knowing. It requires access to the unfamiliar and unnamed, not just the unknows. Answers to the first item can be clarified via discourse with those we don't like to agree with.

---

[217] Brannen, Peter, *The Ends of the World*, Harper Collins: New York, 2017, p. 8.

The second requires reconsideration of what is valued in life. The third requires a great appreciation of the universe, its rule system, and human's role in it, if they have one.

The following book is not an easy or happy read. If you are uncomfortable with questions about long-standing religious beliefs and/or post-Aristotle skepticism about logic and rationality being the foundation of life, then you might not appreciate what follows. The contents give no support to those who prefer the security of Plato's Cave with it providing continual support to two-dimensional images from the shadows on the cave ceiling. The feeling of security from two dimensions is similar yet now given by digital representations on screens. In this way the challenges of the third and threats of the fourth dimensions are obscured. This protects you from visualizing and experiencing consequences of prior actions. Creators of Apple, Microsoft and Amazon "created" it. All you did was use it so as in Plato's Cave you can forget any responsibility.

Humans are becoming less tolerant of each other, while being more accommodating of their own weaknesses. This is seen in how they exhibit anger, ignorance, silliness, irreversibly wrong endeavors, and dislike of difference in others. Why? Donald Trump, a spokesperson for the phenomena, illustrated the meaning of being in an era of hatred of life, as did his "followers." It was as if millions discovered that they were mortal, and in fact rather insignificant in the universe, and became damned angry. Dreams of a long-term immortality were dashed. Industrialization, the great human achievement, was beginning to be seen for its long-term expenses.

Industrialization was driven by dreams of short-term gains characterized by writers in *The Economists* arguing to increase productivity as a basis for happy economics. Such came to be the accepted standard of the knowledge managing the private sector. In general we can see that much of what was accomplished came via extensive use of cause-effect thinking. Now we see where many problems accompanied such thinking.

Now we can move on to inclusion of time as a major variable in the research and practice of what was learned and what awaits our learning. We might well come to call it 'Effects of Effects" thinking.

In this was we seek the prior effects, not causes, of prior systemic processes in our environment. This will open more interesting and helpful doorways into the future. Dimensionality will be crucial to understanding future effects of past effects. From this we can see what an individual or social ground thinks and speaks arises from where they stand, sit or lie. Much of what you represent can be seen to come from the dimension you have chosen to occupy.

Dimensions Beyond Space, Time and Matter

Having given up on finding meaning in the significant humans then turn to ideas for managing the insignificant. This shows up most clearly in the course on how to use case studies to understand strategic thinking. Many job applications now require applicant knowledge of case study education and an understanding of strategy. To see why this is an obvious problem read from the strategic gospel of Carl von Clausewitz. His chapter ten explains the fundamental importance of deceit in being strategic. Titled "cunning," Clausewitz offers examples of military actions that require deceit. For him, and his followers, deceit is an essential means to winning. MBA students in business schools learn much about this in their courses as well as in their program. As such they are preparing to move beyond business as usual, with changes essential to business as unusual requirements.

Careful examination of marketing syllabi shows how advertising is important to get customers away from thoughts of long-term problems with products. During product design entropy is put aside while ads focus on perpetual motion. Thus, with an MBA, graduates are prepared to engage in Faustian negotiations. This becomes key to innovative industrialization that strives to continually improve productivity at doing the wrong thing.

This book uses the philosophical frame of Goethe and his classic work, the Faustian Tragedy, to clarify the meaning of why climate change is not a hoax and will turn business as usual into no business. The emergence of conditions of climate change raises questions about from where it comes, to where it will go, and why it's now beyond traditional management to avoid it.

This process presents humans with a serious problem as power over the environment and timeliness turn out to be helpful in life, but relatively worthless to life. Time, for example, is of supreme value to life. As the home of entropy, it governs the cosmos, is ominous. Within the 4th dimension, it reveals the rule systems of life, and death. It is as significant to humans as is their effort to ignore it. This is a pity as it comes to resolve the dilemma of climate change conditions and how they became too late to manage.

Is there anything humans can do now to avoid climate change? No. If not, what should they do? Can humans manage the consequences of unfortunate human behavior by changing the values that managed to create them? Can we step outside their little Euclid created boxes to understand their context in a larger reality, before they have no reality? As I used to ask my architecture students in getting them to design spaces without parallels, "How often have you seen parallels in nature?"

Finding love or seeking love are meaningful events yet can seem trivial in some contexts. To manage either, or both, and make sense of things human we can face a significant challenge. Management may be unhelpful. In dealing with events of passion management rules can become relatively trivial. From episodes of passion, we often end up at why. Using why to understand relations of passion, which are inherently systemic, and not open to analysis, can worsen things. Much of being human is different, and inherently analytic. As such it's almost trivial while appearing very insightful and leading to power over the subject being analyzed. Context, where parts become systemic, is far more important to the meaning. The problem for human nature in this is that the analytic implies great power, in the Faustian sense, while context tends to trivialize power and those who aspire to manage it.

Learning to appreciate context is meaningful to life's unfolding. From examining the social context, we see how humans seek short-term results and thus create longer-term consequences from producing and using the results. Understanding context then helps us understand management and its alternatives. Knowledge of context informs process and should inform those choosing behaviors.

Humans seem very attracted to a pattern of behavior that has long been with humans but came to be called Faustian in the 16th Century. It came from ethical discourse in religious teaching, focusing on the centerpiece of ethical discourse, the soul, and who would own it. It was about each person having a discussion with the devil about who really owned the soul, or if anyone cared. The discussion was called the Faustian negotiation. It was a central management theme for human bargaining with their reality over being good, or bad. From ideas about humans' needs, or wants, humans devised ever shorter-term gains in accessing their needs and wants within brief lives. They were willing to let the costs arrive later, assuming they knew there would be costs humans calculated how such would not arrive until they were dead. In this way ethics were structured around accumulation of gains, not the longer-term cost, i.e., pain, associated with their behavior.

Understanding Via Dimensional Appreciation

Continuing research describes climate change as seriously emerging, with ever greater clarity we see human activities to be the sponsor of climate change. What is difficult is why humans continue their fateful activities behind the impending situation despite knowing more of its probable end. Humans are increasingly aware this is coming and that they are responsible but seem unable to change their role. As climate change approaches it seems ever more difficult to understand why humans would create such a serious long-term paradox knowing it ends as catastrophic for life.

It seems clearer with time that humans occupy several dimensions of existence. While they have very different properties and support different activities, they all support some aspects of consciousness. They are not hierarchical yet substantially different. Each involves aspects of management between humans and their contexts, although the qualitative differences are great. Herein these are outlined as dimensional locations. They offer a variety of contexts where humans are drawn to behave differently in each.

There is some urgency to humans waking from their current state of misplaced stability, that might best be called changelessness. Since my climate change research of the nineteen-seventies two issues seem consistent in results of general climate change research. One is that the consequences become more serious with time. Two is that they are arriving sooner than anticipated in earlier research on the same topics. This is explained in the following via a dimensional array. It allows us to clearly see the basis of many traditional human behaviors as sponsored by a context. This allows access to more of the how and why that allows humans to continue to contribute to causes of climate change.

As a backdrop to the larger process of climate change emerging to define the context of life, we see governmental management being changed. *Somehow governments are shifting in many parts of the world from attempts to become more democratic to the dangerous situation of fewer humans having more control of what is done, and perhaps of more importance, what is not being done.* Leadership, an aspect of management, had become a serious impediment, just as it seems to have been a sponsor of the situation needing resolution.

It might be helpful to begin to shift towards a dimensional context to better understand where we are, and more important, to where we must go. To learn more about such a dimensional basis to our context for thinking then acting I offer this section. I will outline 0 through 4 dimensions that are easily available to consider and act out within. This is distinctly not a hierarchy schema. It is a way to include greater amounts of context in thinking and deciding. Regulations, due to the education and practices of lawyers, is mostly restricted to the *one dimension* of a line with two ends. Selection of on which end to stand comes to depends how to arrive at some truth via what attract, where attraction comes from many items, including payments from interested parties. Due to the intrinsically low quality of legal truth a lawyer can easily switch ends. Then, when a person with legal training is drawn into political activity, he easily moves down to stand on 0-dimensional points, depending on where the most interest of the moment is. In this way the process can move down to a minus 0 dimension and become pointless.

Humans, under leadership, attempt to dwell upon the *two-dimensional* world of "Flatland." On such it is very hard to distinguish differences making a difference, such as between the nature of male and female. Male leadership becomes a given when males decide in Flatland.

Three-dimensionality is the land of mother nature and her systems of life, as managed by mother nature. *Four-dimensionality* is the atmosphere of father time who shows little respect for mother nature to ensure life dies out via the entropic guardian of lifelessness. Then, we see beyond hierarchical signs that most humans insist on seeing a very different place. Beyond hierarchical it is where all meaning and the information on which meaning is based dwells. We might call it the world of *fifth dimensionality,* where all information about the third dimension as governed by the fourth dimension is widely known. Therein humans do not have more, or less, intelligence than trees although they can still argue they do when its needed. The 5th is well *outside human understanding* via the limits of rationality humans rely on to make dollars even when such makes no sense. Mathematics becomes an incidental clue, centers on zero, but has no equal's sign. Traditional math is used to keep the non-rational from the rational within the truth of the 2nd dimension. Where this fails, we see the emergence of the importance of the irrational emerge on pointless lines in the 1st dimension prior to seeking true pointlessness beneath the 0th dimension. The 4th dimension is thus used to clean up the considerable mess found in the consequences derived by the 0th dimension politics, economics, and truths that come to threaten the existence in the 3rd dimension. The entertainment value of all this is considerable but provides no doorways out from the hierarchy of a Catch-22.

If you have trouble with the above, you are in good company. Please refer to your instruction manual as given at birth.

Herein the how is used to examine the why. These contents are about the soul of the *human project,* something that does not rationally exist in human systems of industrial management, but which may well be the major occupant of the fifth dimension, a place where the restrictions imposed by rationality are disregarded, while recognizing that such restrictions are crucial to meaning in other dimensions of thought and action.

> 0 - Zero is only a point which we often find ourselves trapped on or around in space. We see this with humor where lawyers argue the truth of a point that doesn't exist. Given self-defined regulations it's easy to see when a point is being made that there is no alternative for the lawyer, or the lawyerly trained judge, to escape to as a truth. Points seem simple but can have very dramatic consequences, even providing a rationale for warfare. A zero-dimensional point provides a place on which the rational can stand, no manner the quality of what informs. Zero dimensionality is only a point. On this point one can stand and make pronouncements. They can seem clear and appear secure as they involve essential changelessness. If you change your position too much your point has lost you, much like the ground beneath a politician who changed his mind. Finding your point, and what you might stand on, can be best gained from examination of evidence in the 1st dimension. From such you can see which end of the line seems most popular with a larger social group. As a person wanting to be a political leader you can thus pick your point on which to stand. The danger in this is that the ground beneath can move or the popularity of one end of the one-dimensional line can fade and drift to the other end. The result can be that you seem and look pointless, i.e., without a point. It is easy to see why the 0th dimension is the primary realm of politics and politicians in society. If you are looking for serious substance you might avoid this dimension. Those who attempt to use fear of

climate change as their immortality project tend to be found herein.

1 - The First dimension is a simple line. It can be curved but is generally straight to not confuse those living herein. Many living here went through education to become lawyers. Those so trained are often drawn to life in the 0th dimension as they can stake out a position based on interpretation of arguments on this 1-dimensional line. They are the lawyers most drawn to false clarity in the extremes of each end of this line. They take up point a or b as the basis for gaining political control via attracting votes for it. The dilemma from these two dimensions ends in the Mark Twain commented: "If voting mattered, they wouldn't let us do it." This is seen in always moving to the extreme clarity of the extremes at the left or right side of the line. What such does is prepare the public to accept voices of the authoritarian. They speak with the clarity of a one-dimensional political leadership over those with little time and few resources to think. Selecting the end on which you will stand, from the one-dimensional line, and moving it down to a point to stand on, regardless of the precarious balancing act required, demonstrates your will to power. Later, those who believed in the line approach to clarity can stand in lines awaiting food, shelter, banking, or flights to somewhere nicer. Someone saying, "Climate change as a hoax." is an early indicator of one end of such a line. At the other end is another person who says, "If you just follow me, we will make it."

2 - The Second dimension is more expansive and complex. It offers power of much greater potential than the politics of left and right. It opens a "flatland" terrain where man-made laws beginning as conjecture can be specified as true on two-dimensional, man-made papers. Ideas for designs of the artificial, such as buildings, cities, and video games, can be realized via ever wider expansion into the flat plain thinking. Euclid is seen to have provided many of the tools for managing this dimension, where most encourage further anti-natural behavior. The non-natural law of parallels illustrates the extreme power of such tools. Being in the natural beauty of a natural space lacking parallels illustrates the potential of leaving the second dimension.[218] Finding meaning upon a two-dimensional plane, while highly rational, is very flat. It involves many differences that make no difference except that their implied meaning can fuel great anger about the irrelevance of life upon flatland. There are serious problems herein, such as not recognizing sexual differences yes being able to own dirt as real estate.

3 - Moving up and down, and around in three-dimensional space is more exciting yet brings mysteries into life above 2-D rationalities. Herein change begins to be avoidable. One must learn about the non-rationality of change and

---

[218] The 1960s building on Helsinki University of Technology campus was designed as a student center; to inspire students to feel they were in another dimension and needing less alcohol to get there. Lacking many of the normal parallel surfaces of most buildings it was also used for continuing education to engineers who needed to become more innovative about their work. Called Dipoli, this became very interesting.

its appreciation. The Third dimension is fundamentally different. It is normally occupied by the natural processes of birth, life, death of systems of life. This is where the happiness, trauma, and sadness of glimpses of life are seen. With time humans have added a great deal of their artificial existence to this dimension via first and second dimensional ideas. Holographic thinking is possible thus we can believe we are part of a three-dimensional existence while restricted to two. This has become expensive for the larger three-dimensional context, especially as zero, first and second dimensional operations have come to manage relations to the fourth dimension, that of irreversible time. The danger to this, as well as how we managed to arrive here, provides the subject and primary concern in this book.

4 - Change is not only present in 4-dimensional existence but comes a one-way existence defined by the vagaries of time. Change can be dramatic with consequences as unfortunate. It challenges the existence of life. Herein the results of limited rationality in the first four realms of existence appear, as do the consequences of ignoring change. This explains much about human affairs and the misguided pathways they follow or create. Political arguments are mostly posed as a pathway to leadership which always ends as a hollow immortality project that becomes motivated by evil and ends in disaster. It is easy to see soulless to the extreme. Such arguments end as pointless via the 0-dimensional points made and the end-of-line 1-dimension track they eventually fall from. The best test is to judge their com-

ments in the 4th dimension, the home of entropy, which offers no escape from irreversibility.

5 - The 5th dimension, home of the soul, offers a different form of hope. Access to a soul suggest the supernatural that encloses the natural while running counter to Darwin, especially as interpreted by Social Darwinists who cherish authoritarian governance over human behavior, and counter to the injustice in humans' judicial system under the title of democracy. Via their attempts at problem solving politicians fall off the extreme left or right end of their one-dimensional life. Via the soul truth replaces intolerance. The soul has been and is mysteriously important to evaluating the worth of our occupancy of the earth, although we are more devoted to being an occupant than having a soul. Many argue that there is no 5th dimension, but many others argue against the 0th through 4th. The essence of the 5th dimension is implied in the Nick Cave song, "Death is Not the End."

Arguing simply means that someone cares about something that they do not know about beyond what they see in one dimension and feel a need to make a stand in the 0th dimension. On the other hand, if the soul and its deep feelings are present and accepting the dilemmas of life, they need to move on to the home of the soul, a 5-dimensional place. Thus allows an appreciation of the costs to life of actions taken in the more restrictive dimensions of existence. Herein we seen the resulting change from what humans did to protect themselves from seeing change as vulgarities. Herein all entities know what all others are thinking, thus they act differently to each other.

Humans have learned to accept the thinking of economists as governed by lawyers. This is like being protected as you hide in the wrong cell. To be where they are, humans are concerned about their 0-Dimensional leadership (those walking a 1-D line with yes/no, republican/democratic, Marxists/Fascists, evil/righteous, male/female, continuation/completed that become dichotomies of non-existence. Humans tolerate the limits of 1-D leadership as it seems simple. In fact, it is simple-minded and obscures their occupancy in a 2-D wasteland of mobile phone screens as flatland existence. When excursions are made into the 3rd dimension humans mostly confine themselves to the artificial and avoid the natural as consumed to create the artificial. Contemplation of the 4th dimension (entropy as time) is totally avoided or even disallowed. It's like taking a second-rate college course on thermodynamics.

The 5th dimension, from where there is hope, is, thankfully, assumed beyond human management skill, or even knowing of. That is where we find a storehouse of common and widespread knowledge about meaning and exchange of the meaningful. Doorways into science of the edge, religions defining pre and post life potentials, are therein found. The concerns about management of the Human Project come from experiences, colleagues, friends and especially students I've been allowed to work with for many years. Those often seen to be losers, misfits or trouble-seekers were the most illuminating as to how we should change management. The communication taking place in this 5th dimension seems to explain why youth are so upset, hope being played out via having children is being suspended, and humans are acting out the extremes of their thoughts. Good and bad are revealed via extremes.

Yes, the above provides an updated image of Plato's Cave in his "Allegory of the Cave," Therein the dilemma of human life becomes self-generated as a not so funny contradiction in two dimensions, just like Plato's shadows on the cave ceiling. Humans have moved from emphasizing management of the soul to things for the body. Their search for meaning, in an afterlife, has transformed into the economics of today's ownership. This change has occurred in the shadows surrounding the quest to trap change in an artificial container. It's noteworthy that what we do to protect ourselves from change seems to result in environmental changes that are ominous.

We are nurtured by the corruption encouraged in thinking strategically, i.e., via lies. Can humans now learn to be less strategic and more serious in managing the consequences of prior strategics? Perhaps humans became arrogant from being allowed to negotiate with "the holy" then using the same process allowed to negotiate with product making, use and disposal. This arrogance allowed them to feel they could arise from entropic death, then expand to conquer many laws of the natural. Resources were shifted from a quest for the holy to scientific conquest of the natural. Resources were thus taken from nature to provide for human needs and their psycho wants. Expansion of this allowed human activities to shift from discussing dilemmas to creating them.

Within a particular definition of well-being humans became significant users, i.e., modifiers, of the natural environment on which their lives depended. Development of the industrial was an earlier stage. Development of modified life forms via science and technology is the current stage. Vacuous dreams of permanence, as promised by prophets of, and then profits from, the gospel of *changelessness* emerged. Rejection of natural change arose from the arrogance of humanism. Projects titles changes but the central mission remained constant. Erwin Chargaff, one of the fathers of nucleic acid and gene research, stated the human problem:

> "Our time is cursed with the necessity for feeble men, masquerading as experts, to make enormously far-reaching decisions. Is there anything more far-reaching than the creation of new forms of life? ... You can stop splitting the atom; you can stop visiting the moon; you can stop using aerosols; you may even decide not to kill entire populations by the use of a few bombs. But you cannot recall a new form of life...The hybridization of Prometheus with Herostratus is bound to give evil results."[219]

---

[219] Chargaff, Erwin, "On the Dangers of Genetic Meddling," *Science* 192, (1976): P. 938-940.

Prometheus was a Titan God who took fire from the Gods to make it available to humanity. Herostratus, on the other hand, was an Ancient Greek arsonist who destroyed one of the seven wonders of the Ancient World so that his name would forever be remembered. Does this matter to us? Cohen suggests it matters much to the human project in that it changed the definition of success, reducing the souls' role in change. Our souls, should they exist, encourage risking the present to meet future success. The transaction is bathed in guilt relative to opportunities lost. Religious leaders, political followers, management theorists, and managers make use of the soul in managing our wants in life. For them, its virtual existence awaiting our future is more powerful than an actual existence in need of daily maintenance. The idea of it is instrumental to the unfolding of the human life.

0,th 1,st and 2nd Dimensional are Mostly for Humor

Was the use of artificial rationality to manage the natural and good idea? Probably not. Now, with climate change's consequences approaching, it looks to have been a seriously bad idea. Gregory Bateson, an anthropologist, argued in 1973 that such would expand on "unaided rationality," a limited brain approach to problem generation. West Churchman in 1979 raised the issue 90% of human reality being non-rational thus was the thinking of Aristotle limited to 10%? Systems thinkers of the seventies raised related concerns for the human condition. If the mentality of humans continues to move to the limits of the artificial than a price will be paid. If might even prove to endanger the natural or cause the natural to endanger of human?

Signs are abundant that a price will be paid by humans for their artificial. This is beginning to appear in the humanly designed context, especially where the industrial has deteriorated the natural via the artificial. There is even evidence that uses of the products made in the industrial are endangering the contextual stability required of life. Context is passing beyond human understanding and management. Can humans manage to find a way out from what is increasingly being called a "problematique," a system of problems that cannot be solved in detached isolation? Current contextual conditions begin to be like what Emery and Trist labeled as a "turbulent environment" in 1965. Via the current emergence of climate change conditions, the context may we become what Trist later called a "vortex environment."

Several questions arise in the following pages. The answers are not apparent. Significant consequences are clearly emerging for human futures and conditions required for life. They increasingly appear as a contradiction to the natural with time. Humans metaphorically resemble the energy system of the cosmos as an entropic process acting out in the 4th dimension. This is seen in how humans rely on techniques of segmented analysis and results creation to inform management. In this, humans avoid appreciation of contextual consequences from human endeavors.

Humans have shown much progress in meeting their needs via ignoring longer-term consequences in concentrating on short term achievements. Will there be a price to be paid for this manner of management? Has short-term gain to now be paid via longer-term pain? Even posing such questions might imply a fateful pathway for humans. What role does management play in the question, and its answers?

Clearly there are weaknesses in management, whatever it might be defined to be. Management has come to define our relations towards much, including nature, technology, others, and ourselves. Several options are available for humans to respond to apparent weaknesses in management; weaknesses that now endanger life on the planet. We can:

1)   Simply abandon all conceptions of business and how to manage it. Change human interpretations of their lives, their economic drivers, their values, and current definitions of life from which they draw meaning. Presume that are limits to growth, regardless of what is being grown, and work to manage systems to be and have less over time. Strategic wars

can be used to limit, then reverse population growth and the business associated with it. A few humans can move to Mars and keep the idea of a species as important alive. The qualities of current management can be retained. Only the quantities will need to be changed.

2) Develop *business-as-unusual* approaches to life and their management. One approach to such is via systems thinking, context appreciation, and rethinking the results from segmented analysis divorced from context, then content. Invest more resources in confronting then reconciling difficulties between humans and nature. Or,

3) Continue with *business-as-usual* and its management via traditional ideas. Close your eyes and simply trust that solutions will keep arriving in a timely manner, as they always seem to. This involves expanding the business-as-usual application of the sciences of the artificial, expanded recycling, and selling sustainability. Design and implement ever more technologies of happiness and entertainment. Ever more widely distributed IT systems of observation and control will resolve management issues where those in disagreement with management can receive needed therapy more quickly.

The first option presumes engaging hopelessness for life on our planet. The third posture presumes the opposite where the espoused threats to planetary life are the threat. Climate change is thereby a hoax to be mostly ignored by real men. Proponents of this often reference the non-existent record of humans having met and managed more serious situations, such as winning world wars and having nuclear and bio-chemical weapons available to resolve future wars. They argue against consideration of the consequences of present actions. Consequence considerations take too much time for these people and can become impediments to their artificial progress. They point to the inherent confusion awaiting those who see context as important to decisions. As context is systemic, complex, and non-causal it only leads to complexity of thought. These souls argue that to respond to perils of climate change only endangers stable economics. Many in this group keep management and the business as close to usual as is possible. Changelessness is the rule.

The subject of dimensionality provides several clues about contemporary attitudes in parts of every social group, attitudes that seem to be growing, not just remaining as items of curiosity making comments from the edges of reality. The following outlines a sense of how these emerge in much political discourse in our day.

- I have a point.
- From where comes your point?
- It arises from observation and helps me understand.
- Please explain what your point.
- I forgot, just let me be.
- Please go away.

Continuing research describes climate change as seriously emerging, with ever greater clarity we see human activities to be the sponsor of climate change. What is difficult is why humans continue their fateful activities behind the impending situation despite knowing more of its probable end. Humans are increasingly aware this is coming and that they are responsible but seem unable to change their role. As climate change approaches it seems ever more difficult to understand why humans would create such a serious long-term paradox knowing it ends as catastrophic for life.

It seems clearer with time that humans occupy several dimensions of existence. While they have very different properties and support different activities, they all support some aspects of consciousness. They are not hierarchical yet substantially different. Each involves aspects of management between humans and their contexts, although the qualitative differences are great. Herein these are outlined as dimensional locations. They offer a variety of contexts where humans are drawn to behave differently in each.

There is some urgency to humans waking from their current state of misplaced stability, that might best be called changelessness. Since my climate change research of the nineteen-seventies two issues seem consistent in results of general climate change research. One is that the consequences become more serious with time. Two is that they are arriving sooner than anticipated in earlier research on the same topics. This is explained in the following via a dimensional array. It allows us to clearly see the basis of many traditional human behaviors as sponsored by a context. This allows access to more of the how and why that allows humans to continue to contribute to causes of climate change.

As a backdrop to the larger process of climate change emerging to define the context of life, we see governmental management being changed. *Somehow governments are shifting in many parts of the world from attempts to become more democratic to the dangerous situation of fewer humans having more control of what is done, and perhaps of more importance, what is not being done.* Leadership, an aspect of management, had become a serious impediment, just as it seems to have been a sponsor of the situation needing resolution.

Herein the how is used to examine the why. These contents are about the soul of the *human project,* something that does not rationally exist in human systems of industrial management, but which may well be the major occupant of the fifth dimension, a place where the restrictions imposed by rationality are disregarded, while recognizing that such restrictions are crucial to meaning in other dimensions of thought and action.

Arguing simply means that someone cares about something that they do not know about beyond what they see in one dimension and feel a need to make a stand in the 0th dimension. On the other hand, if the soul and its deep feelings are present and accepting the dilemmas of life, they need to move on to the home of the soul, a 5-dimensional place. Thus allows an appreciation of the costs to life of actions taken in the more restrictive dimensions of existence. Herein we seen the resulting change from what humans did to protect themselves from seeing change as vulgarities. Herein all entities know what all others are thinking, thus they act differently to each other.

Humans have learned to accept the thinking of economists as governed by lawyers. This is like being protected as you hide in the wrong cell. To be where they are, humans are concerned about their 0-Dimensional leadership (those walking a 1-D line with yes/no, republican/democratic, Marxists/Fascists, evil/righteous, male/female, continuation/completed that become dichotomies of non-existence. Humans tolerate the limits of 1-D leadership as it seems simple. In fact, it is simple-minded and obscures their occupancy in a 2-D wasteland of mobile phone screens as flatland existence. When excursions are made into the 3rd dimension humans mostly confine themselves to the artificial and avoid the natural as consumed to create the artificial. Contemplation of the 4th dimension (entropy as time) is totally avoided or even disallowed. It's like taking a second-rate college course on thermodynamics.

The 5th dimension, from where there is hope, is, thankfully, assumed beyond human management skill, or even knowing of. That is where we find a storehouse of common and widespread knowledge about meaning and exchange of the meaningful. Doorways into science of the edge, religions defining pre and post life potentials, are therein found. The concerns about management of the Human Project come from experiences, colleagues, friends and especially students I've been allowed to work with for many years. Those often seen to be losers, misfits or trouble-seekers were the most illuminating as to how we should change management. The communication taking place in this 5th dimension seems to explain why youth are so upset, hope being played out via having children is being suspended, and humans are acting out the extremes of their thoughts. Good and bad are revealed via extremes.

Yes, the above provides an updated image of Plato's Cave in his "Allegory of the Cave," Therein the dilemma of human life becomes self-generated as a not so funny contradiction in two dimensions, just like Plato's shadows on the cave ceiling. Humans have moved from emphasizing management of the soul to things for the body. Their search for meaning, in an afterlife, has transformed into the economics of today's ownership. This change has occurred in the shadows surrounding the quest to trap change in an artificial container. It's noteworthy that what we do to protect ourselves from change seems to result in environmental changes that are ominous.

We are nurtured by the corruption encouraged in thinking strategically, i.e., via lies. Can humans now learn to be less strategic and more serious in managing the consequences of prior strategics? Perhaps humans became arrogant from being allowed to negotiate with "the holy" then using the same process allowed to negotiate with product making, use and disposal. This arrogance allowed them to feel they could arise from entropic death, then expand to conquer many laws of the natural. Resources were shifted from a quest for the holy to scientific conquest of the natural. Resources were thus taken from nature to provide for human needs and their psycho wants. Expansion of this allowed human activities to shift from discussing dilemmas to creating them.

Within a particular definition of well-being humans became significant users, i.e., modifiers, of the natural environment on which their lives depended. Development of the industrial was an earlier stage. Development of modified life forms via science and technology is the current stage. Vacuous dreams of permanence, as promised by prophets of, and then profits from, the gospel of *changelessness* emerged. Rejection of natural change arose from the arrogance of humanism. Projects titles changes but the central mission remained constant. Erwin Chargaff, one of the fathers of nucleic acid and gene research, stated the human problem:

> "Our time is cursed with the necessity for feeble men, masquerading as experts, to make enormously far-reaching decisions. Is there anything more far-reaching than the creation of new forms of life? ... You can stop splitting the atom; you can stop visiting the moon; you can stop using aerosols; you may even decide not to kill entire populations by the use of a few bombs. But you cannot recall a new form of life...The hybridiza-

tion of Prometheus with Herostratus is bound to give evil results."[220]

Prometheus was a Titan God who took fire from the Gods to make it available to humanity. Herostratus, on the other hand, was an Ancient Greek arsonist who destroyed one of the seven wonders of the Ancient World so that his name would forever be remembered. Does this matter to us? Cohen suggests it matters much to the human project in that is changed the definition of success, reducing the souls' role in change. Our souls, should they exist, encourage risking the present to meet future success. The transaction is bathed in guilt relative to opportunities lost. Religious leaders, political followers, management theorists, and managers make use of the soul in managing our wants in life. For them, its virtual existence awaiting our future is more powerful than an actual existence in need of daily maintenance. The idea of it is instrumental to the unfolding of the human life.

Reality Via Dimensional Perspectives

To elaborate a bit, I offer 7 bullet points to suggest there is a dimensional way to understand what men have done and how they might change their manner of conceiving what ought to be done with less emphasis on their superiority and immortality, and more concern for their approaching weaknesses and grave mistakes in how they think.

-Birth implies access to a 1st dimension on a line to the future.
-Exaggerating a line end deposits you on 2nd dimensional flatland.
-Life can rise to 3rd dimensional life via multi-dimensional experience.

---

[220] Chargaff, Erwin, "On the Dangers of Genetic Meddling," *Science* 192, (1976): P. 938-940.

-The 3rd D becomes lessened via 4th dimensional changes.

-Entropy dissipates potential of the 3rd via the unfolding of the 4th.

-Upset by the 4th humans act up to increase entropy in the 3rd.

-Do humans search for hope or seek immortality via hopelessness.

We devote much to the 0th and 1st dimensions, then the 4th dimension eliminates much of what we should care about in the 3rd dimension. We come to define our existence via the limits of 1 and 2 while helping the 4th destroy much of the hope offered in the nature of the 3rd. Eventually, we see aspects of greater hope in the nonexistence (in normal terminology) of the 5th dimension.

Within it we raise the questions at the edge of existence that attract new explanations and move from historic answers from the core of 1 and 2 via routinized memorization. Therein learning becomes exciting. Results passed on via parents and schools seem like baggage to pack up, declare, check in and forget about while on a journey to find what is. The 5th may be where those who needed a drink were when they chose a name for that esteemed container?

Limiting our existence in the 3rd dimension, even knowing there is such, opens up the universe. Staying in the 1st and 2nd seems to allow avoidance of fearful uncertainties, self-imposed complexities, and all that we do not know. Once firmly in the 3rd dimension we can see that complexity was mostly the manufacture of the 1st and 2nd as found in Plato's Cave and/or in our trusting of those Heavenly promises of immortality. Can we do better? Just now things are sufficiently precarious in life and too life that we need to attempt the better. The idea of a soul may help.

Via Darwin we are taught that differences have more value than commonalities, even though most of those differences have been shown to not make a difference. None-the-less, humans define their lives via differences such as height, width, wealth, and other attractions or distractions. Via social-Darwinism we see survival of the fittest translated into survival of the fattest. Such thinking in 1-dimension allows 10% of a nation to "own" 70% of it, until the 4th dimension sends them away. Yes, it makes followers of Ayn Rand with immortality projects in their minds, e.g., politicians, popular with some. It guards against the funny ideas of another life, one where people are concerned for the well-being of each other and insure pay to workers that earned it, not collectors that count it.

While being educated in why the rich and the beautiful are rich and beautiful we are nagged by funny questions about human endeavors. How is it that we all know so much in common, yet have not spoken to each other about it, nor watched others experience what we have? How we come to know much in common, even outside families and schools, is a key question. We seem to have a collective consciousness, yet we listen to those who give emphasis to differences, differences that in fact do not make a difference that is good, only differences that are used by some to create bad. This is how we create the basis for a war, while knowing collectively that we all lose in a war and continue to lose when we think it's won.

Most question the idea of a soul at least some of the time. They avoid such most of the time as they frantically consume products made from nature's recourses to fill out a 3-dimensional existence, such as stylish homes, clothes, cars, and foods. Additional escapes are invented via artificial devices that allow us to devote hours in negotiating with the simple-minded artificial images of a 2-dimensional existence.

The idea of a soul was long a part of the human existence, but during recent centuries it turned into a 1-dimensional conception, useful for acting strategically. Strategic activities are best seen in political discourse as a line of reality in 1-dimension. One end is defined by humans as bad; the other is good, and humans walk back and forth on it seeking the truth of end points. A politician always pretends access to the good end, and will take you there for a small fee, to tolerate him as your leader. Sometimes that price is extremely high. Democracies and authoritarian states both rely on 1-dimensional thinking.

While trapped in these dimensions we go for a) short-term gains ending in long-term pains (wanting urgent results, while ignoring the consequences of results); b) negotiating with the meaningful via reliance on Faustian bargaining so our nature can create what does not naturally occur (artificial loyalty to an industrialization ending in changed conditions of climate); and c) hiding ignorance behind arrogance that allows avoidance of natural laws that give definition to the fourth dimensional temporal operations (thus making the entropic process more productive via unfortunate economics).

Management involves short-term challenges we can see as of the 1st Order. Beyond them we see consequences to their achievement. These might best be called of the 2nd Order. The 2nd Order arises via unintended systemic consequences from interconnections its achievement of 1st Order results. The process is organized around analytic thinking, working, and managing.

The 1st Order is to meet daily human needs. The largely unconsidered 2nd Order is above the 1st Order. While mostly unseen, the 2nd Order is in fact more ominous to humans. The 1St is clearly heavily managed, which the 2nd is mostly ignored. One of our questions herein is can we learn to manage the 2nd Order? The situation is like going on an expensive 1st order shopping tour, then expanding life into a wildly expensive night on the town, prior to 2nd order results of the following day(s). You had just lost your job, wife, or basis for living so it seemed right, and memorable, to party. What then do you do when 2nd order consequences arrive? The second domain is not singular and isolated problems but becomes a systemic network of problems from prior solutions woven together by reality. Credit card bills, interest rates rising from lowered credit ratings, loss of home and car, etc. As consequences they were not given prior consideration.

From deep sorrow, or great anger, new initiatives can then be undertaken that can lead to further unfortunate consequences growing in the future. The often happens when situations are managed without context in mind. Consequences lie in context until they are disturbed and woken up. Was the individual at fault, or was the model of management used? Can consequences of management be avoided by different management. Does difference require different people or different processes, or different ideals and ideas to motivate the entire process? What do terms like consequences, context and systemic thinking mean to management?

> "Conclusions: 1st order results are intentionally analytic, as derived to gain access to 0th order posturing. We then begin to see the consequences in the 2nd order and become surrounded with them in the 3rd order, with the help of entropy of the 4th order. Therefore, consequences are seldom recognized or even considered in efforts to achieve intended results. Bringing strategic thinking out as an emphasis to improved leadership is simply adding the evil potential in secrecy to the problems of management. Emphasis must move towards appreciation of the systems, and from worship of the analytic. During bipolar situations, leadership pays no attention to the beliefs of the majority. The secrecy encouraged by the strategic enhances this process. Finding systemic views and their management will be crucial to human survival by 2100".[221]

Management of changing traditional presumptions, such as those of Taylor, seems key to the human future if they have one, although the change management has mostly been managing to not change. such. Over time management adopted more of "The Artificial" in attempted control of "The Natural." This is most clearly seen in "The Industrial" approaching its ending in a "Great Failure of Climate Change." The ensuing war between the artificial and the natural is most clearly seen in the industrialization of agriculture, where food becomes increasingly artificial and industrialized healthcare manages the discomfort. At present, problems with diseases and

---

[221] David Hawk, LinkedIn, posting on October 1, 2020, in a course on principles of system's management.

healthcare shortcomings is being overshowed by changing the climatic conditions essential to life. Considering this history of management can the human project be re-managed to avoid a chaotic conclusion.

Is management crucial to continuation of the biological and psychological dimensions of a five-dimensional life? Management, as mostly a 2-dimensional exercise, is the means to create, organize, and direct the why, where, and how humans live. It's at the center of moving the 3-dimensional human project forward. Conceptions of management gained great authority 200 years ago. Adopting the services of the technological management became omnipresent. From the authority during an industrial age technology management moved to structure the content of social-political-economic endeavors. Under closer inspection we can now see the human excitement in hoping to manage continuous technological phenomena to direct economic and political ideologies away from a natural context for creating an artificial world.

Denoted by the Aristotelian call for strict rationality in 350 BC Greece, that basis for industrialization later attracted the mathematizing support of England's Newton in the 17th Century. Implicit, and often explicit, Newton's thinking allowed the *industrial* to oppose, then increasingly manage, the *natural*. Late in the continuation of Newton's process industrial management ends in the tragic consequences human efforts to ignore the natural while building the artificial. Thus, the dictates and consequences of the industrial regime against natural processes, as in the analytic versus the systemic, provides the theme herein.

For Aristotle, the technological served the homocentric by focusing on "the arrangement of technics managed to serve human ends." Centuries later, Newton was inspired by Aristotle and added deep religious beliefs, extreme anger at human competitors, and rudimentary mathematics to the homo-centricity of Aristotle. He joined in the crusade of the industrial coming to control the natural.

Aristotle's demand for strict rationality, as also adopted in early development of computer science in the 1940s, needed the thoughts of Newton. From Newton's humans came to expand management of technics into management of technology. With time, the same model was expanded to include management of humans needed to accompany technology. Faithful to Aristotle, Newton and computer science followers focuses on service to human ends. They mostly blocked out the confusing natural processes providing the context for humans and human ends. The human agenda became disconnected from context and adopted analytic definitions.

Further development of technology and industrialization demanded increasing material and energy inputs from the nature being ignored or desecrated in a derogatory manner. The role of management was stripped of context. Its mission was to improve labor productivity, not consider that natural context from which resources were taken. Management knew nothing of entropy, nor its most fundamental of roles in managing the earth and the universe. This has ended with humans facing significant threat to their continuance.

Ideas, conceptions, measures, formulations, and principles provided the basic language for management of industrialization as well as management of the humans required to provide their work to improve the economics of others. Humans came to be seen, then managed, as machinery in the industrial process. For a few decades after WWII this attitude and its costs were questioned by a few social scientists. In their research it was shown why the social quality needed to be included in governance. The social temporarily gained ground against the technical from 1950.

Appendix:
Into Life's Continuance

Context: A Basis for the Meaningful

Gregory Bateson noted the dilemma between productivity in normal human activities and their being paused to reflect on the meaning of such to life. In his anthropological view of the world, he advised us to weave knowledge of context back into directing activities to improve:

> "Without context, words and actions have no meaning at all." [222]

The stability required by life seems to be long gone. Much of our life now seems to lack the context inclusion Bateson mentions and seems to move faster and more unsettled each year. With this, our context has thus gone into motion from our movement. This is clearly seen in the greater difficulties humans have each year in accessing required sleep. We seem to be acting ever crazier each day from our lack of reflection invited in deep dreams that sort out our superficial challenges.

Our context has passed from the Trist idea of "disturbed reactive" onto environmental turbulence. Irritating storms have become hurricanes and tornadoes. We now see early signs of an approaching

---

[222] Bateson, Gregory, et.al., "Rigor & Imagination: Essays from the Legacy of Gregory Bateson," Int. Comm. Association, New York: Praeger Publishing, 1981,

vortex.[223] Is there a technological possibility to bring life out from a contextual black hole? Probably not. If we can go back, in the US Republican sense of survival, can we go somewhere else? Where? In a recent meeting centered on political arguments becoming more dangerous with time I suggested the two parties each find a mission worth having. For example, the Republicans could take responsibility for drought problems while the Democrats could take responsibility for flooding. Each might them come to understand the overwhelming importance of climate change over the whole.

Humans design, produce, and consume, all to expand their lives. Most avoid thinking of the cost to themselves and the surroundings of such a life. Many seek entertainment to forget the downside of doing what they do, i.e., acting in ways that have future costs. Their emphasis is instead on illustrating power over an environment, which can be considerable. Production and Consumption (P&C) activities consume their resources, including time to reflect on what it all means, and how it ends. Meanwhile, fundamental costs pile up in nature from the P&C and add to the naturally advancing entropic process.[224]

Nature governs the context of life. To counter such agreed upon science human argument with the not so agreeable science that proposes a redesign saying nature is an open system thus it can replenish itself from the outside thus entropy is not a relevant aspect for criticizing the human project. The natural is the central subject herein. We traditionally assumed the artificial to be well-managed, or so the negative effects of P&C would not be very harmful to life. As such we could ignore the costs. The harm from the artificial was a hard to distinguish aspect of the context of life. If such was hidden from sight, we could concentrate on human development of the industrial to bring pleasure to humans via ever better meeting of bio-needs and

---

[223] Emery, F.E., & Trist, E.L., Eric, "The Causal Texture of Organizational Environments," *Human Relations*, 18(1), pp. 21-32, 1965.

[224] Entropy is a measure of the randomness or disorder of a system where it can have a positive or negative value. Important in this is the 2nd Law of Thermodynamics that says entropy is always and irreversibly underway and can only be reversed in one system only if it is increased elsewhere.

psycho-wants. Costs of this, should they exist, were off in the context, acting as a backdrop to existence.

Humans could safely concentrate their limited attention span to sketches running across the foreground of existence. The waste dumps piling up behind and the CO_2 aggregating overhead could be ignored. Life's value came to center on the desired output of the industrial and who could arrange to own the most of it prior to death. Even those investing their education, work, and life in the domains of design, production and consumption would argue how the results were worth the gains. The pains were far in the future, if anywhere.

The industrial process was to serve and support the important performances in life. Humans could thus act out as they searched for what was said to be meaningful by leadership, thus having a doorway to fulfillment, happiness, and self-actualization. Such was the perception of life's meaning in the natural until WWII. That global war over manly differences illustrated that the technological dimension of human existence had been greatly expanded. Richard Garwin, author of the first hydrogen bomb design, became a very strong advocate of disarmament of such and rethinking of the technology of warfare[225].

WWII demonstrated how science and technology can greatly improve the productivity of humans killing of each other. More recently we began to the same in the killing of nature, even if less intentional, but that will be discussed later. For now, it's important to note that in the period after WWII we could see how the theme of industrial overpowers humans and their ambiguous purposes. Very important to this was the work of Eric Trist in his creation of social-technical systems. He studied and documented the relative importance of the social and the technical in the workplace. He showed how the technical was de facto manager of the social, then established experiments to show the gains from reversing such. His thesis helped many industries until the expansion of computers in the work restored the technical as key to management.

---

[225] Richard helped me stage conferences at my university in New Jersey and in New York City on this subject in the eighties. He worked to present his deep concern in ways that would expand knowing what a great threat to life some technologies pose.

Eric Trist went wider via his social psychological view of the world. He agreed with Bateson on the importance of context but then he and Fred Emery went on to see context as a "stage-set for the plays of life." As with Erwin Goffman the Trist approach to context was as a backdrop for humans to reveal meaning via performances. From his experiencing the politico-technological mistakes before, during and after WWII he became concerned with the expanding technological control looming over humans via production and consumption as directed to support life. Erving Goffman would later arrive at the early Trist model for accessing meaning in human affairs. Both were my teachers beyond their classrooms.

Trist's concern for the expanding power of technology from rational ideas and clean logic was growing. The technical was sent to manage what was said to be a non-rational world in a natural setting. It was seen as too unpredictable. Trist saw logical analysis opposed natural reality, and its human occupants. He was very concerned that the dictates of the technical imposed limits on human thinking and feeling. Using unaided rationality to limit values was seen by Trist as damaging then destroying qualities of life. As such, humans moved from the early socio-natural context, based on collaboration, and references by Kropotkin,[226] to a structured, hierarchical, authoritarian, and centralized focus on "the one." The stream of life within societies in nature was becoming lost to the hierarchies of the one.

In his attempt to return to a focus on natural diversity Trist developed a now famous socio-tech model of life. Trist was putting the social back in charge, not allowing technology to control more of human life. He included the potential of the natural context as basic to his socio ecological ideas. His 1973 book[227] on such was not well received, even noted in some reviews as including outrageous ideas. One was where people should move away from their fantasy of connecting individual status representation via status of the autos they drove. Trist had even recommended humans begin to not use,

---

[226] Kropotkin, Petr, *Mutual Aid: A Factor in Evolution*, Boston: Extending Horizons Books, 1914.

[227] F.E. Emery and E.L. Trist, *Towards a Social Ecology: Contextual Appreciation of the Future in the Present*, New York: Plenum Press, 1973.

and maybe lease, not own private automobiles. Fifty years later it's interesting to see such outrageous ideas as beyond prophetic. Leasing autos is obvious to many. While now seen as a very valuable guide to the future, that book is no longer available, but well-used copies can be purchased for $800 to $1000 each.[228]

By the twenty-first century social scientists noted that need to reverse the acceptance of technology as a meaningful context. To not change such was seen as a clear threat to the human future. Younger humans were beginning to seek redefinition of life in nature and its management. By 2025 those youth now see much of their future as a threat. The continuance of life is now threatened by the natural environment on which their life is seen to depend.

A few students now look into historical records of industrialization from 1850 on and see how those activities designed to manage nature become a great threat to the life in nature. This was most clearly seen in the science of that noteworthy American farm girl introduced in the prior section, Eunice Foote.[229]

Searching: Meaningfulness in Meaninglessness

Human beings have significant problems being human. The difficulties are manifest in many ways but are clearly seen in the way in which humans relate to each other and their surroundings. The potential for improvement in these relations is very great, but so too are the difficulties in finding success. In part this is because of serious shortcomings in how humans conceptualize reality (i.e., as changelessness) and in part due to how material resources essential

---

[228] My copy, that I shared with many students at New Jersey Institute of Technology, was seized along with many others from my office under orders of President Joel Bloom, Governor Chris Christie, and a NJ judge they were paying $500/hour. They declared all my books, my files on past research and a daughter's stuffed animal to be "state property." The daughter continues to be sad about such behavior.

[229] Foote, Eunice, "Circumstances Affecting the Heat of the Sun's Rays," Washington D.C.: *Science*, American Association for the Advancement of Science (AAAS), 1856.

to human existence are conceptualized (i.e., as infinitely recyclable). Problems with humans relating to their environments begin with their attitudes towards themselves and their environments, especially as those two things relate to change and entropy.

This shows up most clearly in the entropy construct and how we choose to interpret it. Alternative interpretations of entropy are available. Just as with the concept of change, how a nation, group or individual chooses to interpret entropy provides an important clue to how they will manage their relations to their environments. The dominant attitude is that entropy doesn't matter, and where its influence cannot be avoided, the consequences can be recycled. This attitude stems from an interpretation of entropy from the ideas set by James Clerk Maxwell (1831-1879) and Ludwig Boltzmann (1844-1906). Each, in a different way, felt that entropic processes might somehow be reversed, with the major reversal mechanism being human intellect. This homocentric scenario is like that found throughout industrialization.

This prevalent attitude towards entropy allows for belief in reversing it, known as negative entropy. This is overly optimistic. It tends towards arrogance and is generally ignorant of evidence of change, decay, time, irreversibility, and other realities of nature. Systems theorists are guilty of the same bias. They should be the first to experiment with alternative "attitudes" towards entropy, especially those coming from more holistic visions than what was offered by Boltzmann. This would allow appreciation of deeper interpretations of how humans relate to their environments. This would allow serious critic of utopian dreams associated with concepts of "recyclability" and "sustainability," and more recent requests to being sustainable. All these are simply revisitations and continuances of the 2,500-year-old decision for homocentric control by advocating changeless systems.

An endearing and enduring aspect of the system's approach is that it encourages one to see relations and connections to a larger system of order. It encourages a more holistic stance and innovative, alternative viewpoints. Early on, GST recognized the critical role of attitude in shaping and setting viewpoints. As was pointed out in the first section, attitude helps determine what we see and fail to see. In its favor, the systems' attitude has encouraged many researchers to stretch their thinking. This appears as fundamental and explains the innovative nature of doorways opened by systems thinkers into the arena of scientific discovery and innovation. None-the-less, the system's viewpoint has had its own flirtations with changelessness. An important symptom of this is seen in the early attitude of GST towards entropy where life-forces were felt to exhibit neg-entropy phenomena.

Believing that something is possible, as well as desirable, is a precursor to humans making investments to bring it about. For good as well as bad ends these beliefs can become a magnet for the enthusiasm and other resources needed to work towards accomplishment. This generally beneficial process can sometimes be counter-productive, depending on the ideals. The changeless attitude in negative entropy is one example.

Many researchers believe that the entropic processes can be negotiated with, and, where sufficient intellect is applied, even reversed. This has been a GST attitude since the nineteen-fifties, is consistent with the changelessness agenda of 500 BC, and supports the Middle Ages religious belief that via information from God humans could create perpetual motion machines. In all three ways the significance of the 2nd Law of Thermodynamics could thereby be ignored, and humans could continue to do well whatever they wanted. If we now add the possibility to recycle things, if they can't be reversed, we have escaped all responsibilities.

How the system's perspective views these ideas is critical. Current indications are worrisome. Systems people somehow have developed attitudes like the reductionistic groups that they initially criticized. They had some trouble in the late nineteen-sixties in responding to the AAAS challenge of Garret Hardin when he criticized the fundamentalistic political-economic belief system of the day that felt Adam Smith's ideas were sacred. In 1968 he asked scientists to reconsider the environmental dilemmas that resulted from the individualistic, results-oriented focus of their individual activities. He restated the challenge in 1998 where he argued why. As posed in a 1968 issue of *Science*: "Freedom in the commons brings ruin to all."

> "It is easy to call for interdisciplinary syntheses, but will anyone respond? Scientists know how to train the young in narrowly focused work; but how do you teach people to stitch together established specialties that perhaps should not have been separated in the first place? With Adam Smith's work as a model, I had assumed that the sum of separate ego-serving decisions would be the best possible one for the population as a whole. But presently I discovered that I agreed much more with William Forster Lloyd's conclusions, as given in his Oxford lectures in 1833. Citing what happened to pasturelands left open to many herds of cattle, Lloyd pointed out that, with a resource available to all, the greediest herdsmen would gain - for a while. But mutual ruin was just around the corner." [230]

Hardin argued for the need to rethink the underlying assumptions about human problems then shift to a more interdisciplinary approach that included their context. As such he was supportive of the systems agenda. He felt context to be the provider of clues to the "underlying nature of things." His depiction of the situation that underlays the key human problem was care of the commons that underlay all planetary life. He saw the commons, the context, to have limits.

This depiction is like my long-held concern with the entropic process as inherent to the operations and management of life's context, Hardin's commons. Human arrogance and/or ignorance comes to encourage humans to ignore context, or the commons, as they

---

[230] *Science*, "Tragedy of the Commons, Hardin, Science 162, 1968.

work to expand their advantages in the commons. In so doing, they come to seal the terminal fate of the species.

Key is the role of selfish economics is how it encourages expansion and rate of entropy. Greed in the self that in fact can find support in greed, not the greed that pushes Hardin's conceptualization. From a system thinking basis the entropy process now is seen as consistent with the concerns of scientists like A. Rapaport and K. Boulding. For example, Boulding proposed a model of human activities that would dampen the economic enthusiasm for competition and increase the concern for resources entering and exiting socio-economic systems. He argued how inputs could be seen in an alternative, more dynamic, system of value and how externalities of outputs should be factored in. This approach lost to the dream of negative entropy possibilities associated with resource recycling and even creation. The concept of sustainability seems to take us even further down to the utopian dream world where under the banner of everything matters nothing in fact does matter.

One of the founding fathers of the General Systems Research Society, Ludwig von Bertalanffy, appeared to accept the attitude of life being in opposition to entropy. As mentioned before, others around him were not so convinced but the optimism was too great to be ignored. Boulding was concerned about negative entropy not because resources were infinite or finite, but because of the consequences of resource use. Recycling them only led to them being even more used (Laszlo, 1972). None-the-less the possibility of neg-entropy was widely adopted in the thinking of the Society's membership. Most of the second-generation systems thinkers adopted this stance without thinking.

Most interesting science and technology development now takes place outside discrete disciplines via an interdisciplinary approach, but seldom by systems scientists. The prior comments may provide some hints as to why.

The idea, i.e., possibility, of negative entropy is a problem in several ways. These can be seen easily in specific research to deal with specific environmental problems. This author is involved with two such projects currently. Both began with a criticism of the limits of the forced regulatory structure to get an industry to improve itself. Both required using a model of change dynamics. Both called for an appreciation of the situations of which they were a part, as well as a high level of innovation for redesigning them. The idea of entropy was found to be a critical indicator of such appreciation. The idea of negative entropy was found to be a major impediment to success. It provided an escape hatch to ensure that the only approach that would get anyone to move would be forced regulation, although, of course, not far.

Accessing the More Outside the Hierarchical

We need to seek dimensions elsewhere from our current settings. Many of us spend much time in management within the limitations of 0th dimension (pointlessness). The 1st dimension is a line with two ends, representing a normal 1-dimensional argument. The resulting polarization begins as a digital dichotomy in argumentation over the best direction left or right. The 2nd dimension is best described within Abbots 1908 *Flatland*. Within those limitations humans have trouble distinguishing much, including sexual aspects of reality. The 3rd dimension is where reality as we commonly perceive it unfolds to entertain while avoiding the termination scenario of the 4th dimension. The 4th dimension is defined as an irreversible time which is governed by the singly dimension of entropy via time. The 2nd Law of Thermodynamics is often noted by physicists as one undisputable law of the universe. Outside of entropy roams the 5th dimension. It is like the innards of Hawking's blackhole where spirituality transcends the mental resides.

Humans seem aware of the 5th dimension but mostly reference it to avoid the termination implied in the 4th dimension relative to their existence in the 3rd dimension, as argued over in managing the 1st dimension. The 1st dimension is the home of the ethics as negotiated over the good and bad in the Faustian bargain. Humans can't seem to manage their way out of the 2nd dimension without a normative map showing where they are and should being going.

Fundamental to systems of life just now is the question: Will humans act to show their power via removal of life from our planet via a nuclear war with each other or will they await a longer-term removal of life via the evolving war with nature now seen in consequences of climate change. Using rational industrial logic, the first is far more efficient. It offers clear productivity in riding the planet of life. Needing only a few minutes of expressing their genius via extensively using nuclear weaponry the planet can be changed via human capabilities very productively.

Climate change appears to be much slower. It could require fifty to seventy-five years of continuing expansion of industrialization and the human power such illustrates. Much has been learned about the details found in: "On the Origin of the Species." Now someone can write a final episode to Darwin's drama, "On the End of the Species." Which approach will humans take? The quick via going for the short-term seems fun and colorful. The long-term does not seem very human. Just ask Faust which we will take?

To commemorate Russ Ackoff's death to the NJIT students he had helped I gave a NJIT- wide lecture in the Fall of 2008 titled "It's Too Late." It was to explain the potential in such to achieve significant change in the face of hopelessness. The subject line meaning was when things get bad try to wait until they become so bad that it seems too late to repair. Then, those responsible for the bad will go underground or simply disappear. At that point, with leadership gone, you have a chance to improve things if you work fast with a high degree of innovation. You can then make a difference.

The danger is when things look good again, idiot leadership which I called "leadershit," tries to retake reins of power. There are many examples of this, including Texaco via a project I ran. Via a project it went from being the worst of the oil companies to the best oil company, then returned to the worst once again prior to its disappearance. Via climate change this may well become the model for the industry.

Potential in the "Both" Beyond the Digital

Describing differences became key to learning from an historic battle between beliefs in regulation and beliefs against -regulation. Each side described a very different view of the environmental problem of human activities. Soon we discovered that such a difference was quite irrelevant to improved pollution control. If anything, that difference became a barrier to discovery of deeper and more meaningful differences. Early study evidence illustrated how activities on both sides of their combined wall, built by pro and anti-regulators, often led to increases in pollution in a larger context.

This was seen as continuance of usual differences used in societal management. Historic cultural differences between blacks and whites, Asians and others, tall and short, rich and poor, male and female, etc. Illustrate the folly and damage of such differences. They do not make a difference in any known good sense. Such differences were seen as politically meaningful yet largely irrelevant, then counter-productive, then dangerous.

Their study thus expanded to seek other kinds of differences, those that would be able to manage environmental dangers awaiting human continuance of the more trivial problems of pollution piled outside a factory. The study of deterioration of areas surrounding production was expanded to include areas of product-use. This second posed a much larger threat to life on the planet.

Early in the study I pointed out that humans can best "learn" via experience that appeared rude. We then discussed why learning was needed in the fundamental differences used in national politics. This focused-on differences between those on the hard right and then on the hard left. Via rudeness from the environment both sides can learn to talk together to fashion a more innovative response to danger. I thus told a story of how advanced technology could help. This might include advanced driverless autos. I then showed them humorous pictures of how "right-leaning" people would be given "right-driving" autos. Such would automatically turn only to the right at each intersection. In this way the passenger could learn a lot. The same logic would be used for those proud of being extremely "left" and thus would be in autos that would only turn left at each intersection. Learning would take place as the two groups would crash into each other, thus losing their insurance coverage and/or lives. Those surviving might then see a reason to seek a better way.

Participants laughed at the story but eventually came to understand it's a metaphor on why humans need to find better differences on the way to finding a better way. In the study we move on from those simple-minded dichotomies to see significant and urgent threats to life on our planet. My deepest appreciation goes out to those involved in the study. Our beginning assumption was that humans had created the processes and products leading to environmental deterioration. As such we needed to get them to change their work by redesigning processes and products to stop or slow the harm from human endeavors. As the dangers would dissipate, a safer business-as-usual could be instituted to help all concerned. As such, humans would regain control and reduce the negative aspects of 19th Century industrial production. We hoped that by the 21st Century the threats will be reversed, or at least dissipated much like negative entropy pushes back on the relentless threat of entropy. This assumption was soon found to be quite misguided, even to be wrong.

As the study proceeded it became clear that a cloud was forming on the horizon called climate change. It would cause the initial problems to be addressed in the study to become trivial much like the 2nd Law of Thermodynamics treats the outcomes of significant research to create negative entropy. It began to seem that there was an emergent phenomenon in our world and early indications were that it was of a different logical type. Once it has expanded sufficiently it would reach a tipping point where humans would no longer have control over its evolution, dangers and end state. Even though human activities had initiated the approaching harm they would no longer have access to control it beyond a break point. Frankly, the group found this to be scary. Thus, the project became changed.

Fear of deterioration transforming into climate change terror changed the nature of the project. We learned much from one of the participants in the study relative to the significance and end state of industrial pollution from production and use of what was thus produced. James Black, Senior Scientist of Exxon, taught me and the research group much. He gave much credit for the linking of CO^2 to moisture to global heat buildup to work of Eunice Newton Foote, especially to her 1856 science paper on the question. His work on the project brought us to think on what would happen to the planet's thin life support atmospheric system if it began to change and humans could not intervene to manage the change. He asked what we would do if our changes created a climate change process not susceptible to human management. Participants in the research came to be very concerned about the scale and dept of climate change hardships, suggested by CEO Howard Kauffmann from his reading of the careful articulation of James Black. At the time serve threats to planetary life were beginning. They have greatly expanded since.

We should note that the leader of a university I was teaching at in 2009 had the hundreds of files and documents I had saved from the 1975-77 Swedish Study, including Black's copy of Foote's research from 1856, "Seized and confiscated as state property and not the property of David Hawk." I had used them in my teaching of architectural design and business courses. An administrative official of that university at that time believed that all such documents of Hawk had been destroyed. The rationale was unclear, but the leader of that university did comment prior to the seizer that he "Never hated anyone as much as he hated David Hawk." I have no idea of where such hatred comes in those aspiring to be noteworthy leaders yet are seen to have nowhere to go. Such leadership exists but remains sad.

To better respond to climate change threats today via understanding its history such a statement from leadership is sad. His comment was not isolated as the man who replaced him as university president had previously tried to get Hawk banned from teaching honors courses. "Hawk's emphasis on the implication of climate change for future societies is problematic in all courses he teaches." Youth, on the other hand, came to be very interested in the subject.

Our concern articulated in the results was with _how humans would come to change their behavior,_ to avert a tragedy for life on earth. Most working in the study, including me, felt humans could and of course would change to avert the impending disasters for life on earth. A book on the work was published by students in the Social Systems Sciences Program at Wharton in 1979. It immediately met opposition to its grim forecast from the public, some educators, and the boards of directors for some of the companies involved.

Many felt the climate change consequences we described in our study were a hoax, as created by a group of left-wing scientists. There was little sign that such minds would or could change. Thus, my concern shifted down to a more elemental concern in *can human's change*. The evidence for such a concern was seen in humans being challenged by harsh consequences from prior actions. Even with evidence clear, the humans involved tended to not accept the indictment and refused to change. Climate change evidence via early condition changes began to demonstrate the severity of forthcoming change. Six of the climate change ten tipping points have been crossed. For those six there will be no reversal of process. There is no negative entropy to save the day. A line has been crossed. There are now signs that the last four tipping points are about to trip and initiate their consequences.

Infrastructures required of society will thus be damaged or destroyed including those on which current society is based. These include economics and business (first the insurance industry and then more inflationary aspects), shelter (location and strength of buildings), food (availability, quality and price), medical provision (availability of facilities and medicines), transportation (that defines and connects society), defense (from internal as well as external dangers), political (via a tendency to drift towards a totalitarian state during miserable conditions), and family (via heart-felt sadness for the state of the world for the children).

Russ Ackoff was an important part of my final lecture to NJIT students, just prior to my leaving. The photos below were included and illustrate one of the travel programs I instituted for students. These helped students understand leadership.

DAVID L. HAWK

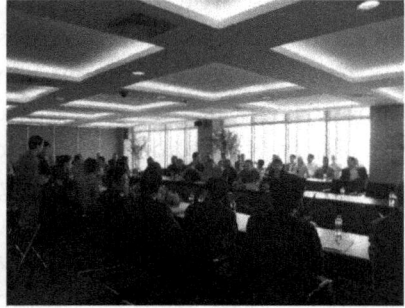

Hawk's class meeting with NJ Congressmen, Washington, D.C.
Then to Beijing for a meeting with Jack Ma and
Chinese Business Leaders of the day

I was offered a job at Boston Consulting Group along with teaching a course each year at Harvard Business School about my "negotiated order" dissertation for "fluid organizations." A student of mine at the Stockholm School of Economics, then teaching at Harvard, arranged the offer. While discussing the details of the job another friend I was staying with in Boston invited me to help create a new school that he was the dean of, titled the New Jersey Institute of Technology. He asked me to come teach in NJ what I taught at ISU. He wanted my help in giving the school an accreditation status, thus becoming an important school in the NYC Region.

After meeting with students, I could not resist. They had limited funding, were very bright and clearly able to survive bad teachers and their worse teaching. Students had heard of my architectural entropy design work at ISU and liked the banner my students had hung outside my design studio at ISU. The banner in the photo they had said: "It's hard to kill a talent." NJIT offered me $27,500, Boston Consulting Group offered me only $81,000. My needs were few. The choice was obvious, Ackoff style.

I spent a decade developing two graduate degrees, thirty foreign study trips, 256 courses, and thus attracting the best students from the best schools. With this we created a network of support from companies in the New York Region. In 1989 I took a two-year leave to run a project in Sweden. Upon my return the provost asked me to become a joint professor in his new School of Management. It had been struggling to begin. He thought my work just finished in Sweden would help motivate it.[231]

Conditions of Success ended with a meeting titled the "Grand Hotel Symposium." Each CEO was to present their views on the state of the future. Most felt emerging environmental conditions would come to redefine their industry and their role in it.[232]

Potentiality in It Being Too Late

This book is for the children of the "so what parents" who created our "too late environment" as a context for life in tomorrow. As will be explained in some detail, the 1965 forecast of Emery and Trist about the approach of un-manageable turbulent environments is our current context. Back then it was called fearmongering but by 1995 it was clearly emerging. It now seems that we will encounter the much greater instability of a vortex environment, as also suggested in 1965 by Trist, by 2030. We have clearly entered the context of the chaotic, beyond the irregular fluids that turbulence was first defined around. Metaphorically, we are part of life moving into a Hawking black hole.

The contents found here come from gifted teachers I had an opportunity to work with and share ideas about the human situation. I then became very appreciative of my students that suffered through my complex courses on interconnected subjects at various colleges in various countries. They argued with me about what was, wasn't and

---

[231] Back at the Stockholm school of Economics I had designed and ran an alternative to the World Economic Forum, titled "Conditions of Success." It was to study the emerging conditions of international business to help CEOs stop wasting their time inventing new strategies that mostly destroyed context. Sixty CEOs joined the project, took an active role, and paid for it. I knew many of them from prior advisement work.

[232] It was held as an alternative to the WEF Annual Meeting. The WEF was upset about this until 2007 they came to visit me to ask for help in the replication of the 1991 study. I joined them for their annual meeting in Dalian, China in 2007 and asked Russ if he would like to come along. He did not feel up to it.

should be, they were they thought was coming. I was very fortunate to have such phenomenal students, and very happy that university administrators seldom managed what we were learning[233].

My description of a forthcoming book on climate change in 2019, "Too Early, Too Late, now what?", was posted in the American Association for the Advancement of Science. It was a republishing of my dissertation of 1979. On May 1, 2019, an abstract form of it was posted, ending in a question for the AAAS Science Community: "Humans are changing the context for life on our planet to the negative. Does anyone see a source for hope?"

There were more than 800 responses in the next three months. The expressed deep concern for climate change, how scientists had addressed it in various ways, yet it continued to expand.[234] Responses totaled 2,100 pages of print-out. Many saw the 1979 thesis as having been too optimistic about humans and their ability to change.

AAAS then changed their requirements based on the posting. Thereafter the discussion would be limited to 150 entrees. They argued that their computer system could not easily accommodate 800 responses. So be it.

Even beyond articles in journals such as *Science*, we see the growth of horror stories of humans waking up in conditions outside life. We feel bad about and for the future. Alongside these feelings we see articles on why it's a waste to spend time feeling bad about the human future. They say it's too long-term to worry about, and it will simply depress people. Youth need to instead concentrate on continuation of human progress. Technological development is said

---

[233] In 1986 the Provost at NJIT insisted that I give a usual end of term exam to base grades upon, to replace grades being based on each student giving a "final presentation" of what they learned, and letting the class evaluate such. When told of this the students design a phenomenal "final exam." It came to be used at various of the leading universities in the world for a few years thereafter to locate who you would love to work with.

[234] Science, AAAS.com, Posted by David Hawk, "RE: AAAS Member Community: Humans are changing the context for life on our planet to the negative. Does anyone see a source for hope?" You can enter the site as a member of AAAS, at the following site: https://mail.google.com/mail/u/0/#inbox/ FMfcgxwChSJjHhGQFpcdmJlmtGvjTxGb

to be able to fix it. In the history of philosophy there is much to say about such undue optimistic being a problem in the longer-term.[235]

On the other hand, we hear stories of the sheer terror that will redefine life and its context. We see images of storms, floods, rising oceans, extending droughts, starvation, migration, natural viruses, and unforeseen diseases. The impending dangers from these are in our collective consciousness, with no advice on how to respond, or escape. We can watch what we call the real men responding to such with fierce anger as they walk away swearing and sweating, then shaking their heads about those damned fairytales that take up their time. Their real women humbly walk behind saying yes dear, and dutifully follow the man's wishes per the Bible's instructions. Conclusion: "It will all be fine. If not, heaven awaits on the other side."

The few who pay attention see troubling data, then note how it seems to get worse in that prior scientific data about the timeline for planetary life is a bit wrong. It is always too optimistic about the timetable of terror.

> "Those who know the most about the human condition repeatedly say: …the situation is worse."[236]

This following arises from a 4,000-page report published in August 2021 as summarized in The Atlantic Daily publication of that month. It seems climate change was different than thought earlier; it was approaching much faster.

> "Where scientists once warned of disasters in the distant future, now they strive to understand what has already happened—and what is too late to save says Robinson Meyer, who covers climate change."[237]

---

[235] Ackoff, R.L., and Churchman, W., "*Methods of Inquiry*," University of Pennsylvania Dissertation, 1950.

[236] A pessimistic book, *Too Soon, Too Late, Now what?* was reviewed in *Science* in Spring, 2020. Of the more than 800 scientists commenting on the posting 75% saw it as overly optimistic towards the climate change future.

[237] *The Atlantic Daily*, Page 1, August 13, 2021, Caroline Nyce.

The young are the most upset with this humanly generated spectacle. When they see the above, and ask why, they see adults being upset with the question or pushing their heads ever more deeply into the Florida sand, or further up into that unmentionable body part. Youth ask: "What can we do about life?" Parents then respond with two directives: "Study hard and obey your parents." Meanwhile, the abyss of life takes the form of a Hawking black hole as it draws closer. The eyes of youth reveal a deep anger while their actions imply a need to leave. What shall we do?

The human project was established to support and aid human life on earth. It was developed to ease access for humans to their needs and wants, and confused attempts to integrate the two. Now the same project appears to be the major threat to the continuance of that life. How can this be happening? It will be argued herein that the attitude and intellect of what is represented by the first three letters of management needs change. The human project and its management appear to be responsibility for where humans are and are going.

Since 500 BC men have arrogantly assumed responsibility for deciding what humans are, where they should go and how best to get there. This is seen in Aristotle, in the Garden of Eden Story and can be seen most clearly since 1850 in a particular form of industrialization of productions, products and lifestyles. Just as mechanization of the industrial was key to realizing human potential it has become the essence of the problem standing in the way of the human future. Herein an argument is made to apply the values of fem-agement.

There are many perspectives on the impending future. They draw from segmented analysis of a part of the problem. The cause, logic, origination, direction, and end-state define each. Our problem is that each is based on a segmented sense of partial analysis to access knowing. As the trees are cut down and examined in parts it becomes increasingly difficult to see or even conceive of the forest, and its more fundamental importance. Few see the overtly clear connection to industrial processes and products as the basis for the impending harm. Most are caught up in examining the proverbial glass. Is this glass full, half full, or half empty? Can we invent another technology, a new one based on AI, that will fill it with even better stuff?

The herein avoids most of those nuances and their feel-good possibilities. It looks at the total situation and its context and sees the human future as bleak. It uses a systems appreciation approach and thus sees the parts of the problem as reassembled. It appreciates how the Human Project as an operating system needs stability over time to continue. Forces, mostly from the technological, introduce considerable instabilities. In their design and construction there is little to no consideration of their consequences. As such the activities to provide goods and services to the Project prove to be its greatest threat in the longer term.

Climate change conditions are increasingly feared as humans see glimpses of their consequences for life. We thus sense a grave threat to life as we know it. In IT terms we concentrate on managing the first order desired results fulfillment while second order feedback operates in the background. From it we sense an undesired instability that arrives via the feedback. All that life needs is in motion or gone. To prepare we make things worse by looking for harsh governance to restore human order and impose the stability essential to human endeavors.

Our model of governance is almost as counterproductive as the model of industrialization it is to govern. It is steeped in enforcement via threats to do things that are mostly unknown and/or unworkable. We see a problem in the system. We stop the system and remove the part (the cause) that our data says is responsible. We change the part and put it back into the system, a system that has since moved on. We thus face an unknowable dilemma of did we make things better or worse via our governance, regulation, and management routine? We don't even know how or what to blame for the resulting mess getting worse.

As part of the Human Project, governance is developed around this funny human idea of leadership from others, not self. Leaders are to set the direction then management arrives to realize the ends. The larger pool of participants then picks up the ques from leadership and follows the demands of management. When the end is important in a different way, this process seldom works. It works well when the ends are a continuation of the past thus management is not needed. No, the future is not open to management via plans and planning. Plans are mostly to identify what you will not during times of instability. Planning is mostly for sessions of humor while on break from surviving.

Systemic Images of the Holistic in Life

Using Sir Geoffrey Vickers's terminology, we can see how an early version of the European International Business Academy (EIBA) was very innovative. It offered the freedom of a rocking boat like the experiences of the early Vikings. While some early participants became sea-sick others developed very agile sea-legs. The EIBA emphasis has shifted over time from agility to seaworthiness. The result is an EIBA that has become more like its U.S. sister ships - unsure of to where they are going but damned difficult to rock. Their emphasis shifted to rigor over imagination. The same tendency is omnipresent these days. Many leaders now seek to crawl into the middle of things. Ernst Fisher's paraphrasing of a key literary theme poetically describes this:

> "Hamm, whose name hints vaguely at myth, literature, and cheap histrionics, is rotting alive in his refuge. The world from which he came is dead. After an unspeakable catastrophe, all that remains are objects, only the inorganic, nothing that grows or breathes. 'End, it is the end, it's coming to an end, perhaps it's coming to an end.' There is no world left, no future, only the hiding-place in the middle of nothing."[238]

This situation is not unlike the quite humorous and deadly serious discourse of an EIBA member, of the Viking variety, who in a late-night EIBA episode speculated on the limits of analysis via using two-by-two matrices - "hell is getting stuck in the middle of those

---

[238] Fischer, Ernst, *Art Against Ideology*, New York: George Braziller, 1969, p. 7.

two-by-two crosshairs, much like Jesus." As most members of EIBA acknowledge, the interesting thing about EIBA meetings, as well as those in the business conferences of other world regions,[239] is what happens outside the securely assembled sessions of management ideology that result from peer scrutiny. This danger to management learning was poetically criticized a decade ago when a very gifted EIBA member distinguished between traditional business principles, that relied on old, sleepy, peaceful, agricultural idioms, and new principles that continually seek the alertness required by those on the move, such as a hunting party.[240]

Regardless, EIBA's membership moves ever closer to the model of American business education organizations - entities that are sufficiently large so to be steady, yet capable of going half-way to the bottom prior to the passengers realizing that something is seriously wrong.

For those concerned about renewal, regeneration, and responsiveness there are several options. One is to systematically abandon organizations after a period, so their membership becomes the fertilizer needed for new beginnings, i.e., this is known as the winter-kill model.[241] Two is much less dramatic although probably more sinister. It involves working on the inside of an organized entity, with a fixed smile and lots of friendly gestures, while planning to bury the whole lot under their comments when the time is ripe.

The problem with the first model is it attracts people who like fertilizer. The problem with the second is that it relies too much on the exit and loyalty options to keep an institution alive. In the A.O. Hirschman sense of the terms, an approach is needed that can tap

---

[239] This cannot be said for all society meetings. Sessions of the American Association for the Advancement of Science Annual Meetings are more interesting than the hallway meetings outside.

[240] This notion was clearly articulated by Gunnar Hedlund in 1987 while on Sabbatical at Stanford, and then publicized by Tom Peters in one of his by-lines.

[241] This approach was used effectively a few years ago in Finland's effort to improve the "too secure" VTT national labs. The results of what the Government and TEKES did could teach those dealing with the relevance problem of the $30 billion U.S. national labs a great deal.

into the considerable powers of voice,[242] instead of relying on exit and loyalty to maintain status quo. Voice is acceptable to those who do not appreciate fertilizer who do not suffer fools well, and who are not well insulated from rapid change rates.[243] The remainder of this paper is for the voice option of the heretic.

A heretic must access the most closely held assumptions in real time.[244] If voice is crucial for institutional renew, and if a heretic is important to the process, then how can they be stimulated? History demonstrates that the most effective way to stimulate discourse is to cut off debate. Sacred topics that are non-debatable become the center of discussion. Choice of sacred management topics depends on location and time frame.[245]

---

[242] Hirschman, Albert O., *Exit, Voice and Loyalty*: Responses to Decline in Firms, Organizations, and States, Cambridge, Ma.: Harvard Press, 1970.

[243] This insulation comes in universities via tenure where those having it can avoid the changes impacting others, e.g., students.

[244] This simply means that you will have to temporarily stop playing with digitally based multi-media for a while and read passages on history.

[245] I cannot personally demonstrate management heresy because of my lack of appropriate credentials. My activities are not and have never been near its legitimized core of management lore. A heretic must come from that center and have a great deal to lose by questioning the assumptions of the endeavor. He also can't be a whistle-blower.

Biography

To Improve Human-Nature Relations

My architectural engineering degree was completed at Iowa State University in 1971. Then I went back to Germany to continue working on the Munich Olympiad Project with my professor friend Gunter Behnisch. After that I worked in London, then moved back to the US. I left the US again in 1975 by moving to work in Sweden at the Stockholm School of Economics. Prior to that I had completed my master's degrees in architecture and city planning, at the University of Pennsylvania, and then the course work for a PhD from the Wharton School. My attraction to Sweden was to work with a very close friend, Gunnar Hedlund.

In 1975, when arriving in Sweden, I drew up a model for researching relations between human business activities and processes that deteriorate nature. The previous model relied on standard analysis and was shown to be irrelevant except for adding to the problem of environmental deterioration. Instead of studying business as usual I switched to seeking examples of business as unusual, that could better relate to nature. In the alternative model analytic subdivisions were avoided. Integration of parts was shown to be superior to adding to piled pieces.

The analytic tradition concentrated on partial analysis of segmented parts of parts. A systems perspective was needed yet the system's science model was still unacceptable in 1975 business education. This was the major reason for moving ed away from the US schools of business. The model I used relied on identifying the effects of causes, not the causes from effects. Such thinking was accepted in Sweden at the Stockholm School of Economics. As such, my Swedish friend, Dr. Gunnar Hedlund and I formed a new institute of the unusual. It was to seek students to help with research of new business ideas for bringing the world together. As such, the growing dominance of nationalism could be lessened. Titled, the Institute of International Business, we began a project into how nationalistic regulation emphasizes nationalistic differences, and largely ignores the need to reduce environmental deterioration.

The concern for the natural environment I had arose while working on a farm about 1950. I noted how agriculture was becoming industrialized by giving emphasis on mechanical logic. It concentrated on singular crop production in straight rows, and destruction of nature, all via a simple cause-effect logic. Hundreds of acres of corn and soybeans were grown in segments while protecting them from the surrounding nature. Nature was increasingly seen as the enemy of humans and the progress they sought. Nature was kept at bay via extensive use of ever more machines, fertilizers, and pesticides.

My concern grew in 1966 -68 while in a war in Vietnam seeing the extensive and willful destruction of forests and their human occupants. My concern went deeper in 1969 while spending a semester in Yucatan studying the demise of the Mayan civilization from human behavior. Along with 22 other students I studied the archeology of a Mayan civilization from 600 to 900 AD. The early example of humanly created climate change resulted from millions of Mayans clearing nature in the region, all to produce artificial foods for human consumption.

Millions of Mayans had established complex cities to improve human life, but only in the short term. My concern was in the effects of this process in creating conditions of longer-term climate change. Desertification of the region was the result of that human model of development. Eventually, the land had to be abandoned then the highly developed urban areas. I argued that humans needed to come to see longer-term costs of environmental deterioration from short-term gains in business-as-usual expansion.

In later projects of others concern gradually expanded to include fragmented dangers to life from related pollution and destruction of nature, with no systemic research into the connections. At that time there was no study of how extensive use of materials and energies, as taken from nature to become economic products for consumption, somehow resulted in irreversible deterioration.

Some small projects had been undertaken from 1968 to 1975 but with little financial support and no call for a more systemic approach. My leaving the US in 1975 was in search of support of the more systemic attitude. The Chair of the Systems Sciences Program at the Wharton School supported the central idea but had no funding for such and advised me to somehow change my articulation of the key problem. My critic of "business as usual" was seen as a problem in a business school.

My concern for business as usual in human affairs emerged during my time in the Vietnam war. I became concerned about there not being a human future. I had become concerned about "the environment," as defined as a location of resources for human use, as context of life, but which humans openly destroyed in war. I was concerned that humans might not have a future via their attitude about themselves and their context for life.

It was hard to collect interest for such from research agencies in the US. Government agencies, corporations and the public found such concern to be a doorway into becoming anti-business. They did not understand the meaning behind a search for "business as unusual" to improve relations between humans and the environment that sustained such. My advisor, Eric Trist, did understand but he was becoming discouraged by business research. My focus was on the intellectual and moral limits of laws for environmental protection of nature from humans. I felt that humans creating legal regulation to protect the environment from human behavior was a way to camouflage a problem, not resolve the processes initiating it - manly actions of men at war with nature in the name of progress was far too systemic to be managed via the analysis of fragmented and mostly incompetent legality. The legislation as designed by those limited by law school instruction would not protect what men were passionate about destroying. From visiting several law school classes

From visiting some law school first semester classes I learned how students were encouraged to separate laws as written from ethics that may have initiated the writing. Their advice was, concentrate on the law as written, not the ethics behind writing; the law is clear while ethics is complicated and can become contradictory. My prior work with environmental law showed how the law can thus become cynical. I felt a new attitude and approach was needed.

I managed Environmental Impact Statements writing in 1972 for a design firm. Via this I worked with many designers, lawyers, and scientists. The work involved extensive analysis added to even more extensive legal posturing intended to make use of the analysis with no hint of synthesis. The designed results consistently looked like a cynical resolution of opposites. I found no sign of hope in the resulting plans. Perhaps there was a temporary posture of feel good, prior to construction, but later the results were seldom better than business as usual.

During interviews after project openings, I heard the argument that "this may not be perfect, but we need to do something until we figure it all out." This included a key US Senator who had drafted the key 1969 legislation behind the strategic failures. I saw this as a forewarning of what would follow. The seventies dream of second-order recycling would do little except make the first order damage less apparent. I found Adam Smith's reliance on capitalism calling for reuse of materials and energy needed in production to be an impossible caveat to an unfortunate economic model of motivation. I thus moved to Sweden with my good friend Gunnar Hedlund who understood my problem and felt it fit within his dream of creating businesses as unusual in an international business model, one that was global as one world not a conflicted theme of international friction in the national. We thus launched the Institute of International Business at the Stockholm School of Economics.

Upon arriving in Sweden I found they were about to adopt the US rule-making system known as environmental protection. I commented on what this might mean for the subject in Sweden in a Swedish magazine. I illustrated in that article how and why there was cynicism behind the complex set of formal US rules and regulations.

I argued that they should instead look for a more natural, more fluid, changing, evolving approach. It needed to oppose the implied arrogance of the American approach to environmental protection.

Yes, the article contained humor linked to pessimism. The Head of Sweden's Environmental Protection Division thus asked me to design a project to compare different national approaches to environmental protection challenges. My two friends, Gunnar Hedlund and Lars Otterbeck, were in the process of beginning what came to be the world leader in international business research and advisement. As funded by major industrialists of Sweden the Institute of International Business, Stockholm School of Economics, was strongly supported by public and private sectors of society. It came to be known as IIB. My project came to be the research that launched the Institute. It was advertised as a project on the environmental costs of business as usual in our world. The Board of the Institute gave it their strong approval. It soon came to include numerous country governments and companies.

Much of the 1975-77 time was invested in traveling to meet government and company people, and document production facilities and practices. The focus was on similar production plants with the same products, owned by the same company, to then measure results of differences in regulation. Governmental, corporate, and third-party measures and their differences were systematically described. Issues such as centralization/decentralization of management, understandability of laws, and learning soon became key to explaining different results.

The results were surprising to almost all involved. The US approach was the least successful in controlling pollution. Results ended up being presented to the Organization for Economic Cooperation and Development. From this many nations turned away from the US model of regulation, and environmental concern. The US kept with it, paying no attention to anything recommended by the study. Results were published in three volumes.

Via the OECD Presentation Russ came across a copy of the report given to OECD and then sent me a warm note of approval. He commented at the time saying those three volumes served as my completed dissertation. He said no further writing was required for the PhD. He concluded his letter by saying he was proud of my work, and my demonstration of what additional knowledge was needed to survive in the future. He felt I illustrated why he had established the Wharton PhD Systems Science Program. He seemed to love the reports: "Environmental Deterioration: Analytic Solutions in Search of Synthetic Problems, I, II, III."

My other advisor, Eric Trist, felt there must also be a document presenting the thesis behind the research and its conclusions. I spent three months writing such than two more years trying to relate to an ever-expanding committee set up by the University to review the subjects in the reports. Russ Ackoff continued to support me and the project, as well as its method and its results until 2006 when I last met with him. A newer replacement Wharton Dean began to accept the climate change from business activities project, and dissertation, t but with some residue concern if it should be a Wharton product.

The Director of the US EPA in 1977, Doug Costle a Harvard trained lawyer, who had been the architect of the laws coming out from the agency called EPA, remained concerned about the thesis. He had helped design the legislation that the agency relied on, and the dissertation came to be critical of. He thus sent me a clarifying letter in 1979, along with a box of final reports he had collected from within EPA (there were about 20 copies of the 3-volume final report found at EPA). His cover letter seemed harsh: "Dear Mr. Hawk, we have no further use of these reports, your research, nor you. I will insure you are never supported to do environmental research in the US."

The Director seemed to forget that he and EPA had attempted to kill the project in 1975. They had offered financial support but officially withdrew it the morning when the research was to begin. It was later learned that this was a strategy to kill off the study. It didn't. Swedish Parliament moved quickly to supplement the work with additional funding.

The dissertation was then republished in 2019, on its 40th Anniversary as "Too Early, Too Late, Now what?". Questions remain about the subject matter, but it clearly is not seen to be a hoax to those who still have a mind. In March 2024 the document was said to be placed in the display room of the Library of Congress. It continues to be widely sold. One organization produced 10,000 copies that it gave away to interested academics.

To Whom Much Is Owed

I am grateful to the many teachers I met and gained from. This begins with my 2nd Grade teacher in Burlington, Iowa. She taught me about the joys awaiting discovery in reading books. She introduced me to dealing with the books, then reflecting on the books of each year. Second was the motivation provided by my best friend in life, Gunnar Hedlund, who grew up in the North of Sweden and had time in Lapland's seeming isolation to read books that mattered, then reflect on what was gained. When I met him at the University of Pennsylvania, he felt sorry for my limited experiences in Iowa from dealing with the contents of books. He immediately then took me to the University bookshop and bought me six books to begin an expansive journey into literature.

On this basis I acquired 5,000 books for my library, where the majority remain. The few that were borrowed and not returned were later replaced. They are very important to me and my students. My best professors and classmates continued illustrating the rewards from books that are loved, more so than from conversations, lectures, TVs and movies. Books, and the ideas found therein, underlie most of the research questions that rose to attract me. Via my 1979 book Russ Ackoff came to agree with me on climate change coming to be the central subject for humans in the 21st Century. There had been much opposition to that being a meaningful question back then. In addition to Russ these people came to support my concern and gave support to me: Prof. Karl Kochimski, Prof. Tony Catterwell, Prof. Edmund Bacon, Prof. Ian McHarg, Prof. Eric Trist, Prof. Hasan Ozbekhan. Their teaching and support, when I felt down and saw little reason to continue, were essential. I thank them dearly.

What to do When Its Too Late: A TV Show

Preamble to the TV Series

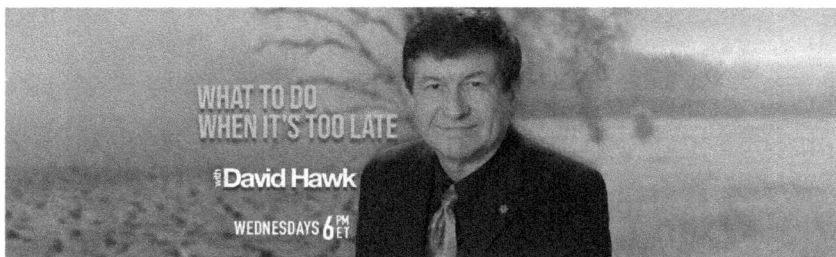

"The continuance of the human future is in doubt. The unfortunate implications of past actions seem omnipresent, perhaps irreversible. Currently titled *climate change* it begins to appear as fatal as widespread radiation from weak leadership initiating a nuclear war in defending their masculinity. The nuclear option will not be discussed but the misguided thinking of the masculine aspect as seen in the shortcomings of the first three letters of management relative to misguided industrialization will be. Much technology that was to enhance life has been redirected to its destruction. What to do? Business as usual as seen in headquarters, labs stores and classrooms is now seen detrimental to life. In part this comes from ignoring the half-empty glass and seeing it as physically half-full and spiritually about to brim over. This is the religion known as negative entropy."[246]

---

[246] From the TV Ad for the program on BOLD BRAVE TV, at BoldBraveTV.com

Presentation of the impact of presumptions and consequences of climate change began in January 2024 via a BoldBraveTV.com series as based in New York. Titled: "What to do when it's too late" almost fifty weekly sessions offered a forum to present how major tipping points of environmental damage had been crossed, thus it was too late via them, before moving to what can be done about the resulting situation. I key question became the search for changing business as usual, that had been a major contributor to climate change, into business as unusual. The mission was expressed as moving from denying to nurturing life on the planet.

The prospects for success did not instill optimism.

www.ingramcontent.com/pod-product-compliance
Lightning Source LLC
Chambersburg PA
CBHW062113020426
42335CB00013B/943